M.E.S.-115

COMMUNICATION TECHNOLOGY FOR DISTANCE EDUCATION

Chapter Wise Reference Book
Including Many Solved Sample Papers

Based on

I.G.N.O.U.

& Various Central, State & Other Open Universities

By: *Kshyama Sagar Meher*

Serving Education for Last 40 Years

NEERAJ PUBLICATIONS
(Publishers of Educational Books)

Retail Sales Office:
1507, First Floor, Nai Sarak, Delhi - 6
Mob.: 8510009872, 8510009878
E-mail : info@neerajbooks.com
Website : www.neerajbooks.com

MRP ₹ 300/-

Published by:

NEERAJ PUBLICATIONS

(Publishers of Educational Books)

Retail Sales Office : 1507, 1st Floor, Nai Sarak, Delhi-110 006

E-mail: info@neerajbooks.com | Website: www.neerajbooks.com

Typesetting by: Competent Computers, Printed at: Novelty Printing Press

CONTENTS

COMMUNICATION TECHNOLOGY FOR DISTANCE EDUCATION

QUESTION PAPER
(December – 2022)

(Solved)

COMMUNICATION TECHNOLOGY FOR DISTANCE EDUCATION

M.E.S.-115

Time: 3 Hours] *[Weightage: 70%*

Note: All questions are compulsory. All questions carry equal weightage.

Q. 1. Answer the following question:

Describe the role of educational television in the context of distance education. Discuss how it can be utilised effectively in distance education in future.

Ans. Ref.: See Chapter-7, Page No. 80, 'Potential of Educational Televsion', Page No. 83, 'Future Trends in Educational Televsion'.

Or

Explain the concept and means of communication. Discuss how different means of communication play an important role in distance education.

Ans. Ref.: See Chapter-1, Page No. 1, 'Communication: The Concept'.

Q. 2. Answer the following question:

Describe major strands of television production.

Ans. Ref.: See Chapter-8, Page No. 92, 'Major Strands of TV Production'.

Or

What do you mean by media selection? Describe the criteria for selection of media for distance education.

Ans. Ref.: See Chapter-5, Page No. 54, 'Media Selection', Page No. 57, 'Bates, Criteria for Decision Making'.

Q. 3. Answer any four of the following questions:

***(a)* Describe the advantage of teleconferencing in distance education.**

Ans. Ref.: See Chapter-14, Page No. 163, 'Advantages of Teleconferencing'.

***(b)* Explain the various stages of video recording.**

Ans. Ref.: See Chapter-12, Page No. 132, 'Studio Recording', Page No. 135, 'Field/Location Recording'.

***(c)* Describe the important points to be considered while planning and producing the audio-cassette programmes.**

Ans. Ref.: See Chapter-6, Page No. 72, 'Designing, Programmes on Audio Cassettes'.

***(d)* Describe the procedures of post-production editing.**

Ans. Ref.: See Chapter-12, Page No. 136, 'Editing'.

***(e)* Mention the features of World Wide Web.**

Ans. Ref.: See Chapter-15, Page No. 177, 'World Wide Web'.

***(f)* Differentiate between Satellite and Terrestrial Communications.**

Ans. Ref.: See Chapter-14, Page No. 160, 'Satellite versus Terrestrial Communcation'.

Q. 4. Answer the following question :

Identify a topic for an educational video programme. Describe the steps you will follow while developing the same video programme.

Ans. Ref.: See Chapter-8, Page No. 93, 'Programe Production Process', Chapter-11, Page No. 121, 'Production Planning', Scheduling and Execution'.

■■

QUESTION PAPER

Exam Held in
July – 2022

(Solved)

COMMUNICATION TECHNOLOGY FOR DISTANCE EDUCATION **M.E.S.-115**

Time: 3 Hours] ***[Weightage: 70%***

***Note:** All questions are **compulsory**. All questions carry equal weightage.*

Q. 1. Answer the following questions:

What do you mean by non-print media? Describe pedagogic uses of non-print media in distance education.

Ans. Ref.: See Chapter-5, Page No. 52, 'The Non-Print Media'.

Or

What are the factors that influence the adoption and growth of new communication technology in India? Discuss those factors.

Ans. Ref.: See Chapter-2, Page No. 17, 'Growth of Communication Technology: Problems'.

Q. 2. Answer the following question:

Describe the uses of audio-radio in education. Give your views on future uses of radio in distance education system of India.

Ans. Ref.: See Chapter-6, Page No. 71, 'Uses of Radio/Audio Medium', Page No. 74, 'Future Trends in Educational Radio'.

Or

Describe the specific uses of computers focused in pedagogic process in distance education system.

Ans. Ref.: See Chapter-13, Page No. 145, 'Specific Uses of Computers'.

Q. 3. Answer any four of the following questions:

***(a)* Describe the process of writing a video script for an educational programme.**

Ans. Ref.: See Chapter-10, Page No. 113, 'Script Writing'.

***(b)* Write a short note on satellite-based communication.**

Ans. Ref.: See Chapter-14, Page No. 162, 'Satellite Based Communication and Distance Education'.

***(c)* Discuss the advantage of teleconferencing in distance education.**

Ans. Ref.: See Chapter-14, Page No. 163, 'Advantages of Teleconferencing'

***(d)* Describe the uses of computer networking in distance education.**

Ans. Ref.: See Chapter-15, Page No. 173, 'Computer Netowrks'.

***(e)* Discuss the uses of graphics in video programme.**

Ans. Ref.: See Chapter-11, Page No. 123, 'Graphics'.

***(f)* Explain the role of interactivity in distance learning.**

Ans. Ref.: See Chapter-5, Page No. 61, 'Interactivity and User Friendliness'.

Q. 4. Answer the following question:

Suppose you are assigned to teach a topic of your choice at the under-graduate level. Select the media appropriate to teach the same topic. Discuss the factors that you would consider while selecting the media.

Ans. Ref.: See Chapter-5, Page No. 54, 'Media Selection'.

■■

QUESTION PAPER

Exam Held in

March – 2022

(Solved)

COMMUNICATION TECHNOLOGY FOR DISTANCE EDUCATION **M.E.S.-115**

Time: 3 Hours] ***[Weightage: 70%***

Note: *All questions are* ***compulsory****. All questions carry equal weightage.*

Q. 1. Answer the following question:

What is the role of educational television in distance education? Describe the future of educational television in the era of Internet.

Ans. Ref.: See Chapter-7, Page No. 80, 'Potential of Educational Television', Page No. 83, 'Future Trends in Educational Television'.

Or

What are the characteristics of satellite communication? Describe the specific uses of satellites in communication in educational institutions.

Ans. Ref.: See Chapter-14, Page No. 160, 'Characteristics of Satellite', Page No. 162, Satellite Based Communication and Distance Education'.

Q. 2. Answer the following question:

What do you mean by 'Computer Assisted Learning' (CAL)? Discuss its uses in distance education.

Ans. Ref.: See Chapter-13, Page No. 147, 'Computr Assisted Learning (CAL)'.

Or

Explain the concept and the advantages of communication technology. Identify the major problems in implementing it in teaching-learning process.

Ans. Ref.: See Chapter-3, Page No. 29, 'Uses of Communication Technology', Page No. 30, 'Applications of Communication Technology: Problems'.

Q. 3. Answer any four of the following questions:

(a) **Write a short note on editing of video programme.**

Ans. Ref.: See Chapter-12, Page No. 136, 'Editing'.

(b) **Write any two major categories of resources for which a producer has to plan and budget.**

Ans. Ref.: See Chapter-11, Page No. 122, 'Budgeting', 'Resource Planing and Scheduling'.

(c) **Write a short note on 'Field Recording'.**

Ans. Ref.: See Chapter-12, Page No. 135, 'Field/ Location Recording'.

(d) **State the strengths of radio/audio medium.**

Ans. Ref.: See Chapter-6, Page No. 70, 'Strengths of Radio/Audio Medium'.

(e) **Why do we need 'Media Integration' in distance education?**

Ans. Ref.: See Chapter-5, Page No. 57, 'Media Integration'.

(f) **Describe the process of estimating the cost of video programme.**

Ans. Ref.: See Chapter-11, Page No. 122, 'Budgeting'.

Q. 4. Answer the following question:

Identify a topic of your choice for an educational video programme. Describe the steps you would follow to develop the script for the same video programme.

Ans. Ref.: See Chapter-10, Page No. 113, 'Script Writing'.

■■

QUESTION PAPER

Exam Held in
August – 2021

(Solved)

COMMUNICATION TECHNOLOGY FOR DISTANCE EDUCATION **M.E.S.-115**

Time: 3 Hours] *[Weightage: 70%*

Note: All questions are compulsory. All questions carry equal weightage.

Q. 1. Answer the following questions:

Differentiate between Computer Managed Learning (CML) and Computer Based Learning (CBL). Describe the significance of using computer in distance education to perform the pedagogical functions.

Ans. Ref.: See Chapter-13, Page No. 148, 'Computer Management Learning (CML)', 'Computer Based Training (CBT)'.

Or

Critically discuss the criteria for making decisions about media selection for distance education.

Ans. Ref.: See Chapter-5, Page No. 57, 'Bates, Critaria for Decision-Making'.

Q. 2. Answer the following question:

Explain the functions of the production team members for producing audio-video programmes.

Ans. Ref.: See Chapter-8, Page No. 93, 'Functions of Team Members'.

Or

Define satellite-based communication and its importance in distance education.

Ans. Ref.: See Chapter-14, Page No. 162, 'Satellite Based Communication and Distance Education'.

Q. 3. Answer any four of the following questions:

(a) **Explain the role of communication in distance education.**

Ans. Ref.: See Chapter-1, Page No. 6, 'Role of Communication'.

(b) **What are the strengths and weaknesses of video cassettes?**

Ans. Ref.: See Chapter-7, Page No. 84, 'Strengths and Weakness of Video Cassettes'.

(c) **Mention the major stages in writing for an educational programme.**

Ans. Ref.: See Chapter-10, Page No. 18, Q. No. 2.

(d) **Write a short note on Shooting Plan.**

Ans. Ref.: See Chapter-12, Page No. 136, 'Shooting Plan'.

(e) **Differentiate between Teletext and Video-text.**

Ans. Ref.: See Chapter-7, Page No. 84, 'Teletext', 'Videotext'.

(f) **Discuss technologies for people with disability.**

Ans. Ref.: See Chapter-4, Page No. 42, 'Technology for People with Disabilities'.

Q. 4. Answer the following questions:

Describe the process of organising a teleconferencing session using a two-way audio and one-way video system.

Ans. Ref.: See Chapter-14, Page No. 163, 'Organising Teleconferencing Sessions'.

■■

COMMUNICATION TECHNOLOGY FOR DISTANCE EDUCATION

BLOCK-1 COMMUNICATION TECHNOLOGY : BASICS

1 Issues in Communication

INTRODUCTION

Communication is a part of all human activities. The effectiveness of communication is becoming more and more important in social interactions and specifically, in educational institutions. The concept of communication, especially educational communication and the process of communication will both be covered in this chapter. Additionally, an effort has been made to connect the idea of general communication with education in general and communication in remote education, in particular. In this chapter, we will study issues related to communication and related aspects of educational communication.

CHAPTER AT A GLANCE

COMMUNICATION: THE CONCEPT

There are numerous ways to define communication. Some claim it is a science—a learned behaviour or skill—while, still others describe it as an art—something creative. Broadly speaking, communication encompasses much more than just art. Due to the fact that it requires a number of teachable techniques and psychomotor skills, it is a combination of a skill and a science. However, because it is founded on certain principles that can be tested and applied to make it effective, communication is best characterised as a science. Here, we assume that communication is a field of study that yields experts in the field. In order to find a scientific explanation for the concept of communication, we will examine communication as a science.

People interpret communication differently depending on the context, provided by the varied locations or surroundings, where communication takes place. Communication has been defined to meet situational needs, ranging from the sharing of meaning to convincing others to elicit the required planned responses.

Three components make up communication are the source, the channel and the receiver. According to the source, persuasion is at the heart of communication. As a communicator, she/he feels certain that the conversation occurred or that the anticipated results were obtained. Communication, from the perspective of the receiver, is a procedure to elicit the intended reactions. If the recipient acts in the manner that you expect, the source will be pleased. Communication is a medium, a carrier of information from the source to the receiver and/or vice-versa from the perspective of the channel. As a result, communication is defined in terms of the tasks to be completed or the goals to be attained.

According to Shannon and Weaver (1949), the primary concern of communication is to reproduce as faithfully as possible a message sent from one place to another place. On the basis of different explanations, Schramm (1973) defined communication as the functions of persuading, informing, teaching and entertaining people. Therefore, communication is a process by which people create and share information with one another to reach a common understanding.

Functions of Communication

Communication performs various socio-psychological functions. MacBride (1980) has discussed some functions of communication in a social system. The main functions are as follows:

***(i)* Information:** The collective storing and dissemination of information for wider human use is referred to as communication. This makes it possible for people to engage in and make informed decisions about any topics with social relevance. Information has been utilised as a socio-cultural and economic development resource.

***(ii)* Socialisation:** Individuals who are active in their communities benefit from communication. People pick up social customs, so they can coexist peacefully. People in a social system have possibilities to comprehend one another and appreciate the sentiments, emotions, ideas and expectations of others because they have access to a variety of information.

***(iii)* Motivation:** A society develops in large part due to the individual motivation of its members. Individual and group activities are encouraged by communication, which also inspires people to achieve predetermined goals. People with knowledge take the lead in social welfare efforts.

***(iv)* Education:** Information dissemination fosters intellectual growth and aids in developing the abilities and skills necessary to contribute effectively to society. In this sense, education and communication are complementary concepts. The level of communication between society's citizens and educators determines the quality of education.

***(v)* Entertainment:** Recreation and entertainment are crucial for maintaining the health of both individuals and society. Through a variety of communicative activities, such as dance, drama, sports, music, etc., people find delight and entertainment. These communication channels offer amusement on an individual and group level.

Means of Communication

There are various tools and media, which serve as means of communication among human beings. Starting from the signs - the primitive means, to super computer-based-communication, there are various techniques, technologies and materials generally used to collect, produce, carry, receive, store, retrieve and disseminate information. All human beings make use of one or the other means of communication depending upon their accessibility and effectiveness. The potential of each means of communication, as well as its weaknesses are discussed below:

***(i)* Signs and sounds:** Simple signs have been used by humans as a form of communication since prehistoric times. Different communities employ body language and other non-verbal languages like facial expression, gestures, music, songs, drawings and paintings. Despite limitations, these communication methods are used for a variety of purposes in primitive societies. With time, these means of communication improved and their application range expanded to more extensive uses.

***(ii)* Language:** All around the world, a variety of languages and dialects are utilised for communication. There are approximately a thousand dialects spoken in India, in addition to the 18 official languages specified in the Eighth Schedule of the Constitution. At both the national and international levels, language is crucial for communication in both face-to-face and remote settings. Language use also plays a significant role in communicating in the classroom. The inability of a substantial portion of the population to communicate effectively with one another due to linguistic barriers causes issues.

***(iii)* Postal system:** The most important network for delivering information from point to point is the postal system. It is used as the centre of remote communication on a global scale. The most widely used form of communication, in both developed and developing nations is the postal system.

***(iv)* Telephone:** The telephone system is one of the networks used for interpersonal communication. In India, telephone use in the classroom is still uncommon. The biggest obstacles to using the telephone extensively in distance education are its limited network, expensive expenses and the lack of initiative on the part of the country's educators. But in recent years, telephone communication has expanded, rather quickly in our nation.

In comparison to other nations, our nation's telephone network infrastructure is extremely subpar. One telephone connection is accessible for every 2, 2, 1.5 and 1.3 people in Australia, Japan, Canada and the United States, correspondingly.

***(v)* Mass media:** The development of radio waves and the printing press has completely changed how people communicate globally. Communication now has a wider audience and is more efficient. Mass education has expanded to include textbooks, newspapers, radio and television broadcasts. Broadcasting is a successful method of distributing information to an infinite audience by bypassing geographic restrictions. It transcends international borders. New possibilities have been made possible by advancements in communication technology.

***(vi)* Satellites:** The world has come together, thanks to satellites. In a flash, information can be sent or received from anywhere in the world. There are communication satellites in several nations. India is one of the few nations, which have own satellites. The satellites that India has so far launched are mostly employed for a variety of domestic objectives. The Indian National Satellites are equipped to offer services for meteorological data, telephone networking, remote sensing, in addition to television and radio broadcasts.

***(vii)* Computers:** The computers are the most advanced and sophisticated means of communication. They are a force in education, as they perform a number of functions with complete efficiency. They have made communication more interactive and individualised.

Process of Communication

The communication process, as Shannon and Weaver proposed in 1949, involves five elements—the source, the receiver, the channel, a coding scheme and noise.

***(i)* Source and Receiver:** There will be no communication without the source and the recipient. Humans, animals, or even inanimate objects can be the source and the receiver. For instance, an information source can be a computer, a non-living mechanism. In the context of educational communication, the sources are the institutions and the recipients are the students.

***(ii)* Channels:** The channels of communication are the means through, which information is transmitted from the source to the receiver. We communicate via a variety of methods, including touch, drumming, spoken words, written words and electrical devices. Even non-verbal and verbal communication can be carried out through facial expressions. The old forms of communication, such as sound signals conveyed across great distances, are still used by tribal groups. Today, we communicate via radio, television, cassettes, telephone, computers, video discs, videotexts and satellite. The following diagram illustrates how the source, receiver and channel are related to one another:

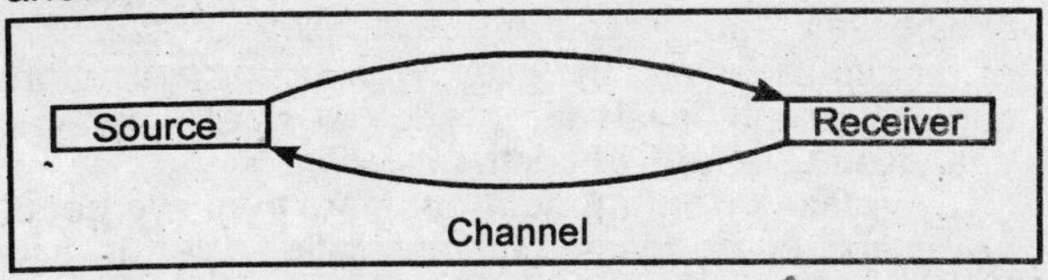

There are direct and indirect communication channels. In the direct channel, we communicate thoughts and information using spoken words, gestures and facial expressions. Electronic and non-electronic communication channels are used in the indirect channel. In the classroom, for instance, we frequently rely on direct communication, or face-to-face instruction, whereas in distance education, we also use non-print and print media in addition to speech communication. In a certain method of education, the curriculum design is significantly impacted by the choice of communication channel.

***(iii)* Code:** A set of signs or symbols used in communication produces meaning for both the sender and the receiver. Word-of-mouth, written material and pictures are all forms of coding used to convey thoughts, feelings and opinions. We use a number of verbal and non-verbal communication signals in our social interactions. The source and the receiver should both be able to access the code being used for successful communication.

***(iv)* Noise:** Effective communication might be hampered by a few issues. When something interferes with or blocks the transmission of information from the source to the receiver, it is called a noise or a barrier. Noise is any component, excluding those introduced by the sender and the receiver that interferes with the accurate transfer of information. Overloading on information is one possibility, as are reception-related technological problems. The example below demonstrates how noise becomes a communication barrier:

A multitude of noise types can obstruct the flow of information. The three types of noise covered are as follows:

(a) **Poor Reception:** Poor reception distorts or lessens the effectiveness of the message. Poor audio quality for audio resources, distorted pictures for video programmes and subpar paper and printing for text materials are a few examples. These pauses make users less inclined to participate in the communication process.

(b) **Overloaded/ambiguous Information:** Information that is excessive or unclear can reduce the effectiveness of a communication. For instance, a course unit containing too much material may distract students and make it difficult for them to comprehend the meaning of the message.

If there is too much information being aired on the radio or TV all the time, the audience may start to become passive users. Similar to this, communication is hampered by confusing information.

(c) **Environmental Distractors:** Noise is frequently a byproduct of environmental disturbances. Consider watching or listening to audio or video cassettes as an example. Communication is less effective when there are interruptions, such a ringing phone or typewriter noise. Even watching television at home is impossible because of the kids running around the house, the phone ringing and family conversations. Environmental distractions should be eliminated or minimised to ensure that they do not impede the consumer's ability to pay attention to the content being provided in order to facilitate effective communication.

This is how the educational programme's materials should be studied as well.

Both the phrases "noises" and "barriers" relate to any interference in communication (whether one-way or two-way) between the source and the receiver (s). The interruptions or noises have an effect on how successfully the student and teacher connect pedagogically in both face-to-face and mediated education.

***(v)* Feedback:** Feedback is a communication in reaction to a prior message from the source. Any technique that allows the sender to determine whether and how the information was received by the intended receiver is considered this. The recipient, in turn, communicates any queries or worries, requests further clarification and requests confirmation that he or she has understood the information correctly or in line with the intent of the author.

In addition to letting the source know how well the information was received by the recipient, feedback enables both the source and the receiver to correct errors and omissions. Feedback affects one's communication style now and in the future. In a face-to-face situation, feedback can be both verbal and non-verbal. Either the sender or the recipient can quickly accept or reject the communication. A straightforward smile could indicate the source's or the receiver's reaction. A single head nod is all that is required to start a two-way conversation. In situations like remote schooling, feedback is occasionally given through written communication. While communicating virtually, feedback can come in a variety of methods.

There are two types of feedback-immediate feedback and delayed feedback. When learning in person, the student receives prompt feedback from his or her teachers. Even when using a computer to aid in learning, the student can get quick feedback on how they are doing. Though the student prepares their assignment responses and submits them to the assessors for their comments and grading, they don't receive feedback on their work for a few days. After a brief break, remarks are given to the teacher and the student in radio and television broadcasts as well. Instantaneous or delayed feedback is essential for effective communication and to ensure the desired effect on the students. It also implies that we are concerned with having the desired effect on the receivers by raising feedback frequency and systematising it.

***(vi)* Context:** The environment in which communication occurs is essential to the exchange of information. Environments that are social, physical, or culturally specific, might affect how something is transmitted. In our daily lives, we constantly overhear people saying, "You misconstrued what I said. You've given my request a lot of thought. I jokingly said" ... and so on. The effectiveness of communication is also impacted by factors pertaining to behaviours, attitudes and values. Similar to this, the mental and physical well-being of the participants affects how well they communicate.

Types of Communication

Communication can be discussed at four levels:

(i) Interpersonal Communication
(ii) Group Communication
(iii) Organisational Communication
(iv) Mass Communication

***(i)* Interpersonal Communication:** This is a typical form of communication when two people exchange ideas, feelings and opinions. Interpersonal communication includes interactions between friends, between teachers and students, between mothers and children and other situations. Another instance of interpersonal communication that takes place remotely is talking to someone on the phone.

***(ii)* Group Communication:** In this kind of communication, a team's members decide together on a challenge, an issue, or a topic of shared interest. To achieve a set of objectives, to forge new social connections, or to find a solution to a challenge the group is facing, the participants in a group communication play an active role in communication. The diagrammatic representation of group communication is shown below. Group communication systems can be found in places like the family, a particular area of an office and a classroom.

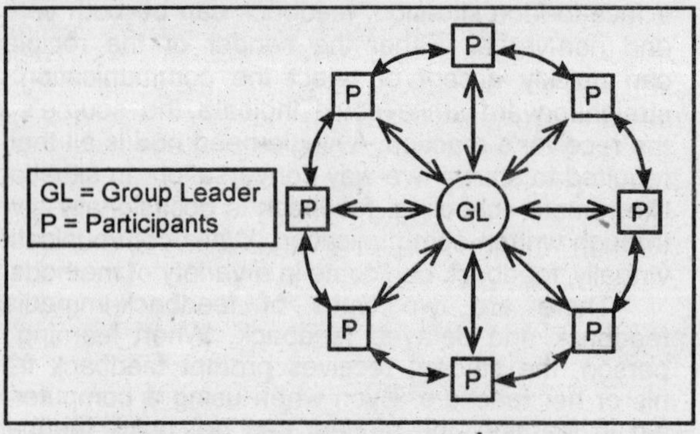

***(iii)* Organisational Communication:** It is centred on a single organisation. Any organisation can be considered a multiple group communication system because it is made up of groups of people interacting with one another. Anywhere within the organisation may initiate communication but the only direct channel for information is within the organisation. Schools, businesses and offices are examples of this form of communication. In this type of organisational communication system, notifications are typically employed as a form of communication.

***(iv)* Mass Communication:** More than two people are involved in mass communication, yet it goes beyond group and organisational communication. As the name "mass" suggests, this kind of communication always involves a sizable group of people exchanging knowledge, concepts and ideas. In this instance, we communicate with a sizable audience through the mainstream media. Face-to-face interactions, as well as print and non-print media, can all be used in mass communication. For instance, radio and television programmes are transmitted to inform, educate and/or entertain a sizable audience.

Three features of mass communication are covered below:

***(i)* The audience is large and heterogeneous:** There is a sizable and diverse audience. Being mass communication mediums, radio and television have a sizable audience with a variety of origins, tastes, ages and jobs. These mediums are accessible to both uneducated and literate people. A similar mass medium, newspapers have a somewhat smaller audience.

***(ii)* The source is an institution or a group of people:** A Company or a group of individuals are the source. For instance, the Indian government's Ministry of Information and Broadcasting broadcasts radio and television programmes all over the nation. One of the private organisations in India that participate in printed mass communication is The Times of India group.

***(iii)* Some kind of mechanism is used to reproduce information:** Information reproduction involves some sort of mechanism. The printing press, the television and radio receivers, the studio where programmes are produced and the transmitters, all serve as mechanisms.

Educational Communication

The Latin verb "communicate", which means "to share", is the source of the English term "communication". Sharing knowledge, abilities and attitudes is a part of the teaching and learning process. The act of exchanging content with pupils remotely is known as distance education. As a result, communication between society and people can be viewed as a process of education (Hills, 1986). Hills adds that the effectiveness of education in conveying societal standards should be regularly assessed. The process of how professors and students behave and interact to advance the knowledge of the latter is at the heart of educational communication. Teachers and institutions serve as the sources in educational communication and the communications are curriculum-related (the content, the skills and the attitudes and related activities which educate, inform, train, enlighten, inspire and entertain the students). Students serve as the receivers and a variety of instructional techniques including textbooks, assignments, audio-visual aids, demonstrations and tutorials are employed as media to communicate the information. In distance learning, communication is accomplished through self-directed learning using a variety of teaching-learning configurations.

Through satellites, which have the ability to transmit even live events to the students at their place of employment, it is now possible to deliver education to all corners of the globe. Education has thus, transcended numerous limitations of location and time. As a result, modifications have been made to both teaching and learning strategies. Technology has stepped in to improve the nature of educational communication, including computers, videotapes, videodiscs, teletexts, communication satellites and teleconferencing services. The teaching and learning processes are now more engaging and interactive, thanks to these technology. They have accelerated learning, as well as improved methods for storing and retrieving information. According to Hills (1986), the computer sits alongside the cerebellum, optic lobes and cerebrum as the "fourth brain" of man.

One such is the communication model developed by Shannon and Weaver in 1949. In this concept, the agency responsible for passing on knowledge, skills, values and culture to the next generation is the teacher or educational institution. Teachers manage and provide information in a way that helps pupils understand it. By encoding their thoughts in a set of symbols, such as spoken or written words, written sentences, or visual cues, the teachers make their ideas apparent. There are many communication channels utilised in education today; the key to choosing the right channel is determining if it accurately and clearly conveys the message to the students as intended by the source (teacher/educational institution).

As was previously said, the teacher or institution providing distant education should ensure that the students receive the information intended for them. They should have the necessary knowledge and abilities to do this, including the ability to understand the content, take notes, respond to self-assessment questions and build on the students' past knowledge. In other words, the course materials ought to be based on the prior knowledge or background of the intended pupils. In order to improve the course materials' quality and meet the set objectives, feedback is crucial.

The teacher should learn how the students are responding to and absorbing his or her lessons, modules, audio, or video programmes. By eliminating errors in decoding and issues brought on by "noise", such information will improve communication throughout the teaching and learning process. On the other side, the students should also receive feedback on how well they are understanding the material being covered. Students will be inspired to learn more by feedback on their performance and the course material. The following diagram can be used to describe the educational communication process for the sake of clarity.

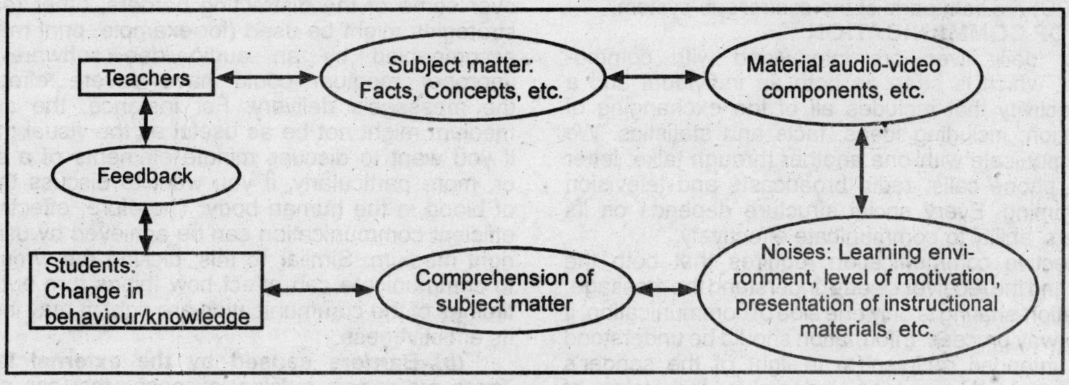

Educational Communication Process

The students play a dual role in educational communication, since they serve as both sources and receivers. In order to assist the students in meeting the goals of the course, the instructor assumes the position of a "manager" and employs a variety of teaching strategies. The learning materials are interacted with by the students, who extract the intended meaning from them. Students must therefore, be given more consideration in educational communication since they actively engage in learning, rather than simply being the recipients of information. In a distant learning setting, students are self-directed, independent learners. It is even more crucial that the media utilised for them to be noise-free. Education is described by Tiffin and Rajasingham (1995) as a communication system that is purposeful, receives specific inputs like students, teachers, knowledge and problems and processes those inputs at various communication levels so that the learners become knowledgeable to apply learned skills and knowledge to given problems. The features of an open system, such as negative entropy, feedback, steady state, differentiation, equifinality, teleology and hierarchy, are also shared by education as a communication system.

To comprehend and use the ideas in distant learning, have a discussion about them.

***(i)* Negative-entropy:** Open systems tend to be more organised and resist the trend toward disorder. They rely on the environmental suprasystem and the feedback system to accomplish this.

the system to adjust them by taking remedial action.

***(iii)* Steady state:** This dynamic equilibrium state occurs when the system maintains its structural stability despite changes in the external environment.

***(iv)* Differentiation:** Open systems move towards a greater level of organisation or growth, in addition to adapting to their changing environment. Growth results in function differentiation and specialisation.

***(v)* Equifinality:** This refers to an open system's capacity to arrive at a specific state or condition via a number of alternative routes.

Due to their innate resilience and flexibility in adapting to shifting environments, open systems can reach a given goal state using a variety of alternate strategies.

***(vi)* Teleology:** This attribute of open systems shows their purposefulness and how they function, in accordance with their goals.

***(vii)* Hierarchy:** Open systems are hierarchical, meaning that each of their numerous integral lower level subsystems is a dependent component of the higher level system. They are both autonomous frameworks. It is simple to apply all these qualities to education as a communication system. The figure that follows, shows distance learning as a communication system with open system characteristics. The picture depicts processing at several fractal levels that represent various communication modalities. In distance learning, the study centre, regional centre and material delivery system are support subsystems. The administrative sub-system, which manages the system as a whole and institutional design (ID) are both parts of the control sub-system.

ROLE OF COMMUNICATION

Our daily lives are intertwined with communication, which is seen as both an individual and a group activity that includes all of the exchanging of information, including ideas, facts and statistics. We all communicate with one another through talks, letter writing, phone calls, radio broadcasts and television programming. Every social structure depends on its members' ability to communicate effectively.

Effective communication requires that both the sender and the receiver clearly understand the message. Information-sharing is only one side of communication, it is a two-way process. Information should be understood by the intended recipient(s) in light of the sender's objectives(s). We cannot undervalue the value of communication in our lives because we are all involved in one form of communication or another. Therefore, a thorough examination of the idea is necessary. We can make sure that the information is conveyed by having a thorough understanding of communication as a process. The communication will fail if the recipient does not understand the message from its proper angle. Consider the significance of educational communication as it relates to complex information. It is challenging to provide instructional content in a way that each student fully comprehends it. We can say that educational communication is successful if the learner is able to demonstrate a behavioural change or improvement. It is more challenging to communicate with online students than it is with those who study in person. There are a number of obstacles standing in the way of remote learning students and institutions. For instance, there is typically no provision for immediate feedback from either party. Most of the teachers and students are strangers.

BARRIERS TO COMMUNICATION

A message goes through a number of steps on its way from the sender to the recipient and vice versa. This causes a number of interference in effective communication. According to Sillars, two different sorts of barriers, frequently obstruct communication.

***(a)* Barriers caused by the senders and receivers:** The senders and the receivers themselves disrupt communication. The reasons could be a lack of understanding between the parties, poorly stated goals, an inability to understand the language used, etc., or a lack of clarity on the part of the sender and the recipient. The communication might not appear to the recipient in the way that the source intended (communicator). Defensiveness, a persistent attitude, a situational misunderstanding and unwarranted certainty are among factors that can hinder successful communication between participants. The communication is also influenced by the person's background and experience. The efficient flow of information can be disrupted by personality traits, such as aptitude, attitude, interest and motivation.

Similarly, covert distractions like student tension, frustration, anxiety, etc., might reduce the impact of educational communication. As a source, you cannot compel a student to participate in the planning and creation of the teaching materials. To go around or over some of the distracting barriers, other teaching strategies might be used (for example, print materials accompanied by an audio-video software). The improper medium could have severe effects on the message's delivery. For instance, the auditory medium might not be as useful as the visual medium if you want to discuss minute elements of a system or, more particularly, if you want to discuss the flow of blood in the human body. Therefore, effective and efficient communication can be achieved by using the right medium. Similar to this, picking the wrong time to communicate can affect how things turn out. If the timings of the communication are right, it may increase its effectiveness.

***(b)* Barriers caused by the external factors:** There are certain outside influences that can obstruct communication. Noise such as mechanical noise from moving automobiles, typewriter noise, contradictory messages, bad printing impressions and poor sender and receiver reception. Lack of sufficient motivation is on the part of the recipient. The participants might not be prepared to pay less attention than they would normally. Similar to this, a lack of incentives, such as poor work prospects upon course completion, may render communication useless. The method of communication. Effective communication is hampered by inadequate maintenance, inferior tools, faulty receiving sets, weak transmission waves, etc. Following are some possible actions that could be taken to interfere with some barriers:

(i) Both parties should be aware that effective communication is necessary. Both parties should take the initiative to communicate on the same page.

(ii) In order to comprehend each other, both parties must be able to think and feel somewhat similarly. If not, they will not be able to communicate effectively.

(iii) Both parties should collaborate on a deliberate communication act. Understanding the message alone is insufficient. There must be a result for communication to be successful and participants must exhibit the precise expected behaviour.

CHECK YOUR PROGRESS

Q. 1. Define the following terms:
***(i)* Channel *(ii)* Code *(iii)* Noise.**

Ans. *(i)* Channel: The method by which information is sent from a source to a receiver is referred to as the communication channel. Many techniques are used by us to communicate, such as touch, drumming, spoken words, written words, and electrical equipment. Face expressions can be used to convey both spoken and nonverbal messages. Tribal tribes continue to employ the antiquated methods of communication, such as sound signals transmitted over enormous distances. Radio, television, cassettes, telephone, computers, video discs, videotexts, and satellite are all common forms of communication nowadays. There are both direct and indirect channels of communication. Through direct communication, we express our ideas and information using spoken words, hand gestures, and facial emotions. The indirect channel uses both electronic and non-electronic communication channels. For instance, face-to-face instruction is usually used in the classroom, although in remote learning we also employ non-print and print media in addition to spoken communication. The selection of the communication channel has a considerable impact on the curriculum design in one particular educational approach.

***(ii)* Code:** In communications and information processing, code is a system of rules to convert information—such as a letter, word, sound, image, or gesture—into another form, sometimes shortened or secret, for communication through a communication channel or storage in a storage medium. An early example is an invention of language, which enabled a person through speech, to communicate what they thought, saw, heard, or felt for others. But speech limits the range of communication to the distance a voice can carry and limits the audience to those present when the speech is uttered. The invention of writing, which converted spoken language into visual symbols, extended the range of communication across space and time. The process of encoding converts information from a source into symbols for communication or storage. Decoding is the reverse process, converting code symbols back into a form that the recipient understands, such as English or/and Spanish. One reason for coding is to enable communication in places, where ordinary plain language, spoken or written, is difficult or impossible. For example, semaphore, where the configuration of flags held by a signaller or the arms of a semaphore tower encodes parts of the message, typically individual letters and numbers. Another person standing a great distance away can interpret the flags and reproduce the words sent. We use a number of verbal and non-verbal communication signals in our social interactions. The source and the receiver should both be able to access the code being used for successful communication.

***(iii)* Noise:** Every element that prevents an accurate transmission of information—apart from those introduced by the transmitter and the receiver—is referred to as noise. One possibility is information overload, as well as technological issues with reception. The following are the three categories of noise:

(a) **Bad reception:** Bad reception, on the other hand, distorts or diminishes the message's effectiveness. A few examples include poor audio quality for audio resources, distorted images for video programmes, and poor paper and printing for text materials. Users are less likely to join in the communication process when there are these interruptions.

(b) **Excessive or unclear information:** Excessive or unclear information might lessen the effectiveness of a communication. For instance, a course unit with too much information may divert students and make it challenging for them to understand the content.
The audience may start to become passive users if there is constantly too much information being broadcast on the radio or television. Similar to this, unclear information hinders communication.

(c) **Environmental disturbances:** Environmental disturbances frequently produce noise as a result. As an illustration, think about watching or listening to audio or video cassettes. When there are interruptions, such a ringing phone or typewriter noise, communication is less effective. Because to the children running around the house, the phone ringing, and family conversations, it is impossible to even watch television at home. To guarantee that they do not impair the consumer's capacity to pay attention to the content being supplied and to promote effective communication, environmental distractions should be eliminated or minimised.

Q. 2. Write two educational implications of interpersonal communication.

Ans. Interpersonal communication is at the core of the classroom process or teaching and learning. This is so because this type of communication happens between people and forms a personal tie between them. It is the exchange of information between two or more people sending and receiving the messages. In the context of teaching, interpersonal communication refers to the interaction that occurs among students and their teachers, which seeks to convey meaning, perform academic tasks and establish relationships. The type and degree of interaction in the classroom as a micro-social context varies across cultures, individuals and subjects. Effective interpersonal communication means effective teaching and learning.

The students play a dual role in educational communication, since they serve as both sources and receivers. In order to assist the students in meeting the goals of the course, the instructor assumes the position of a "manager" and employs a variety of teaching strategies. The learning materials are interacted with by the students, who extract the intended meaning from them. Students must therefore be given more consideration in educational communication, since they actively engage in learning rather than simply being the recipients of information. In a distant learning setting, students are self-directed, independent learners. It is even more crucial that the media utilised for them be noise-free. Education is described by Tiffin and Rajasingham (1995) as a communication system that is purposeful, receives specific inputs like students, teachers, knowledge and problems and processes those inputs at various communication levels so that the learners become knowledgeable to apply learned skills and knowledge to given problems. The features of an open system, such as negative entropy, feedback, steady state, differentiation, equifinality, teleology and hierarchy, are also shared by education as a communication system.

Q. 3. Give at least one example each of different types of communication.

Ans. Communication can be discussed at four levels:

(i) Interpersonal communication
(ii) Group communication
(iii) Organisational communication
(iv) Mass communication

***(i)* Interpersonal Communication:** Interpersonal communication is an exchange of information between two or more people. This type of communication takes place between people who are interdependent and have some knowledge of each other. For example, communication between a son and his father, an employer and an employee, two sisters, a teacher and a student, two lovers, two friends and so on. Although interpersonal communication is most often between pairs of individuals, it can also be extended to include small intimate groups, such as the family. Interpersonal communication can take place in face-to-face settings, as well as through platforms such as social media.

***(ii)* Group Communication:** Group communication is the act of sending and receiving messages to multiple members of a group. In a business environment, groups often use this type of communication to exchange ideas, determine goals and motivate other members. The size of groups can vary but they typically comprise at least three members and up to 20 members. Group communication can be beneficial for groups of all sizes, from smaller focus groups to entire departments. When groups communicate effectively, they can share necessary information as they work to accomplish mutual goals. There are many types of group communication channels and it's important to choose a method that works for most members to ensure everyone receives and understands the shared messages. Members of the group may have different styles of communicating, so more than one type of communication may be necessary to reach the group's mutual goals. For example, a group leader may choose to hold a weekly meeting to discuss the team's progress, while also using emails to communicate on a more regular basis.

***(iii)* Organisational Communication:** Organizational communication refers to the communication that takes place between people who are working towards common goals within an organization. It consists of the interactions that take place for the purpose of working together towards these goals or conducting business in general. Effective organizational communication methods and strategies can help a business flow and become successful. Organizational communication has many purposes as it aims to convey what the organization stands for and why it exists. It is also used to communicate how the work is to be completed, the levels of authority within the organization and how to identify the customers of the organization among many other topics. A company sending an email to all its employees is an organizational communication.

***(iv)* Mass Communication:** The process of disseminating information to a large audience via various communication channels is referred to as mass communication. The word "mass" describes the fact that the message is meant for a broad audience rather than a single person or group. Print media (newspapers, magazines, books), broadcast media (radio, television), digital media (websites, social media), and outdoor advertising are all examples of mass communication channels (billboards, posters). Mass communication examples include: *(a)* Television newscasts like CNN or BBC News, *(b)* Radio shows like BBC World Service or NPR, *(c)* Publications like The New York Times and The Guardian.

Q. 4. Define 'feedback' in three lines.

Ans. The feedback is the final step of the process that ensures the receiver has received the message and interpreted it correctly as it was intended by the sender. It increases the effectiveness of the communication as it permits the sender to know the efficacy of his message. Feedback is an essential part of the communication process. It represents the missing link in the sender-receiver loop, recruiting a response from the receiver to the sender. Therefore, the two-way communication process ends with feedback. Some of the reasons why feedback is important are:

- Feedback shows if the recipient has received the message and whether the message has been understood in the same terms as intended by the sender.
- Feedback signals the level of effective communication between the two parties.
- Feedback is a valuable communication skill that helps improve human relationships.
- Being the final component of communication, feedback helps break communication barriers between the sender and the receiver.
- Feedback is an excellent tool for continuous learning.
- Constructive feedback motivates the sender.

Q. 5. Why is 'feedback' so important in educational communication?

Ans. In an educational setting, feedback is any response regarding a student's performance or behaviour, or it can be a student's response to a teacher. It can be verbal, written or gestural. The purpose of feedback in the assessment and learning process is to improve a student's performance, not put a damper on it. It is essential that the process of providing feedback is a positive, or at least a neutral, learning experience for the student. Negative feedback can discourage student's effort and achievement. Instructors have the distinct responsibility to nurture a student's learning and to provide feedback in such a manner that the student does not leave the classroom feeling defeated. Providing feedback means giving students an explanation of what they are doing correctly and incorrectly, with the focus of the feedback on what the students is doing right. It is most productive to a student's learning when they are provided with an explanation as to what is accurate and inaccurate about their work. One technique is to use the concept of a "feedback sandwich" to guide your feedback–Compliment, Correct, Compliment.

When student feedback is given immediately after showing proof of learning, the student responds and remembers the experience about what is being learned more positively. If we wait too long to give feedback, the student might not connect the feedback with the learning moment.

It is vital that we take into consideration each individual when giving student feedback. Our classrooms are full of diverse learners. Some students need to be nudged to achieve at a higher level and other needs to be handled gently so as not to discourage learning and damage self-esteem. Studies of effective teaching and learning have shown that learners want to know where they stand in regards to their work. Providing answers to the following four questions on a regular basis will help provide quality student feedback.

OTHER IMPORTANT QUESTIONS

Q. 1. Write the meaning of communication.

Ans. The Latin term communis, which means common, is where the word "communication" gets its etymological roots. In order to develop "commonality" with someone, we communicate. In other words, we're attempting to spread knowledge, a concept, or a mentality. The common usage of the term is reflected in the definition of communication. To impart, bestow, or convey, to make known, or to supply by way of information is what is meant by the verb "to communicate." "The act or reality of communicating transmission, the imparting or interchange of thoughts, opinions, or information by speech, writing, or signs anything, which is communicated or imparted; a document or message conveying views or information" is how the New Webster's dictionary defines communication.

The Oxford Dictionary states that "communication is the imparting, conveying or exchanging of ideas, knowledge, etc., through speech or writing. Any attempt to define communication has to take into consideration the idea of mutuality and commonness, an exchange, a shared environment, a social relationship among the participants and the existence of a common need, urge, aim, or goal. When there is a shared experience, communication is said to occur. There are many different ways to define communication but they all share the idea that it is "a social process of interaction through messages." Charles Morris gives two definitions of communication — one broader than the other. Broadly, communication is "the establishment of a commonage." In the limited sense it means, "use of signs to establish a commonage of signification."

George Lundberg uses communication to designate interaction by signs and symbols.

Baker Brownell uses the terms "direct" and "indirect" communication. Direct communication is a function of 'identification of people with one another.' Indirect communication is a "process, wherein something converted into symbols is carried over from one person to another."

Theodore Newcomb defines communication as that process by which people influence each other or leave impression on others.

Shannon's is perhaps one of the most comprehensive definitions. According to his Mathematical Theory of Communication, communication includes "all of the procedures by which one mind may affect another or one mechanism affects another mechanism."

Q. 2. Discuss the components of communication. Explain the importance of each of them.

Ans. Communication involves following five components:

(i) Communicator or the sender
(ii) Message
(iii) Medium/media — verbal, non-verbal, symbolic, visual
(iv) Receiver
(v) Feedback

***(i)* Communicator:** When a message is sent, communication officially starts. The capacity to articulate ideas clearly is just as important as having clear ideas themselves, therefore the communicator must be aware of his or her goals, comprehend the audience, grasp the topic, organise the message methodically, choose the best channel and present the message successfully.

***(ii)* Message:** The communicator needs to be extremely clear about the message they want to get over to the audience or receiver. He must identify the subject because clearer communication results from proper specification. It is crucial for the communicator to be convinced in his own mind because if he is not, he will not be able to persuade others. The communicator should master the content before delivering it. To understand the receiver, communicator should think very carefully on the following: The receiver's knowledge and education, power of comprehension, ability in grasping message, their common standard of living, whether the message is adoptable and practicable for them.

***(iii)* Media:** The communicator should be judicious and selective in choosing the media of communication. There are four major steps involved in communication. The first is attention.

(iv) **Receiver:** The receiver receives the message and understands the content. The objective and the expectation from the receivers determine the goal of the communication. For the communication has to be effective, the receiver has to use the message.

(v) **Feedback:** It is important in communication because it enables the sender to evaluate the effectiveness of its message. Without feedback, the communication process would be incomplete.

Q. 3. What is the importance of sender in communication process?

Ans. A person, group, or organisation that starts the communication is known as the sender. The success of the message stems primarily from this source. The communication is influenced by the sender's experiences, attitudes, knowledge, competence, perspectives and culture. The message may be communicated orally, in writing, graphically, or via symbols. Communication efficacy is influenced by the sender's aptitude for communicating, attitudes and convictions, understanding of the subject matter and goals, socio-cultural context, etc. A message's sender encodes a concept. Encoding entails breaking a message down into a set of codes and words that have significance. The sender must encrypt the communication before it can be delivered to the recipient. Because it's the sender who initiates the communication process, he/she is primarily responsible for its success or failure.

Q. 4. Write the significance of message in a communication process. What are the conditions a message must fulfil to arouse the desired response in the receiver?

Ans. Signs, symbols and codes are used to create messages, which serve as signals and convey meaning. Ink on paper, sound waves in the air, electric current impulses, a wave of the hand, a flag in the air, or any other sign capable of being meaningfully deciphered can all be used to convey messages. Messages are encoded and the recipient must decode them in order to grasp or comprehend the content. The primary element of communication is the message. To achieve the desired result, it must be constructed to specifically address the needs of the recipient and be conveyed in a way that is understandable. According to Wilbur Schramm, the message must fulfil certain conditions if it is to arouse the desired response in the receiver:

(i) The message must be so designed and delivered as to gain the attention of the intended audience.

(ii) The message must employ signs that refer to the experiences common to source and the receiver, so as to get the meaning across.

(iii) The message must arouse the needs in the receiver and suggest some ways to meet these needs.

(iv) The message must suggest a way to meet these needs, which is appropriate to the context in which the receiver finds himself/herself at the time when he/she is moved to make the desired response.

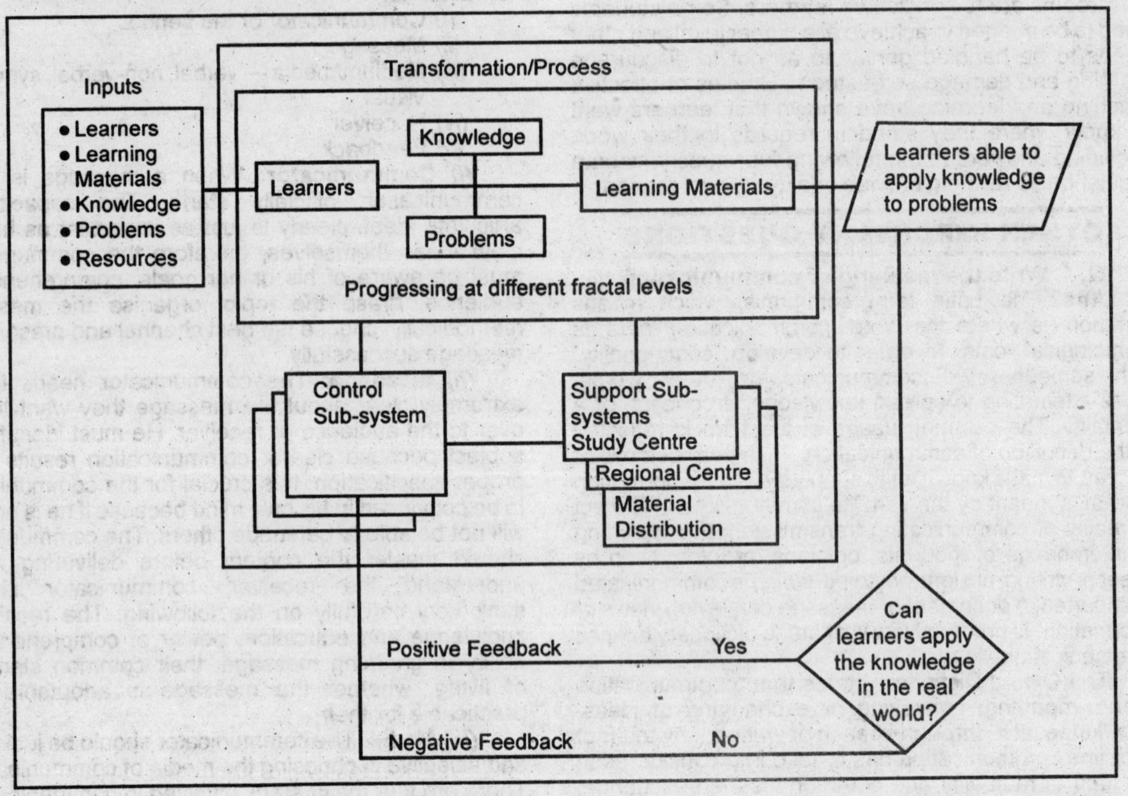

Q. 5. Explain the role of channel in communication process.

Ans. The term "channel" describes the method used to send or receive messages. The five senses—sight, touch, hearing, smell and taste—are mentioned. Any of the aforementioned sensory perception methods can be used to receive a message. Media in print or on screen can convey a message. It may be audible through audio, speech, or musical instruments. As with movies, television and other audio-visual media, it can be seen and heard. With the aid of models, demonstrations, specimens and tests, it can be handled, odoured, or tasted.

The communication process frequently involves numerous sensory faculties. When several sensory faculties are involved in receiving meaning, communication is more effective and long-lasting, meaning clearer. Mechanical devices are also included in channel. No message can be transmitted unless they are encoded. When we communicate through language or speech, we encode the message into written or spoken words. We use signs and symbols to communicate. The deaf and mute are taught to follow the sign language. In order to communicate messages to a distance we use sound waves. In order to make them last, we use writing. In order to complete the act of communication, the message must be decoded.

Q. 6. Write a brief note on the role of receiver in communication process. What is the significance of experience in effective communication?

Ans. The receiver, also called a destination, may be an individual or a group, a crowd, or a mob, reading, listening or watching. The receiver is the object in the communication process. The sender must constantly keep the needs, aspirations, knowledge, socio-cultural milieu and background of the receiver if the message is to have the desired objective. Wilbur Schramm speaks of the field of experience as an important factor for effective communication. The source can encode and the destination can decode only in terms of the experience each has had. If there has been no common field of experience, communication is impossible. Schramm illustrated this with the experience of an African tribesman who sees an aeroplane for the first time. The plane may seem to him to be a bird and the aviator a God born on wings. The film "God's Must be Crazy" illustrates this idea. Here the experience of the source and the destination are strikingly different. This difficulty persists when we try to communicate with cultures that are much different from ours.

The 'sender-message-channel-receiver' model has been criticised for presenting communication as linear and definite. Communication is an endless process and hence it is misleading to think of the communication process as starting somewhere and ending somewhere. The science of cybernetics has provided important insights into the process of communication by making available analytical tools like signs, symbols, feedback, redundancy, noise, etc.

Perhaps the greatest contribution of cybernetics to the communication process has been that of feedback. Feedback not only makes communication circular but also enables modification possible at different stages in the process of communication.

Q. 7. What do you know about the barriers of communication?

Ans. Barriers make the communication imperfect. The sender has no control over the barriers. There are three types of barriers:

(i) Psychological — emotional, perceptual and selectivity,

(ii) Semantic.

(iii) Physical.

Emotional is psychological block. The sender and the receiver both may have emotional blocks. People also perceive things differently. Another perceptual problem occurs when people tries to fill in information without checking its accuracy. Perception is based on people's own experiences. One perceives what he expects to perceive. A final set of psychological blocks exist because of competition for people's time and attention — the question of selectivity. The selection factors are: timing, context and content (how much positive/ negative).

The semantic barriers happen during choice of words for a certain message. Since words can mean different things, these create a block. Block in communication may also be created by physical appearance, the audience and context of the message and presentation.

Q. 8. Noise plays a role in communication process. Explain.

Ans. Anything that hinders or interferes with our ability to send or receive messages is considered noise. By drawing attention away from the communication act, noise diverts communicators' attention. Effective communicators figure out how to make sure their messages are accurately received, despite any background noise. Both internal and external sources produce noise. Noise can come from the spoken words, the surrounding circumstances, physical discomfort, psychological state and intellectual capacity. It becomes less and less likely that we will be able to negotiate or share meaning as the noise level rises. The environment's sight, sound, smell and feel are examples of external sources of noise. A drab room, an overly warm space, a loud siren, an offensive odour and too many conversations occurring at the same time are all examples of environmental noise.

Among the internal sources of noise are personal thoughts and feelings. Racism, sexism, feelings of inadequacy, hunger, excessive shyness or extroversion and deficient or excessive knowledge can all interfere with the ability to send and receive messages effectively. Most of us find it easier to cope with external noise than with internal noise because closing a window, for example, is usually a lot easier than opening a mind or changing a personality.

Q. 9. Discuss how channel affects the communication process.

Ans. Similar to how a bridge connects two sites, messages are sent and received over a channel. Face-to-face communication uses all five senses to transmit and receive signals. In practice, we may use several channels at once to send a single message. In reality, interpersonal communication is typically a multichannel guided interaction using situational/manipulative means, visual, auditory, tactile, olfactory and ways to transmit both verbal and non-verbal messages.

Channel-switchers are skilled communicators. They understand how to convey ideas through traditional words and non-verbal cues, as well as through sound, sight, touch, taste, smell and the surrounding environment. However, if you find yourself consistently tuning in on just one channel, you might miss the most salient parts of a message.

Today, with computer-mediated communication, we have a richness of channels to choose from. In addition to face-to-face contact, we have texting and instant messaging. For example, if one channel is closed or damaged, we can open another to compensate. For instance, rather than assuming that a blind or sight-impaired person will be able to recognize us by our voice, we should also name ourselves. Since the blind person is unable to see the visual cues we use to colour in or shade the meaning of a verbal message, we may also need to take special care to ensure that the meanings we want conveyed are contained in the words we choose and the expressiveness of our voice.

Q. 10. Feedback is important in communication process. Explain.

Ans. Feedback informs the source of his accomplishment in achieving his goal and helps him determine the best course of action moving forward. The messages that individual encodes are fed back into his system by his decoder when he communicates with himself. For example, by writing himself a letter. However, he needs feedback from those he speaks with in order to know whether he was successful in getting his point across and whether it had the desired impact. The receiver's response is impacted by the source's activity and vice versa. The responses of the other can be used by either the source or the receiver. Feedback is provided by responses. A newspaper might influence its readers by deciding, what news they can read. Similarly, the readers also affect the newspaper. If readers do not buy the paper, it may have, to change its selection criteria of news and presentation of news. An experienced communicator is attentive to feedback and constantly modifies his message in the light of what he observes in or bears from his audience. Person to person communication channels permit maximum feedback. The source has an opportunity to change his message immediately as a result of feedback he gets. Mass communication channels have minimum opportunity for feedback, since the source and the receiver are separated in time and space. They have little opportunity to get feedback from each other.

MULTIPLE CHOICE QUESTIONS

Q. 1. Who says the primary concern of communication is to reproduce as faithfully as possible a message sent from one place to another place?

(*a*) Shannon (*b*) Weaver
(*c*) Both (*a*) and (*b*) (*d*) None of these

Ans. (*c*) Both (*a*) and (*b*).

Q. 2. Who defined communication as the functions of persuading, informing, teaching and entertaining people?

(*a*) Shannon (*b*) Weaver
(*c*) Schramm (*d*) None of these

Ans. (*c*) Schramm.

Q. 3. Who discussed some functions of communication in a social system?

(*a*) MacBride (*b*) Weaver
(*c*) Schramm (*d*) Shannon

Ans. (*a*) MacBride.

Q. 4. Indian National Satellites (INSATs) are capable of providing facilities for:

(*a*) Meteorological data
(*b*) Telephone networking
(*c*) Remote sensing
(*d*) All of these

Ans. (*d*) All of these.

Q. 5. A communication code is a set of signals or symbols that creates meaning for

(*a*) Both the source(s) and the receiver(s)
(*b*) The source(s)
(*c*) The receiver(s)
(*d*) None of these

Ans. (*a*) Both the source(s) and the receiver(s).

Q. 6. Which is not a code in communication?

(*a*) Word of mouth (*b*) Written material
(*c*) Visuals (*d*) Channels

Ans. (*d*) Channels.

Q. 7. Communication between a student and a teacher is:

(*a*) Interpersonal communication
(*b*) Group communication
(*c*) Organisational communication
(*d*) Mass communication

Ans. (*a*) Interpersonal communication.

Q. 8. Which of the following is not interpersonal communication?

(*a*) Interaction between two friends
(*b*) Interaction between teacher and student
(*c*) Interaction between mother and child
(*d*) Interaction between employer and employees

Ans. (*d*) Interaction between employer and employees.

Q. 9. Communication between a teacher and students in a class is:

(*a*) Interpersonal communication
(*b*) Group communication
(*c*) Organisational communication
(*d*) Mass communication

Ans. (*b*) Group communication.

Q. 10. Communication in an office is:
(a) Interpersonal communication
(b) Group communication
(c) Organisational communication
(d) Mass communication
Ans. (c) Organisational communication.

Q. 11. In comparison, which have a large audience with different backgrounds, tastes, ages and occupations?
(a) Radio and television
(b) Radio
(c) Newspapers and magazines
(d) Television
Ans. (a) Radio and television.

Q. 12. Which of the following step is not taken by the communicator?
(a) Formuiating the message by putting thoughts into words
(b) Passing the message through various psychological or internal communication barriers
(c) The message is encoded for transmission
(d) The message is decoded
Ans. (d) The message is decoded.

Q. 13. Which is engaged in broadcasting television and radio programmes all over the country?
(a) Ministry of Information and Broadcasting
(b) Ministry of Finance
(c) Ministry of Small-scale Industries
(d) None of these
Ans. (a) Ministry of Information and Broadcasting.

Q. 14. Newspaper is a:
(a) Message (b) Sender
(c) Medium (d) Receiver
Ans. (c) Medium.

Q. 15. Hills regards the __________ as man's 'fourth brain'.
(a) Computer (b) Message
(c) Satellites (c) Channels
Ans. (a) Computer.

Q. 16. The smiling of a person after listening to a comedian is a:
(a) Message
(b) Sender
(c) Medium
(d) Feedback
Ans. (d) Feedback.

Q. 17. Illiterate and the literate can make use of which media?
(a) Radio and television
(b) Radio
(c) Newspapers and magazines
(d) Television
Ans. (a) Radio and television.

Q. 18. Which is not true about communication?
(a) Failure to understand the receiver may result in failure in the communication process
(b) An illiterate cannot understand a written message but can understand if it is explained in spoken words
(c) A good communicator does not require good communication skills
(d) Communication becomes effective when both the sender and the receiver understand the same information
Ans. (c) A good communicator does not require good communication skills.

Q. 19. Verbal, written or electronic are:
(a) Different feedbacks of communication
(b) Different types of message
(c) Different barriers of communication
(d) Different channels of transmission
Ans. (d) Different channels of transmission.

Q. 20. Which of the following is not a verbal communication?
(a) Face-to-face meetings
(b) Telephone conversations
(c) Video conferencing
(d) E-mails
Ans. (d) E-mails.

■■

Growth of Communication Technology

2

INTRODUCTION

When people first began writing on stone or wood in ancient times, communication was only movable within a small region. Various other forms of communication were also developed as civilisation advanced. The printing press, which is by far this field's most impressive invention, revolutionised mass communication. The written words, whether they were on paper, wood, or stones, reached everyone who could read what had been written there. The printing technology became more effective as a result of technical advancements. The most cutting-edge communication technologies, both print and non-print, are available today. Common folks are now more able to share other people's experiences and feelings. This chapter will examine the development of communication technology globally and in India, in particular. Additionally, a number of issues with the adoption and transfer of communication technologies are discussed.

CHAPTER AT A GLANCE

DEVELOPMENT OF COMMUNICATION TECHNOLOGY: AN OVERVIEW

A key human and societal process is communication. It enables communities to exist and by definition, distinguishes between humans and other species. Thus, the effectiveness of interpersonal communication within any culture is dependent on that communication. In other words, the degree to which a society's citizens can afford and utilise different forms of communication, such as written text, radio, television, video cassette recorders, video text, computers, etc., is a measure of that society's prosperity. Due to this, more focus is being placed on the creation, storage, processing, editing, interpretation and dissemination of information to all parties nowadays. We are transitioning to an information-based society as communication technologies progress and become more widely available. People have evolved their own strategies for communicating as effectively and efficiently as possible throughout history, depending on the conditions. The earliest forms of communication were signs, symbols, gestures and facial expressions, which were widely used in prehistoric communities. It took many years for print to be created and employed as a mass medium of communication.

Print Medium

The development of printing technology marks the beginning of modem communication technology. It eventually gave rise to more specialised print materials, such as religious and political literature that aided in human transformation. The most potent and common teaching technology, even in the era of computers and satellite communication, is written text. The printed word continues to be a fundamental educational instrument. Papyrus, bark and leaves were employed in ancient times for writing. Before an emperor instructed his courtiers to find a more practical writing medium around 100 AD, the Chinese wrote on flat pieces of bamboo or on silk fabric. Chinese paper technology emerged as a result.

The first written words were used for educational purposes around 105 AD, when the Chinese invented paper and ink. In the past, it was necessary for the writers to manually copy the written words to produce numerous copies of a written text. This made reading materials exceedingly expensive and only accessible to a select few. Large-scale duplication of original works began as a result of the demand for more copies of reading materials, particularly in subjects relating to religion. Consequently, printing began. The Buddha's teachings were published in book form via movable type printing in China, as early as 868 AD.

For the purpose of creating printing blocks that could be put together to create a printed page of a book, the Chinese experimented with using wood, clay and tin. By the 1400s, printing had become a common practice throughout Europe and printing presses had become a skilled trade. As a result, western printing began to become more automated. The mass printing of books began in the middle of the fourteenth century, thanks in large part to John Gutenberg of Germany. It was Gutenberg who worked on putting the concept of moveable type into practice. Following then, a number of advancements in printing technology were created in order to boost both its efficacy and efficiency. The evolution of printing technology over the past few centuries led to modern printing.

And today, hundreds of books are printed every day in numerous languages and for a variety of purposes. As a result, the printed word has replaced other forms of information storage and transmission. Newspapers, magazines, journals, pamphlets, handbooks, dictionaries, atlases, encyclopaedias, workbooks and other print media are used in a variety of ways. Technology is constantly evolving and getting better. With time, it got simpler to publish a book and the results were of higher quality. Computers and laser technology were introduced in printing and distribution of print media in the 1980s.

The ability to save printed text items in huge volumes and use them as needed is made feasible by computers and other electronic devices. The following is a concept map of the history of print:

On September 6, 1556, the first printing press was nearly, accidentally introduced to India. It's interesting to note that the press was being sent to Ethiopia, then known as Abyssinia, for use by Christian missionaries. The reporters stayed in India as the Jesuit priest who was travelling with them passed away during a brief layover in Goa, India. Printing thus, became possible in India by accident. The first book printed in India was entitled Doctrina Christiana. Near the Tamil Nadu district of Thirunelveli, in the village of Punikael, the second printing press in India was established in 1578. The Christian missionaries built the press, which was used to print holy books. In Bombay, the third printing press—as well as the first non-missionary press—was established in 1672. The first newspaper was published in India in 1780, more than two centuries after the printing machine was invented. On January 29, 1780, The Bengal Gazette, the first newspaper, was published. After that, numerous presses were established and newspapers were published. The Dig Darshan, a Bengali monthly launched in 1818, was the first periodical in the English language to be published in India. Other newspapers and magazines in several other Indian languages thereafter, followed. Hindi printing only recently became available. In 1826, Oodunt Martand became the first newspaper to be printed in Hindi.

Audio Media

A phenomenon of the twentieth century is the radio. Between the 1920s and 1940s, the radio experienced tremendous expansion. With the discovery of radio waves, radio technology has been continuously improved, and broadcasting facilities have expanded quickly. Radio technology first advanced quite slowly, but this changed after World War II, and it ultimately had a very rapid expansion in recent decades. More people are having access to the radio as a means of listening to news and entertainment. Election campaigns after the World Wars became potential factors in the global and especially American radio industry's continued expansion. So, those in positions of authority showed a keen interest in commissioning new radio stations to broadcast political propaganda. Together with political propaganda, the ability of radio to disseminate economic news encouraged the planners to set up an increasing number of radio stations across the world. 564 licenced radio stations existed in the USA alone in 1922. The radio medium's potential for commercial information and entertainment value led to its quick development. Even now, listening to the radio is mostly for enjoyment, then for information and news. Certain nations, like France and Hong Kong, heavily rely on radio for entertainment (70 and 72 per cent of total broadcast hours respectively). The required advancements in radio technology were achieved in order to reach and enlighten an increasing number of people.

The size and price of the radio sets decreased as a result of these advances. Transistor technology helped make the radio become a mass medium, which is today used in practically every nation on earth. Nowadays days, people with limited incomes may purchase radio sets and carry them around with them. The use of radio in education—in a more general sense—came later. It was realised that the radio may be a possible tool for increasing public understanding because it is widely accessible to so many people. Radio started to face significant competition from television.

The radio therefore started to modify. The radio technology as well as the transmission methodology underwent a lot of refinements. The radio's popularity increased as a result of a number of technical advancements, including multiplexing, stereophonic transmission, and the widespread availability of transistors. The Digital Audio Broadcasting (DAB) technology is now undergoing global al.1 testing. The audio medium has expanded significantly outside of radio because to advancements in technology like phonograph records and tape recorders. Although phonograph discs have nearly been superseded by cassette tape technology, these media have increased the popularity and accessibility of the audio medium for the general public. The audio cassette has a lot of instructional potential while being mostly utilised for pleasure purposes due to its mobility and simplicity. The most popular audio format right now is the audio CD, which, because to its digital recording, produces sound that is incredibly clear.

Audio-visual Media

Following the radio, came television. In the late nineteenth and early twentieth century, advancements in the field of television were accomplished. After further investigation, the Bell Telephone Laboratories were able to transmit an experimental television programme from New York to Washington in the United States in 1926–1927. There were 17 experimental television stations in operation in the USA by 1930, when important technological advancements in television were made. Globally and especially in developed nations, audio-visual technologies are growing quickly. Since the invention of broadcast television, we have had access to video-tapes, cable TV, computers, video text, video discs and many other forms of media.

Digital broadcast television is replacing analogue broadcast television. TV's audience is expanding every day. Around the world, more and more advanced technologies are being used, including talk-back capability, videophone systems, facsimile, etc. Different nations are competing to acquire as many audio-visual technologies as quickly as possible, depending on their economic circumstances, level of technological development and requirements. Since the use of communication technology in education is predicated on the idea that audio-visual media are beneficial for teaching, distant learning is where it really shines.

Telecommunication

The earliest advancement in telecommunications was the transmission of telegraphic signals through wires. Alexander Graham Bell first showed off his telephone in 1876, opening up the possibility of long-distance voice communication through telephony. Bell's demonstration of a point-to-point telephone link marked the birth of the modern telecommunications industry, which has nearly completely transformed how people interact. Since then, after going through different development stages, telecommunication technology has also changed from amazing switching systems. The technique, which was initially developed as a means of long-distance audio transmission, can now transmit full multimedia, including audio, video, pictures and text. This ability has a wide range of applications in online learning.

Multimedia Communication

Telecommunication networks now have more capacity, particularly in terms of bandwidth, the rate at which data is transmitted. The high-speed transmission signal channel, which is measured in megabits per second, is referred to as "broadband" (Mbps). The classic telephone services are typically referred to as "narrowband" and operate at a speed of kilobits per second (kbps). Multimedia communication is now possible, thanks to the development of very small aperture technology, Integrated Services Digital Network (ISDN) and Broadband ISDN. The development of the Internet and computing technology, both significantly contribute to multimedia communication. This is due to the Internet's more interactive architecture. Any number of services can be requested and offered at once in the context of multimedia communication. All of the media listed above are moving towards convergence due to the potential for multimodal communication at very high speeds.

Convergence of Communication Technology: The World Communication Report from 1997 paints a very clear picture of the convergence of communication technology. Interactive services are in demand and technology is advancing in that direction. Through a wide range of media, including mass media, interactive media and self-media, computing power, telecommunications technology and media skill are all coming together to provide interactive services. The advancements in microcomputer technology have made it possible for different communication systems to converge. You can now access instructional programming online at your home, thanks to advancements in communication technology. A convergent technology that can handle text, images, audio, video and animation all at once is the Internet. Additionally, it can make synchronous interaction easier. The convergence has changed the computer into a device that can provide education, information and entertainment right at your door.

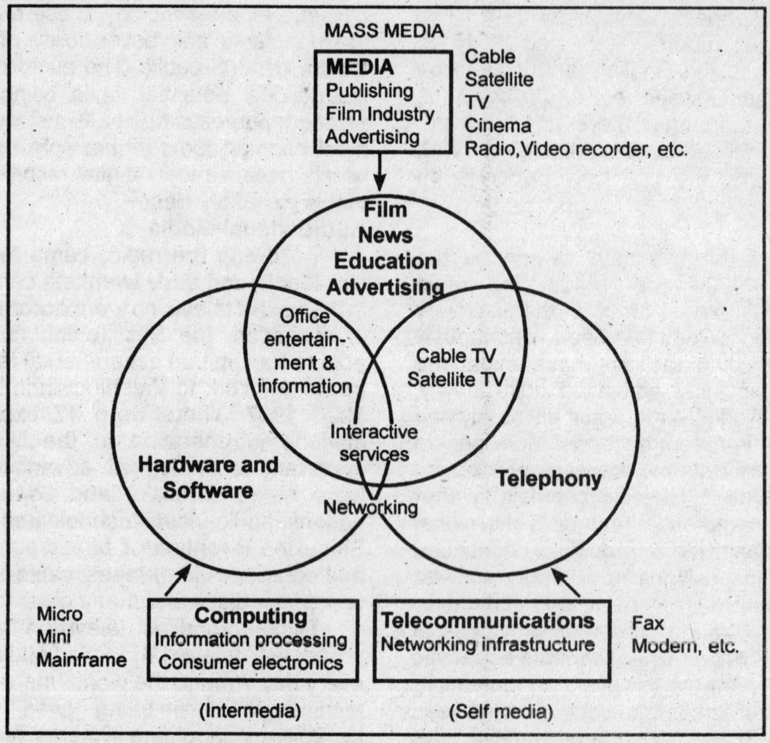

Convergence of Communication Technology

GROWTH OF COMMUNICATION TECHNOLOGY: PROBLEMS

Different underlying factors can affect how a specific type of technology is used to address educational issues. The requirements for the development of technology are essentially the same for both industrialised and developing nations. For instance, both scenarios experience the same influence on the adoption of new technology from the strength and zeal of society's economy and policymakers' attitudes.

Political Factors

In developing nations, communication is not just a socio-economic necessity, but also a political one. A political system, or a group of individuals in power, can influence the uptake and development of a specific communication technology in a nation. The adoption of new technology to promote social change and education depends on the political structure of the nation in question and its underlying purpose or desire. The adoption of technology in India was driven by political decisions, which allowed the country's computer sector to grow significantly. India is currently one of the world's top exporters of software. Some societies may absorb technology more readily than others because of their potential for greater information processing adaptability in their linguistic and cultural frameworks. Comparatively, more quickly than other Asian nations, Japan embraced technology. In a nation, the top classes and the wealthy adapt technology more rapidly and easily than the middle and lower classes and urban residents adopt it faster than rural residents. Additionally, social prejudice has an impact on how each person adopts technology. For instance, younger people adopt technology more quickly than older people. Males adapt to it more quickly than females do.

Economic Factors

Cost is a significant issue that affects a nation's adoption and development of communication technology. And in the case of emerging nations that acquire technology from developed nations, this is unquestionably true. They don't have enough money in the budget to support or finance technology-based projects. Some nations have spent a lot of money purchasing various technologies without putting in place the infrastructure required to make those technologies useful. These nations are therefore, heavily indebted. The country's economic development should be considered when making investments in new technology. The benefits of spending the same amount of money on other measures for social development are the same as the benefits of communication technology in rupee terms.

We largely refer to Thomas' (1987) discussion, which focuses on four important economic factors that influence a nation's usage of communication technology. These factors are as follows – societal financial stability, policymakers' attitudes and budgetary and technological resources allocated. There are some nations with higher per capita income, that are more prosperous economically. The developed nations have significantly higher per capita income than the emerging nations. Since technologies are extremely expensive, it goes without saying that the nation with the greater per capita income will be better able to purchase more communication technology. Conversely, the majority of poor countries lack the necessary communication technology.

They continue to rely on their conventional communication channels. This is not meant to imply that the conventional approaches are ineffective. However, we think that those techniques have some limitations, especially in terms of their effectiveness and reach. Additionally, civilizations must modernise their communication and technological systems if they are to work on the modern social agenda. The way policymakers view new technology, affects how quickly it is adopted and developed in a nation. They would notice that the necessary technology is adopted and applied in numerous areas, including the educational systems, if they view the adoption of communication technology as aiding in the growth of the nation.

The decision-makers in charge of making policy, determine the amount to be allotted or the priority order for developing or importing a specific technology for a given purpose. Given their favourable attitudes towards their use, decision-makers in our country tend to be relatively lenient when suggesting and putting communication technology into practice. They occasionally adopt technology at various levels of education with extreme fervour, while without having put in place the essential infrastructure in the form of the required resources, such as skilled labour, upkeep systems and group communication.

The main economic challenges that emerging countries face are recognised to be a shortage of capital, a lack of foreign exchange and the inevitable difficulties associated with the balance of payments. The amount to be set aside for the adoption of communication technology is determined using the overall budget allotted for the education sector. The initial cost of installing a technology, is extremely high. However, once a nation has access to communication technology, it can't communicate with and educate an infinite number of kids without spending a lot of money. However, ongoing costs are necessary for the receiver equipment and experienced staff. The cost-effectiveness of a given technology is the final issue to be discussed here. In terms of the amount of money, time and effort invested, we must evaluate whether the stated goals have been optimally attained by adopting the technology. Therefore, the efficiency of the technology being recommended for various target groups must be evaluated by educational planners.

Cultural Factors

Both fostering cultural activities and spreading awareness about cultural heritage are greatly benefited by communication technology. The broad definition of culture encompasses information, ideas, art, morality, laws, conventions, as well as any skills and behaviours that a person picks up from being a member of the community. These cultural characteristics are present to differing degrees in many communities around the world. These elements cause social divides between different societies. As a result, it is thought that the diverse cultural systems have an impact on how technologies are implemented, developed and used.

One of the most crucial elements in the transfer of educational software from one nation to another is the cultural component of language. The radio and television shows, computer programmes and even written texts are created in several languages in numerous nations with various cultural traditions. The same is true for how intellectual traditions affect technological exchanges. Thus, a country's population's attitudes, values, beliefs and lifestyles will determine how quickly new technology are adopted. For instance, the intrusion of many technology from the industrialised nations has recently sparked a conflict between modernity and traditionalism in India. While some people have embraced innovation and implementation, others have remained loyal to the old ways. Even in the middle of the 1980s, when computers were first installed in Indian banking institutions, there was uproar. To protest automation, the bank employees went on strike. One of their worries was that they might be replaced by computers. Another concern was that the computer will lengthen the already lengthy lines of young people without jobs. But the usage of computers created more career opportunities. The teachers' resistance and attitude of non-cooperation to any innovation or change in their current teaching-learning practices is a significant cultural component in the formal education system.

They appear to be content with the way they are now teaching. Therefore, they see no need to adopt a new technology and subject themselves to needless financial, time and energy burdens. This is a significant factor in the underuse of modern mass media, despite its availability in some nations. Under the new circumstances, technology should promote our culture and beliefs. According to Contractor, Fulk, Monge and Singhal (1986), a homogeneous culture considerably facilitates the adoption of communication technology. The values of the two nations—the borrower and the donor—must coincide for the adoption of communication technologies to be successful.

Second, the use of technology to support traditional cultural activities and enable development in accordance with its values and norms is necessary for it to be successful. These findings apply to all civilizations. For instance, the Satellite Instructional Television Experiment (SITE) initiative was a success because it allowed the peasants to watch television without upsetting their sense of cultural balance. The viewers engaged in a group discussion about television messages in relation to the customs of the rural community. They either approved or rejected the transmitted messages based on their conversations. The use of television programmes was successful in this way because it allowed for changes in viewers' attitudes, knowledge and abilities.

Technological Factors

The development and uptake of communication technology in a nation is influenced by a variety of technological factors. According to studies, technology itself acts as a hindrance to its own development. For instance, a regular supply of electricity is necessary for technology to function. The intermittent supply of energy was one of the main causes of the under-watching of television programmes in Indian villages during the Satellite Instructional Television Experiment (SITE) and Indian National Satellite (INSAT) projects. The following are some issues that are particularly important to the use of technology in education.

Appropriateness: The technology selected should be appropriate for the nation's geographical setting. Large growing nations with challenging geography requires technology that works for them. India's decision to have her own communication satellite to cover the entire nation is justified in light of these factors. For large-scale operations, cable or microwave networking are unaffordable due to their restricted coverage and high costs.

Accessibility: There won't be equal access to communication tools for education across a nation. In the near future, there will be many homes without any, primarily in the rural and urban parts of the developing globe. For many years to come, the public's access to modern communication tools like computers and video text will continue to be very restricted. This does not imply that we have a negative outlook on things. Far from that, we believe that in many of our nations, the earliest uses of communication technology will be for commercial and non-educational purposes.

The availability of a technology to the educational sectors will necessarily be impacted by certain constraints, such as a lack of appropriate funding, a lack of enthusiasm among educators and administrators, a lack of sufficient software or courseware, or a lack of political will.

Handling: If we do not understand how to use an electronic equipment, it will no longer be useful. While some gadgets are sophisticated and require particular handling techniques, there are some devices that may be managed with basic knowledge. For instance, even though computers are simple to use, they require specialised expertise. Even more so, one finds it challenging to keep up with handling and maintaining them because technology is developing so quickly. A case in point is updating to new operating systems.

Maintenance: It has frequently been seen that different technologies are imported or adopted from industrialised nations without the necessary maintenance plans in place. Once such gadgets experience technological issues, they are permanently rendered useless. Poor maintenance facilities may be the result of a lack of knowledge, resources or infrastructure, the absence of spare parts, or the uncaring attitude of users. For example, even the most widespread and well-liked of gadgets, like the television set installed in a rural primary school in many developing nations, are not covered by an efficient maintenance programme.

Software/Courseware: It is a truth that the educational sectors around the world, particularly those in affluent nations, suffer from a lack of pertinent software courseware. Additionally, developing nations have a major software quality issue. The majority of these nations rely on imported textbooks from developed nations. These curricula might not meet the socio-cultural and academic requirements of the pupils in the borrower nations. One issue with this is that the courseware's language may be challenging for the students to understand. The real use of such courseware thus, becomes questionable. We must acknowledge that creating educational courseware is a difficult task that requires a lot of knowledge, resources and funding. It can be difficult to create curriculum for contemporary communication devices like computers, video text, video discs, etc. The skill with which the courseware has been created will determine how well the students learn from a lesson. Even though some developing nations have advanced in the production of general radio and television programmes, they lack a sufficient supply of educational programmes. The development of communication technology in the educational sectors is hampered by the lack of pertinent courseware. Therefore, careful planning and software design for the new communication technology (such as the talk-back system) are required. Otherwise, the introduction of the new technology will take an excessively long period.

Educational Factors

The development and uptake of communication technology are influenced by a few educational aspects. These elements are connected to the socio-cultural and economic norms present in a community. A technology or innovation is more likely to be adopted if teachers, a key element of the educational system, are involved. We must keep in mind that teachers can harm any media's success at the institutional and practical operational levels. They may or may not be ready to adapt their position or their current procedures to meet the demands of the technology. Thus, their perspective on technology plays a crucial role. The use of communication technology requires that teachers' roles evolve.

They should realize that they are no more the only source of information required to transmit knowledge. In other words, new communication technologies will ask the teachers for new roles of teaching managers, facilitators, individualisers of teaching, advisers and so on. This is not something new we are talking about. A number of research studies on the educational media have provided empirical evidence to show that these devices demand that the teachers should play new roles. There is an undercurrent of scepticism among some educators that the adoption of a technology may lead to further elitism in education – widening the gap between those who have access to resources and those who do not have.

Technology adoption requires a lot of money and every institution cannot afford to purchase such expensive equipment. Additionally, the government is unable to provide every student with access to technology. If technology is introduced selectively in schooling, a new privileged class will be quickly created. The primary purpose of communication technologies is to help people achieve their educational goals. The language of education, in addition to the software's or courseware's other features, determines whether it is successful or unsuccessful. Even identical course materials created by foreign and local organisations in the same language have varied effects.

For instance, an Indian study by the University Grants Commission (UGC) Research Advisory Committee for INSAT-IB programmes found that the English-language programmes imported from other nations made relatively little difference in how well students understood the subject matter when compared to the English-language programmes produced in India. Due to the pronunciation of the foreign specialists, the students had trouble understanding the language. The UGC imports a lot of programmes from the US, the UK, Japan and other nations. However, due to issues brought on by linguistic and cultural differences, Indian students are unable to properly utilise these programmes.

In addition, there are certain other elements that affect decision-makers' choices on the use of technologies in education. Here are a few examples: The majority of the time, teachers are not involved in the development or creation of the courseware (there is a distinction between courseware and software; the former refers to any instructional materials that contain content, such as student radio and television programmes). It's possible that the producers' and teachers' perspectives will diverge. This is the reason why educators do not favour these gadgets. The course material also has another issue. The courseware's content scope may be constrained and its presentation may be insufficient from a qualitative point of view. It is exceedingly challenging to cover the full curriculum with just one technology from a quantitative standpoint (medium). Therefore, additional media are needed to fully realise educational objectives, yet many nations find it extremely challenging to embrace a multimedia approach to teaching and learning. In poor nations, the course materials are insufficiently diverse. It's possible that the developed-country curriculum and tools that are being used in developing-country classrooms aren't appropriate for those children. Both the professors and the students might believe that oral and written communication are still common in the classroom. Students are discouraged from using modern communication technology because of their reliance on textbooks and lectures. As an illustration, while living in a highly-industrialised world, the Japanese still rely on instructors to facilitate teaching and learning. As a result, intellectual imperialism still affects education, with professors believing they are the only qualified individuals capable of instructing students. For pedagogical objectives, some communication systems are superior to others. The technology is preferred by educators because it has the power to address issues in education and as a result, enhance the calibre of instruction.

COMMUNICATION POLICY

Broadcasting was initially established by private organisations in various nations of the world, but over time, government organisations either directly or indirectly, wholly or largely, took control of it. A person or group of persons started the less resource-intensive radio broadcasting system on their own initiative. The television, on the other hand, began on a very small scale because it was an expensive medium for private initiative. Another intriguing fact is that in some nations, including the Philippines, the Netherlands, the United Kingdom and Italy, religious organisations have been granted permission to broadcast for the general public. In India, the government has complete control over the broadcast system for the entire nation and regulates the electronic mass media, including radio, television and telecommunication. Similar to how the press, which is owned privately, is utilised to serve the public and political interests, so are these media. The regulation and use of radio and television in the nation has been the subject of intense debate during the past ten years. To explore the policy concerns surrounding the electronic mass media, a number of debates were held (and are still being held) at various public forums, including the Parliament.

The idea that the electronic media should be an independent organisation accountable to the people, free from any political meddling, is clearly on the rise. The Ministry of Information Broadcasting has permitted the private, public and autonomous agencies to make programmes due to the availability of the direct broadcast capability and the requirement for an increasing number of programmes to feed the transmission. The Ministry of Human Resource Development, the Ministry of Agriculture and Rural Development, the Ministry of Health and Family Welfare and the Central Institute of Educational Technology have all started creating instructional programmes for their respective target audiences as a result. Applications of theory to reality are known as policies and they typically take the shape of social, political, economic and cultural action. A clear and comprehensive policy is necessary for large-scale communication action. "Sets of rules and norms developed to guide the behaviour of communication systems", according to UNESCO, are what constitute communication policy. Globally, the topic of communication rules has been hotly debated and contentious for a very long time. Technology used for communication is not an incidental service. Its governing laws are the result of social pressures.

In other words, the relevant policies are dependent on the social function that we anticipate communication technology will play in the intricate transformation that society is undergoing. Their execution should make clear the goals to be reached, the strategies to be used and the tasks to be completed. It requires deliberate planning to undertake activities involving communication technology and to identify social objectives. They ought to encourage more educated and involved citizens. With these facts in mind, policymakers should develop an overarching framework for policy in the public interest and focus on problems with communication disparity both, within and across countries.

However, in actuality, technological advancements have also pushed the creation of communication policies. The main goal of these policies is to find ways to ensure that the flow of information and communication does not exacerbate social class differences and that all social groups equally share in the benefits. However, in practice, the politically and economically dominant classes often slant these policies in their favour. This necessitates re-evaluating the function of information and communication in a democracy. The duty of the government to enlighten the people and provide access to information sources has long been recognised in democratic societies. The goal of communication is to reach out to individuals using all of the media at hand to advance societal progress. Along with our commitment in our constitution to freedom of speech and expression, communication is a way to encourage societal advancement. For social development, including official and informal education, radio and television are used. Dr. Vikram Sarabhai foresaw the use of television as a tool for education and social transformation and as a result, the SITE project was carried out in rural areas to benefit the entire country. Therefore, it is not only desirable but also vital to use a broad-based approach when formulating communication-related policy. Various communication-related policy decisions have occasionally been made. Compared to electronic media, print media policy has a longer history. In India, guidelines are being developed for the use of electronic media, particularly radio and television.

Communication Policies and Development: The type and flow of communication and information have a considerable impact on developing countries' key priorities of social, educational, cultural and economic development. Since, communication is a tool to advance social development and education, policies on communication should be developed to provide the entire or integrated growth of society with the desired structure. In other words, communication should be connected with the overall developmental goals of the nation. The development strategy should decide the kind of communication system needed. The system must ensure that the populace actively contributes to achieving the development objectives. Instead of being the end aim in this case, communication technology is a tool for growth. Therefore, having control over technologies amounts to potentially having a say in how development will proceed. The creation of communication policies and development strategies, which are viewed as essential tools for tackling many national concerns, should be prioritised in order to ensure that the medium of "information" becomes the medium of "communication". Since communication depends on individuals having access to information and participating in a common cause, many media should be included in the development process. But unless "education is one of the major aims of these programmes under debate", this cannot be done fully. Indian space research and application programmes' main objective is to use communication for development, or to raise India's standard of living. In India, many communication technologies are embraced and used to the fullest extent feasible. The stated goal of our broadcasting services has been to support mass education and development. Because of the policy decisions made, a variety of information resources, including audio and video, are being used for the benefit of the people, bringing them closer to the information age. India has three key goals, despite its limited resources:

- To speed up the pace of development by informing, educating and motivating the people for development.
- To ensure that these technologies benefit a large number of people.
- To provide efficient communication facilities to the masses.

Narula wishes to draw attention to the fact that the government's main efforts have been focused on ensuring that the technologies available to the nation reach the majority of people, transmit the best and most relevant information and demonstrate the people's physical and financial accessibility. Therefore, it is predicated on the idea that technological advancements will close the gap in communication and the disparity in developing advantages among people.

Communication Policies and Demographic Factors: The demographic aspects and their effects on various levels of development plans must also be included in the communication policies. When formulating policies with the intention of offering suitable solutions for the expansion of resources, facilities, equipment, etc. with the passing of time, it is important to take into account the population of the nation. The population expansion and its impact on various development and educational initiatives should be included in communication plans, especially in developing nations, according to UNESCO. Indian educational system, for instance, is experiencing issues as a result of growing population, which also has an impact on the distribution of educational resources. The infrastructure for communication must be able to meet the needs of the many demographic sectors, which are expanding at an alarming rate. In this aspect, an effective communication approach will undoubtedly aid in promoting education.

Integrated Approach to Communication Policy

An integrated strategy is advised by Mowlana and Wilson (1988), who analyse communication strategies and planning for development. They contend that because communication and development are strongly intertwined, national communication strategies should take into account all economic, political and cultural challenges at the national, international and global levels.

As such, communication policies should consider the following elements:

Stages in the Process of Communication: *(i)* the source, *(ii)* the process of production, *(iii)* the process of distribution and *(iv)* the process of use. Distribution and use have become most crucial areas in communication policies because of the technological advancements.

Factors Affecting Communication: They include issues related to: *(i)* ownership and control, *(ii)* capital formation, *(iii)* bureaucracy, *(iv)* technology availability, *(v)* message integration, *(vi)* message development, etc.

Balance of Modern vs. Traditional Channels: The communication policy should ensure that modern technologies do not sever traditional and indigenous communication channels that are ingrained in a culture and community. Instead, a nation's communication system and policies should be set up so that both modern and conventional channels work well together. The primary goal of communication technology is effective societal growth, which is ensured through an integrated approach to communication policy.

CHECK YOUR PROGRESS

Q. 1. Identify and write the current trends in each of the following media:

***(a)* Print**
***(b)* Audio**
***(c)* Radio broadcast**
***(d)* TV broadcast**
***(e)* Telecommunication**
***(f)* Multimedia communication.**

Ans. *(a)* Print: Print media is implementing innovative digital printing trends like customised URLs (PURLs) and QR codes on everything from brochures to magazines to attract customers to their online platforms. These digital components provide a lot of advantages, with their intrinsic trackability being one of the most important ones. Businesses receive information when a person clicks on a PURL or scans a QR code with their smartphone. This information may be used to track conversions and determine, which print features are popular and with whom. Additionally, they don't need much tracking beyond a certain analytics tool and are simple to construct and integrate into any print feature.

It's challenging to stand out in a stack of papers. Businesses are employing textured features in print media to improve their chances by appealing to the senses and evoking awareness and recall. Some of these techniques, such as die-cutting and embossing, practically elevate printed materials off the page, whereas foil stamping is a more subdued method of adding texture to print materials. It's a style that makes use of developments in digital printing that make it simpler than ever to produce print features that stand out, not just in terms of text and colour but also in terms of unexpected details that grab the attention right away.

The latest trend in printing is augmented print. In a nutshell, augmented printing combines the greatest aspects of print and virtual ads. Innovative packaging is a very common trend in print marketing. Although it's often taken for granted, packaging has long been among the most effective ways to promote items. This unconventional approach has acquired a lot of traction recently, particularly with customised posters.

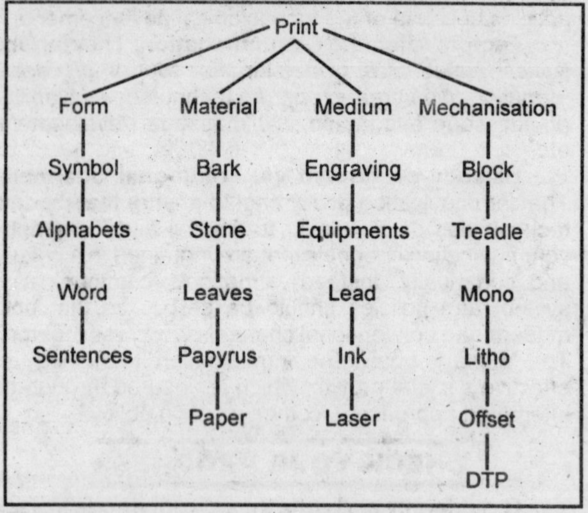

***(b)* Audio:** People now listen to news, music, podcasts and books, among other types of auditory information. The popularity of podcasts is skyrocketing. Around the world, 4,449,114 podcasts have been registered. More than one-third of adults in the United States, listen to podcasts each month, with 90% of those listeners doing so at home. Popular audio companies like Spotify, iHeartRadio and Pandora have become household names and are only getting more well-known. For instance, 90% of Americans listen to the radio every day.

According to Nielsen, 40% of people who work from home each day and 75% of them each week stream music. A hybrid work style is evolving as the globe learns to live with the pandemic, with people dividing their time between their home and work offices. Voice assistants and smart speakers are becoming typical home appliances. 44 per cent of American adults use voice assistants and one-third of American families have smart speakers.

By 2022, over 870 billion voice assistant-enabled devices have been utilised by American consumers. As more consumers use smart speakers for research and shopping, these figures will rise. As a result, there will be a rise in the demand for audio content, which will give marketers more chances to interact with consumers.

Prior until recently, there were few options for ad formats and programming and advertisers had limited options for measuring audio commercials. Leading audio firms are starting to solve these issues by creating live audio content and offering new ad forms, which is another development boosting the development of digital audio. Better targetting and measuring tools are also being developed by them. Programmatic advertising (also known as automated buying, selling and fulfilling of commercials) is a crucial aspect of display advertising that is increasingly gaining traction in audio advertising.

***(c)* Radio broadcast:** Radio broadcasting is evolving due to emerging technologies. While it has slowed down for FM, digital growth is now accelerating. Nowadays, a sizable portion of music is consumed in cars, which are becoming digital. Hybrid radio's enabling technological advancements are changing the business in a variety of ways. Radio no longer has a competitive advantage due to distribution. For newcomers to radio's market of content creation and distribution across many channels, there are now no entrance hurdles. And content is king. Because of this, radio stations that produce original, speech-based content have a considerable edge over those that only play recorded music.

At this point, the conversation turned to indexing, one of the most unexpected uses of developing technology. Radio stations ought to be indexing content so that it may be found and used across various platforms. If no one can find a station's mine of valuable programming, that doesn't help. However, broadcasters must also use indexing technologies during live events. Cramer observed that "so much of what radio does is lost after broadcast." After stations have transcribed content, it can be reused and programmatically monetized in the future. This gave rise to AI-driven translation programming, an unexpected and mostly unnoticed emergent technology with value for radio stations with unique content. Some radio stations utilise synthetic speech translation technology to translate English broadcasts into Spanish in the U.S., where Spanish is the second most spoken language after English. Stories and content that speak to consumer needs are still used by brands to forge deep and genuine connections with their audience. Delivering information in the listener's language of choice is still a successful strategy for promoting your audio material. According to a developing audio trend, in-store playlists will be purposefully used to influence consumer behaviour, attract new customers and enhance the shopping experience for customers. Consumers continue to use ethics as a guide. Radio and messaging will continue to adhere to the strategy of sustainability as a core objective. Due to the pandemic, people are splitting their time between home and work. Voice assistants and smart speakers are becoming more and more common household appliances as a result.

***(d)* TV broadcast:** Over the past few years, entertainment services like Netflix, Disney+ and Prime Video have mostly displaced traditional television networks. OTT technology, which is media distribution software that permits the transmission of video information over the internet without the use of dated streaming technology, is one of the newest trends in broadcast media. The market for video streaming services has been completely transformed by Netflix.

As a result, viewers have been forced to "cut the cord" on cable. The forecasts also state that by 2023, a fifth of cable consumers are anticipated to cancel their subscriptions. While the world fights to contain the greatest pandemic of the century, the change is already underway owing to virtual cloud technology. This new broadcasting media technology has already been included using the cloud, an IT-enabled technology. Amazon Web Services (AWS), Rackspace and Microsoft Azure are a few of the Cloud Service Providers (CSPs) that provide both public and private cloud services. Use of these services necessitates a steady internet connection. To offer a seamless experience for creating, sharing and viewing content, while managing both time and cost, almost all broadcasters have switched to cloud computing. Therefore, broadcasters must incorporate some of the current trends in broadcast media, in order to stay relevant. If you can recognise the significant changes in broadcasting and embrace new trends, you'll prosper and be prepared for the future.

(e) **Telecommunication:** As the process of the global economic recovery moves on in this digitalized and competitive environment, businesses in the telecom sector face new opportunities as well as challenges. As a result, they are forced to reinvent themselves and this time, major changes are anticipated. The scourge of never-ending seem has accelerated digital transformation and adoption. Additionally, in a relatively short amount of time, IoT technologies were adopted and gradually applied, radically changing how businesses operate in today's society. It is a fact that businesses that aren't original, or creative, won't exist in the next years. Consumer behaviour is also evolving as a result of the importance of the 5G network, IoT and IoB, Assets Management and Big Data, among other factors.

In order to capture a larger share of the market, MNOs are increasingly carving out Towercos in the telecom industry, a novel style that will be popular for a long time. One of the most important trends for telcos right now is without a doubt the fact that telecom companies are increasing the capacity of their networks. As a result, the biggest investment cycle in the history of fibre-optic deployment is starting. The benefits provided by this incredible technology can meet all client needs and expectations because it outperforms all other broadband technologies. Studies from the Fiber Broadband Association predict that during the next five years, more fibre will be installed than has been done thus, far.

Innovations like the 5G network, Fiber to the Home (FTTH) and Fiber to the Building (FTTB) have boosted the placement of these network systems due to the 3 billion internet users throughout the world who are yearning for greater speed access. If used effectively, this solution also streamlines corporate procedures and cuts expenses in any industry, as we previously covered in the 2021 telecom trends. In addition, a CCS insight analysis projects that 1.34 billion connections to 5G would exist by 2022.

Similar to this, fibre deployment, a crucial issue in the digital development of regions, ensures that everyone has extensive access to very high-speed internet. The Organization for Economic Co-operation and Development (OECD) has released data that demonstrates the uneven deployment of fibre optics among its member nations. Using LoRaWAN, IoT is transforming crucial infrastructure.

A remote monitoring solution for the telecom sector is required for large-scale IoT adoption. To manage assets effectively, there is a propensity to combine various business divisions into a single platform. TREE, created by Atrebo, is the ideal option for telco infrastructure. Additionally, this platform can make extensive IoT installations simpler. Innovation in IoT mechanical design is embracing innovation and creating new, better UI/UX designs as one of the top telecom trends for 2022.

IoT Internet Security: As the number of cyber attacks rises yearly, IoT devices may provide access to private and sensitive information. As a result, IoT makers are creating multi-layered security protocols to take the role of conventional passwords.

LPWAN sensors can be used to measure the air quality in confined places. LPWAN stands for Low Power Wide Area Network. Healthcare is playing a significant role in this pandemic world, accelerating the development of the Internet of things at all levels.

In conclusion, LoRaWAN networks are operational in more than 160 countries globally and have a wide range of advantages, including secure bidirectional connections, low power consumption, long communication range and low data rates. These are the IoT trends for the telecom sector that we anticipate in 2022. More details regarding these ideas will surface as 2022 comes to a close.

For the same target demographic, telecom carriers are up against a lot of competition. Furthermore, the industry's high overhead costs make it extremely harder to survive in this competitive market. Communication Service Providers (CSPs) are therefore, required to automatically gather data and increase profit margins in order to cut costs. With the help of algorithms, the integration of AI, machine learning and process mining makes it possible to foresee and anticipate problems before they negatively affect customers.

To achieve enormous rental optimization for MNOs and Towercos, for instance, Atrebo creates Telco Site Rental Savings, a Celonis' Execution App.

On the other hand, the introduction of the meta-verse, 5G and edge applications and the necessity for high-performance telecom networks have all grown. In this new world, constant connectedness has no place.

Without a question, blockchain has established itself as the cornerstone of the digital era. In particular, it streamlines day-to-day communication activities, boosts information and transaction security, improves supply chain transparency and lowers operational expenses.

The global blockchain in telecom market is anticipated to increase at a CAGR of 77.9% between 2022 and 2030, reaching $1.37 billion by 2024, according to Report Ocean Research. The rising number of blockchain consortia is the main factor fuelling this enormous expansion.

In this particular market, IBM, SAP and Microsoft are major participants. Atrebo made the decision to participate in this technology. We are employing TrustOS, a Telefónica blockchain solution that is connected with Atrebo's TREE platform, along with Telefónica Tech to digitalize 2,00,000 telecom infrastructures with blockchain.

Last but not the least, communication tower safety and durability depends on a sturdy and adequate tower design. The deployment and optimization of tower sites will be a growing trend in telecom in 2022. To ensure adherence to industry design standards, sophisticated communication systems are designed and analysed. A fantastic way to strengthen engineering integrity.

In this case, we can demonstrate the TREE inventory model's ability to construct, calculate and analyse structures using a cutting-edge 3D model, allowing us to provide the best feasible solution.

In conclusion, we anticipate that the telecom sector will undergo a significant corporate digitalization this year. A significant development will undoubtedly be the integration of IoT solutions into business operations, not to mention the growth of telco carve-out and the significant investment in fibre.

(f) **Multimedia communication:** Whether it's a personal conversation with friends, family and coworkers or a major brand's communications to a customer base, multimedia communication is more varied than ever. Early in the 1990s, the internet became widely used, bringing with it a variety of innovative communication tools, including digital media channels that enable users to send messages more swiftly and across longer distances.

These technological advancements opened the door for digital media to have a significant impact on how companies and brands build relationships with their customers. They have an effect on conventional communication careers as well. New job descriptions and a new communication environment are the results. An illustration of an email outreach system for client relationship management. For entertainment, news and business purposes, the media's continued reliance on technological advancements presents enormous financial prospects. Future communication professions are expected to be shaped by some main areas of growth, as specialists with degrees in communication look to the future. Executing communication strategies through digital channels, such as social media posts, blog posts, landing sites, videos and other formats is a common focus for social media managers, digital media managers, content strategists and communication specialists.

American information consumption and sharing are dominated by digital media. As a result, significant factors that will probably have an effect on the field's future are beginning to emerge. When it comes to media, innovation has become the new standard and this tendency isn't going to reverse as we consider potential media ideas. Media trends have been influenced by social media, digital advertising and easier access to the internet via multiple devices. Digital media will change in the future as new tools become available, customer needs change and technology quality and accessibility rise. Future developments in digital media will be influenced by the growth of mobile video, virtual reality (VR), augmented reality (AR) and more sophisticated data analytics.

The methods used by advertisers to reach consumers must change as well because the future of media is constantly changing. A poll found that 74% of American families with adults between the ages of 18 and 34 no longer have cable TV service, have no plans to, or have never had it. Due to the fact that adults in this age bracket are increasingly using streaming services like Netflix, Hulu and Sling, advertisers must create new approaches to connect with them. More customers are preferring online video platforms over traditional television every year and many of them are doing so, while utilising mobile devices. This suggests that a mobile-first approach is necessary for the future of media, especially video. This demands companies to assess how they present themselves in the marketplace and go beyond advertising on well-known streaming channels. Having mobile-friendly, accessible video content is essential because videos are now accessible across platforms.

Public relations has embraced big data and used the insights gained from it to enhance PR strategies. Analytics from online advertising track more than just a campaign's effectiveness. Additionally, they can spot changes in the campaign. Marketing professionals can use the data gathered to improve their ads' messages, choose the best distribution methods and learn more about the audience. PR experts are using data analysis to design outreach initiatives that are more successful. Communication specialists may now predict news cycles and interest, find out which media outlets cover their business the most, find potential connections with media outlets, other companies and influencers and more thanks to the abundance of data that is currently available. Data is shaping the future of media concepts in PR by being able to make sense of all the (ethereal) noise, even though some of the metrics related to public relations may seem intangible. While AR enhances real-world photos, VR recreates scenarios using specialised software and gear. These two industries, which have developed side by side, have recently received new attention and each is expanding swiftly. The global VR and AR industry is anticipated to increase from $37 billion in 2019 to

$1.3 trillion by 2030, according to market research, firm Research and Markets. Many experts believe that new technologies will enable consumers to engage fully with products prior to purchase, assisting in the conversion of advertising budgets into actual consumer purchases.

Additionally, by combining print and digital media, these technologies may offer customers compelling, individualised experiences. The COVID-19 pandemic has maintained the rapid acceleration of digital media use in both personal and professional communication in recent years. People are using the internet more frequently now due to lockdowns, infection worries and limitations on in-person business. For instance, according to statistics from market research firm GlobalWebIndex (GWI), the epidemic caused 43% of customers to use social media more frequently in August 2020. A RAND American Life Panel Survey also revealed that 25% of participants indicated they have increased their internet buying since the pandemic began.

Q. 2. What are the four major economic considerations that influence the use of communication technology?

Ans. Cost is a major factor that influences how quickly communication technology is adopted and developed in a country. This is undoubtedly true in the case of developing countries that import technology from advanced ones. The budget does not provide enough funds to support or finance projects involving technology. A lot of money has been spent by certain countries on various technologies without the infrastructure necessary to make those technologies functional being put in place. As a result, these countries have high debt levels. While investing in new technologies, one should take the nation's economic growth into account. In rupee terms, the advantages of communication technology are equivalent to those of spending the same amount of money on other social development initiatives.

Thomas' talk, which focuses on four important economic elements that affect how communication technology is employed in a country, serves as our main source of inspiration. These elements include the societal financial stability, the viewpoints of legislators, and the amount of funding allocated to technology. Some countries with greater per capita incomes are more prosperous economically. The per capita earnings in industrialised nations are significantly greater than those in emerging nations. Given the high cost of technology, it is obvious that the country with a higher per capita income will be better able to afford more communication technology, and the majority of poor nations don't have enough of it.

They still rely on their traditional methods for communication. This is not intended to suggest that the traditional methods are inadequate. However, we believe that such methods have certain restrictions, particularly in terms of their potency and range. If civilizations want to advance the contemporary social agenda, they must also modernise their technology and communication systems. The speed at which new technology is embraced and developed in a country depends on how politicians interpret it. If people see the use of communication technology as assisting in the development of the country, they would see that the essential technology is accepted and utilised in many sectors, including the educational systems.

The decision-makers in charge of making policy choose the amount to be allotted or the priority order for developing or importing a certain technology for a given purpose. Given their favourable attitudes towards their use, decision-makers in our country tend to be relatively lenient when suggesting and putting communication technology into action. They occasionally embrace technology at various levels of education with extreme fervour, while without having put in place the essential infrastructure in the form of the required resources, such as skilled labour, maintenance systems, and Gc. The primary economic issues that developing nations deal with are generally acknowledged to be a lack of capital, a lack of foreign currency, and the inescapable problems related to the balance of payments.

The entire budget given for the education sector is used to calculate the amount to be set aside for the adoption of communication technologies. You are aware that installing a technology entails a sizable up-front expense. But, once a country gets access to communication technology, she would find that it is very expensive to connect with and teach an unlimited number of children. But, the receiver hardware and knowledgeable employees require continuing expenses. The last topic to be covered in this article is the cost-effectiveness of a certain technology. We need to evaluate if using the technology has best achieved the stated aims in terms of the resources applied (money, time, and effort).

Hence, educational planners must assess the effectiveness of the technology being offered for different target groups. They must provide convincing answers to a variety of questions, such as whether receiving instruction in person is more successful than receiving it over the radio and if television is more effective than radio or vice versa. These problems need to be resolved before investing in particular communication technologies. Because adopting a technology for public use would be worthless otherwise, it is the responsibility of the technologists to ensure that the investment in technology helps more students overall.

Q. 3. What are the main cultural and technological factors that influence the adoption and growth of communication technology in a country?

Ans. Communication technology has a huge positive impact on both promoting cultural activities and disseminating knowledge about cultural heritage. Culture is a broad, complex system that includes knowledge, morality, laws, conventions, and any habits or skills that a person picks up while residing in a certain culture. Many civilizations throughout the world have different versions of these cultural characteristics. These factors result in social divisions between various societies. As a result, it is believed that how technologies are implemented, created, and used is influenced by the various cultural systems. In other words, both individual and societal views towards various communication technologies are influenced by these elements or variations.

The cultural aspect of language is one of the most important factors in the transfer of educational software from one country to another. Radio and television programmes, computer programmes, and even written texts are produced worldwide in a wide range of languages and cultural traditions. In terms of how intellectual traditions influence technical exchanges, the same is true. The attitudes, values, beliefs, and lifestyles of a nation's people will thus affect how rapidly new technologies are embraced. For instance, a recent clash between modernism and traditionalism in India was provoked by the introduction of much technology from the industrialised countries.

Because of this, some individuals have welcomed innovation and implementation while others have stuck with more traditional methods of doing things. There was controversy even when computers were initially introduced to Indian banlung institutions in the middle of the 1980s. Employees in the banking sector went on strike to protest industrial automation. One of their worries was being replaced by computers, although this did not come to pass. Another worry was that the computer will add to the already long queues of young people around the country without work. The use of computers has, however, resulted in more career prospects.

When computers were initially utilised to run a convoluted examination system in the Central Board of Secondary Education, questions were once more raised regarding the necessity and utility of such a move by certain higher level executives, financial advisers, and people in general. Nevertheless, as soon as they started using the computers, their concerns disappeared.

Technology-related elements Several technological elements have an impact on the growth and adoption of communication technology in a country. There are technical problems with new communication techniques. Several studies demonstrate how technology itself impedes its own advancement. It's possible that there have been occasions when handling, utilising, and sustaining new technology has been difficult.

For instance, technology cannot operate without a steady flow of power. During the Satellite Instructional Television Experiment (SITE) and Indian National Satellite (INSAT) initiatives, one of the primary reasons for the under-watching of television programmes in Indian villages was the erratic electricity supply. The following are some issues that are particularly important to the use of technology in education:

(1) Appropriateness: The technology used should be suitable for the country's climate. Big, developing countries with difficult geographic conditions need technology that is suited to them. In view of these elements, India's determination to create her own communication satellite to cover the entire nation seems reasonable. Due to their limited reach and high prices, cable or microwave networking are prohibitive for large-scale businesses.

(2) Accessibility: We are convinced that there won't be a national standard for who has access to communication technologies for educational reasons. Many residences may soon be without any, mostly in the rural and urban areas of emerging countries. The public's access to contemporary communication technologies like the computer, videotext, and vide will continue for a long time. This in no way implies that we have a pessimistic viewpoint. Far from it, we think that the first uses of communication technology in many of our countries will be commercial and not educational.

Some limitations, such as a lack of enough money, a lack of excitement among educators and administrators, a lack of acceptable software or courseware, a lack of political will, etc., will inevitably have an influence on the availability of a technology to the educational sectors.

(3) Handling: If we don't know how to utilise an electronic device, it loses its usefulness. While some devices are complex and need specific handling methods, others may be operated with only a few fundamental skills. For instance, although being easy to use, computers still require specialised knowledge. Because technology is evolving so fast, it is much more difficult to keep up with handling and maintaining them.

A case in point is updating to new operating systems.

(4) Maintenance: Many technologies are routinely imported from or adopted from industrialised countries without the required maintenance plans in place. When such devices encounter technical problems, they become permanently unusable. Lack of spare parts, inadequate infrastructure, a lack of expertise, inadequate resources, or a careless attitude on the part of users can all contribute to poorly maintained facilities. Even the most popular and widely used equipment, such as the television set put in a rural elementary school in many poor countries, is not properly maintained.

(5) Software/Courseware: It is undeniable that there is a global shortage of relevant courseware, particularly in industrialised countries, for the educational sectors. Developing countries also face a serious problem with software quality. Most of these countries rely on imported textbooks from industrialised countries. The social and intellectual expectations of the students in the borrowing countries may not be met by these courses. The language of the courseware may be difficult for the students to understand, which is one problem with it. So, the actual use of such courseware is called into doubt. We must admit that developing educational courseware is a challenging endeavour that needs a lot of expertise, materials, and cash.

The development of curricula for modern communication tools like computers, videotext, and video discs can be challenging. How well students learn from a lesson depends on how well the courseware was developed. While some developing countries have made progress in the creation of general radio and television programmes, they are severely lacking in instructional programming. The absence of suitable courseware hinders the advancement of communication technology in the educational sectors. Consequently, careful planning and software design are needed for the new communication technology; otherwise, it will take too long to introduce the new technology.

Q. 4. As a teacher you want to introduce computers in your institute. List the problems you may face in doing so.

Ans. There could be students who have very little experience with computers in their daily lives. As a result, not only are teachers often tasked with training students, in addition to teaching their own coursework, many of them are also just learning the systems themselves.

Even if you students and teachers that are completely comfortable with computers, there is still the issue of technical support. Computers break down and software installs and upgrades can fail. If there isn't an adequate support staff on hand, that equipment will sit unused. Unfortunately, not all schools can afford to have a technical person on site, which requires extra expenses and the institution has to bear. Some districts may have no tech support, relying instead on teachers and administrators troubleshooting problems, which disrupts the learning process. Some students may not be interested in learning computers. The management may also oppose because they do not want to incur the expenses in computers.

Q. 5. What are the three main priorities India has set up to use communication technology for social development?

Ans. The three main priorities India has set up to use communication technology for social development are:

(a) Reach the majority of people and inform, educate and motivate them.

(b) Ensure that the technologies convey relevant information for the benefit of masses.

(c) Make communication technologies accessible both physically and financial to the masses.

The goal of communication is to reach out to individuals using all of the media at hand, in order to advance societal progress. Along with our commitment in our constitution to freedom of speech and expression, communication is seen as a way to encourage societal advancement. For social development, including official and informal education, radio and television are used. The renowned Indian scientist Dr. Vikram Sarabhai foresaw the use of television as a tool for education and social transformation and as a result, the SITE project was carried out in rural areas to benefit the entire country. Therefore, it is not only desirable, but also vital to use a broad-based approach when formulating communication-related policy. Various communication-related policy decisions have occasionally been made. Compared to electronic media, print media policy has a longer history. In India, guidelines are being developed for the use of electronic media, particularly radio and television. One crucial thing to remember is that communication policies and development strategies, which are seen as crucial tools for addressing many of a nation's issues, should be created first and foremost to make sure that the medium of "information" become the media of "communication".

Q. 6. Which is the most important demographic factor we should take into consideration, while framing a policy of communication?

Ans. The communication policies must take demographic factors and their impacts on different levels of development plans into account. It is crucial to consider the population of the country when creating policies with the goal of providing appropriate solutions for the expansion of resources, facilities, equipment, etc., over time. According to UNESCO, communication planning, especially in developing countries, should take the population growth and its effects on various development and educational activities into consideration. For instance, the Indian educational system is having problems as a result of population growth, which also affects the allocation of educational resources. The communication infrastructure must be able to accommodate the demands of the numerous demographic sectors, all of which are rapidly developing. In this regard, promoting education will unquestionably benefit from an efficient communication strategy.

MULTIPLE CHOICE QUESTIONS

Q. 1. The first written words were used for educational purposes around:

(a) 105 AD *(b)* 405 AD
(c) 608 AD *(d)* None of these

Ans. *(a)* 105 AD.

Q. 2. The first written words were used for educational purposes in:

(a) Britain *(b)* China
(c) Iran *(d)* Egypt

Ans. *(b)* China.

Q. 3. The Buddha's teachings were published in book form via movable type printing in China as early as:

(a) 605 AD *(b)* 405 AD
(c) 608 AD *(d)* 868 AD

Ans. *(d)* 868 AD.

Q. 4. By the 1400s, printing had become a common practice throughout ________ and printing presses had become a skilled trade.

(a) Asia *(b)* Europe
(c) China *(d)* None of these

Ans. *(b)* Europe.

Q. 5. On September 6, 1556, the first printing press was nearly accidentally introduced in:

(a) India *(b)* Britain
(c) America *(d)* France

Ans. *(a)* India.

Q. 6. Between the 1920s and 1940s, ________ experienced tremendous expansion.

(a) Radio (b) TV
(c) Print media (d) None of these
Ans. (a) Radio.

Q. 7. The latest medium for printing is:
(a) Papyrus (b) Laser
(c) Lead (d) Paper
Ans. (b) Laser.

Q. 8. Which is the latest material for printing?
(a) Papyrus (b) Laser
(c) Lead (d) Paper
Ans. (d) Paper.

Q. 9. Which is the latest mechanisation for printing?
(a) DTP (b) Offset
(c) Litho (d) Mono
Ans. (a) DTP.

Q. 10. The earliest form of printing was:
(a) Symbol (b) Alphabets
(c) Word (d) Sentences
Ans. (d) Sentences.

Q. 11. SITE is:
(a) Satellite Institutional Television Experiment
(b) Satellite Instructional Telecom Experiment
(c) Satellite Institutional Telecom Experiment
(d) Satellite Instructional Television Experiment
Ans. (d) Satellite Instructional Television Experiment.

Q. 12. The audio medium has grown tremendously because of the developments of:
(a) Gramophone records
(b) Tape recorders
(c) Both (a) and (b)
(d) None of these
Ans. (c) Both (a) and (b).

Q. 13. ISDN is:
(a) Internal Services Digital Network
(b) Internet Services Digital Network
(c) Integrated Satellite Digital Network
(d) Integrated Services Digital Network
Ans. (d) Integrated Services Digital Network.

Q. 14. Who defines communication policy as "sets of principles and norms established to guide the behaviour of communication systems"?
(a) UNESCO (b) WHO
(c) UNO (d) None of these
Ans. (a) UNESCO.

■■

Applications of Communication Technology

3

INTRODUCTION

We frequently discuss the revolution in communication. We do sense and realise that something truly amazing is taking on in the communication sector. But many of us might not be able to understand the whole range of the technology being considered. There are many technologies that can be used to improve human communication. We'll talk about and examine their ramifications in this chapter. The technical details of how a computer works may not be necessary, but in this day and age, it is important to understand what computers are capable of and how they work. We should also be aware of modern means of communication and the means by which they might be used to educate students who are enrolled in remote learning programmes. We will therefore, concentrate on the theoretical features and applications of various communication technologies.

CHAPTER AT A GLANCE

USES OF COMMUNICATION TECHNOLOGY

We use communication technology for effective communication. Now communication technology has influenced the lifestyle and habits of all who are exposed to it.

Reaching

The intrinsic urge of humans to express their pleasures, tragedies, thoughts and visions to as many people as possible is manifested in ancient writings, paintings and cave inscriptions. Modern communication technologies have made it possible for us to efficiently communicate with a big audience. The entire world has become a global village, thanks to technology. Radio may now be heard over the entire country of India because to satellite based communication and terrestrial transmission networks. The telephone and its upgraded variants make it possible for individuals to communicate quickly across the globe.

The communication networks have become more effective, thanks to telephones with fax machines. Messages can be sent and received instantly by people in faraway locations. People now have access to incredible efficiency, thanks to computers. A keystroke on the keyboard can access vast amounts of data contained in tiny microchips. The ability to access more information is added via videotext technology, which converts the home television into a computer interface. With the use of this technology, consumers can view numerous information frames on a home television screen that is wirelessly connected to a computer data base, as well as text, numbers and graphics from remote data bases.

Telephones with fax machines have helped communication networks become more efficient. People in distant places can instantaneously send and receive messages. Computers have given people access to remarkable efficiency. A keyboard input can access enormous amounts of data stored on tiny microchips. With the use of videotext technology, which turns the home television into a computer interface, it is now possible to access more information. Customers can view a variety of information frames, text, numbers and graphics from remote data bases, as well as multiple information frames on a home television screen that is wirelessly connected to a computer database, using this technology. Reaching people around the world has never been easier, thanks to the invention of the Internet and the World Wide Web. Email, which is quick and inexpensive, has taken over as the preferred method of communication.

Teaching

Technology development has altered how teaching and learning are thought of. Learning is now possible everywhere and at any time. One illustration is distance learning. Technology in communication has a powerful multiplier impact. Teaching now takes on different forms and perspectives. Now, a social worker does not have to physically visit each community and hold in-depth discussions about a social issue. To spread messages to the intended audience, a social worker can use audio cassettes on the topics that are most important to him or her. Posters, filmstrips, audio and video films can help a health professional communicate messages regarding illnesses, preventive measures and the nursing process more effectively.

A very low power radio station was established by a Catholic Bishop in North Luzon of the Philippines primarily to disseminate biblical teachings as an illustration of how technology has been used to deliver messages. Most of the attendees were fisherman. These fishermen occasionally spend days at sea without ever learning, what is happening on land. They are to be reminded of the Christian faith's principles during this period. Imagine sending the following message to the sea for a small cost in between religious teachings "Your elderly mother, Mr. Lopes, is gravely ill. She wants to see you right away. Please depart right away for home. Your family members are waiting for you on the beach".

Utilizing communication technologies can help the teaching-learning process, deliver developmental messages and disseminate information about a range of concerns and challenges. In industrialised nations, modern communication tools including videotext, teletext, video discs and computers are employed in the classroom. These technologies are not typically used in developing nations for educational reasons due to their high cost and sophistication. However, some underdeveloped nations are testing and using them—albeit in a limited capacity. As a result of cost reductions, radio is now available to more individuals and locations, which is rapidly changing the situation. In developing nations in general and in India in particular, broadcast technology has been and is still being employed for educational and developmental purposes. For instance, the radio is being utilised as India's national classroom, a tool to combat illiteracy and for development as a way to enhance the country's standard of living.

Specific Uses

Communication technologies can be used by students to seek information or clarification to resolve doubts or queries. For example, telephone can be used for this purpose. Students can listen to radio to increase their knowledge, watch TV to learn new things and use computers to gather, process and store information. Videotext and teletext can be used to gather specific information. Some specific educational uses of communication technology are:

Course Planning: In terms of course design and planning, computers can be a huge assistance. Teachers and students can swiftly and successfully develop and learn a course using the computer at their disposal. The benefit it offers is that it can finish and carry out activities far more quickly and efficiently than humans could ever do manually. The authority in charge of the computer, however, determines how effective a course plan will be.

Course Management: Course management is a crucial process that begins concurrently with course preparation and lasts until the results, or the students' successful completion of the course(s), are announced. The computer is an essential component in course management. All of the data created throughout the course's preparation and implementation can be stored on the computer. Any necessary adjustments can then be made to boost the course's effectiveness. The effectiveness of management will entirely depend on the individual(s) in a position of authority and the people operating the machinery.

Student Support Services: With the development and accessibility of electronic media, distance education has advanced significantly, since the 1980s. In the past, distant learning relied primarily on printed materials and sporadic face-to-face encounters between the teacher and pupils. A two-way dialogue with the pupils became possible because of communication technologies.

Print Material: Practically, all universities offering distance learning, printed materials serve as the main instructional input. The print medium has undergone a second revolution with the introduction of laser printing and desktop publishing. Before, students received print materials that were cyclostyled (sometimes of extremely poor quality) for their own study. There was frequently no pedagogical support, included in these items.

Radio Broadcasting: Radio has always served as a valuable tool in development and education. Radio may be a huge aid in attaining the goal of democratising education by delivering it to the homes of all the country's residents. Students' access to remote learning would increase as a result. Distance learning institutions offer essential administrative inputs through radio broadcasts in addition to course based programmes.

Telecasts: The genuine experts, subject matter, locations and activities can all be seen on the television screen in addition to the audio facility. Since the laboratory can be brought to the student's study table, television is a better medium for teaching science subjects. Through television, students can access expensive experiments, real-world fieldwork or sports, tiny elements, vintage video, sophisticated equipment and notable figures. Students can interact with the nation's best educators through radio and television broadcasts.

Audio and Video Cassettes: Students can have access to the audio and video programmes at the study centres. If a student cannot watch a particular broadcast, she/he can go to the study centre and watch it there. The cassettes and pen drives are also very handy. They provide the facility of learning at your own place.

Telephone: Telephone is mostly used for inter-personal communication. A telephone line can be used for using devices such as fax, e-mail and computer. Telephone can also be useful if audio conferencing is conducted for the students.

Computer: CAI, or computer-assisted instruction, is a very useful tool in remote learning. Computer diskettes have the capacity to gather, process and store a lot of data for dissemination. But remote learning institutions in India are not yet making widespread use of computers for teaching and learning. However, the advent of computers is quickly altering society. Now, classes can be found on the network as well.

Videotext and Teletext: Teletext and videotext are examples of cutting-edge communication tools. A master computer and a home television can be linked and the master computer can be used to retrieve the needed data. Teletext utilises the home television as well and receives information from the master computer's transmission as needed.

APPLICATIONS OF COMMUNICATION TECHNOLOGY: PROBLEMS

These technologies have a great deal of promise to benefit humanity. Some of the new technologies simply cannot be used because of the physical and mental conditions, which may not allow them to function. There are a number of technological, software, cultural, social and economic issues. Here, we go over a few of the issues with using communication technologies in India.

Socio-political Factors

In India, it is said that telephone networking did not expand in the past because some people at the top deliberately did not want it to expand. Scholars say that development communication failed in the 1960s and 1970s because there was not enough political support.

It is an undisputed fact that the communication technologies will not benefit people unless there is a strong political will to support them. With the enthusiastic support of the government in 1980s computer revolution entered India. Since then the computer industry is growing by leaps and bounds. It is becoming more and more acceptable in educational institutions. Similarly, the telephone accessibility has also increased. There are various direct and indirect problems, which may crop up due to the application of the new communication technologies. Some of these problems are discussed below.

Decentralization and Isolation: If embraced, communication technology could result in an informed nation. Information is a resource that improves decision-making and likely increases independence. The nation's political structures may need to shift significantly as the current power dynamics between the centre and the periphery are questioned and challenged. Additionally, the change could usher in a very troublesome topsy-turvy time of transition. But such a change must be welcomed if a truly democratic and egalitarian society is to be established. The citizens are also given the ability to operate freely, thanks to the availability of multiple communication channels. Lack of physical interaction can lead to psychological isolation, which can lead to social issues.

Information 'haves' and 'have-nots': Lack of infrastructure and high equipment costs prevent those with limited financial resources from even imagining adopting new technologies. The wealth disparity in society is widened as a result. The vast majority of developing nations lack the terminals, networks and communication channels required to participate as equal partners in the global economy of information generation and delivery. Around 95% of computers are found in industrialised nations, whereas three-quarters of telephone connections are found in ten of these same countries, which together make up only 20% of the global population. Currently, India has 1.5 telephone lines per 100 people. It was less than one per 100 people up until 1994. E-mail and Internet access are not readily available at many institutions. Some have connections with 1.2 or 2.4 kbps. One can only send and receive e-mails with such limited bandwidths and a bad terrestrial phone connection; they cannot browse the internet or conduct online searches.

Interpersonal Relationship: While building an educated society, communication technologies also distance people from one another. The frequency with which technology is used separates people. For instance, viewing television may cause family members to interact less.

Human and Administrative Factors

Students must have access to the required technology in order to use communication technologies in remote education. If the pupils cannot use the technology, it could lead to significant administrative issues. Thousands of staff needed to be trained and oriented on how to use computers when Indian Railways adopted its computerised reservation system. Since the employees who had previously worked manually for years, now had to adapt to the new circumstances and adopt new functions of highly intelligent computers, they must have fought the shift, which must have led to numerous administrative issues. However, these circumstances are typical of any change, therefore it is our responsibility as educators to bring about change in a systematic manner to reduce resistance and enable the advantages of the technological revolution.

Economic Factors

People's financial capacities become a barrier to accessing technologies. Any communication technology application is an expensive endeavour. The exchequer of the countries involved is under a lot of strain as a result, especially if they are developing nations. Many of them are unable to use the technology due to the enormous investment requirement. As a result of their inability to afford the essential gadgets, the common people frequently miss out on the benefits of technology. When people lack access to TVs, the benefit of the Doordarshan network growth, for instance, is diminished. Purchasing a TV is difficult and painful for the average person. And this is valid for all forms of communication.

Equipment-related Factors

The implementation of foreign technologies is the main cause of the equipment-related issues. The machinery is imported from other international organisations or from industrialised nations. As a result, the adopting nations depend on international organisations for maintenance. This dependence produces chaos because the governments of the adopting nations are unable to fully control every facet of such technologies. The legal processes of the nation might occasionally complicate the import of replacement parts and consulting services, leading to unforeseen delays and irritation.

SKILLS OF USING COMMUNICATION TECHNOLOGY

According to the requirements and characteristics of a particular civilization, technology evolves and expands. However, the barriers dividing society and communities are breaking down in modern times. The exchange of products, materials, information and people across the nations occurs frequently and virtually without barriers. All of these things have happened so simply and fast because to communication technology and the communication revolution, albeit the transformation is still far from complete. As a result of the frequent transfer of communication technology, several governments are pooling their resources to support research initiatives for the creation of new technologies. This spread of communication technologies has encouraged nations to train their citizens in the new skills needed to use these technologies for commercial, educational and entertaining objectives.

For Education

To accomplish the goal, the educator must be thorough in his or her planning and techniques. This will enable the teacher to make the best use possible of the technology used. He or she can employ a variety of communication channels to influence students' knowledge, abilities and desired attitudes as a cohesive force. Every tool or medium used, must add to the overall cumulative effect. Sometimes utilising a single technology will suffice. Therefore, technology should not be employed merely for its own sake. The improper use of technology must be taught.

Three general categories can be used to categorise the abilities needed to use communication technologies:

(a) **Hardware-related:** It is the knowledge or understanding how each piece of equipment functions.

(b) **Software-related:** It is understanding of the content/software and the range of formats that can be employed to accomplish the goal.

(c) **User-related:** It is information pertains to the target market and those who must understand how to utilise both the hardware and the software.

Radio and television:

(a) The following hardware-related abilities are needed:

- Installing, running and maintaining transmitters, antennas and studios.
- Recording software programmes in proper formats to meet discipline-based criteria.
- Repairing or replacing worn-out hardware components.

(b) Software-related skills needed by educators/ teachers include the ability to:

- Clearly understand how hardware functions
- Be familiar with instructional designs.
- Be aware of the specific strengths and weaknesses of each individual medium being used.
- Judge the quality of voice, visuals, music, etc. Write scripts.

(c) User-related skills are those that students must possess in order to use technology:

- Understand how operating systems work.
- Know how to get the most out of media.

Computer:

(a) Hardware related skills:

- Teachers must have the ability to operate a computer using a keyboard and mouse
- Fix basic issues, such as weak connections.
- Maintain the computer.

(b) Software-related skills include:

- The ability to use a variety of software programmes.
- Create programmes that are tailored to the needs of certain students.

(c) User-related skills include.

- Knowing how to operate a computer.
- Understanding computer-assisted or computer-managed learning.

For Development

All communication technologies used for educational purposes are also applicable to development purposes also. The skills required to apply communication technology for development purposes are similar.

For Entertainment

Communication technology can be utilised for enjoyment, as well as for learning and growth. In order to maximise learning, programme creators should create their materials in a way that grabs and holds students' attention. There is no educational programme that can be successful without the motivational component. Games and simulations that present powerful educational inputs, such as reasoning and the potential for problem solving, are played on computers. The necessary talents would be the ones that were previously listed.

For Commercials

The development of communication technologies has made business the top focus in our society. The communication channels that are used to promote any company activity will have a significant impact on its success. Although the technologies would not change, how they were used would depend on the need. For the use of communication technologies in the corporate environment, the selection of media and message processing are essential. Software specialists with talent are required to promote commercial goods. Different forms of communication, including text, audio and video, are widely employed in daily life for business objectives. Numerous organisations, both governmental and private, are involved in creating programmes for profit.

COMMUNICATION TECHNOLOGY AND SOCIETY

Technology, according to Rogers (1986), is a plan for instrumental activity that lessens ambiguity in the cause-and-effect relationships necessary to achieve desired results. A tool for knowledge and information collection, processing, storing and dissemination is referred to as communication technology. The needs and personalities of a society's citizens play a role in the development and adoption of various technologies. Each segment of the greater human society is unique and has its own demands and character. As a result, meeting a society's needs through importation from the other group is impossible. For them to have value and be helpful in the society in question, they must develop from the society itself.

However, when knowledge between many communities increases, innovations created in one community can be successfully and consciously applied in others. One of the fundamental traits of humans is the need to interact with other people. Additionally, each group of humans has been able to successfully create a suitable form of internal communication. Over a lengthy period of time, languages were created through the methodical production of sounds. Every community has its own distinct demands and characteristics, which have resulted in a variety of languages with their own phonologies, syntaxes and vocabularies. A society's demands and characteristics change with time and therefore, so do its members' communication techniques.

In fact, communication methods and patterns have gained so much significance that they are no longer seen as the "other part" of society but rather as its central component. We can argue that the history of communication technology dates back to the period when people developed sign languages and drew pictures on cave walls to communicate with one another and future generations, while keeping in mind the essential idea of technology. We can assume that every civilization will have its own communication technology depending on the characteristics and requirements of its members because we are living at the dawn of the 21st century and seeing rapid improvements in communication technologies.

Take the nation's population issue as an example. The family planning programme was implemented in India as early as the 1960s. The implementation of numerous initiatives for this programme received significant funding and resources. Various organisations, both official and non-governmental, have employed a variety of communication methods and technology to inform the public about the risks of unregulated population growth. Perhaps people are now aware of the issue, yet on average, parents still have three or more children in each marriage. This may be due, at least in part, to the fact that our media or media strategies failed to adequately inform the public and as a result, failed to inspire them to adopt family planning. The common people in rural areas could not identify with the individuals (characters) depicted in the advertisements in this regard. Today's civilization is dominated by information, rather than the technological sector. As a result, it is known as the information era. The rise of computer and communication technology is largely responsible for the information age. People will undoubtedly become more isolated from one another as a result of options for teleworking, telecommuting, virtual conferences and other such situations in an information society. Additionally, it might enable us to maintain our balance with the natural world.

ACTIVITIES

Q. 1. Take an evening off from your other activities. Monitor – watch the television programmes and document each of the programmes by topics and duration, including the advertisements. Having done this, try to calculate the time given and identify the topics devoted to education, development, entertainment and commercials.

Ans. Doordarshan National devotes about 12 hours to entertainment programmes, about six hours to commericials including advertisements and other six hours to education and development.

CHECK YOUR PROGRESS

Q. 1. Name five communication technologies, which are used to reach a large audience.

Ans. Communication technologies used to reach a large audience are – radio, television, video, videotext and teletext.

Q. 2. Tick the best word/expression.

***(a)* The reach of broadcast increases manifold when it is hooked to:**

(a) Radio
(b) Antennas
(c) Satellite

Ans. *(b)* Antennas

***(b)* A fax machine is connected with a:**

(a) Telephone
(b) Television
(c) Radio

Ans. *(a)* Telephone

Q. 3. Given below are two categories — one has clusters of users/audiences/people/institutions and the other has clusters of communication technologies. Please match the user clusters with appropriate technology clusters.

Category A	Category B
(i) A village school without electricity	A. Radio, television, video cassette player
(ii) A small company in a medium sized town	B. Telephone, videotext, telex, television, radio, fax machine
(iii) A very big commercial firm in a metropolitan city	C. Telephone radio
(iv) A family of four, earning Rs. 15,000-a month, living in a rural locality	D. Radio, posters

Ans. *(i)* D, *(ii)* C, *(iii)* B *(iv)* A.

Q. 4. Notes: *(a)* Write the code of skill (H, S or U) in the box given in front of each statement.

Compare your answers with those given at the end of the Unit.

The following is a set of ten statements. Each statement is related to one of the following skills — Hardware skill (H), Software skill (S) and User skill (U). Now you have to indicate in front of each statement, the skill it belongs to:

(i) **Repairing the needle of the meterband in a radio set is a**
(ii) **Directing a television drama is a**
(iii) **Switching on the knob of a television set is a**
(iv) **Using 'a computer' programme is a**
(v) **Checking a photograph is a**
(vi) **Dialing a telephone number is a**
(vii) **Producing a greeting card in a computer is a**
(viii) **Reading news for radio broadcasts is a**

(ix) Taking a long shot, mid shot and a close up with a video camera is a
(x) Putting on a video film is a

Ans.
(i) Hardware skill (H)
(ii) Software skill (S)
(iii) User skill (U)
(iv) Software skill (S)
(v) User skill (U)
(vi) User skill (U)
(vii) Software skill (S)
(viii) Software skill (S)
(ix) Software skill (S)
(x) User skill (U).

Q. 5. Fill in the blanks. Whether these are hardware, software, application or technology.
(i) Technology is __________ of a machine for a specific output.
(ii) A radio set is __________.
(iii) Manufacturing a radio set is __________.
(iv) Farm forum of All India Radio is __________.

Ans. *(i)* Application, *(ii)* Hardware, *(iii)* Technology, *(iv)* Software.

OTHER IMPORTANT QUESTIONS

Q. 1. Discuss the uses of communication technology.

Ans. To communicate effectively, we employ communication technology. All people who are exposed to communication technologies now live different lifestyles and have different habits.

1. Reaching: Old texts, paintings and cave inscriptions all demonstrate how humans have an innate need to share their joys, tragedies, thoughts and visions with as many people as they can. We can now effectively communicate with a large audience, thanks to modern communication tools. Thanks to technology, we now live in a global village. Due to terrestrial broadcast networks and satellite-based communication, radio may now be heard throughout the entirety of India. People can communicate swiftly around the world, thanks to the telephone and its improved versions.

To communicate effectively, we employ communication technology. All people who are exposed to communication technologies now live different lifestyles and have different habits.

Reaching: Ancient writings, artwork, and cave inscriptions all show how individuals have an intrinsic need to share their triumphs, sorrows, ideas, and dreams with as many people as they can. Thanks to contemporary communication techniques, we may now efficiently communicate with a huge audience. We now reside in a global community as a result of technology. Radio is now audible throughout all of India because to terrestrial broadcast networks and satellite-based connectivity. The telephone and its upgraded variants allow people to converse quickly throughout the globe.

Networks of communication have been more effective, thanks to phones with fax machines. Instant messaging allows people in remote locations to send and receive messages. People now have access to extraordinary efficiency, thanks to computers. Countless gigabytes of data are accessible via keyboard input and are housed on tiny microchips. More information is now accessible, thanks to videotext technology, which converts the home television into a computer interface. Customers can use this technology to display several information frames on a home television that is wirelessly connected to a computer database, as well as a range of information frames, text, numbers and graphics from remote databases.

The development of the Internet and the World Wide Web has made it simpler than ever to communicate with individuals all over the world. Email has replaced other forms of communication as the most convenient and affordable option.

2. Teaching: The rise of technology has changed the way that teaching and learning are viewed. Nowadays, everyone can learn anywhere at any time. Distance learning is one example. Communication technology has a significant multiplier effect. Nowadays, teaching takes on new guises and angles.

A social worker no longer has to physically visit every town to conduct extensive conversations about a social issue. A social worker can use audio cassettes on the subjects that are most important to him or her to distribute messages to the target audience. A health practitioner can communicate information about illnesses, preventive measures and the nursing process more effectively by using posters, filmstrips, audio and video films. As an example of how technology has been utilised to communicate messages, a Catholic Bishop in North Luzon of the Philippines founded a very low power radio station, primarily to disseminate biblical teachings. The majority of those present were fishermen.

On rare occasions, these fishermen will spend days at sea without ever learning what is going on ashore. During this time, it is important to remind them of the fundamentals of the Christian religion. Imagine, for a nominal fee, sending the following message to the water in between religious discourses. "Mr. Lopes, your old mother is very sick. She needs to see you immediately. Please head home immediately. Your family members are waiting for you on the beach ". Communication technology can facilitate teaching and learning, convey developmental messages and distribute knowledge about a variety of issues and difficulties. In industrialised countries, the classroom makes use of contemporary communication, means including videotext, teletext, video discs and computers.

Due to their high cost and sophistication, these technologies are not frequently used in developing countries for instructional purposes. However, even in little doses, some developing countries are testing and employing them. Radio is increasingly accessible to more people and places due to cost reductions, which is quickly changing the scenario. Broadcast technology has been and is currently used for educational and developmental reasons in underdeveloped countries, particularly in India. For example, radio is used as India's national classroom, a tool to fight illiteracy and for development to raise the level of living in the nation.

3. Specific Uses: Students might use communication technology to seek information or explanation to clear up any doubts or questions. For this, the telephone might be used as an example. Students can watch TV to learn new topics, listen to the radio to expand their knowledge and utilise computers to obtain, analyse and save data. Specific information can be gathered via teletext and videotext. Communication technology is used in education in the following specific ways:

4. Course Planning: Computers may be a big help with course design and planning. Using the computer at their disposal, teachers and students may quickly and successfully construct and learn a course. Its advantage is that it can complete tasks far more swiftly and effectively than people could ever accomplish manually. The effectiveness of a course plan, however, is decided by the authority in control of the computer.

5. Course Management: The critical process of course administration begins at the same time as course planning and continues until the outcomes, or the students' successful completion of the course(s), are made public. The use of a computer is crucial to effective course management. The computer can save all of the information generated throughout the planning and delivery of the course. The course's effectiveness can then be improved by making any necessary revisions. The person(s) in a position of authority and the people running the machinery will both have a significant impact on how well management is executed.

6. Student Support Services: Since the 1980s, distant learning has come a long way because of the growth and accessibility of electronic media. Printed materials and infrequent face-to-face interactions between the teacher and students were the mainstays of distance learning in the past. Communication technologies made it feasible to have a two-way conversation with the students.

7. Print Material: Almost all universities that offer distant learning use printed materials as their primary teaching tool. Laser printing and desktop publishing have brought about a second revolution in the print medium. Before, pupils were given cyclostyled print materials for their own study that were occasionally of very poor quality. Pedagogical support was usually absent from these items.

8. Radio Broadcasting: Radio has always been a useful medium for growth and education. By bringing education to every person in the nation, radio may be a key tool in achieving the goal of democratising education. As a result, more students would have access to online education. Along with course-based programmes, distance learning institutions provide vital administrative inputs through radio broadcasts.

9. Telecasts: In addition to the audio feature, the television screen also shows the actual experts, topics, settings and activities. TV is a better medium for teaching science courses, since it can bring the laboratory to the student's desk. Students have access to pricey experiments, real-world fieldwork or sports, minute details, vintage video, cutting-edge technology and famous people through television. Through broadcasts on radio and television, students can engage in conversation with the top teachers in the country.

10. Audio and Video Cassettes: The study centres offer students access to audio and visual programming. A student may visit the study centre to watch a programme if she is unable to do so at home. Pen drives and cassettes are both highly useful. They offer the option of learning at your convenience.

11. Telephone: The majority of telephone usage is for interpersonal conversation. A telephone line can be utilised with fax, email and computer equipment. If students are involved in audioconferencing, telephone might also be helpful.

12. Computer: CAI, often known as computer assisted instruction, is a fantastic resource for distance learning. A lot of data can be collected, processed and stored on computer diskettes and then distributed. However, there is still a limited usage of computers for teaching and learning at India's distance learning institutes. But the introduction of computers is swiftly changing society. Classes are now accessible on the network as well.

13. Videotext and Teletext: Examples of cutting-edge communication tools include teletext and videotext. The required data can be retrieved using the master computer, which can be connected to a home television. Teletext uses the home television as well and if needed, obtains data from the transmission from the master computer.

Q. 2. Discuss the issues that arises due to the applications of communication technology.

Ans. These innovations hold out a lot of hope for the future of humanity. Some of the modern technologies are just not usable by some people due to their physical or mental limitations. Many technological, software, cultural, social and economic problems exist. We discuss a few of the problems with employing communication technology in India, in this article:

1. Socio-political factors: In India, it is alleged that some influential individuals purposefully prevented telephone networking from growing in the past. According to experts, the 1960s and 1970s saw a failure in development communication due to a lack of political backing.

Unquestionably, unless there is a strong political desire to promote them, communication technologies won't help people. The 1980s saw the entry of the computer revolution in India with the enthusiastic assistance of the government. Since then, the computer sector has experienced tremendous growth. The acceptance of it in educational institutions is growing. The accessibility of the phone has also improved.

The implementation of new communication technologies could lead to a number of direct and indirect issues. The list below discusses a few of these issues.

2. Decentralization and Isolation: Communication technology has the potential to create an informed society. Information is a tool that enhances judgement and probably raises independence. As the current power relationships between the centre and the periphery are questioned and challenged, the political structures of the country may need to change considerably. The transformation may also usher in a very difficult transitional period that is topsy-turvy. But if a really democratic and egalitarian society is to be developed, then such a transition must be accepted. Because there are numerous communication channels available, citizens can also move about freely. Psychological isolation brought on by a lack of physical contact might result in social problems.

3. Information 'haves' and 'have-nots': The adoption of new technologies is unthinkable for individuals with limited financial means due to a lack of infrastructure and hefty equipment expenses. As a result, the wealth gap in society widens. In order to engage as equal stakeholders in the global economy of information generation and distribution, the vast majority of developing countries do not have the terminals, networks and communication channels necessary. Ninety-five per cent of computers are situated in industrialised countries, yet only twenty per cent of the world's population—ten of these same countries—have telephone connections. India now has 1.5 telephone lines for every 100 residents. Up until 1994, it was less than one per 100 persons. Many institutions lack easy access to e-mail and the Internet. Some connections have speeds of 1.2 or 2.4 kbps. With such constrained bandwidths and a poor terrestrial phone connection, one can only send and receive emails; they are unable to surf the internet or perform online searches.

4. Interpersonal Relationship: While building an informed society, communication technologies also distance people from one another. The frequency with which technology is used, separates people. For instance, viewing television may cause family members to interact less.

5. Human and Administrative Factors: Communication technologies must be available to students in order for them to be used in distance learning. If the students are unable to use the technology, it could cause serious administrative problems. When Indian Railways implemented its computerised reservation system, thousands of employees needed to be trained and given computer usage orientation. Employees must have resisted the move because they had to get used to the new circumstances and embrace new computer functions after years of working manually. This is likely what caused many administrative problems. These conditions, though, are typical of any transformation. To lessen resistance and permit the benefits of the technology revolution, it is our duty as educators to implement change in a methodical way.

6. Economic Factors: The ability of people to pay becomes a barrier to obtaining technologies. Any use of communication technology is an expensive project. As a result, especially if the involved countries are developing ones, their exchequer is greatly strained. Due to the significant expenditure needed, many of them cannot use the technology. The regular people frequently miss out on the advantages of technology because they cannot afford the necessary gear. The benefit of the Doordarshan network expansion, for instance, is lessened when people lack access to TVs. For the typical person, buying a TV is complex and painful. And all types of communication fall under this.

7. Equipment-related Factors: The key reason for the equipment-related problems is the adoption of foreign technologies. The equipment is imported from industrialised countries or from other international organisations. As a result, the maintaining countries rely on international organisations. Because the governments of the countries who adopt these technologies are unable to properly regulate every aspect of them, this dependence results in anarchy. The nation's legal procedures could occasionally make it difficult to import replacement parts and consulting services, causing unanticipated delays and annoyance.

Q. 3. Discuss the skills of using communication technology.

Ans. Technology develops and grows in accordance with the needs and peculiarities of a specific culture. But in contemporary times, the partitions separating society and communities are dissolving. People frequently and almost without obstacles exchange goods, materials, information and ideas across borders. Though the shift is still far from complete, communication technology and the communication revolution are to blame for all of these things happening so quickly and simply. Several governments are pooling their resources to support research projects for the development of new technologies as a result of the frequent transfer of communication technology. The expansion of communication technologies has prompted governments to educate their people in the new skills required to use them for business, education and entertainment purposes.

1. For Education: The educator must be meticulous in their planning and execution if they are to succeed in their purpose. This will make it feasible for the teacher to utilise the technology in the optimal way. He or she can use a range of communication techniques to exert a unifying effect on students' knowledge, skills and desirable attitudes. Each method or tool employed must contribute to the overall cumulative effect. Sometimes relying solely on one technology is sufficient. As a result, using technology for its own sake is not appropriate. Technology misuse needs to be educated.

The skills required to use communication technology can be divided into three general categories:

(a) **Hardware-related** knowledge or comprehension refers to knowing or comprehending how each piece of equipment works.

(b) **Program-related:** Understanding the software, the material and the variety of forms that can be used to achieve the objective

(b) **User-related:** This information is relevant to the target audience and those who need to know how to use the software and hardware.

Radio and Television:

(i) The following hardware-related skills are required: setting up, operating and maintaining transmitters, antennas and studios; recording software

programmes in the appropriate formats to meet discipline-based standards and repairing or replacing worn-out hardware components.

(ii) **Software-related** skills required in educators/ teachers include the capacity to judge the calibre of voice, visuals, music, etc., clearly understand how hardware works, be familiar with instructional designs, be aware of the specific strengths and weaknesses of each individual medium being used and write scripts.

(ii) **User-related** skills are the abilities that students need in order to use technology, comprehend how operating systems operate and make the most of media.

Computer

(i) Teachers need to be able to operate a computer using a keyboard and mouse, troubleshoot simple problems like faulty connections and maintain the computer.

(ii) Software-related abilities include the capacity to use a range of software applications and the capacity to design applications that are specific to the requirements of certain students.

(iii) Computer proficiency and knowledge of computer-assisted or computer-managed learning are two examples of user-related skills.

2. For Development: All communication technologies that are utilised in education can also be employed in development. Applying communication technologies for development requires similar skills.

3. For Entertainment: Technology in communication can be used for enjoyment, as well as for learning and development. Programme designers should make their materials in a way that captures and keeps students' attention in order to maximise learning. Without the motivational element, no educational programme can be successful. On computers, people play games and simulations that offer strong educational inputs like reasoning and the potential for problem-solving. The skills previously mentioned would be considered to be necessary.

4. For Commercials: The growth of communication technologies has elevated business to the top of our society's priorities. The success of any firm initiative will be significantly influenced by the channels of communication that are employed to promote it. The technology themselves wouldn't change but how they were applied would depend on the situation. The choice of media and message processing are crucial for the usage of communication technology in a corporate setting. Talented software specialists are needed to advertise commercial items. Text, audio and video are just a few of the several types of communication that are frequently used in daily life to achieve business goals. A large number of organisations, both public and commercial, are engaged in developing programmes for profit.

Q. 4. Discuss communication technology and society.

Ans. Rogers (1986) defined technology as a strategy for instrumental activity that reduces uncertainty in the cause-and-effect relationships required to get desired results. Communication technology is a term used to describe a device used for gathering, storing, processing and disseminating knowledge and information. The development and uptake of various technologies are influenced by the demands and personalities of the people who live in a society. Each component of the larger human society is distinct with its own needs and characteristics. It is therefore impossible to satisfy a society's needs by importing from the other group. They must emerge from the society in issue in order for them to be valuable and beneficial.

However, ideas developed in one group may be successfully and intentionally applied in another as information between numerous communities grows. Humans need to engage with other people because it is one of their basic characteristics. Each human group has also been effective in developing a suitable method of internal communication. Languages were developed by the deliberate production of sounds over a long period of time. Every society has unique requirements and traits, which have led to the development of numerous languages with unique phonologies, syntaxes and vocabularies. The needs and traits of a society evolve throughout time and as a result, do its individuals' communication styles.

In fact, communication patterns and procedures have become so important that they are no longer considered to be the "other part" of society but rather its core. The development of sign languages and the painting of images on cave walls to communicate with one another and future generations, while keeping in mind the fundamental principle of technology might be considered the beginning of communication technology. Since we are at the dawn of the 21st century and are witnessing significant advancements in communication technologies, we may infer that every civilisation will have its own communication technology depending on the traits and needs of its citizens.

Consider the country's demographic problem as an illustration. In India, the family planning programme was put into place as early as the 1960s. Numerous initiatives for this programme received a sizable amount of funds and resources for implementation. To educate the public about the dangers of unchecked population growth, a variety of organisations, both official and non-governmental, have used a variety of communication strategies and technology. Though parents continue to have three or more children per marriage on average, perhaps individuals are becoming more aware of the problem. This could be at least partially attributable to the fact that our media or media techniques did not effectively inform the people and, as a result, did not encourage them to undertake family planning.

In this respect, the common people in rural areas were unable to relate to the persons (characters) shown in advertising. Information, not technology, is the dominant force in modern society. It is referred to be the information era as a result. The information era is largely due to the development of computer and communication technology. Due to possibilities for teleworking, telecommuting, virtual conferences and other similar situations in an information society, people will surely grow more alienated from one another. Additionally, it might help us stay in harmony with the environment.

MULTIPLE CHOICE QUESTIONS

Q. 1. Which of the following is not a category of teleconferencing?

(a) Audio-conferencing
(b) Video-conferencing
(c) Computer-conferencing
(d) Radio-conferencing

Ans. *(d)* Radio-conferencing.

Q. 2. CAI is:

(a) Computerised assisted instruction
(b) Computer affiliated instruction
(c) Computer assisted institution
(d) Computer assisted instruction

Ans. *(d)* Computer assisted instruction.

Q. 3. In India, it is said that telephone networking did not expand in the past because:

(a) Some people at the top deliberately did not want it to expand
(b) Of lack of resources
(c) Common people were not interested
(d) None of these

Ans. *(a)* Some people at the top deliberately did not want it to expand.

Q. 4. Scholars say that development communication failed in the 1960s and 1970s because:

(a) There was not enough political support
(b) Of lack of resources
(c) Common people were not interested
(d) None of these

Ans. *(a)* There was not enough political support.

Q. 5. According to Bruce Girard, former director of Latin America's computer radio Pulsar, what is the per centage of computers in the developed countries?

(a) 95% (b) 85%
(c) 75% (d) 65%

Ans. *(a)* 95%.

Q. 6. According to Arunachalam, teledensity in India today is about ________ per 100 person.

(a) 1.5 lines (b) 2.5 lines
(c) 3.5 lines (d) 4.5 lines

Ans. *(a)* 1.5 lines.

Q. 7. Till 1994, teledensity in India was less than ________ per 100 persons.

(a) One (b) Two
(c) Three (d) Four

Ans. *(a)* One.

Q. 8. The features of distance education have proved that learning is possible:

(a) Anytime (b) Anywhere
(c) Both *(a)* and *(b)* (d) None of these

Ans. *(c)* Both *(a)* and *(b)*.

Q. 9. A very low power radio station was set up by a Catholic Bishop in the Northen Luzon of the Philippines primarily to impart:

(a) Biblical teachings
(b) Teachings for children
(c) Teaching workers
(d) None of these

Ans. *(a)* Biblical teachings.

Q. 10. Installing, running and maintaining transmitters, antennas and studios are:

(a) Hardware-related abilities
(b) Software-related skills
(c) User-related skills
(d) None of these

Ans. *(a)* Hardware-related abilities.

Q. 11. Familiar with instructional designs is:

(a) Hardware-related abilities
(b) Software-related skills
(c) User-related skills
(d) None of these

Ans. *(b)* Software-related skills.

Q. 12. Know how to get the most out of media is:

(a) Hardware-related abilities
(b) Software-related skill
(c) User-related skill
(d) None of these

Ans. *(c)* User-related skill.

■■

Future of Communication Technology

4

INTRODUCTION

While several of the technologies we have described here are employed elsewhere, such as for business purposes, they are not currently available for educational usage. However, we expect that as soon as the right environment is established for such uses, these technologies will be utilised in education. Here, we'll learn about how communication technologies are used in education, with a focus on the circumstances in developing nations like India. Because technology develops so quickly, it's possible that some of the debate you read here is now out of date.

CHAPTER AT A GLANCE

COMMUNICATION TECHNOLOGY IN DEVELOPING COUNTRIES: A CHALLENGE

Recently, there has been an increase in the need for communication technologies in developing countries as well. The information age has been extremely beneficial to every country. The development of communication technologies has accelerated in India. To name only a few of its frequent applications, it is successfully employed in production units, planning and development processes, education, human resource development, banking, telecommunication, rural development, weather forecasting and managerial functions. The atmosphere in India is great for the successful production and application of communication technologies in a wide range of fields. They require increased access to communication technologies in addition to the motivation and necessary initiation to use them strategically if they are to benefit from this advantageous environment.

Even though they are diverse, developing nations have some commonalities. The main issues that most developing nations face are economic, political and social. The rapid expansion in their populations has exacerbated their economic and social issues. Additionally, they struggle with issues like illiteracy, inadequate technical training, widespread child labour, low status for women, etc. These issues can be resolved by introducing and utilising appropriate technologies. One of the crucial aspects that needs to be emphasised is the difficulty in obtaining communication technologies. They need to be created, adopted, mastered, controlled and put into practice. To make and use such technology, individuals (both producers and consumers) must be mentally prepared.

The use of communication technologies depends on the human capacity already in place. The great majority of developing nations lack the necessary readiness. Second, we need to make sure that new technologies do not damage the cultures of developing civilizations by being incorporated into their socio-economic structures. Intelligent use of new technologies in emerging nations can in fact hasten the process of development without interfering with the nation's socio-cultural framework. Another area of importance is research and development. Research and innovation must receive the proper focus from developing nations if communication technologies are to become flexible and accessible to the general public.

It appears that only nations with a strong scientific foundation will be able to gain competitiveness and the necessary vigour to keep up with the rapid rate of progress. Therefore, resources (*i.e.* investments) must be redirected to the improvement and innovation of communication technologies in order to see developing countries take the first steps towards full industrialization. These nations must come up with innovative plans for maximising their meagre resources, including science and technology, in order to support indigenous forms of growth. Universities and other higher education institutions have a significant impact on technological innovation and transfer.

But let's not lose sight of the fact that emerging nations have ambitions to leapfrog industrialised nations into the information era, skipping the latter's protracted industrial phase despite their limited resources and slow adoption of new communication technology. Many emerging nations are introducing new communication technologies as they experience rapid changes in technology, communication and lifestyles with far-reaching social repercussions. Communication technology has been expanding quickly in emerging nations despite the challenging economic environment. Today, a large number of individuals have access to various communication technology. Additionally, they are prepared to make additional investments to ensure that they do not miss out on the advantages of the information age.

As a result, certain nations are rapidly advancing towards becoming information societies. India is a good illustration. The means and techniques of education and development have been significantly impacted by communication technologies. In emerging nations as well, the future is very promising for new innovations and breakthroughs in communication technologies. It is hoped that educational institutions will demand communication technologies more frequently. In conclusion, there are many concerns about how communication technologies are evolving in relation to the establishment of a new kind of society in the developing world. These nations present us with both a huge task and a huge opportunity. It is crucial for us to make sure that technology significantly advances us.

ASSESSMENT OF COMMUNICATION TECHNOLOGY

We shall critically assess some of these achievements and limitations of communication technologies.

Achievements

Communication technology is used to support conventional teaching strategies and media. The flavour of the message to be delivered and the knowledge to be learned is improved through media. Additionally, they offer additional ways to deliver the information. Technologies for effective and efficient communication can take the place of face-to-face interactions.

Technologists are working to give students the tools and resources they need to succeed in their academic endeavours without placing an undue load on them. The individualization of learning is one of communication technology' most significant contributions to education. Plannings for individualised learning takes mastery-based learning into consideration.

A human aspect is provided by group projects and other activities that promote social interaction. We must first ensure that a technology, or combination of technologies, performs properly and improves the pedagogical process in order to achieve the end goals defined for the students, the institution and the country. We want to emphasise right now, nevertheless, that communication technologies aim to make educational opportunities for students not only more accessible but also tremendously enticing. They get students involved in the learning process by inspiring them, maintaining their interest for the best learning and helping them to retain the knowledge they have acquired.

With the right technologies, learning is no longer restricted to the school's four walls. It doesn't matter where you are or when it happens; neither does your age, your gender, or your socio-economic or demographic limitations. A genuine contribution of communication technology is the development of an informal learning environment specifically created to offer a high-quality educational experience, which is accessible anytime the students wish to learn. Thus, it is envisaged that communication technologies would lead to more productive time for education, training and employment when combined with flexible homework (*i.e.*, assignments) and learning schedules (i.e., study habit skills). As a result, the potential for lifelong learning will lead to reliable delivery methods and curriculum that spans the lifespan.

This is the area where educators must make a significant contribution to creating the most suitable curricula to satisfy the changing needs of the general public. According to futurists, social demands in the 21st century will be substantially dissimilar from those that the majority of us currently experience. Learning will be a diverse, lifelong process that concentrates on each student's unique needs at every given moment in any given circumstance.

Limitations

In poor nations, communication technology encounters some challenges. There are three interrelated reasons that are primarily responsible for the slow expansion and subpar performance of telecommunication services in developing nations. These are listed below:

(a) The key factor contributing to its subpar performance is a lack of investment funds. Communication technology has always been criticised for being too expensive for underdeveloped nations to use.

(b) Inefficient internal organisation and management of operational components of educational systems that extensively rely on communication technology, leads to expensive expansion and running expenses, subpar maintenance and constrained capacity. The use and application of communication technology determines its efficacy. It is unreasonable to anticipate returns and the successful results that their developers had in mind if it is not performed properly and adequately.

(c) The third and most prevalent barrier to telecommunications development is inadequate sector policies. As a result, there isn't much incentive to increase performance or to generate funding for telecommunications expansion in the field of education and training.

In addition, the following factors also work against communication technology:

***(a)* Planning, Monitoring and Evaluation:** Communication technologies struggle with a lack of precise planning, inadequate monitoring mechanisms regarding their use and inadequate evaluation to offer feedback services to enhance the system.

***(b)* Quantity:** For communication technology to succeed, there must be a sufficient quantity of telephone connections, TV and VCRs access. The communication of technology is extremely elitist due to poor teledensity and the widespread inaccessibility of new technologies.

***(d)* Quality of Services:** Subpar services have an impact on the success of communication technologies. For instance, telecom services are unreliable and of poor quality. The technology in use in underdeveloped nations is outdated.

***(d)* Price:** Communication technology is relatively expensive, making it challenging for the majority of people in poor nations to use. For instance, the cost of communication facilities in India is 100% greater than the global average for identical services.

(e) **Instructional Design Knowledge:** Lectures and the "talk and chalk" method are both convenient for teachers. They find using communication technology to be quite uncomfortable, which prompts an initial resistance to its use in teaching.

The preparedness and readiness of the implementers—the teachers—who form an essential part of any innovation in the educational enterprise—are crucial to the successful implementation of any educational media in a nation. Their participation in and attitude towards using technology is a key component of its success. The creators of new communication technologies thought that one of the main applications of their discoveries would be to make education accessible to everyone, or at least to those who want it.

But we must re-examine the nation's educational system to determine if the potential of the technology at our disposal for educational purposes was completely realised.

The preparedness and readiness of the implementers—the teachers—who form an essential part of any innovation in the educational enterprise—are crucial to the successful implementation of any educational media in a nation. Their participation in and attitude towards using technology is a key component of its success. The creators of new communication technologies thought that one of the main applications of their discoveries would be to make education accessible to everyone, or at least to those who want it. But we must reexamine the nation's educational system to determine if the potential of the technology at our disposal for educational purposes was completely realised.

FUTURE TRENDS

The way that communication technologies are being employed in education and development will decide how they are used in the future. Today's educators must balance the need to steer technology down an evolving educational path with the need to guarantee that all users and students who are interested in it have access to it. It is a fact that modern communication technologies are available to business organisations for commercial use. However, keeping up with technological changes and assuring the optimal pedagogical use of relevant technologies are educators' key priorities.

Communication Network

The characteristics of transmission networks have a major role in determining how well communication technology operates. The need for telecommunications networks is always rising from the general public and educational institutions in particular. They require the most cutting-edge technological gadgets and systems, such as videotext, video-disc and videophones for quick access to documents and data processing, as well as for personalised services and assistance. A nation's ability to advance hinges on how adaptable and powerful its communications infrastructure is. Based on the nation's rapidly expanding technological networks, this futuristic vision was created. Satellites, computers, fibre optics and other devices will make it possible to transmit text, voice, photos and videos at a faster rate.

Because a sizable number of people, institutions and business houses already have them on a sizable scale—a process that is difficult due to a lack of resources—the possibilities of acceptance and success of such devices are fairly high. Among the technology alternatives are satellite, optical fibres, VSATS, ISDN and others. For instance, fibre optic cables can be utilised to improve user access to technical networks so that consumers can instantly access information through adaptable, affordable networks. Fibre optic cables will be able to accommodate the wide range of needs of people whose access to mobile phones, mobile television and other mass communication tools is rapidly expanding.

A computer or other machine, such as a human interface, can control a communication network. Due to the trend towards a greater emphasis on distant education and open learning to suit the communication needs of the information society, these requirements will only increase in the future. Three fundamental challenges, nevertheless, will always be in the spotlight. These are cost effectiveness, connection and bandwidth. The ability of a system to transfer lots of data quickly is referred to as bandwidth. The amount of data transfer increases with bandwidth. Similar to connectivity, interactive connectivity allows users to interact with anybody, anywhere, at any time. Finally, there is the cost, which will decrease in the next years.

Satellite Communication

With the help of communication satellites, time and space have virtually vanished, allowing people to connect and share experiences even in the most remote regions of the globe. Telephone service provided by satellite has long been considered the answer for remote locations with low population densities. Satellite based remote calling has various advantages. Signals are delivered directly into the corporate telephone networks when using satellite telephone, which functions much like a regular public telephone network. Satellite phone systems are not susceptible to long-distance environmental conditions, unlike terrestrial cable networks. The widespread use of satellite telephony in modern society is evidence of its success on a global scale. For instance, satellite telephony is used for communication in China's coal mines, Taiwan's police, India's government and networks in Germany, Denmark, Canada and the Commonwealth of Independent States.

Satellite Radiotelephone Projects

The world of telecommunications is poised to revolutionise the whole global network, thanks to the potential of satellites. This technique uses a significant number of small portable terminals and low-earth orbit satellites. It aims to introduce a variety of reasonably priced, increasingly portable and practical international personal communication services. This is done by utilising advancements in mobile satellite capabilities and technology. Global personal communication is made independent of national networks like India's VSNL by such a method. The satellite-based technology will track the receiver telephone anywhere in the world, in contrast to conventional communications networks. These systems are made to transfer multimedia-based information, speech, data, fax and other types of information quickly. Several companies compete in the satellite radiotelephone market at the moment.

Integrated Services Digital Network (ISDN)

The Integrated Services Digital Network (ISDN) is a digital phone connection system that supports a wide range of services, including voice and non-voice services and allows data to be transmitted using end-to-end digital connectivity. Users have access to these services through a small number of standard multi-purpose user network interfaces. With ISDN, a bearer channel with a 64 kbps bandwidth carries both voice and data. Depending on the service type, a data channel can handle signalling at a speed of 16 kbps or 64 kbps. ISDN services come in two fundamental categories. Primary Rate Interface (PFU) has 23 or more B channels in addition to one 64 kbps D channel, while Basic Rate Interface (BRI) has two 64 kbps B channels, one 16 kbps D channel and one.

Customers must be within 5.5km of the telephone switching centre and have an ISDN phone connection in order to get BFU service. Beyond that, specialised repeater equipment is required. A simple two-wire phone line known as a U-interface, is extended to your premises from the telephone exchange after you sign up for an ISDN connection. This terminates into a unit known as a "Network Terminator" (NT1) to which numerous ISDN devices may be connected via the SIT interface, allowing for a maximum of seven ISDN devices to be connected.

Advantages of ISDN:

(a) **Speed:** The rate of data transfer is incredibly fast. Additionally, since the data has already been converted to digital form, a modem is not necessary. While ISDN allows speeds up to 64 kbps, standard modems have a maximum speed of 56 kbps.

(b) **Multiple devices:** A number of devices for each gadget to be utilised in the past, a separate telephone connection was required. For instance, one for email and one for fax services, etc. Seven devices can be connected to an ISDN line at once.

Broadband ISDN: Broadband ISDN (BISDN) is defined as a network capable of supporting data rates greater than the primary rate supported by ISDN. The main aim of BISDN is to support wide and image based services. The broadband channels proposed for BISDN are:

- H2, channel, 30 – 45 Mbps
- H3, channel, 60 – 70 Mbps
- H4, channel, 120 – 140 Mbps

The services on BISDN can be both interactive as well as distribution oriented. This will allow real-time teaching using video conferencing at low costs.

Internet

E-mail, which was once only a text-based medium for sending and receiving messages, has evolved into a fully multimedia platform with the ability to transmit audio, video, pictures and other visual content. This technology offers a significant amount of interaction. These days, this is how many colleges around the world conduct their courses. E-mail, the World Wide Web and Internet phone are the three fundamental services that will revolutionise the entire communication system, thanks to the Internet.

E-mail: A store-and-forward message service is email. The user's mailbox is where the messages and data are electronically sent and kept. Email offers a high-speed information sharing service by utilising computer, text-processing and communication facilities. One computer user can communicate with another user or a group of users via the user's terminal using the e-mail feature on the computer system.

WWW: World Wide Web (WWW) is a graphical user interface based and allows audio and video to be used. Web combines text, text-based interaction, multi-way interactive audio and video.

Internet phone: Internet phones, also referred to as broadband phones, are digital communication tools used to make phone calls via the Internet. As a Voice over Internet Protocol (VoIP) application device, it is also widely used. When a call is placed, the VoIP phone processes the user's voice using an analog-to-digital conversion circuit before converting it into multiple digital packets. The data is then sent over the Internet to be received by the other user.

Technology for People with Disabilities

In the underdeveloped world, there are many millions of people who need specialised and improvised communication technologies. The computer screen can be divided to display both incoming and outgoing messages and it can keep the incoming text so you can read it later when you're back in the office or your study. The system's usefulness for inter-disabled communication is an intriguing feature. The use of telephone networks by the deaf and the hearing allows for communication. The computer would translate both speech and text into one another. Typing the message enables it to be transformed into a synthesised voice. Given the rapid advancements in technology, it is believed that speech-generated text will enable a deaf person to use a phone to communicate with other phone users without the need of a professional operator. Another option — voice-encoded written printed communications, like fax messages, will be sent to you over a cordless or mobile phone. These services have been shown to be theoretically possible and may materialise within the next ten years. A flexible keyboard is being created for computers so that physically challenged people can use them more readily.

Enabling Technologies: Wagner (1992) investigates a number of ways to assist the disabled. He believed that society's first priority should be finding technology that can help those with disabilities. Wagner provided a further illustration in this regard. To help individuals with disabilities overcome barriers to communication, education and work, John Hopkin University's Search for Computing Applications to Assist Persons with Disabilities, U.S.A. aimed to use computer innovation.

Networked Society

Net worked society is a broad framework. A summary of the lecture on this topic by an eminent computer and communication technologist is given below:

Networked Society: Vision and Technology Option By Prof. T Vishwanathan

THE WORLD IN TRANSITION

The world is changing. According to the big bang hypothesis of the universe's genesis, the universe was created with a huge bang from an egg-shaped shell and has been expanding ever since. The rate of growth will eventually reach zero, at which point the contraction will begin. A form resembling an egg will emerge from the universion. Here, the old Indian creation hypothesis is also applicable. One world order is dissolving and another is emerging. Networked Society is discernible in this setting.

NETWORKED INFORMATION SOCIETY OF TOMORROW

With the expansion of the Global Information Infrastructure (GII) and the widespread use of networks, although there are significant societal challenges that need to be addressed, certain macro shifts seem to be occurring.

COMMUNICATION TECHNOLOGIES

Optical fibres, satellites and short-range radio are the three communication technologies that are anticipated to play complimentary roles in defining the networked society of the future.

Optical fibre: Due to its extraordinarily high data carrying capacity, optical fibre is quickly replacing conventional copper lines in some telecommunications applications. Fibre has the advantage of complete immunity to electromagnetic interference, is lightweight and is less expensive than copper wires. A single optical fibre may theoretically support 10 tera (1013) bits per second of bandwidth.

Satellite systems: Although installing fibre optics might seem like a difficult process, satellite links are by far the fastest way to create access. By leveraging satellite connectivity, even the most isolated regions can be included to the world network map in a matter of hours.

Short-haul radio links: Satellites and fibre optics both have the capacity to connect faraway locations. Fibre laying issues prevent its arrival at homes anytime soon. Except for one-way broadcast reception applications, a dish could not be installed on top of every house due to the satellite's limited bandwidth. The end user (homes and offices) must be connected to the network in a different way in the network society's requirement for interactive connectivity. Short-distance microwave radio links hold significant promise in this area.

BROADBAND INFRASTRUCTURE

The majority of today's internet services are text and data-oriented, with sporadic graphics and still images. Future services would handle full-featured voice, motion video and all other types of information and they would be generically categorised as Interactive services and Distribution services. A broadband infrastructure is required to support these services and the Broadband Integrated Services Digital Network is the most promising infrastructure globally (B-ISDN).

Broadband ISDN

A network able to handle data rates higher than the main rate provided by ISDN is referred to as broadband ISDN (BISPN). BISDN's primary goal is to assist services that use video and images. For BISDN, the following broadband channels have been proposed: * H2, channel, 30–45 Mbps * H3, channel, 60–70 Mbps * H4, channel, 120–140 Mbps

Both interactive and distribution-focused services are available on BISDN. This will make low-cost real-time video conferencing possible for teaching.

Asynchronous Transfer Mode (ATM)

A new technique for simultaneously transferring plenty of audio, data and video via a network is defined by a set of international standards called ATM.

COMPUTER TECHNOLOGIES

Personal computers or computer-based systems would constitute bulk of end equipments in the network society. With the continuing advancements in microprocessor technology, the personal computer systems are undergoing substantial changes.

Network Computers (Net PCs)

Conventional PCs are undergoing a metamorphosis to accommodate the connectivity and access requirements as network computing is given more attention. In order to achieve optimum efficiency in a network context, network personal computers, or simply NetPCs, are built on cutting-edge microprocessors and are uniquely architectured employing hardware and software techniques.

Multimedia PCs

Multimedia PCs will have specially built architecture and setup on the line of network computers intended for the network environment to handle multimedia applications. Having sufficient local processing power to run multimedia programmes is the focus of multimedia PCs.

Transputer PCs

A little thought will reveal that what is desirable is a balance between network access and local processing power. The United Kingdom's transputer technology held great promise as a great way to integrate both computation and communication capabilities on the chip.

LANGUAGE FOR MACHINE COMMUNICATION

Finding a suitable language for machine communication is necessary. English is not the best option. Sanskrit is a good choice for machine communication because of its structural, grammatical and semantic characteristics.

INFORMATION AND KNOWLEDGE MANAGEMENT

Powerful personal computers and communication infrastructure only tells half of the tale of the networked society. Data, information and knowledge bases, as well as the accompanying data management strategies and the navigational tools necessary to access these bases are additional crucial elements.

Knowledge Warehousing

Massive volumes of data can be archived and stored using techniques called data warehousing. Improvements in optical storage technology are predicted to result in a notable increase in hard drive capacities. Optical discs with capacities of 50 Gigabytes and greater are anticipated to become commercially available shortly, thanks to the development of Digital Versatile Disks (DVD) and the use of blue lasers in place of infrared ones. Optical storage is without a doubt the most promising data warehousing technology for the networked society.

Knowledge Mining

There is a need to hunt for new strategies because the current data mining methods are not best suited for finding information and knowledge. It is hoped that the traditional methods of knowledge organisation and classification will serve as a foundation for cutting-edge automated methods of information and knowledge mining.

POSSIBLE ILLS OF NETWORKED INFORMATION SOCIETY

The pinnacle of networked society's progress is regarded as virtue reality. When we are particularly worried about not cooperating with nature enough, it is unclear whether one should even consider virtual reality.

CONCLUDING REMARK

With the trade, economy, occupation, development, education, culture and leisure all centred upon networking, a networked society would emerge as the main topic of living.

CHECK YOUR PROGRESS

Q. 1. Why is research and development an area of concern to technologists in developing countries?

Ans. Research and innovation are of fundamental importance to reducing poverty and building stronger economies and societies. For solutions to be truly sustainable, the skills and expertise for such research and innovation need to exist within developing countries. Nonetheless, investments in building such capacity continue to be limited. Developing countries invest far less in research and development (R&D) as a share of their GDP than developed countries. Even middle income countries often invest well under 0.5%, compared to 3% and above in advanced countries.

Developing countries are a heterogeneous group, extending from the least developed countries to emerging economies. Consequently, their innovation systems and associated R&D measurement systems exhibit wide variety both internally by institution, sector and region and internationally. In addition, despite the increasing presence of developing countries in global R&D, there is still a marked lack of demand for science, technology and innovation (STI) indicators from policy-makers in developing countries. Even if the demand does exists, there are often significant problems with compiling the data due to a lack of coordination at the national level, a lack of cooperation by research institutions, universities and businesses and a generally weak statistical system in the country.

In 1973, developing countries as a whole accounted for 5% of the world's scientific publications and only India, South Africa and Argentina made the list of top 25 countries. In 2006, scientific publications from developing countries accounted for 20% of the global share, largely due to Asia (14.8%) and in particular to China (7%). China experienced a growth in publications of over 100% in the last decade while in Latin America, Brazil has increased its contribution to global publications by almost 50% during the same period.

In many developing and emerging economies, the business sector performs much less R&D than the government and higher education (public) sectors. This is particularly evident in agricultural and natural environment research where there may be strong links between local research institutions established before independence with parent institutions abroad. In effect, this likely means that more 'R' than 'D' occurs. However, where there are large inflows of funds for health R&D – especially for clinical trials – it is more a case of less 'R' and more 'D'.

The lower emphasis on R&D in the business sector may reflect organizational issues. When business enterprises cater mainly to the local market, competitive pressure may be reduced so that systematic R&D would be the exception not the rule. R&D projects may therefore be commissioned ad hoc to deal with production issues making it infrequent, informal and difficult to capture. This is quite a different issue to the (possibly rare) occurrence of R&D in the informal sector.

Establishing a sound and sustainable R&D statistical system requires dedicated political support as well as a predictable budget, infrastructure, a stable staff complement and provision for continuous training. Ideally, the responsibility for the surveys should remain vested with a dedicated agency for periods in excess of five years so that methodological stability may be attained. Migration of responsibility for the survey carries the risk of inconsistency.

In some developing countries, large public enterprises in different sectors that intensively develop research activities dominate R&D expenditure. In some cases, these enterprises may create "independent" R&D institutes where research efforts are undertaken in an autonomous way with significant R&D budgets. They have their own financial resources, receive funding directly from supporting agencies and may enter into their own contractual arrangements. This sub-sector includes state utilities both at the national and secondary level that are registered as enterprises. They are 'corporatized' with a single shareholder and also operate independent research centres or R&D departments as cost centres that may receive funding agency support.

Q. 2. Identify three major contributions of communication technology to education. Also identify three major problems in implementing such technology in a given situation.

Ans. Major contributions of communication technology to education are:

(a) The use of communication technologies to support traditional educational methods and media. Media improves the flavour of the information to be learned and the message to be conveyed. They also provide other means of disseminating the knowledge. Face-to-face encounters can be replaced by technologies for effective and efficient communication.

(b) Technologists are aiming to reduce the burden on students, while still providing them with the tools and resources they need to excel in their academic endeavours.

(c) One of communication technology's greatest contributions to education is the personalization of learning. Mastery-based learning is taken into account while planning for individualised instruction. Group projects and other activities that encourage social interaction give activities a human element.

Major problems in implementing such technology in a given situation are:

(a) Shortage of finances: A lack of investment funds is the major reason affecting its poor performance. Communication technology has long been criticised for being out of reach for developing countries due to its high cost.

(b) Poor internal organisation and administration of operational elements in educational systems that heavily rely on communication technology results in high expansion and operating costs, poor maintenance and limited capacity. The effectiveness of communication technology depends on how it is used and put to use. If it is not done correctly and adequately, it is unreasonable to expect returns and the successful outcomes that its developers had in mind.

***(c)* Service Quality:** The success of communication technology is impacted by poor services. For instance, telecom services are unreliable and of poor quality. The technology in use in underdeveloped nations is outdated.

Q. 3. Outline briefly three major educational uses of communication satellites.

Ans. The use of satellite communication in education is widespread. In places where it is impossible to provide an effective formal education due to location and demography, satellite and interactive television broadcasts are used. As a result, numerous inventions have been tested.

By establishing a private network of Satellite Interactive Terminals (SITs) and Receive Only Terminals (ROTs) located throughout the nation, India's satellite is able to provide high bandwidth two-way contact. The Hyper Text Transfer Protocol (HTTP), which is widely used on the Internet and in online applications, provides the foundation of the interaction method. Consequently, the satellite enables us to establish a network through which we can exchange already-existing resources (often referred to as digital repositories), in text, graphic, audio and video formats; and also, we can create real-time interactive virtual classrooms (often referred to as synchronous e-learning) across the nation. The potential for this country's educational progress with either of these options is huge. The satellite includes six extended C-band transponders for the regional beam, one Ku-band transponder for the national beam and five Ku-band transponders for spot beams. Through national and regional beams, everything combined covers the entire nation. The National Council for Educational Research and Training, the Consortium for Educational Communication, Visvesvaraya Technological University and Vigyan Prasar are a few of the significant organisations that use the Edusat network. It is now feasible to communicate with pupils in real-time using a two-way video and two-way audio system, thanks to satellite connectivity.

The satellites have made teleconferencing—a real-time information exchange between people—possible. The satellite has made it feasible to take classes online. Meetings, training, demonstrations, data transmission and other activities are all possible. Teleconferencing for education is a useful tool for online learning. Multiple media are utilised and a two-way broadcast allows for participatory group conversation.

These days, reliance on this technology is growing. The popularity of distant learning may be related to the desire in employing audio and related visual data that may be transmitted over normal telephone lines.

Q. 4. Describe briefly the special features of ISDN.

Ans. The first public digital network is the Integrated Services Digital Network (ISDN). It was made to accommodate a wide range of data kinds, including sound, video and data. Circuit-switched synchronous communication is the foundation of it. ISDN employs D channels for return signalling and B channels for basic traffic. Each B channel offers 64 Kbps of data rate, while each D channel offers 16 Kbps. B channels are multiplied to accommodate p 4 Kbps. The 2B+D channel offered by the basic rate interface (BRI) can be used to transport signals at a rate of 128

Kbps. High-quality video communication cannot be supported at this level. By employing the primary rate interface, communications based on ISDN can use a larger bandwidth (PRI). Up to 24 B channels can be used by PRI communications to transmit data at 1.5 Mbps rates. A communication system standard for video conferencing over ISDN is provided by H.320. The great majority of currently in use video telephony and video conferencing systems rely on H.320.

Narrowband ISDN is currently a common name for ISDN (N-ISDN). The telephone industry's current twisted pair copper wiring can be utilised to provide it. Broadband ISDN is the name given to the second generation of ISDN (B-ISDN). It offers transmission paths that can accommodate substantially greater rates. Similar to N-ISDN, B-bandwidth ISDN's is defined in terms of multiples of 64 Kbps. N-ISDN is restricted to 1–24 multiples of 64 Kbps channels, whereas B-ISDN has a multiplier range of 1–65,535. The coaxial cable of optical fibres is the physical conduit needed for B-ISDN. By utilising ATM packet switching technology, B-ISDN can be implemented effectively.

OTHER IMPORTANT QUESTIONS

Q. 1. What is satellite communication? What is the significance of Satellite Instructional Television Experiment (SITE)?

Ans. Satellite communication is the use of man-made satellites to establish communication linkages among various locations on Earth. The global communications network is not possible without satellite communications. Around 2,000 man-made satellites circling Earth transmit and receive voice, video and data signals in analogue and digital formats to and from a single or a network of locations globally.

Signals used in satellite communications are transmitted and received in the very high-frequency range of 1 to 50 gigahertz (GHz; 1 gigahertz equals 1,000,000,000 hertz). Larger antennas are required to receive signals in the lower frequency area of the satellite frequency spectrum since they are broadcast at low power levels.

As a result of the stronger signals at the higher end of this spectrum, dishes as tiny as 45 cm (18 inches) in diameter can pick them up. Due of this, the Ku-band and Ka-band spectrum are perfect for mobile phone and data applications, broadband data communications and direct-to-home (DTH) broadcasts.

The largest satellite-based communication experiment in support of educational and developmental initiatives was SITE.

Prof. V.A. Sarabhai served as the project's primary catalyst. An experiment dubbed SIET by way of Applications Technology Satellite was launched by India and the USA in 1969. (ATS-6). The Satellite was launched from Cape Carnival in the United States on May 30, 1974. On August 1, 1975, this satellite started broadcasting in India.

In six states—Andhra Pradesh, Bihar, Karnataka, Odisha, Madhya Pradesh and Rajasthan—chosen on the basis of their educational backwardness, Indian Space Research Organization (ISRO) and All India Radio (AIR) accepted the task of broadcasting ETV programmes to the designated villages. From August 1975 through July 1976, the experiment was ongoing. The subjects of education, agriculture, health, family planning and national integration were the focus of SITE's educational goals. There were about 2400 Direct Reception Television Sets (DRS) deployed for SITE, which were spread out across the nation's many agricultural, cultural and linguistic regions. Additionally, a variety of socio-economic contexts were picked for the project. Four hours a day, one and a half hours in the morning and two and a half hours in the evening, were dedicated to satellite television transmissions. Children's enrichment programmes for the age range of 5 to 12 years were broadcast in the morning, while adult-oriented programmes were broadcast in the evening. Four different linguistic regions were covered by SITE, however on school days, children from other regions also watched these programmes. Even though the shows were aimed towards kids, others in the school watched them as well. These were designed to give general enrichment and were not dependent on course curricula. The electrification of the school, which housed the television receiver, was the responsibility of the governments of each state receiving SITE programmes.

A team of educators from the National Council of Education Research and Training determined the programmes' contents (NCERT).

The State Institutes of Educational Technology (SIET) in each of the separate states' senior department of education officials were then presented with it. A number of science-related programmes established by ISRO with the goal of fostering scientific thinking. ISRO also established a production studio in Bombay and its team created one of the instructional programmes.

The experience gained during the SITE period was very positive for future national television service growth. The government made the decision to launch the SITE community-viewing programme. Three Base Production Centers: Hyderabad, Cuttack and Delhi (Hindi) developed the programmes (Telugu and Kannada). The shows followed a lecture demonstration with a documentary, a play and a debate. A few prototypes were created and pretested in several communities before approaching the programmes for broadcast purposes. This pre-testing was done to gauge how well-liked the programmes were.

Q. 2. Write a note on the development of technology for disabled persons.

Ans. Many different types of technology have been developed to lessen or remove obstacles that individuals with disabilities face, particularly obstacles linked to computers and technology. Assistive technology, which includes hardware and software solutions, can help with activities like reading and creating papers, interacting with others and conducting web searches. Students and workers with impairments are becoming capable of managing a larger variety of activities independently as the varieties of assistive technology increase and mainstream technologies become more accessible. Students with disabilities can access the remote learning centre. Students with impairments can continue to live at home, while they are enrolled in distance learning courses, sharing papers, teaching, exchanging ideas and giving presentations. A common part of training and learning involves using a computer.

Students with disabilities such as dyslexia, poor vision, hearing loss, or intellectual impairments can now access digital and audio libraries' materials, content and resources online to attend educational courses. Without needing to visit the local institution or library, students can connect from their homes and study or listen to the pertinent books.

Today, people with impairments use the Internet, increasing their ability to contact with one another remotely. They may obtain and comprehend public information and news, engage in leisure activities with others, chat, shop, manage their finances and write to authorities and friends, thanks to the Internet.

A computer with a broadband connection gives people the chance to participate more fully in daily life and live independently.

The majority of blind people use ordinary keyboards, however Braille input devices are also available. Keyboard use can be made easier by Braille key labels.

The development of skills can benefit from educational software that uses the computer to deliver multisensory experiences, interaction, positive reinforcement, personalised training and repetition. Computer-assisted writing assignments, tutorial courses and drill-and-practice work can help some children with learning difficulties who struggle to process written material.

Accessibility problems are not completely resolved by providing assistive technology to people with disabilities. All digital tools and materials, including software, websites, papers, online courses and other digital resources, must be created in accessible formats.

Q. 3. What is the Internet? How WWW is different from the Internet? How does the Internet work?

Ans. There are billions of computers and other electronic devices connected to the Internet on a global scale. You can speak with anyone in the world, access nearly any information and accomplish a lot more with the help of the Internet.

By getting online, or connecting a computer to the Internet, you may accomplish all of these tasks. When someone refers to a computer as being online, they are merely referring to the fact that it is linked to the Internet.

The World Wide Web, more commonly abbreviated as WWW or the Web, is a collection of various websites that you may visit over the Internet. Related content, images and other materials come together to form a website. Websites can be interactive in a way that is specific to computers, or they can be similar to other forms of media, such as newspaper articles or television shows.

A website can serve a variety of functions, including serving as a news source, an advertisement, an online library, a place for users to share photos, or even an instructional platform like ours!

The physical cables that make up the Internet, which can include copper phone wires, TV cables and fibre optic cables are distributed throughout the world. These physical cords are necessary for accessing the Internet even with wireless connections like Wi-Fi and 3G/4G.

Your computer sends a request to a server across these cables whenever you view a webpage. Websites are kept on servers, which function similarly to your computer's hard disc. The server retrieves the website and delivers the correct information back to your computer as soon as the request is received. Amazingly, everything takes place in a matter of seconds.

The capacity to speak with anyone in the world virtually immediately is one of the best aspects of the Internet. With billions of users worldwide, email is one of the most established and widely used methods of online communication and information sharing. People can communicate with each other in a number of ways and create online communities, thanks to social media.

You can use the Internet for a variety of additional purposes. There are countless ways to stay up to date on news and do online shopping. You can take care of your financial affairs, meet new people, watch TV, or pick up new skills. Virtually everything may be learned or done online.

Q. 4. What are the characteristics of network society?

Ans. The network society implies that it is for:

- Anyone
- Anytime
- Anywhere
- Any information
- Any format

Every person on the earth would need access to the network in a fully networked society. In the same way that an electricity or water supply connection is a necessary piece of infrastructure, network connectivity to the home would also become such. A person from one of the world's poorest villages should be able to access information resources in one of the world's wealthiest cities when the networked information society is completely evolved.

Time zones and holiday schedules would no longer matter in people's daily lives because of network infrastructures that are planned to run around-the-clock. Resources cost may become independent of access time and day of the week across all countries. The person accessing the information's necessity and convenience would be important considerations. An "anytime" facility would encourage the development of a "on demand" culture, allowing people and communities to live more flexibly. "Anywhere" implies that those who are accessing information resources can do so from anywhere. A person from anywhere in the globe should be able to access a resource for information that is located somewhere else in the world. When a person could access information from anywhere in the globe, regardless of where they were living, the idea of location independent access would become a reality. The implementation of such a plan would necessitate permanent identification of all people for the duration of their lives. In reality, a child may be given a universal code at birth and be recognised by that code for the rest of his or her life on the planet. These concepts may seem improbable, yet they are not impossible to implement.

As the right to access information is being emphasised more and more, all information should be accessible to everyone on the earth. While certain information may be paid for and some may be free, everyone should have access to all information. Different countries' information policies already show a shift towards this scenario.

No transnational boundaries should exist in a networked society and information should be able to be shared in any format that the recipient can understand. The possibility of real-time machine translation exists. An intermediate language to represent information becomes crucial in this situation. The majority of the communication mediums used today are broadcast, including newspapers, periodicals, journals, television and radio. The environment will be primarily interactive in a networked society.

Q. 5. In the networked society, which are likely to be the activity centres?

Ans. In a networked society, households rather than offices will likely serve as the hubs of activity. According to the fact that 35% of business workers in the United States work remotely now, it would appear that a networked society would lead to a society with less travel, if not none at all. Physical location might no longer matter for receiving or providing services. The workplace culture would drastically shift as a result. Flexible work schedules and creative resource and workforce management hold the promise of increased productivity. According to estimates, travel accounts for more than 20% of a working person's daily active time on average. Home-based activities would increase creativity, innovation and productivity because travel time would be avoided. A home-centered economy would eventually result from the telecommuting culture and activities.

Q. 6. How the networked society will help overcoming unemployment problem?

Ans. Massive industrial houses have been built and the previous few centuries have been marked by mass manufacturing. Because of this, there has been power-sharing between the workforce and the management, which has resulted in strikes, lockouts, etc. Small, self-contained communities of homes would develop in a networked world. The local needs of the community will be satisfied by goods found in its natural surroundings. In a networked society, the idea of groups and unions might become obsolete. This would also suggest that production would occur locally, with a sizable workforce involved in creating the necessary items. This concept for widespread employment and overcoming the current unemployment issues is intriguing.

Q. 7. Write a note on optical fibre.

Ans. Due to its extraordinarily high data carrying capacity, optical fibre is quickly replacing conventional copper lines in some telecommunications applications. Fibre has the advantage of complete immunity to electromagnetic interference, is lightweight and is less expensive than copper wires. A single optical fibre may theoretically support 10 tera (1013) bits per second of bandwidth. But the performance of currently on the market equipment is only around 5 Gigabits per second. The biggest obstacle is in electrical-optical interfaces, whose working speeds are constrained by current technology. Bit rates of the order of 20 Gigabits per second or greater are likely to become practical in the near future because of the ongoing advancements in photo electronic technology. Even yet, we are a long way from using the fibre's full potential. This may be advantageous in that fibre technology's growth path seems limitless, at least for the next century or two. The bandwidth requirements for the video services anticipated in the networked society can only be met by optical fibres. Since the advent of modern telecommunications in 1879, it is estimated that the world has buried about 1.8 billion kilometres of copper cable beneath the surface of the planet. In a short period of time, it is nearly difficult to replace all of this copper with fibre for the networked society.

Intercontinental, intercountry and intercity trunk lines are the segments, where fibre can be introduced with ease. Bringing fibre to your home or to the curb seems to be a long-term solution. However, Japan is planning to install fibre in homes soon. It is obvious that, as of right now, optical fibre promises to meet the predicted bandwidth needs of the networked society.

MULTIPLE CHOICE QUESTIONS

Q. 1. The capacity of a system to transfers large amount of data at high speed is called:

(*a*) Bandwidth (*b*) Modem
(*c*) Networks (*d*) LAN

Ans. (*a*) Bandwidth.

Q. 2. ISDN is:

(*a*) International Services Digital Networking
(*b*) Integrated Services Digital Network
(*c*) Integrated Services Digitalised Networking
(*d*) Integrated Services Digitalised Network

Ans. (*b*) Integrated Services Digital Network.

Q. 3. Basic Rate Interface (BRI) has:

(*a*) One 64 kbps B channel
(*b*) One 16 kbps D channel
(*c*) One 64 kbps B channel and one 16 kbps D channel
(*d*) None of these

Ans. (*c*) One 64 kbps B channel and one 16 kbps D channel.

Q. 4. Primary Rate Interface (PFU) has:

(*a*) One B channel plus + one 64 kbps D channel
(*b*) 23 or more B channel plus + one 64 kbps D channel
(*c*) One B channel plus + one 64 kbps D channel
(*d*) 23 or more B channels plus + one 64 kbps D channel

Ans. (*b*) 23 or more B channel plus + one 64 kbps D channel

Q. 5. To access BFU service, it is necessary to have an ISDN phone connection and the customer must be within what distance of the telephone switching centre?

(*a*) 5km (*b*) 10km
(*c*) 15km (*d*) 20km

Ans. (*a*) 5km.

Q. 6. Most of our teachers are not comfortable with:

(*a*) Lectures
(*b*) The 'talk and chalk' method
(*c*) Use of communication technology
(*d*) None of these

Ans. (*c*) Use of communication technology.

Q. 7. Which of the following makes use of satellite telephony system for communication purpose?

(*a*) Coal mines in China
(*b*) Police in Taiwan
(*c*) Both (*a*) and (*b*)
(*d*) None of these

Ans. (*c*) Both (*a*) and (*b*).

Q. 8. Broadband ISDN is capable of supporting data rates:

(*a*) Greater than the primary rate supported by ISDN
(*b*) Less than the primary rate supported by ISDN
(*c*) Broadband ISDN and ISDN have the same capacity
(*d*) None of these

Ans. (*a*) Greater than the primary rate supported by ISDN.

Q. 9. The main aim of BISDN is to support:

(*a*) Video and image-based services
(*b*) Audio-based services
(*c*) Only text-based services
(*d*) None of these

Ans. (*a*) Video and image-based services.

Q. 10. Communication technologies struggle with:

(*a*) A lack of precise planning
(*b*) Inadequate monitoring mechanisms regarding their use
(*c*) Inadequate evaluation to offer feedback services to enhance the system
(*d*) All of these

Ans. (*d*) All of these.

Q. 11. Which is a store-and-forward message service?

(*a*) E-mail (*b*) World Wide Web
(*c*) Internet phone (*d*) None of these

Ans. (*a*) E-mail.

Q. 12. How many devices can be connected to an ISDN line at once?

(*a*) Six (*b*) Seven
(*c*) Eight (*d*) Nine

Ans. (*b*) Seven.

BLOCK-2 MEDIA IN DISTANCE EDUCATION

Media in Distance Education: An Overview

5

INTRODUCTION

This chapter's main topic is a study of how and why different media are used in the teaching-learning process. This discussion's initial phase covers media classification as well as its advantages and disadvantages in relation to teaching-learning interactions. The chapter then moves on to discuss how to choose and use suitable media elements into instructional design as its following stage. Exploring the potential of educational media in instructional design specifically for the setting of distance education, as well as giving an overview of media in distance education, are the main objectives.

CHAPTER AT A GLANCE

ROLE OF MEDIA IN THE DISTANCE EDUCATION

Educational media serves as extensions of the professors and aid in communicating with the pupils. In the context of distance education, the media plays a crucial role in the process of deliberate instruction. Distance education has four essential characteristics: *(i)* the teachers and students are separated by a physical distance; *(ii)* the majority of the educational content is delivered to students through one or more media, such as print, television, radio, etc.; *(iii)* a professional organisation is in charge of the programmes; and *(iv)* the instructional system allows for two-way communication between the student and the teacher, tutor, or administrator. As a result, educational media serves as conduits for transmitting knowledge and teaching from a distance between a DE institution's tutor and its students.

Classification of Media

Taxonomies for instructional media have been proposed by a variety of media experts. Romiszowski (1974) built his taxonomy around the idea of information-carrying sensory channels. The table below displays how he has classified the media.

Table 1: Romiszowski's Classification of Educational Media

Sensory Channels	Major Illustrative Media
Audio	Teacher's voice, language laboratory, audio tapes, radio broadcasts, etc.
Visual	Pictures, charts, models, handouts, film slides, transparencies, progmmed instructional material etc.
Audio-Visual	Open channnel television, closed circuit television, videotape, etc.
Tactile	Working models, simulated devices, adaptive teaching machiners, etc.

The sensory pathways employed to receive information from the basis of Romiszowski's categorisation. As a result, it is viewed as being quite insufficient. According to Schrammn (1977), there are two categories of educational media–big media and small media. The "glamour boys of the field", big media are more expensive and rely on cutting-edge technologies. Small media, in contrast, are generally far less expensive and rely on developing and middle technologies. Transparencies, slides and other types of boards are examples of small media, while sound films, interactive video, interactive television and computers are examples of big media.

The most thorough taxonomy of instructional media, however, was created by Bretz (1971) and the majority of media specialists accept it. The type of information they convey and whether they are primarily recording or telecommunication media are the two criteria on which Bretz's media taxonomy is founded. Bretz separates information into auditory, visual, still and motion. He further divides the visual industry into the categories of image, line art and print. Line drawings exist in the middle of the visual spectrum, between pictures and print at either end. Bretz initially separated the audio industry into four categories, including music, noise and either natural or synthetic sounds. However, he did not separate the audio industry; rather, he treated it as a totality. Bretz divided educational media into seven classes:

Class I: Audio-motion-visual media
Class II: Audio-still-visual media
Class III: Audio-semi motion media
Class IV: Motion-visual media
Class V: Still-visual media
Class VI: Audio-medium
Class VII: Print medium

Media are typically divided into two categories by educational technologists – interactive and non-interactive. These two categories were used to group all educational media. Five categories could be used to classify instructional materials from a different perspective, viz. *(i)* print, *(ii)* audio, *(iii)* video, *(iv)* 3-d models and *(v)* integrated.

The Print Medium

The primary, if not the only, method of formal face-to-face instruction has been print. Recent research has shown that print is still the most often utilised medium in remote education. Dichanz (1982) notes that there is minimal variety in the use of media in West Germany, where 90% of all study materials at the Fern-Universitat are printed materials. According to Hawkridge, who praises the U.K. Open University for its creative use of a variety of educational media, Print is the primary medium through which Open University students learn. All distance education institutions in India use print as their major educational medium.

Limitations of Print Medium: Like any other pedagogical tool, print has advantages and disadvantages. Two reasons account for print's widespread use as a teaching tool: first, it has advantages and second, it is less expensive than other forms of media. Print is frequently referred to as "frozen language", meaning that it is completely dead, cold and disconnected from experience, rendering it irrelevant. It is said that no reasonable and enthusiastic instructor would select print as their first preference because print means "printed languages" and all of language's flaws are likewise attributed to print. The main four of these are:

(i) Direct experience is a poor substitute for language.
(ii) Because language can be deceptive, it should not be trusted.
(iii) Because we engage in and live in an oral culture, receiving an education through print is both unnecessary and unwanted.
(iv) Since fixing problems requires taking action, paper cannot serve as a replacement for taking action.

There are certain practical restrictions:

(i) Because a sufficient degree of literacy among students is required for effective use, print is a demanding instructional medium.
(ii) Print is only useful if the reader has highly developed cognitive abilities for understanding the text and assessing its thinking content.
(iii) Reading is a linear sequential process that requires processing words and lines in a specific order, such as top-to-bottom, right-to-left, or left-to-right.
On the other hand, a visual image can be absorbed holistically and understood nearly, instantly. Depending on the individual's capacity for observation, one need only gaze at it to get its meaning.
(iv) Reading printed material takes far longer than viewing the same information as visuals, such as on television.
(v) Reading is inappropriate for the development of skills, whether they are managerial, psychomotor, or interactive. Reading a printed lesson can give someone theoretical knowledge about driving a car, but it cannot give them the abilities necessary to operate a car.
(vi) The printed lesson's wording was chosen in accordance with the author's presumption about typical readers. Once written, the language of a printed lesson is fixed; it does not change for below-average or weak learners.

Merits of Print Medium: Print is still widely and universally used in all forms of education, including distant learning, due to a number of advantages:

(i) Print offers relatively permanent educational content that is accessible anytime desired and is free from the rigid temporal constraints associated with television and radio that can be used anywhere to process printed content. The least limiting media is print.
(ii) While it is true that television visuals can be processed almost instantly, it is highly improbable that learning from watching television occurs in a similarly quick manner. In actuality, time is the most crucial factor in all learning. The learner is literally inundated with the fast-changing visual images, making the entire process hit-or-miss.
It takes longer to process printed material and more time spent on a task results in more and better learning.
(iii) Because print offers more alternatives for picking a better learning approach or even initially trying out several tactics and selecting the most successful one, print enables learners to learn at their own speed and in a way that is most suited to them.
(iv) The use of print as a teaching tool is completely consistent with our sophisticated cultural environment. In actuality, print is a huge part of every developed society. A primitive, rather than a mature society teaches through imitation, display and spoken word.
(v) Certain ways of thinking that are involved in the educational process almost force the usage of print media. The usage of print is required

when defining, qualifying logical restrictions, developing, or sequencing 'sophisticated reasoning.

(vi) Students who have mastered reading, prefer to use print media. It is well-known that students, who find their teachers' lectures dull, believe that reading assignments help them study more effectively.

(vii) Since symbol systems are used in abstract thought, print is particularly well adapted to this type of thinking. The use of language becomes essential as we move away from actual learning references and print gains particular significance.

(viii) Print is still the most affordable educational tool available. It outperforms practically all other forms of media in terms of price, mobility and the unique freedom from hardware dependence for its users.

The Non-print Media

Although, some non-print media, such as 3-D models and home experiment kits, are loosely referred to as "electronic media", others are not. However, since the majority of these are electronic-based, they have a special way of destroying distance.

Non-print media can benefit distance learning in a number of ways, including the following:

***(i)* Greater Delivery Capabilities:** The non-print media, particularly those in the electronic category, can simultaneously reach students in various locations and give them a sense of belonging, of being a part of a large organisation, alleviating their feelings of loneliness and the notion that they are unimportant to the system, simply because teachers do not instruct them face-to-face. Table below shows the delivery capabilities of different non-print media.

Table 2: Delivery Capabilities of Non-print Media

Individual learners	Medium size groups at one place	Scattered individual or grups
• Telephone • Computer-assisted instruction on sharing basis)	• Films • Videotapes • Film strips • Slides • Audiotapes • Charts, posters • 3-D models • Slow-scan television	• CCTV • Open broadcast television • Radio • Fascimile • Slow-scan television.

***(ii)* A Supplement to the Master Medium:** Print is the primary or master medium for DE institutions. Because of their versatility, the non-print media can support the print media very well. Certain characteristics make educational media work well as a supplement. A case in point is the capacity to use it by an individual in opposition to the group, complete control over when to use it and how it works and portability. The table below makes evident these characteristics of non-print media as tools to complement the master medium.

***(iii)* Greater suitability to Iconic and Enactive Modes of Experience:** Three categories of experience have been postulated by Bruner: enactive (using activity), iconic (using images, graphics, or 3-D representations) and symbolic (based on the use of symbols). Print can be used to express symbolic experiences. The use of non-print media can enhance educational opportunities. For instance, slides, silent or sound films, or tapes can most effectively teach someone how to tie even a simple knot, whereas just verbal description in text cannot.

***(iv)* Feedback through Recorded Performance:** The learner's performance can be recorded on some non-print recording mediums, which can then provide incredibly helpful feedback. For instance, audio cassettes offer helpful feedback regarding one's command of a language's sound system, while video tapes offer much-needed corrective feedback for other forms of performance. Print media isn't very useful in this regard.

***(iv)* Facilitate Diverse Learning Objectives:** To achieve a variety of learning objectives, distance teaching moves away from the traditional face-to-face teaching mode. Instead, it places a reasonable dependence on a variety of other media. Printed material can't very effectively accomplish all learning objectives. This assertion is supported by William H. Allen's (1967) chart illustraties the alleged efficacy of various instructional modalities for various learning objectives.

***(vi)* Contribute to Specific Learning Activities:** Particular non-print media kinds and distribution techniques are especially effective at supporting the learning activities of distant learners. For instance, utilising computers or audiotapes, it is possible to properly drill and provide practice to language and math learners. Electronic media can assist with discovery-based learning. A movie, for instance, could be utilised to teach physical scientific ideas through exploration.

The "real-life" or "laboratory learning" scenarios that demand problem-solving and situational awareness are commonly shown in movies and simulations.

***(vii)* Motivate Learners Psychologically:** Utilizing electronic media has shown to be psychologically interesting for students during both the preparation period and during participation, which promotes learning. While print content presents a challenge for these students, these mediums can capture their interest and appeal to the neo-literate. For instance, Korea's experience using television to deliver non-formal education demonstrates that "participants in a project occasionally perform tasks they may otherwise be hesitant to attempt" because of the thrill of the medium.

***(viii)* Help Learners get Involved:** The non-print medium encourages participation and interaction from the students, which facilitates learning. Heinich et al. (1982-83) cite the research of May and Lumsdaire (1958), who discovered that practising psychomotor skills, while viewing a film in which those abilities are being performed improves learning. Similar findings have been made for overt written or oral short reactions made while watching a movie. It has been discovered that even covert responses, such as silent repeating of important vocabulary and lesson points, are helpful. The usage of a group discussion following the viewing of a video cassette or film can also help to improve learning.

***(ix)* Promotes Participatory Learning:** Because teachers using television for instruction have discovered that televised instruction receives more attentiveness and has fewer diversions than classroom instruction, electronic media directed instruction boosts learners' concentration on a task. The objectives are clearly defined and the instructional environment is designed to fulfil them because media-based learning is structured.

***(x)* Accommodate Individual Needs:** Non-print media can adapt to different requirements and interests, particularly with the use of computers. The development of new technologies and the rising popularity of individualised training have mostly coincided. The flexibility and variety of new media gives me the chance to modify my media mix for use in individualised education. For example, the system of audio-tutorial instructions or programmed instructions are specifically made for individualised learning.

***(xi)* Help Learners Monitor the Information Input:** With certain technical tools, such as audio and video cassettes, students can decide how much material they want to be exposed to. Additionally, they provide people the flexibility to view or listen to a piece of information as many times as they wish. Additionally, these technologies provide them the freedom to select a convenient moment for them to get any given information.

***(xii)* Extend the Role of a Teacher:** With the use of non-print media, a teacher's responsibilities go beyond merely imparting knowledge. Utilizing media enables educators to take charge of the learning process in innovative ways. They will have more time to devote in identifying students' issues, holding private consultations and providing advice and direction.

Applications and Use of Media

Application and use of print and non-print media are given below:

Combined Use of Media: The non-print media, when used in conjunction with the print medium, can play an integrative function to make up for the lack of the typical teacher-learner relationship in distance education and meet the various demands of the students. The following are some examples of various media-mix applications or media-combination techniques:

(i) Integrated
(ii) Complementary
(iii) Supplementary
(iv) Independent.

Each of these approaches are discussed briefly.

***(i)* Integrated Media Use:** Non-print media are combined with the master medium, which is often print media, in an integrated strategy. The use of media integration should be such that students understand that non-print media also offer something unique to teach them and should be given serious consideration. Students are encouraged to watch television because it is an integral component of the instruction. These "non-print" media components are used in assignments and tests. The time allotted to the students for a course includes this media mix.

***(ii)* Complementary Media Use:** In the complementary strategy, the choice is made at the level of the syllabus's design. The separation between print and non-print media for the transmission of all information has been determined upon and is clearly defined. For instance, if 70% of the medium is print, 30% is non-print. Out of ten units/topics, two will be covered through given texts and two more, as is stated very clearly in the beginning. This method is especially appropriate for courses like science or engineering that combine theoretical and practical components.

***(iii)* Supplementary Media Use:** This method's main objective is to improve students' learning experiences. The entire material is contained in the "master-medium" (mainly print) and some portions of that information are also made available through non-print mediums. For instance, in a management course, a case study might be broadcast on TV to help students grasp a theoretical concept that was covered; in a rural development course, a sanitation or nutrition film might be played, following a discussion of the topic. For this kind of media-mix, there is no need for syllabus-level planning because non-print material can be created and distributed afterwards.

***(iv)* Independent Media Use:** The autonomous approach refers to a style of distant learning that largely avoids the use of print media. The primary sources of information in this case are non-print media (except few media notes). If the target audience is undereducated, hasn't mastered reading abilities, or the course is entirely practical, this strategy is particularly suited.

MEDIA FACILITATION

The practice of choosing the best set of media characteristics to promote the most effective learning in a certain context is known as "media facilitation". Two main questions are addressed in this process of "media facilitation":

(i) Which media qualities, *i.e.,* behavioural changes in learners are best suited to deliver and provide for specific learning activities and associated learning outcomes?

(ii) How can it be ensured that the chosen media are integrated with each other and the selected learning outcomes if more than one media is to be used?

Media Selection

The selection of media is mostly based on the characteristics of the medium. A medium's capacity to display qualities like pictorial representation, size (enhanced, reduced, or real), colour (black and white, limited colours, full colour), movement (still, semi-motion, full motion), language (print or oral sounds) and sound-picture relationship are referred to as its "media attributes" (silent or with sound). The selection of the course objectives is the first step in the course design process. The choice of the course material comes next. When learners are exposed to and respond to pertinent course material, course objectives should be achieved. As a result, the course material comprises of a variety of stimuli that students must take in and react to.

Learning activities consist of the process of receiving these stimuli and responding to them. These actions could be overtly utilitarian or internally motivated. If educational media are chosen carefully, students can receive stimuli and respond to them. As a result, an educational medium should only be chosen – *(i)* if it can enable the learner to engage in the planned learning activities and *(ii)* if it can deliver all the required information to the learners.

Establishing the course objectives should be the first step in the media selection process, which should ideally also take media editing into account. Phase I of media selection, however, solely involves matching media to learning objectives. Another name for it is "selection through rejection". It invariably yields a condensed list of carefully chosen educational media. Phase II of media selection is selecting the media based on additional criteria, mostly related to the budgetary outlay and practical limits of learners' preferences and talents and occasionally teachers' as well. The picture below depicts many elements of the second stage of media selection.

If the costing process is to be effective, the unit of costing must be agreed upon. Typically, the "unit of production" is used to calculate the costing unit. According to various perspectives on the unit of output, it can be related to *(a)* producing support material for an hour of student time, *(b)* producing one unit of support material, such as one A4 size sheet for a printed lesson or one 35 mm slide, etc., or *(c)* achieving a specific level of learning for a group of students, i.e. the amount of time required for acquiring a specified amount of knowledge. These three points of view on unit costing have to do with middle unit cost.

A medium's costs might be either "direct" or "indirect." Direct costs are associated with a particular service or good. On the other hand, indirect expenses are those that are incurred across the entire operation but cannot be directly linked to a particular service or product. Costs often refer to the outlays for labour, raw materials and overheads, also known as the cost of capital goods and equipment. Editing is necessary to increase the effectiveness of educational media. Three degrees of editing are possible with this–visual, narrative and engagement. No explanation is necessary for narrative or sound editing. The goal of involvement editing is to incorporate learner activities into a medium's message.

We must select the educational media that can deliver the essential elements of the knowledge to learners in the most effective way. Salomon uses an example to demonstrate the rule he suggests. Language would not be an appropriate medium to convey that sort of information if the simultaneous execution of values in an engine is deemed to be the important feature. Salomon nevertheless recommends including a rider. The code must be in some way isomorphic to the learner's symbolic method of thinking, the author warns, in order to have the appropriate cognitive effects from this fitting of the symbolic qualities of the medium to the essential features of content or message.

Schramm (1977) suggests that instead of asking broad and vague questions like; "Can media teach"? or "What is the best medium"? We would do well to ask smaller, sharper and more specific questions like "How can we best use a given medium for a given act of instruction? Or in a given situation which medium is more cost-effective than another? Or, how do the symbolic coding systems of a given media relate to what a student learns from it?' Answers to these questions can make the process of media selection appropriate as well as effective. Like formal face-to-face education, distance education too is based on educational objectives. These objectives may be from the cognitive domain, affective domain and psychomotor domain.

Cognitive Domain:

Print: Worksheets, textbooks, quick readings, handouts and copies of articles can all be printed.

Slide: For self-instruction, use a slide that is either live-narrated or integrated with audio.

Transparencies: These are used by teachers to encourage students to solve problems and explain complex concepts that call for non-verbal demonstrations.

Instruction tailored to each student, delivered by computer, workbook, audiotape, or film strip

Live instruction: Through contact programmes and counselling at a study centre, there is live training.

TV and CCTV are used to offer new information and to enhance lessons that are printed out.

Videotape: For selected viewing of pertinent information that students have requested or that the course author recommends (s).

Radio broadcast: An accessible yet academic presentation on the radio for further.

Affective Domain:

Live instruction: Because human connection is a potent tool for changing attitudes, live instruction is both effective and essential. A tutor can also help make group discussions organised and interactive for all participants.

TV/movies/Video tapes/Interactive Video: These are the most effective forms of media for presenting global events because they allow viewers to experience real emotions, while seeing staged events.

Radio/Audio tape: For information and empathic sensitivity training, radio and audio tapes give sound-based realism of human events.

Telephone Teaching: Provide assistance or direction over the phone for resolving personal or academic issues.

Print: Books, magazines and handouts with content designed to affect change in learners.

Psychomotor Domain

Audiotape: Provides detailed instructions on how to complete a task; students simply listen and follow along.

Film/TV/Videotape: Videotapes can be used to explain procedures that students can follow along with images in motion make actions that are being modelled or presented seem very natural and presentations in slow motion make accurate and in-depth study and scrutiny easier.

Live demonstration: It is used to analyse model performances and procedures in the actual world and to imitate them.

Language lab: For learning the target language's sound system, for improving auditory discrimination and for improving listening comprehension.

Audiotape: Used to demonstrate sample utterances and practice imitating them, practice stress placement and intonation patterns and record one's voice for later analysis.

Home experimentation kits: These are specifically designed to make it easier to conduct experiments at home as part of technical, vocational, or science courses, can be merged with course materials to increase their efficacy. The advantages and disadvantages of various instructional medium are shown in the table below:

Table 3: Factors affecting the process of media selection

Medium	Merits	Demerits
Print	*(i)* Cheap *(ii)* Easy to prepare *(iii)* Application in a variety of situations *(iv)* No hardware needed for use	*(i)* Study skills required (from the students) *(ii)* Time consuming
Television	*(i)* Quite easy access *(ii)* Mass coverage *(iii)* Combines sound & visual presentation *(iv)* Wide coverage of content and contexts e.g. lecture, narration, demonstration, etc. *(v)* Can shift its focus from extensive to intensive. *(vi)* High-tech appeal *(vii)* Change in image-size possible *(viii)* Information density is high	*(i)* Script-writing and costly production, as well as complex *(ii)* Needs costly hardware at user end as well as transmission end *(iii)* One-way flood of information *(iv)* Prior collaboration between concerned agencies essential *(v)* Fixed schedule *(vi)* Limited air-time
Video tape and Film	*(i)* Wide application range *(ii)* Can be stopped and replayed *(iii)* Allows focus shift-extensive to intensive *(iv)* High-tech appeal *(v)* Combines audio and visual presentation *(vi)* Re-usable *(vii)* Permanent record and storage possible *(viii)* Can be used whenever needed *(ix)* Can be used whenever needed *(x)* Can be used whenever needed *(xi)* Can be used whenever needed *(xii)* Lip sync in learning spoken language	*(i)* Require costly recording presentation equipment *(ii)* Technical and professional expertise is required for production *(iii)* Depends on power supply *(iv)* One-way flow of information

Medium	Merits	Demerits
Overhead Transparencies	*(i)* Helpful in systematic presentation of information; especially in developmental sequences *(ii)* Easy to use *(iii)* Presentation rate can be varied *(iv)* Easy to prepare *(v)* Quite cheap *(vi)* Useful for large groups	*(i)* Need OHP and electricity *(ii)* Need complex skills for advanced level preparation *(iii)* Not easily portable
Audiotape	*(i)* Easy to prepare *(ii)* Re-usable *(iii)* Applications in a variety of situations *(iv)* Equipment & tapes easily portable *(v)* Duplication is easy and cheap *(vi)* Especially suitable for language teaching	*(i)* Tends to be over-used *(ii)* Fidelity decreases with use *(iii)* Recording often faulty *(iv)* Fixed rate of presentation of information
Radio	*(i)* Easy access *(ii)* Portable hardware *(iii)* Relatively affordable because cheap *(iv)* Mass coverage *(v)* Can be edited for easy comprehension	*(i)* Fixed time schedule *(ii)* Depends on power-supply *(iii)* One-way flow of information *(iv)* Script-writing and production quite technical & need advanced skills *(v)* Costly capital hardware needed *(vi)* Involves prior agreement for education use between educational institution and radio agency.
Computer	*(i)* Present verbal, digital as well as graphic information *(ii)* Can interact with learners by asking or answering questions *(iii)* Maintains a record of answers *(iv)* Can control other media hardware as well *(v)* Individualises instruction in terms of learners need(s) and pace *(vi)* Can interface computer and video *(vii)* Can simulate experiences and situations	*(i)* Computer literacy including programming skills essential *(ii)* Requires more capital input *(iii)* Variety of software is essential *(iv)* Suitable only for individual learners or small-size groups *(v)* Use of hardware and software across various systems is often difficult

It is quite astonishing the diversity of media available for use in distance learning and face-to-face instruction. We have a really helpful example from the U.K. Open University experience. The Planning Committee for the Open University reached a temporary arrangement with the British Broadcasting Corporation to provide production and transmission facilities for television and radio, even before the institution was officially constituted. The BBC-2 and Radio-3 channels were made available to the open university, thanks to this deal. More than 4,000 programmes, each lasting 20 minutes, were produced during the first seven years of this relationship for radio and television. Currently, the Open University TV broadcast's total weekly programming time hovers around an astonishing 36 hours; for radio, the number is closer to 30 hours. According to studies, students at the Open University devote not more than 5% of their time to each broadcast medium. These students have easy access to both media on a regular basis and they typically watch two-thirds of TV broadcasts and about half of radio shows. Thus, DE students in the U.K. choose TV over radio as a medium. In the Open University system, utilisation of the broadcast medium, particularly TV, comes in second place to print. In terms of the range of applications, TV has an advantage over other forms of instructional media. The presenter or tele-teacher does not constantly occupy the little screen. In reality, once he appears, his voice accurately portrays him and the screen may be used for a multitude of purposes, while the voice-over offers priceless description, clarification, or focus. Occasionally, the video camera lens may take close pictures to help the students concentrate attention on minute details. It may offer a series of material aids or other visual aids in a planned sequence.

There are currently two issues with the Open University's usage of broadcast media. The first has to do with high production expenses and the second has to do with the availability of airtime being limited. The hunt for substitute delivery methods has resulted from this. The fourth decade of Doordarshan, India's version of the BBC, has passed. It now touts itself as one of the biggest networks in the planet. Information about entertainment is provided through hundreds of its production facilities and about 350 broadcasters. By the turn of the century, 80–90% of its population will be covered, thanks to additional manufacturing facilities and transmitters that are already being built up. The UGC programmes are the most recent addition to Indian educational TV. Additionally, IGNOU programmes are regularly carried on Doordarshan. Thus, the TV has already entered the field of distance education in India as a flexible distribution medium but there are still issues with production costs and the availability of airtime, particularly in terms of suitable time slots. The issues of accessibility and regularity with regard to educational television need to be addressed as a more flexible distribution option. The only practical alternative is to keep a sufficient quantity of diverse video-taped programmes, a video player and a TV monitor in study centres because it is impractical to provide video cassettes and a TV receiver to individual students. Distance learners could make use of this delivery medium to suit their time and needs but questions of easy and regular access shall continue to engage our attention for some years.

Bates, criteria for decision-making

According to Bates, any institution should base its decisions on the responses to questions about actions:

Accessibility: How usable is a given piece of technology for students? How adaptable is it for a certain target audience?

Cost: What is the breakdown of each technology's costs? How much does each learner cost each unit?

Teaching and learning: What types of learning are required in teaching and learning? Which teaching strategies will best satisfy these needs? What technology supports this teaching and learning the most effectively?

Interactivity and user-friendliness: What form of engagement is made possible by this technology? How user-friendly is it?

Organizational issues: What organisational hurdles must be overcome before this technology may be successfully used? What organisational changes are necessary?

Novelty: How recent is this technology?

Speed: How fast can courses be implemented using this technology? How soon can materials be modified?

Access: A distance student may study at home, in their place of employment, or at a nearby centre. Depending on where a student is seated during study time will determine how much technology is available to them. In many nations, open access, home-based learning will be constrained to a small number of technologies. For example, the poorest countries may be in a position to use only print and radio, while slightly wealthier countries may use print, radio, audio cassettes and possibly television.

Cost: A number of general points can be made about the balance of costs for different technologies.

When an organisation has several study centres, for instance, the cost of installing equipment into local centres can greatly outweigh capital expenditures. In general, the recurrent costs of producing high-quality technology-based materials have a tendency to be underestimated. The main cost of using technologies for teaching is in production rather than capital and as a result, it is recurring. For example, the annual recurrent cost frequently exceeds the total start-capital cost.

The fixed and variable costs of various technologies vary significantly:

- Radio and audio cassettes have minimal fixed and variable costs.
- Telecourses with tutor mediation, computer-mediated communication and in-person instruction have low fixed costs but high variable costs.

If workstations are to be used, pre-programmed computer-based learning (CBL) and video discs have both high fixed and high variable expenses.

Teaching Functions: Each medium has a wide range of applications. As a result, differences within a medium (such as those between a documentary and a broadcast lecture) may be bigger than those between media (for example, a face-to-face lecture and a lecture on a radio programme). The ability to acquire abilities and the presentational aspects of the chosen media are key considerations. In connection to the course objectives and the types of learning (comprehension analysis, application, problem-solving, interpersonal, mechanical skills, attitude modification, etc.) that are necessary, the course designer can take advantage of the presentational properties of each medium.

Interactivity and user-friendliness: It is crucial to consider how much a given medium fosters interaction and active learning, as well as how user-friendly it is. While some technologies only offer asynchronous interaction, others offer "real-time interactivity". Some interactive media are one-way, while others are two-way.

Organisational Issues: How to fully utilise the potential of each medium is one of the organisational difficulties. The organisation needs to be prepared to adapt to change and/or accept new technology that will improve how it operates. The organisation wants to successfully use both labour and technology to embrace changes because technologies incur additional costs.

Novelty: According to Bates, originality should be the criterion with the least weight. However, the novelty of the medium occasionally draws financing from other organisations. But before you become intrigued by a medium's novelty, you must be certain of its pedagogical value. Additionally, the institution will ultimately bear the cost of the media if it is not economical.

Speed: It has to do with how rapidly an institution can switch to a new medium, thanks to the medium. Some technologies require longer development times. Multimedia learning programmes, for instance, need more time. It takes a long time to create an audiotape for a videotape. You must also take into account how quickly the materials may be updated and amended.

Media Integration

The use of many media is implemented for efficient learning. Since different media must be combined, one of the media must serve as the "master medium", and other media must be employed as and when necessary to ensure that the presentation quality is as effective as possible. At the curriculum design stage, decisions are made regarding the integration of media. Later, when the courses are designed, different media are assigned their own roles. Decisions on the integration of media are valid for both the content and delivery of the course. Within the overall weight allotted for the non-print category, different non-print medium are allocated different weights. The decision to employ a different form of media than the master medium is made in light of the learning experiences and activities that will be offered to students.

Table 4: Strengths and Weaknesses of Various Technologies

Media	Access	Costs / Students Nos.		Teaching		Interactivity		Organ-isation	Speed
		Large	Small	Presen-tation	Skills	Learning Material	Social		
One-way Media									
Print	Good	Good	Average	Average	Average	Average	Poor	Poor	Poor
Radio	Good	Good	Poor	Poor	Poor	Poor	Poor	Average	Good
Audio Cassette	Good	Good	Average	Average	Good	Good	Poor	Good	Average
Educational Broadcast TV	Average	Poor	Poor	Good	Average	Poor	Poor	Poor	Poor
Pre-recorded TV	Poor	Good	Poor	Average	Average	Average	Average	Average	Poor
Video cassettes	Good	Average	Poor	Good	Good	Good	Poor	Average	Poor
Computer-based learning	Average	Poor	Poor	Average	Average	Good	Poor	Poor	Poor
Multimedia	Poor	Poor	Poor	Good	Good	Good	Poor	Poor	Poor
Two-way Media									
Audio Confer-encing	Good	Poor	Good	Poor	Average	Poor	Good	Good	Good
Live Interac-tive TV	Poor	Poor	Poor	Poor	Poor	Poor	Average	Average	Good
Video Confer-encing	Poor	Poor	Average	Poor	Average	Average	Average	Average	Good
CMC	Average	Average	Good	Poor	Good	Average	Good	Good	Good

Integrated media use – Example 1

Study of the assembly of various components of an oscillator circuit. Watch the technique being demonstrated by starting Section D of Videotape 2.

When the learner plays Section D of Videotape 2, the voice is heard saying:

2nd videotape: You will now see as an oscillator circuit is put together.

Division D: The frequency for which the oscillator will be constructed must be determined initially. Assume the oscillator has a 450 kilo hertz frequency. The importance of circuit components at this frequency is something you already know. Please see page 56 of your manual for information on circuit design 3. Now follow my example. Open your home kit 3, please.

Take out the soldering iron and switch it on .... (The learner does as advise*(d)* .... check that your kit contains the following components. (Each component is first shown and named and the learner checks that he has these in his kit........ this goes on step-by-step and the learner carries out each step as shown).

Your oscillator circuit is now complete. However, its operation has to be examined. The main socket to the supply plug. (The student does this.) Activates the main supply. The red pilot light ought to be on. The student turns on the supply end and examines the red pilot lamp, etc.

Following the presentation and actual experiments: 'Now you have learnt how to construct an oscillator circuit of frequency 450 kilo hertz and how to check its functioning. Please turn to page 58 of Circuit Designs 3 for review exercise on oscillator circuits.

(Student turn to page 58)

Text: "You have now completed the practical activity No. 8 of preparing a 450 kilo hertz oscillator. Write answers to the following review questions on your Review Exercise Sheet No. 8 .... etc.."

This was an illustration of media integration using print, videotape and a hands-on exercise with a house kit. The non-print media were included into the print-based master medium. Another instance of media integration involving print, TV broadcast, radio and practical action is provided by Hawkridge (1978):

Integrated media use - Example 2

The television camera in a geology class closes in on the samples and is later mounted to a petrological microscope. The students can inspect their own specimens and slides following the procedures shown on television because to the McArthur microscope they have in their home experiment kit that was specifically created for the Open University. Students are instructed to examine 19 rocks from the home experiment kit and try to categorise them as belonging to one of the three basic groups of rocks—igneous, sedimentary, or metamorphic—for the comparison radio show. They are encouraged to decide how large the grains are and of what shape and so on".

Another component of media integration is taking into account how and when learners will use different media during instruction. This part of media integration focuses on "Involvement Editing". To *(a)* elicit questions, comments, etc. from the students; *(b)* look for different applications of the material being taught; *(c)* get them to respond to different crucial questions; *(d)* practice different skills and *(e)* provide time cues to signal stopping points so that students can switch to another medium, use it as intended and then return to the original or primary medium.

MULTIMEDIA APPROACH IN DISTANCE EDUCATION

In order to ensure student learning under the (distance education) is equivalent to that under the formal system, it is necessary to find ways and means to ensure that the objectives of formal education and DE are nearly identical for a given level of education. The DE organisations haven't been able to provide DE students with a variety of inputs like live lectures from teachers, frequent and intense teacher-pupil interaction, explanations and clarifications made available by teachers upon request from the learners, live demonstrations of various techniques and procedures, model performances by expert teachers, guided peer-discussions, guided reading assignments, individualised and personalised instruction, field trips and laboratory work.

The requirement for obtaining extra information and classification must be reduced, if not fully eliminated, when writing lessons. Education objectives in terms of the learner's behaviour changes must be developed after the course objectives have been finalised. The primary medium is typically print. This could be explained by two factors: (1) the suitability of print media for various learning objectives and (2) the constraints of time, resources and expertise available.

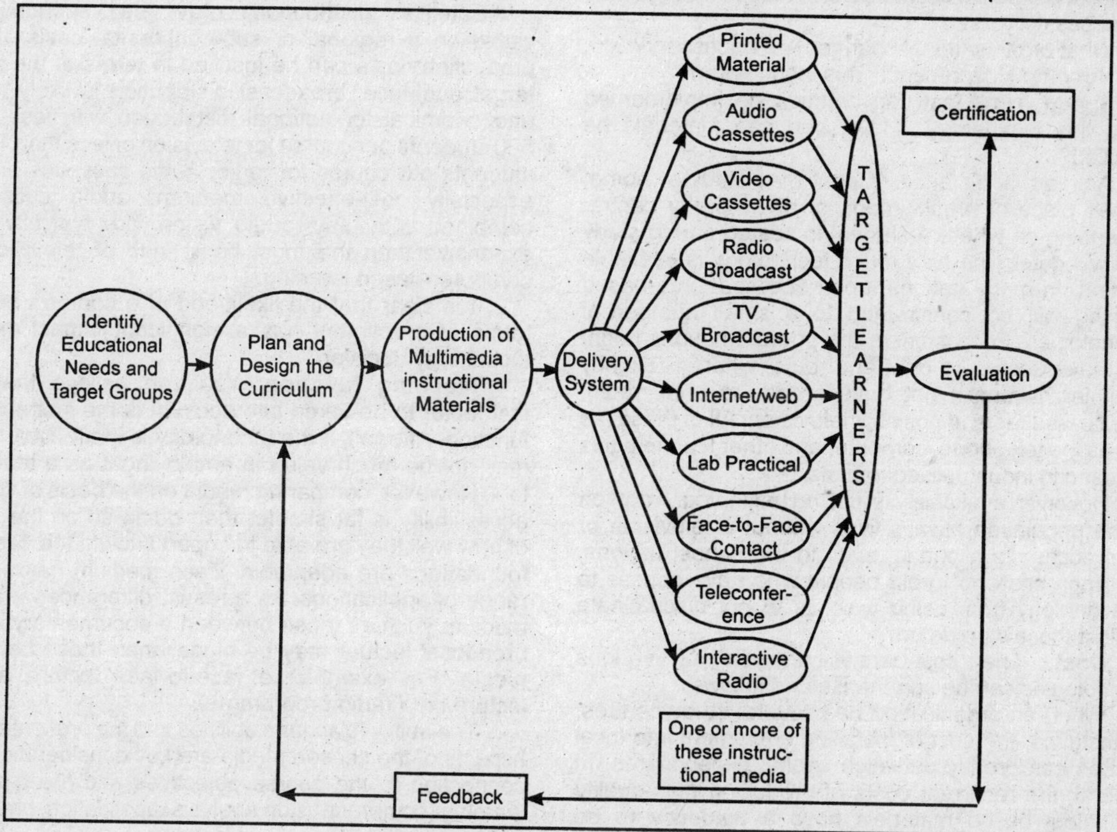

Multimedia Approach of IGNOU

ACTIVITIES

Q. 1. Based on the criteria of Bates, decide on a 'media-mix' for your institution. Provide reasons for each of your decision.

Ans. According to A.W. Bates' "ACTIONS" paradigm, each institution should base its decisions regarding the use of technology in open learning on the responses to the following questions:

Access: How user-friendly is a certain piece of technology for students? How adaptable is it for a certain target audience?

Cost: What is the breakdown of each technology's costs? How much does each learner cost each unit?

Teaching and learning: What types of learning are required in teaching and learning? Which teaching strategies will best satisfy these needs? What technology supports this teaching and learning the most effectively?

Interactivity and user-friendliness: What kind of interaction is made possible by this technology in terms of interactivity and user-friendliness? How user-friendly is it?

Organizational issues: What organisational hurdles must be overcome before this technology may be successfully used?

What organisational changes are necessary?

Novelty: How recent is this technology?

Speed: How fast can courses be implemented using this technology? How soon can materials be modified?

Access: A distance student may study at home, in their place of employment, or at a nearby centre. Depending on where a student is seated during study time will determine how much technology is available to them. In many nations, open access, home-based learning will be constrained to a small number of technologies. For instance, the poorest nations might only have access to print and radio, whereas slightly wealthier nations might have access to print, radio, audio cassettes and possibly television. All of these, as well as the telephone, computer and other technologies are used in industrialised nations.

However, availability is just the beginning. A portion of the population always lives without a television or even access to a phone, even in the richest nations. Is it appropriate to forbid people who have access to a technology from using it so as to not discriminate against those who do not?

Cost: The cost-benefit analysis of various technologies can be summarised as follows:

When an organisation has several study centres, for instance, the cost of installing equipment into local centres can greatly outweigh capital expenditures. In general, the recurrent costs of producing high-quality technology-based materials have a tendency to be underestimated. The main cost of using technologies for teaching is in production rather than capital and as a result, it is recurring. For example, the annual recurrent cost, frequently exceeds the total start-capital cost.

The fixed and variable costs of various technologies vary significantly:

- Radio and audio cassettes have minimal fixed and variable costs.
- Telecourses with tutor mediation, computer-mediated communication and in-person instruction have low fixed costs but high variable costs.

If workstations are provided, pre-programmed computer-based learning (CBL) and video discs have high fixed and high-variable expenses.

The majority of technologies currently used in national distance teaching and open learning institutions have fixed costs that typically far outweigh variable costs because production is the primary cost, which is fixed for any course, this means that economies of scale apply to "traditional" distance education courses: the more students, the more cost-effective technologies become.

While suitable for sources with relatively modest student numbers, some of the more recent interactive technologies, such as computer conferencing and audio-graphics, have substantial variable costs, making them exceedingly expensive for courses with huge student populations.

Satellite distribution may be economically viable on a regional or sub-continental basis, if the production costs can be justified in terms of the likely target audience; broadcast distribution is likely to be uneconomical for national distribution with less than 500 students per course for television or less than 1,000 students per course for radio. Audio cassettes are an especially cost-effective medium; audio cassettes combined with, say, audio vision, are typically less expensive than the most basic kind of television or computer-based learning.

It is clear that the likelihood of a course's size in terms of enrollment has a significant impact on the technology decision.

Teaching function: You can believe that the first factor to be taken into account is the instructional function. After all, if the technology is ineffective, there may not be much value in employing it as a teaching tool. However, comparing media on the basis of cost or accessibility is far simpler than doing so on the basis of how well they are able to impart knowledge. Media's foundations are adaptable. Each medium has a wide range of applications. As a result, differences within a medium such as those between a documentary and a broadcast lecture may be bigger than those between media. For example, a face-to-face lecture and a lecture on a radio programme).

The ability to acquire abilities and the presentational aspects of the chosen media are key considerations. In connection to the course objectives and the types of learning (comprehension analysis, application, problem-solving, interpersonal, mechanical skills, attitude modification, etc.) that are necessary, the course designer can take advantage of the presentational properties of each medium.

Interactivity and user-friendliness: The degree to which a specific medium promotes interaction and active learning, as well as its user-friendliness, are of utmost importance. While some technologies only offer asynchronous interaction, others offer "real-time interactivity." Some interactive media are one-way, while others are two-way. Since the learner in distant education is separated from the teacher, the medium's interactivity is crucial. In terms of user-friendliness, the capability of the medium to give the learner control is important. For instance, you can't go back to a single frame in a TV broadcast since the message simply fades away. On a video clip, however, you can simply fast-forward and rewind to repeat viewings until you fully grasp a topic.

Organisational Issues

Organizational difficulties: How to fully utilise the potential of each medium is one of the organisational difficulties. The organisation needs to be prepared to adapt to change and/or accept new technology that will improve how it operates. The organisation wants to successfully use both labour and technology to embrace changes because technologies incur additional costs. The amount of training the employees would need to use the technology should be considere l, while making a choice about it. Job responsibilities may need to be re-engineered, depending on the necessity and the broader organisational structure.

Novelty: According to Bates, novelty should rank last on the list of considerations. However, the novelty of the medium, occasionally draws financing from other organisations. But before you become intrigued by a medium's novelty, you must be certain of its pedagogical value. Additionally, the institution will ultimately bear the cost of the media if it is not economical.

Speed: This has to do with how rapidly the institution can switch to the new medium, thanks to the medium. Some technologies require longer development times. Multimedia learning programmes, for instance, need more time. It takes a long time to create an audiotape for a videotape. You must also take into account how quickly the materials may be updated and amended.

CHECK YOUR PROGRESS

Q. 1. Define 'educational media' in general and in the context of distance education.

Ans. The term "educational media" describes forms of media that disseminate information for educational purposes. They are typically used only for teaching and learning.

Educational media supports the teaching and learning process from the lesson's inception through its conclusion, or from beginning to end. It offers tangible experiences that act as a foundation for thinking, arguing and problem-solving. It improves both initial learning and learning retention. Print, non-print, electronic, audio, visual, audio-visual and projected media, all fall under the category of education media. Workbooks, instruction books, magazines, journals and newspapers are examples of print media. These are affordable, portable and simple to operate. Projected and non-projected media are non-print media. Audio, visual and audio-visual media, as well as projected and non-projected media, are all examples of electronic media. The teaching-learning tools that appeal to the auditory sense are audio media. These media also carry sounds that can be heard on their own, such as audio tapes, record players and radio. Media that appeals to the sense of seeing (eyes) or that can be seen, such as television, computers and whiteboards, are considered visual media. The term "audio-visual" refers to educational resources that engage students' hearing and seeing senses simultaneously to offer them auditory and visual experiences. Examples include television, videotapes and closed-circuit television (CCTV). Projected media are a kind of educational resources that can only be accessed by projecting their information on a wall or screen using a projector machine made specifically for that purpose, according to Gwarinda. Media that is projected typically combines hardware and software. For projection, these need a light source, such slides from a movie projector, etc. No screen projection is necessary for non-projected media. These don't need a source of light. They consist of two- and three-dimensional items, prints, maps, models and so forth.

Q. 2. Briefly describe Romiszowski's scheme of media classification. Give two examples for each class.

Ans. Rorniszowski's scheme of media classification is a framework that categorizes media based on the degree of interactivity and synchronicity between the sender and the receiver of a message. The scheme includes four classes of media, which are as follows:

***(a)* Linear-Non-Interactive Media:** In this class, the message is transmitted in a linear sequence from the sender to the receiver without any feedback or interaction. Examples of this class include movies, television shows, and books.

Examples:

Movie: The Godfather

Book: 1984 by George Orwell

***(b)* Linear-Interactive Media:** In this class, the message is transmitted in a linear sequence, but the receiver has some control over the pace or order of the information presented. Examples of this class include multimedia presentations and educational videos.

Examples:

Multimedia Presentation: A TED Talk.

Educational Video: Khan Academy's Introduction to Biology.

***(c)* Nonlinear-Interactive Media:** In this class, the receiver can interact with the message, but the sender has no control over the pace or order of the information presented. Examples of this class include video games and hypertext documents.

Examples:

Video Game: The Legend of Zelda: Breath of the Wild.

Hypertext Document: Wikipedia.

***(d)* Nonlinear-Synchronous Interactive Media:** In this class, the message is transmitted in a nonlinear sequence, and the sender and receiver can interact with each other in real-time. Examples of this class include video conferencing and online gaming.

Examples:

Video Conferencing: Zoom.

Online Gaming: Fortnite.

Q. 3. Describe the major shortcomings of "print medium".

Ans. Print is commonly described as "frozen language," which connotes that it is entirely irrelevant, lifeless, and cut off from experience. It is believed that since print refers to "printed languages" and all of language's problems are likewise assigned to print, no sensible and passionate educator would choose print as their first option. They are mostly comprised of:

(i) Direct experience fails to adequately replace language.

(ii) Language should not be trusted since it may be deceitful.

(iii) Print education is neither essential or desirable for us since we belong to and are a part of an oral culture.

(iv) As solving problems calls for quick action, printing cannot substitute for quick action.

There are obviously practical limitations in addition to these ideological criticisms.

(i) Print is a difficult educational medium since its usage requires that students have a sufficient level of literacy.

(ii) When the reader possesses the cognitive skills required to comprehend the text and evaluate its thought-content, print works best.

(iii) Reading requires that words and lines be processed in a specific order, such as top-to-bottom, left-to-right, or both.

On the other hand, a visual picture may be grasped very instantaneously and can be taken in whole. Depending on the person's ability for observation, all one needs to do is stare at it to understand what it means.

(iv) Compared to accessing the same information visually, such as on television, reading printed material takes far longer.

(v) Developing managerial, psychomotor, or interaction abilities by reading is unsuitable. Although reading a written lesson can provide someone with some theoretical information about driving, it cannot provide them the skills required to drive.

(vi) The phrasing used in the printed lesson was selected based on the author's assumptions about typical readers.

After a lesson has been developed, its language cannot be changed to accommodate learners who are poor or performing below averagely. As a result, it is said that print is a poor pedagogical medium for teaching students of different academic levels; weak pupils and students who have reading difficulties often suffer the most.

Q. 4. List any four features of the print medium that account for its wide-spread use in education.

Ans. A few features of print, notably the remote learning mode, contribute to its widespread and all-encompassing use in education.

(i) Print delivers instructional information that is comparatively permanent, available whenever wanted, and free from the strict temporal restrictions imposed by television and radio. Maybe even more significantly, printed content can be processed everywhere, whether a person is travelling by air or by land, at night or in the morning. The least limiting medium is print; other mediums severely impede learning.

(ii) While it is true that television pictures may be absorbed very instantaneously, learning from watching television does not often take place in a similarly rapid fashion. Indeed, the most important aspect of any learning is time. The approach is hit-or-miss since the learner is physically bombarded with the rapidly shifting visual representations. Reading written content requires more time, and studies show that learning increases when time is spent on a job.

(iii) Print helps students to study at their own pace and in the method that is most comfortable for them since it provides more options for selecting a better learning strategy or even initially experimenting with various techniques and choosing the most effective one.

(iv) Our highly developed cultural milieu is entirely congruent with the use of print as a teaching instrument. Print actually plays a significant role in every advanced civilization. A primitive civilization instructs by imitation, presentation, and spoken word rather than a mature society.

(v) Certain educationally related methods of thinking practically mandate the use of print media. For creating, defining logical constraints, developing, or sequencing complex reasoning, print is necessary. It

is unfathomable how literary forms like the novel essay and belles-lettres would develop outside of the print medium.

(vi) Readers like to learn through print media. It is a well-known fact that students who find their professors' lectures boring think that reading assignments make it easier for them to learn.

(vii) Print is especially well suited to this kind of thinking since symbol systems are utilised in abstract cognition. When we move away from genuine learning references, language usage becomes crucial, and print becomes especially important.

(viii) Print remains the most cost-effective instructional resource on the market.

Regarding affordability, portability, and the unique independence from hardware reliance for its consumers, it performs better than almost all other types of media. Print has advantages and weaknesses, just like any other type of instructional media, thus we may conclude that.

Print is incredibly helpful for assisting students in developing understanding of complex concepts and processes, developing fundamental learning skills of reading and writing that help a learner become more and more independent, and assisting students in taking stock of their learning through interpolated questions. In actuality, it would be prudent for us to remember that major media like computer and television technologies still utilise print, albeit rarely.

Q. 5. Briefly describe how non-print media can supplement the print-medium.

Ans. Print is the primary or master media used by institutions offering distance education. Because of their versatility, non-print media offer good support to print media. Certain characteristics make educational media work well as a supplement. A case in point is the capacity to use it by an individual in opposition to the group, complete control over when to use it and how it works and portability. Criteria like portability, control over functions, control over use and individualised use are applicable to media like film, photos, slides, audio tape, video tape, computers and video disc.

Non-print Media as a Supplement: Criteria-based Analysis

MEDIA	CRITERIA			
	Portability	**Individualized use**	**Control-over use**	**Control-over functions**
Television	Yes (portable models only)	Yes	No. TV Schedule pro-determined	No
Radio	Yes	Yes	No	No
Film	Yes (for portable models only)	Yes (though costly)	Yes	Yes
Photographs	Yes	Yes	Yes	Yes
Slides	Yes	Yes	Yes	Yes
Audio Tape	Yes	Yes	Yes	Yes
Video Tape	Yes	Yes	Yes	Yes
Computer	Yes (only for Notebooks)	Yes	Yes	Yes
Videodisc	Yes	Yes	Yes	Yes

Q. 6. Describe three pedagogic uses of non-print media, which are unique to them.

Ans. Non-print media, especially those in the electronic category, can simultaneously reach students in different locations and give them a sense of belonging, of being a part of a large organisation, alleviating their feelings of loneliness and the idea that they are unimportant to the system simply because teachers do not instruct them face-to-face. Some examples of non-print media's pedagogical uses include:

(i) Greater delivery capabilities.

(ii) We are aware that the majority of DE institutions use print as their primary or master medium. The non-print media may assist the print media extremely effectively due to their variety. Media for education that meets certain criteria functions well as a supplement. A few examples are its mobility, total control over when to utilise it, and potential to be used by an individual in opposition to the collective.

(iii) Iconic and active types of experience are better suited. Bruner proposed three forms of experience: enactive (using action), iconic (using visuals, graphics, or three-dimensional representations), and symbolic (based on the use of symbols). It is possible to express symbolic feelings through print.

(iv) Non-print media usage can improve educational chances.

For instance, rather of only verbal instruction in text, slides, silent or sound videos, or recordings can most effectively teach someone how to tie even a simple knot. A student can become adept in applying a variety of strategies in an active mode similarly to how work on home experiment kits can. For providing these sorts of educational possibilities, print is a terrible medium.

(v) A non-print recording media may be employed to capture the learner's performance, which can subsequently be used to provide highly useful feedback. Video tapes, on the other hand, provide crucial corrective feedback for various types of performance while audio cassettes are useful for providing feedback on one's mastery of a language's sound system. In this aspect, print media isn't particularly helpful.

(vi) Distance learning differs from typical face-to-face training in that it relies more heavily than usual on other media to accomplish numerous learning goals. All learning objectives cannot be very successfully met by printed information. This claim is reinforced by a chart created by William H. Allen in 1967 that shows the purported effectiveness of different teaching modes for specific learning goals.

(vii) Take part in certain instructional activities Certain non-print media kinds and distribution techniques are especially effective at supporting the learning activities of distant learners. For instance, utilising computers or audiotapes, it is feasible to properly drill and provide practise to language and maths learners. The use of electronic media can support inquiry-based learning. For instance, a movie might be used to explore physical scientific concepts with students. They continue to view the different parts of the movie after they have an understanding of how the photos relate to one another. They are then interested in the theories that support such links. Similar to this, social science teaching may make use of a number of media to give students visual and aural experiences that convey important information and questions. Movies and simulations frequently depict "real-life" or "laboratory learning" situations that call for problem-solving and situational awareness.

(viii) Students have found that engaging in electronic media is psychologically stimulating, both before and during involvement, which promotes learning. Some of the opening tasks, such as arousing the reader's interest, motivating them, offering a defence, etc., might be accomplished more effectively by nonprint mediums than by printed texts. The diversity and novelty of various mediums grab students' interest and encourage learning. Although these pupils find print information difficult, these media might grab their attention and appeal to the neo-literate.

As an illustration, Korea's experience utilising television to offer non-formal education shows that "participants in a project occasionally execute things they may be hesitate to attempt" due to the excitement of the medium.

(ix) **Promote student involvement:** Many studies have emphasised how non-print media promote student involvement and participation, which in turn aids in the facilitation of learning. Since students' answers to the instructional stimuli and the reward of right replies are delayed, learning at a distance through standard texts lacks continuous active engagement. More than print information, certain digital media promote student involvement.

Heinich et al. (1982–1983) reference May and Lumsdaire's research from 1958, which showed that learning is enhanced by practising psychomotor skills while seeing a video that features those skills being used. Similar conclusions have been reached for overt, brief responses expressed in writing or verbally while watching a film. Even covert reactions, such silently repeating key vocabulary words and instructional points, have been found to be beneficial. Following the watching of a videotape or movie, a group conversation can further enhance learning.

(x) **Encourage active learning:** Teachers that utilise television in the classroom have also found that students pay more attention to it and have less distractions than they do in a classroom, which helps them focus better.

Because media-based learning is organised, the objectives are clearly stated and the instructional environment is created to meet them. The necessary atmosphere is not generated, even though print material is organised and has objectives that are well stated. Non-print media help to create an environment in the classroom where students actively participate in the learning process.

(xi) Non-print media may be tailored to suit various needs and interests, especially when using computers. New technological advancements and the rise in popularity of individualised training have mostly occurred at the same time. New media's adaptability and diversity allow me to change my media mix for use in individualised instruction.

For instance, a system of audio instructional instructions or pre-recorded instructions is especially designed for personalised learning. Audio tutorials use audio recordings to personally guide each student's learning tasks. Individualized training allows groups of students to be taught in accordance with the characteristics they have in common. For instance, customised instruction is provided for disabled pupils who have particular requirements. This is the greatest way to tailor lessons to the requirements of a specific group of pupils. For tailoring training for these various groups, a heavy reliance on technologically advanced media and resources is necessary, along with the right selection of such materials to satisfy the specific expectations.

(xii) With certain technical tools, such as audio and video cassettes, students can decide how much material they want to be exposed to. Additionally, they provide people the flexibility to view or listen to a piece of information as many times as they wish. Additionally, these technologies provide them the freedom to select a convenient moment for them to get any given information.

(xiii) The function of a teacher can now be expanded to include more than just dispensing information with the help of non-print media. Utilizing media enables educators to take charge of the learning process in innovative ways. They will have more time to devote to identifying students' issues, holding private consultations, and providing advice and direction.

Q. 7. Briefly describe complementary and supplementary patterns or media mix.

Ans. In the complementary strategy, the choice is made at the level of the syllabus's design. The separation between print and non-print media for the transmission of all information has been determined upon and is clearly defined. For instance, if 70% of the medium is print, 30% is non-print. Out of ten units/topics, two will be covered through given texts and two more, as is stated very clearly in the beginning. This method is especially appropriate for courses like science or engineering that combine theoretical and practical components.

The main goal of using supplemental media is to improve students' learning experiences. The entire material is contained in the "master-medium" (mainly print) and some portions of that information are also made available through non-print mediums. For instance, in a management course, a case study might be broadcast on TV to help students grasp a theoretical concept that was covered; in a rural development course, a sanitation or nutrition film might be played following a discussion of the topic. For this kind of media-mix, there is no need for syllabus-level planning because non-print material can be created and distributed afterwards.

Q. 8. List any four educational media that can be used for realizing cognitive domain objectives. Briefly describe how each of these can be put to use.

Ans. The following educational media can be applied to achieving cognitive domain objectives:

1. Print: This includes handouts, textbooks, quick reads, worksheets and copies of articles. These may be utilised by the students during or following a lesson, lecture, or teaching session.

2. Slide: Slides can be used for self-instruction along with audio cassette. Slides aid in learning for students.

3. Transparencies: These are tools that teachers employ to help students solve problems and explain complex concepts that call for non-verbal examples.

Individualized training can take place online, in a workbook, on an audiotape, or on a video strip.

4. Live instruction: Live education is provided at study centres through contact programmes and counselling.

5. TV and CCTV: In addition to the material offered in printed lessons, additional information is presented on TV and CCTV.

6. Videotape: This is utilised for the selective viewing of pertinent content that students have requested or that the course author has recommended(s).

7. Radio broadcast: This is used to deliver scholarly material in an accessible manner with additional information.

Q. 9. List any four educational media for developing the psychomotor skills of DE students. Briefly describe how any two of these can be effectively used.

Ans. These instructional tools are used to help DE students strengthen their psychomotor abilities:

1. Audiotape: You can use this to get step-by-step directions on how to do anything. Students only need to listen and act appropriately.

2. Film/TV: Videotapes can be used to demonstrate procedures that students can watch and replicate. Model or demonstration activities look quite genuine when they are captured in motion. Analysis and examination are made easier with the help of slow motion presentations.

3. Live demonstrations: These are used to analyse model performances and procedures in the actual world and to imitate them. Following a live demonstration, students can learn more effectively and perform better.

4. Language lab: Use this to learn the target language's sound system and to improve your auditory discrimination and listening skills.

5. Audiotape: Students can utilise audiotapes to demonstrate example utterances and have them imitated, to practice stress placement and intonation patterns and to record their own speech performances for later analysis.

6. Home experimental kits: These are specifically designed to make it easier for students to conduct experiments at home as part of technical, science, or vocational courses. They can be combined with the course materials to increase their effectiveness.

Q. 10. Why is 'media integration' desirable in DE?

Ans. A multimedia approach is followed for effective learning. Since various media have to be used in combination, it is necessary that one of the media should be the "master medium" as and when needed, other media should be used so that the quality of presentation becomes maximally effective. Decisions regarding media integration are taken at the stage of curriculum design. Later on, when the courses are developed, various media are given their allotted role to play. Decisions about media integration hold good for course material, as well as its delivery. Separate weight is given to various non-print media within the total weight earmarked for the non-print category. Suppose it is decided that 70% information will be presented to learners through 'print' medium and 30% through 'non-print' medium, then 'print' has the status of the master medium and the non-print media are to be integrated with it. The division of information to be carried through various non-print media has to be within the ceiling of 30% already allotted to the "non-print" category. The instructional material in the master medium provides instructions to learners when and how to use other media. Switch-over across media is thus well-integrated. The use of media other than the master-medium is decided according to the learning experiences and activities that are to be provided to learners. If learners are to carry out certain activities by themselves, then home-experiment kits may be used. The written text on a course on "Electronics" provides detailed description of the theory of oscillators in radio circuits and the function of each component. This is to be followed by practical sessions.

This was an example of media integration involving the use of print and videotape and practical activity using a house kit. The non-print media were integrated with the master medium *i.e.,* print. Hawkridge (1978) describes another example of media integration using print, TV broadcast, radio and practical activity:

Q. 11. Briefly describe multi-media approach in distance education.

Ans. The conditions of teaching-learning process in the distance education mode are different from those of the formal campus-based system. In DE, the learners and the teachers are not face-to-face except during the brief period of contact programmes. They are situated at a distance from one another. The organisation of DE does not provide for daily or often not even for weekly meetings between the teachers and the learners even when they reside in the same locality or city. Since the objectives of DE and formal education are more or less identical for a particular level of education, ways and means have to be found to ensure that student learning under the DE is comparable to that under the formal system. Various inputs like live lectures by teachers, regular and intense teacher-pupil interaction, explanations and clarifications made available by teachers on request from the learners, live demonstration of various techniques and procedures, model performance by expert teachers, guided peer-discussions, guided reading-assignments, individualised and personalised instruction, field trips and laboratory work are just not available to DE students, the DE organisations have, therefore, to be a lot more concerned about course planning and the development of instructional material. Lessons have to be written in such a manner that the need for seeking additional information and classification is minimized, if not entirely eliminated. Once the course objectives have been finalised, educational objectives in terms of the learner's behavioural changes have to be worked out. The process of course development and media selection is suggested in earlier.

In most cases, the principal medium is print. This could be attributed to two reasons:

(a) The suitability of the print medium for a variety of learning purpose.

(b) The exigencies of time-cost, resources and expertise available.

In almost all the developing countries, distance education systems operate through print. However, there are institutions in the world, where there is a systematic media mix. The UKOU provides a classic example for the integrated use of various media such as print, broadcast, face-to-face tutorials and practical. The University of Air, Japan and Central Radio and Television University of China use the broadcast mode as the primary medium with print as the supplement.

The approach is supplementary in nature, except for few courses that are offered in single medium through an independent approach. On an average for an eight credit course (one credit is equivalent to 30 hours of study time). Apart from printed text, 4 audio and 2 video programmes are produced to supplement text. Also 20 hours of face-to-face contact at study centre is provided to learners. However, it is optional. Apart from these broadcast radio, TV, interactive radio and teleconference too are provided at regular intervals. Normally, the course development process goes through stages.

MULTIPLE CHOICE QUESTIONS

Q. 1. According to Schrammn (1977), educational media can be categorised as:

(a) Big media and small media
(b) Print media and electronic media
(c) Indoor media and outdoor media
(d) None of these

Ans. *(a)* Big media and small media.

Q. 2. According to Schramn (1977), which media are more expensive?

(*a*) Big media (*b*) Small media
(*c*) Outdoor media (*d*) Indoor media

Ans. (*a*) Big media.

Q. 3. Which of the following is a big media?

(*a*) Transparencies (*b*) Slides
(*c*) Computers (*d*) None of these

Ans. (*c*) Computers.

Q. 4. Which of the following is a small media?

(*a*) Sound films
(*b*) Interactive video
(*c*) Interactive television
(*d*) Transparencies

Ans. (*d*) Transparencies.

Q. 5. Bretz divided educational media into ___________ classes.

(*a*) Five (*b*) Six
(*c*) Seven (*d*) None of these

Ans. (*c*) Seven.

Q. 6. Enactive means:

(*a*) Using activity
(*b*) Using images, graphics, or 3-D representations
(*c*) Symbolic (based on the use of symbols)
(*d*) None of these

Ans. (*a*) Using activity.

Q. 7. Iconic means:

(*a*) Using activity
(*b*) Using images, graphics, or 3-D representations
(*c*) Symbolic (based on the use of symbols)
(*d*) None of these

Ans. (*b*). Using images, graphics, or 3-D representations.

Q. 8. Which of the following is not an interactive media?

(*a*) Print (*b*) Audio
(*c*) Video (*d*) 3-D models

Ans. (*a*) Print.

Q. 9. Individualised instruction is given through:

(*a*) Computer
(*b*) Workbook
(*c*) Audio tape or film strip
(*d*) All of these

Ans. (*d*) All of these.

Q. 10. Slide can be:

(*a*) Narrated live
(*b*) Combined with audio tape for self-instruction
(*c*) Both (*a*) and (*b*)
(*d*) None of these

Ans. (*c*) Both (*a*) and (*b*).

Q. 11. Which of the following is a demerit of print media?

(*a*) Cheap
(*b*) Study skills required
(*c*) Application in a variety of situations
(*d*) No hardware needed for use

Ans. (*b*) Study skills required.

Q. 12. Which is a demerit of TV?

(*a*) Combines sound and visual
(*b*) Needs costly hardware at user end, as well as transmission
(*c*) Wide coverage of content and end
(*d*) None of these

Ans. (*b*) Needs costly hardware at user end, as well as transmission.

■■

Radio and Audio Components

6

INTRODUCTION

Of the other three electronic media, including audiocassette, television and videocassette, the radio is the least expensive and most widely available. In contrast to the audience of other mainstream media, its potential audience is enormous. It serves people of all ages and maturity levels, from elementary school children to grandfathers. In addition to the low cost and broad appeal, its ease of use is another element in its widespread use. While all of these qualities make it a widely applicable mass communication tool, its adaptability also serves as a compelling pedagogical argument for its usage in education. The radio can be used for a variety of things.

In this chapter, we will focus on the development, potentials and future trends and role of educational radio and audio components in education.

CHAPTER AT A GLANCE

ORIGIN AND GROWTH OF RADIO IN INDIA

A new era in communication was inaugurated by the invention of the radio in the first quarter of the 20th century. In the 1920s, radio clubs in Madras (now Chennai) and Calcutta conducted their first experiments out of pure curiosity. Today, radio in India has matured into one of the largest networks in the world. On January 23, 1927, the then Viceroy of India, Lord Irwin, formally launched the first radio station of the Indian Broadcasting Company ((IBC) at Bombay (now Mumbai), marking the start of organised broadcasting in India.

The Indian Broadcasting Service, which was owned by the government and replaced the IBC in 1930, was also shut down on October 9, 1931, as a result of financial difficulties. On May 5, 1932, the government eventually agreed to manage the service on a state level in response to public demand. The company was renamed All India Radio on June 8, 1936. Radio stations were also established in a few princely states, including Mysore (September 10, 1935), which named its station Akashvani, Baroda, Hyderabad (February 3, 1935), Aurangabad and Trivandrum (March 12, 1943). At the time of the partition, AIR had 6 stations (Bombay, Calcutta, Delhi, Madras, Lucknow and Tiruchirapally). Today, AIR has grown by 11 to more than 179 stations.

Presently, AIR airs almost 2000 programme hours daily in 146 dialects and 24 languages. It covers 89.7% of the country's geographical area and reaches 97.1% of the people, including a sizeable portion of the rural population.

Some Major Educational Radio Projects in India

A brief summary of a few major radio projects undertaken in the field of education is given below:

(i) **School Broadcasts:** There were sporadic transmissions from Bombay and Calcutta for schools even before the AIR was established. Calcutta began broadcasting in schools in 1937. Schools received funding to purchase radios. A school programme was launched by AIR from Delhi, Calcutta, Madras and Bombay. With the aid of government organisations like the NCERT's Central Institute of Educational Technology (CIET) and other similar institutions, AIR generated educational programming for schools.

(ii) **Adult Education and Community Development Project:** A broadcasting effort was initiated in 1956 to reach out to rural residents. The programme, dubbed "Radio Forum", was tested in 144 villages, close to Poona. Canada is where this type of software was initially developed and tested. India decided to give it a try with the aid of UNESCO and in each of the 144 villages, "Radio forums" of roughly 20 people each were set up. The participants were instructed to listen for thirty minutes to a radio programme on an agricultural or community development programme before debating whether to act on it in their own village.

(iii) **Farm and Home Broadcasts:** The farm and home transmissions were started by AIR in 1966. These broadcasts were created to offer guidance and information on agriculture and related themes. The intention was to inform the farmers and help them implement cutting-edge methods in their farms. The officials occasionally have agricultural radio schools as well and these have proven to be highly successful.

(iv) **University Broadcasts:** Since the very beginning of organised broadcasting, AIR stations have transmitted radio programmes on topics of academic interest. There was minimal interest among students, according to research done in 1965 to evaluate the effect of these broadcasts on pupils. As a result, two categories of programmes—"general" and

"enrichment"—were created. Public interest issues are included in regular programming. The enrichment programmes assist universities in their various jurisdictions that offer correspondence education. In order to provide options for using radio for its courses, the University of Delhi's correspondence school in Delhi works out the details in cooperation with the AIR. Additionally, the Central Institute of English and Foreign Languages in Hyderabad produces and airs its programmes via AIR.

(v) **Language Learning Project:** The AIR developed and carried out an experiment in 1979–1980 to employ radio broadcasts for language instruction. Together with the Government of Rajasthan's Department of Education, the experiment was carried out. Hindi was attempted to be taught to school-age youngsters. The Radio Pilot Project, as the initiative was known, attempted to reach 500 elementary schools in the districts of Jaipur and Ajmer. Children considered the projects to be helpful and studies have shown how the projects helped children's vocabulary grow. Later, it was duplicated in Madhya Pradesh's Hoshangabad district.

An Overview of the Development

The creation of the broadcast network and the planning and production of particular educational programmes are the two aspects of the growth of educational radio in India. With the ability to reach up to 90% of this vast nation's population, AIR has accomplished an incredible feat. One of the biggest networks in the globe is AIR. The AIR's non-formal education radio programmes have had great success pursuing worthwhile goals in the fields of agriculture and rural development.

AUDIOTAPES AND OTHER DEVELOPMENTS

A few devices with independent and/or auxiliary functions have recently joined the radio in widespread use. These have become popular because they allow us to get past some of the limitations of radio broadcasts, namely their exclusivity to certain hours. They are frequently referred to as radio medium extensions. Furthermore, these devices have been priced affordably enough for a sizeable portion of the population to purchase them. According to Rowntree, the following could be used to summarise the goals of employing audio in instruction:

- To assist students in honing their abilities.
- To give the lesson a more human and intimate feel.
- To offer "aural source material" for the learner to analyse or respond to, such as a dialogue with a client or a fellow student.
- To give concepts discussed elsewhere in the course new vitality.
- To walk students through tasks when having them constantly refer to printed instructions would be disturbing.
- To express ideas that are difficult to convey in writing.
- To inspire or motivate students.
- To introduce novel concepts to students who are illiterate, reluctant, or unable to read due to their circumstances.
- To give learners the required variation in their learning process.
- To affect the attitudes and feelings of the students.
- To solicit valuable contributions to the teaching effort from those who are unlikely to do so in writing.
- To give students the opportunity to hear from knowledgeable users, clients, other students, etc.
- To serve as a catalyst for group discussion and experience sharing.

Radio-Vision

The BBC invented the radio-vision approach, which enables the subject to be conveyed through two channels—the audio and the visual. While the explanation is provided through recorded narration, the visuals are delivered in the form of still filmstrips, charts, slides, models, etc. Educational institutions employ this in place of educational television. Radio broadcasting has its own benefits:

- It is affordable.
- It can accommodate many learner types.
- It is simple to build such programmes at the institutional level or at learning centres.
- It offers visual reinforcement for the concepts being taught.

The National Council of Education Training and Research used radio-vision method as one of the elements of the multimedia package for in-service teacher training that was produced and run during SITE to conduct a pilot experiment in its application in 1975–1976. To the approximately 24,000 participating teachers at 2400 centres, a number of charts and image cards were sent and verbal explanations were given via specially crafted radio broadcasts. The outcomes were discovered to be positive.

Audiotapes

Some of the restrictions of radio transmissions can be solved through audiotapes. The ability to utilise an audiotape whenever and wherever is a significant benefit for learners. The students can use the stop-start approach or any other replay strategy to review the taped content numerous times. Additionally, the audiocassette offers a level of discretion and seclusion that radio broadcasts cannot. The audiotape is quite cheap, easy to use, adaptable and operate. It is an effective teaching tool.

Audiovision

Audiovision is the use of audiotape along with visual media, much as radiovision. When you want the students to look at a series of pictures, follow a set of instructions, check a table, look at a map, etc., this style is quite helpful. You can even perform field studies using audio vision, asking the students to look at real items or specimens.

This shows that "hearing and viewing" are both taken into consideration by audio vision. By having the students complete any of the following tasks, audio vision can be made more engaging, in the opinion of Rowntree (1994):

- writing comments or calculations
- completing a form or questionnaire
- using materials
- operating a model
- carrying out an experiment.

Radiotext

A "radio text" environment has been created by combining radio with text data transport across computer networks. An FM radio station with a data broadcasting facility via a computer network often serves as the teaching end. Through a computer network, the radio broadcast's key messages are transmitted in textual mode to the listener. The learning end has a computer screen to receive the textual information and a radio listening capability. Due to the simultaneous transmission of both audio and text, the student receiving the lesson receives high-quality instruction at a reasonable price. Over 80% of the students at the Yashwant Rao Chavan Maharashtra Open University in Nasik expressed satisfaction with the use of radio text in an experiment. Additionally, it used a peer group conversation at the receiving end after the broadcast, demonstrating the versatility of radiotext.

STRENGTHS, LIMITATIONS AND USE OF RADIO/AUDIO MEDIUM

People have used and continued to utilise the radio to inform, educate and entertain them. The radio is a tool for reaching and educating those who lack access to other informational and educational communication channels.

Strengths of Radio/Audio Medium

Radio broadcasting's potential is derived from two factors: its extensive reach, low-operational costs and high-pedagogical values.

Here are some qualities that add to its potential:

***(i)* Easy Accessibility:** Radio is easily accessible compared to other forms of media, which benefits the bulk of our citizens. There are inexpensive transistors in the market that are easily accessible to even the economically underprivileged strata of people. Therefore, it can be used as a home-based method of teaching.

***(ii)* Wide Coverage:** Due to the availability of radio broadcast facilities across the subcontinent, we currently cover a significant percentage of our territory with radio broadcasts. As a result, because it can readily and rapidly reach the remote rural areas, radio can expand learning at a distance.

***(iii)* Low Capital Investment and Operating Cost:** Radio technology is quite inexpensive. Radio broadcasts require fewer production facilities than other electronic media and are relatively inexpensive to setup and produce.

***(iv)* Easy Learner-reception:** One can listen to radio broadcasts even, while performing manual labour.

***(v)* Effective Thought Promotion:** Radio stimulates the learner's cognitive function, since simultaneous information processing and listening are invariably present during radio listening. With the use of subtle music or the pause method, it can also inspire the imagination of the audience.

When used creatively, broadcasting may make education engaging and entertaining.

***(vi)* Motivative Supportive Facilities:** Music and other sound effects can be used to stimulate the mood and drive of listeners.

***(vii)* Easy Production:** Doing inventive radio programmes is easier than making them for television or video. Such manufacture does not require any specialised machinery or equipment. In comparison to the creation of a television video programme, it also involves less labour.

***(viii)* Effective-creation/Transmission of reality:** A strong audio version effectively establishes "movement" and sharpens the attention of a scene. A live broadcast can allow viewers to experience the authenticity of a situation that is, say, 100 miles away. Additionally, it can transport listeners to a scene from the past that happened, say, 100 years ago.

***(ix)* Feasible Mode of Learner Enrichment:** The most typical use of media in education is "enrichment", which is a feasible method of student enrichment. With the use of radio, this duty can be carried out quickly and affordably.

***(x)* Direct Instruction:** Radio has been used for direct instruction. However, doing so necessitates frequent and deliberate radio use. For specific target audiences, programmes based on the curriculum are broadcast under such programmes.

Limitations of Radio/Audio Medium

The following are the limitations of the radio:

(i) A flexible medium cannot be used with radio. The listener and the speaker/producer do not converse, or discuss in person. The learning environment is not particularly favourable in the absence of inspiration, direction and monitoring and the teaching/learning process turns into a one-way transfer of knowledge.

(ii) A learner's questions and misgivings can wait till later to be addressed. As a result, neither quick feedback to the learner nor assessment of the value of the content are provided.

(iii) It might not be a suitable medium for all course material; for instance, radio is ineffective for teaching courses that require demonstrations or visual aids.

(iv) There aren't enough people with the necessary qualifications to create educational programmes. Personnel with both production and academic training are required for radio programming. Finding someone with experience in this area is challenging. Coordination within the team is challenging when individuals from either line are selected to work together and the output quality falls as a result.

(v) Educational radio programmes haven't gotten enough and the right amount of airtime. The learners

are inconvenienced by this situation because they must be available during the broadcast time, regardless of their current commitments.

(vi) In the majority of emerging nations, educators must build curricula for diverse populations, such as the illiterate, school dropouts, the unemployed, etc. A radio programme of universal utility or appeal is harder to make the more diverse the audience.

(vii) A learner's attention span is limited, thus factual information retained after the programme's initial few minutes is typically poor unless additional efforts are made from time to time to maintain attention.

(viii) The technical team involved in the development and production of radio programmes frequently lacks sufficient knowledge of the pertinent pedagogical requirements of the students and their characteristics.

Uses of Radio/Audio Medium

The radio is a particularly effective mass communication tool since it may instantly reach every person in the nation or perhaps the entire world. It is also a mystical medium where words might vanish into thin air. It has an advantage over other media in disseminating information, education and entertainment because of its immediate nature and comparative simplicity. Three fundamental inputs—human voice, sound effects and music—are used to do all of this. Interpersonal communication, which should be informal and conversational, is what the radio genuinely facilitates. The radio can be a useful tool in instructional technology and the educational system because it is an aural medium. Radio programmes can pique students' interests and inspire their imaginations, while also aiding in the learning process. For both formal and developmental education, the radio is used.

Formal Education: The method is referred to as formal education when the radio programme is a part of a clearly defined curriculum for which students are registered, their progress is monitored and assessed and a certificate is provided upon successfully completing the course. Various educational radio programmes carried out in various nations were analysed by Jamison and McAnany in 1978. They came to the conclusion that the radio serves the following four major purposes:

(i) Enhancing learning involves providing pupils more experience, especially in subjects that the teacher finds challenging to teach. In India, primary school students listen to the radio for enrichment.

(ii) Direct instruction, which entails a teacher bearing the majority of the instructional load. The teacher teaches the remaining material, while a portion of the curriculum is covered by radio. The Radio Mathematics Project in Nicaragua makes extensive use of radio as a teaching tool.

(iii) Extending in-school education, i.e., expanding educational resources to isolated and dispersed communities and therefore substituting the radio for a classroom teacher. Radio instruction is utilised to provide additional educational opportunities to individuals who desire them. For example, Mexico's Radio Primaria (1969) was created to increase access to elementary education in the country's rural areas.

(iv) Distance learning, which substitutes the institution and the teacher entirely, by combining the radio with other media, mainly the print medium and sporadic in-person meetings. The industrialised nations, like the UK, Australia, Canada and Japan, heavily rely on radio for remote learning.

Kenya, Thailand and China have extensive experience using the radio correspondence method of education. A good example of distance education is Radio Santa Maria. Through this programme, people who didn't attend school-based education, can achieve a primary equivalency degree through home study with the aid of radio.

There are two ways that formal education is delivered over the radio: through radio broadcasts and through audiocassettes. In India as well, both types are employed in educational transactions. For instance, the Department of Education (Government of Rajasthan), AIR, Jaipur and the NCERT, Delhi, started a project together called the Radio Pilot Project. The project's objective was to educate Hindi to the primary school students. Radio programmes are also being broadcast for students in secondary schools. During school hours, a large number of radio stations in India air programmes that follow the secondary school curriculum. Some colleges and universities, like the Central Institute of Educational Technology (CIET), have capabilities for producing television programmes. IGNOU is engaged in planning, producing and evaluating both radio broadcasts and audiocassettes for its students.

Developmental Education: The knowledge imparted to the audience during developmental education might not be covered by any set curriculum. The goal of development is to bring about both social and economic transformation in a society. It is a frequently utilised participative approach. The radio programmes for development are broadcast alongside regular programming. Discussions focus on issues of general interest and those that require media attention. Sensitizing individuals to their issues and inspiring them to come up with a solution are the primary objectives of developmental education. These could include initiatives to boost agricultural output, enhance peoples' overall health, combat social ills end illiteracy, spread social education and more. Jamison and McAnany (1978) gives the following three major objectives of the radio developmental education:

(i) **To Inform:** The radio has far better reach to isolated locations. The radio's feature aids in the messages' widespread distribution. The radio has the capacity to make developmental messages more accessible to a huge audience.

(ii) **To Motivate:** One of the main goals of radio programmes is to inspire listeners to act in a way that is socially acceptable. The radio programmes' objectives include enhancing listeners' quality of life and inspiring them to fight against social ills like drug addiction.

***(iii)* To Teach:** The radio assists in organising the provision of educational services. It aids in the instruction of basic skills in vocational courses on food and nutrition, pickle making, biscuit making and other topics. Making people literate is one of the radio broadcast's key goals.

The radio literacy programme was introduced by Radio Santa Maria in 1964. The literacy initiative attracted thousands of adults who participated and profited from it. A wide range of children's programming is carried by AIR. The broadcast fare for kids includes educational programmes, as well as shows about health, cleanliness, national integration and other topics.

On the radio, general interest programmes are discussed for young people.

For the adult audience, programmes on agriculture and related topics, health and hygiene, social education, mass literacy, etc., are transmitted. AIR's farm and home departments create programming for listeners in rural areas.

Cost of Radio Programmes

The audio programmes are a less expensive option when compared to the costs associated with generating audio programmes with other media. A radio often costs one-tenth as much as a television. The price of creating a master's programme varies based on the type of material to be covered and the resources offered by open institutions. The master programme can either be broadcast instantly after completion or replicated onto new audiotapes. The additional costs depend on two additional elements. The cost of producing a radio programme per student will be very low if it serves a huge number of students. The lifespan of a programme is equally significant, in terms of how much radio programmes cost. A software will prove cost-effective if it can be utilised for a long time with only minor revisions or improvements. Additionally, a student must spend money on batteries or electricity, in order to listen to radio programmes, as well as a transistor or an audiotape recorder.

AUDIOTAPES IN EDUCATION

A cassette is a storage medium for information that will be used repeatedly in the future. In India, audiocassettes were first used in the early 1980s. The Governments of India's open electronic policies from the middle of the 1980s fostered cooperation with the developed nations, particularly Japan, for the production of audiocassettes. As a result, the Indian market saw the sale of thousands of audiocassettes. The audiocassette recorder is mostly used to listen to music and is more of an urban phenomenon. Perhaps the first institution to make extensive use of audiocassettes for educational reasons is IGNOU. The advantage of audiocassettes over radio broadcasts are: The students have a lot more freedom with audiocassettes than they would with a regimented radio broadcast since they can choose to listen whenever it is convenient for them. They can use the audiocassettes that are available to them. Because it is more convenient for them, the audiocassette better meets their specific demands. With audio cassette players, the technical features (stop, pause, replay) are available. These tools make it easier for students to study in accordance with their needs. One can learn at their own pace and according to their preferred learning method. Learning from audiocassettes is not limited by time or location.

Designing Programmes on Audiocassettes

The following are two crucial considerations that must be made when organising and creating audiocassette programmes. We must include certain activities in the programmes to make learning interactive. To ensure the students' involvement in the teaching-learning process, an audio programme should be designed in this manner. There are numerous ways to provide built-in activities. Activities and questions can be used to break up a discussion and aid students in understanding concepts, finding solutions to issues and reviewing crucial or challenging subjects. Such pedagogical activities ought to be possible with the audiocassette presentation's layout. The audiocassettes have the ability to help students learn practical skills as one of their educational uses. The audiocassette should therefore allow for the development of skills like diagramming and creating visuals, as well as setting up equipment. In each instance, comments may offer a crucial and encouraging voice as the students get to work on their projects. But in order to accomplish these goals, we must use a multimedia approach to education.

Combining Audio Programmes with Other Media

Compared to other forms of media, audio cassettes are simple to incorporate into any other teaching tool. The combination of audiocassettes and printed text can enhance learning to the fullest extent. The students at the British Open University have found this strategy to be quite effective. With the use of audiocassettes that are merged with the printed text and are provided in the form of pictures and diagrams in a sequential order, each illustration is backed by a potent commentary, many subjects, including engineering and science, are being taught. Frame-by-frame, presentations of illustrations in the form of visuals are made and each frame is accompanied by voiceovers that increase the impact of the visuals.

Cost of Audio Cassettes/Programmes

For both the radio broadcast and the audiocassette, the master tape preparation process is the same. When the master tape is prepared, it can either be broadcast immediately or converted into audiocassettes. As a result, the expenses associated with producing programmes for radio transmission and audiocassettes are nearly identical. The institution must buy blank audiocassettes and have the master tape replicated in case of the audiocassettes. The audiocassettes may be distributed to students, as part of their course materials or made available at study centres, where students can access the necessary programmes. It relies on the price and availability of suitable technology for the pupils in both scenarios. As a distance educator, it is your responsibility to make sure that the majority of your students can access the teaching materials you plan to employ. You need to consider if the radio is reachable, whether the students have audio cassette players and whether the study spaces you intend to stock with audiocassettes are accessible to the students. The students must purchase an audiocassette recorder in order to use the audiocassettes at their place of employment. Additionally, they must spend money on batteries or electricity costs. As a result, both institutional and individual costs are included in the overall cost of making and using the audiocassettes.

LEARNING FROM AUDIO MEDIA

Radio programmes are created and broadcast for kids at various educational levels in developed nations. Some developing nations, including Kenya and India, broadcast instructional programmes for their citizens' students. Many universities throughout the world have their own small campus radio stations that broadcast instructional radio shows for the enrolled students.

Radio has the power to affect people's attitudes, knowledge and consciousness. This is based on the following characteristics of radio as a teaching tool:

(i) The radio exposes the kids to fresh materials.

(ii) It removes the children from the confines of the school or classroom.

(iii) It has a strong ability to go to far-off places.

(iv) It carries the responsibility of a teacher because it can transmit information to everyone (distance teaching via radio).

(v) It works wonders for teaching some subjects, such languages, history and environmental studies.

(vi) Because it is so good for encouraging creative thinking and emotional learning, teachers and students are able to accomplish higher-level objectives.

(vii) The radio is a very versatile medium. Information that is current is presented. Instantaneous broadcasting is possible for messages relating to agriculture, weather, market prices, etc. Similar to how public service information can be quickly distributed to the populace.

(viii) The radio's ability to work well with other media, notably written texts, is another illustration of its adaptability. The radio's efficacy will depend on how effectively it meets the needs of the topics being covered or lessons being taught.

As a uni-sensory medium, radio only offers voice information, leaving it up to the students to conceive what the things, people, locations and events in the programmes would look like. Thus, the radio encourages kids' imagination and helps educators achieve their objective of fostering their visual creativity. The audio medium is not appropriate for any of the subjects.

For instance, unless the necessary supplementary materials, such as workbooks, are available, it is impossible to demonstrate specific objects, charts and diagrams as illustrations. In 1977, Searie and Sipper discussed some guidelines for effective instruction when utilising radio as a teaching tool. These values are listed as follows:

When students participate actively in their learning, it is more effective. Students should respond to radio instruction by taking some sort of activity. You can actively respond verbally, physically, or in writing. If the student is informed of his or her progress in the programme, learning will rise. Feedback will therefore quicken the pace of learning. As a result, each programme needs to have a feedback option.

More learning will result from listening to the radio if the information is provided in a logical order, from simple to complicated, tangible to abstract.

Learning is facilitated through practise with study materials. The pupils should have the chance to put their new knowledge into practise through the radio programmes. They have the chance to review it during practise. In his research, Meed (1977) discovered that the majority of radio programmes required students to engage in tasks outside listening.

Learning Patterns

The radio is used for individual as well as group listening.

(i) **Individual listening:** Using the radio to tailor education is crucial. The radio can be used in a variety of ways to aid learning. I saw three of them.

(a) The students listen to particular programmes on the radio, which provides the actual content. This is the case for the majority of AIR instructional programmes.

(b) In conjunction with other media, the radio is utilised to direct the instructional process. For instance, audiocassettes are utilised in conjunction with print materials like workbooks, notes and textbooks. Each student works on the printed materials after listening to the programme. Individualized learning is included in these fees.

(c) The radio is employed as a tool for participatory learning in which each student engages directly in the exchange of information. She/He engages in pedagogical activities to aid in learning. The student completes built-in exercises that are included in the audiocassettes.

(ii) **Group Listening:** The radio might be helpful for this type of listening as well. It can be applied in at least two different ways as a group listening tool: The radio serves as a means of distributing information for communal consumption. A section of the population in a region that is concerned, receives news about the weather conditions.

The radio is employed as a means of directing a group through typical exercises. A community is targetted and guided for certain goals and behaviours as a whole. People can work on some group projects, while listening to the radio. Through interaction, they pick up particular behaviours. This group includes social education and general cleanliness programmes.

Students do not utilise programmes in the same way during group listening as they do during solitary listening. For instance, a single listener utilises the relay/control facility more often than a group of listeners. Individual students are free to fast-forward through or skim any portion of the programme but doing so in a group setting is troublesome. Similar to how the individual listener is aware of how to operate the equipment, he or she is also able to search for the necessary materials and start, pause and replay the equipment. In a group setting, the listener typically does not have access to such chances. Another crucial distinction is that while a group situation might inherently be distracting for a listener in a group, the individual learner pays greater attention to the discussion or transactions. Group listening is not, however, less effective than individual listening. Both have advantages of their own. During group listening, a student can debate the material with both his or her tutor and other classmates. The student is free to ask a question, seek clarification on something and express an opinion about the topic under discussion. If there is a discussion after the lesson, the pupils are more assured of their understanding. In a circumstance where only one person is listening, this benefit is absent.

FUTURE TRENDS IN EDUCATIONAL RADIO

The future of radio appears to be dismal with the rise of television, video and more advanced technology mass media. We question how long radio will be used as a tool for teaching, given the advantages, sophisticated features, innate desire for the "new" and appeal in urban areas that recently produced media enjoy. However, we think that the radio will continue to play a significant role in advancing education, at least in India and other developing nations. Our conviction is supported by economic factors and the fact that remote rural populations still lag significantly behind urban populations in terms of development.

We cannot overnight make the transition to modem technology, in order to meet the educational and entertaining needs of all these rural residents. Any attempt to do this could severely strain our budget. As a result, for quite some time to come, we will unavoidably have to stick with the less expensive and more practical medium of radio for the diffusion of knowledge.

ACTIVITIES

Q. 1. For Indian students: Find out how educational radio is being used by open universities in India. Develop a case description of any one open university using radio. For this activity, try to make use of your nearest library or any other source.

Ans. Beginning in January 1992, AIR stations in Mumbai, Hyderabad and Shillong began airing IGNOU programmes on the radio in cooperation with the institution. The primary target audience for this project was students at traditional and open universities. Although Shillong began this, it was later abandoned. As a result, it is currently, exclusively broadcast from AIR Mumbai and AIR Hyderabad. The local area continues to enjoy the popularity of this show. Interactive Radio Counselling on IGNOU-AIR (IRC). This programme, which was started in 1998 for students at Open / Conventional Universities, is also incredibly successful.

IGNOU, in partnership with AIR Bhopal, launched this project in May 1998 as an experimental programme for a year in an effort to close the gap between educational institutions and learners by quickly replying to their enquiries and providing academic counselling in subject areas.

Due to the experiment's effectiveness, it was expanded to eight additional AIR stations (Lucknow, Patna, Jaipur, Shimla, Rohtak, Jalandhar, Delhi and Jammu). Currently, 186 radio stations of All India Radio offer interactive radio counselling every Sunday from 4:00 PM to 5:00 PM for an hour. Two Sundays on the National Hook-up are included in this. Since February 2001, 80 cities have toll-free telephone services that allow learners to communicate with specialists and get explanation without having to pay for their calls. On the first and third Sundays of each month, AIR stations in Kolkata and Delhi broadcast in English and Hindi, respectively, via a nationwide hookup, which is relayed by 186 radio stations.

Programmes at various regional IGNOU and State Open Universities are scheduled for the second and fourth Sundays, respectively. Region-based programmes of IGNOU have also been assigned the slot of the fifth Sunday (if any). This programme's popularity is growing every day. The Gyan-Vani (Educational FM Radio Channel of India) project was started in 2001 and once more, students from Open and Conventional Universities were the intended audience. Gyan Vani (Gyan = Knowledge, Vani = aerial broadcasting) is an educational FM radio channel in India. It is a special decentralised idea for spreading mass media for empowerment and education that is tailored to the educational needs of the neighbourhood. It is now transmitting in test mode across the Allahabad, Bangalore and Coimbatore FM stations in India. By June 2002, the network is expected to grow to 40 stations altogether. IGNOU, NCERT, UGC, IIT, DEC and other national level universities will contribute daily programming to the Gyan Vani stations, which would function as media cooperatives. Each station will have a range of roughly 60 km, providing comprehensive access to the entire city or town, as well as the neighbouring areas. It acts as the perfect vehicle for addressing the socio-cultural and educational demands of the local community.

Gyan Vani is a key tool in realising the goal of education for everyone, not just for the regular educational system. Gyan Vani's primary goal is to deliver education to people where they live. Along with providing a rigorous education, Gyan Vani will also focus on awareness campaigns for Panchayati Raj employees, women empowerment, consumer rights, human rights, children's rights, health education, science education, continuing education, extension education, vocational education, teacher education, non-formal education, adult education, education for the handicapped and education for the underprivileged. Gyan Vani can be accessed via a commercial FM station.

Q. 2. For other students: Find out the use of educational radio in your country. Discuss any one educational radio project in detail. For this, you may use your nearest library or any other source.

Ans. African language radio stations have a strong aversion to adding formal educational programmes to their schedules, since South Africa Broadcasting Corporation radio has a long history of being associated with apartheid educational policy. This dissatisfaction was made worse by high levels of centralization, a lack of autonomy and the low status given to black employees. In response, radio stations broadcasting in African languages created their own unofficial instructional programmes. These historical patterns still have an impact on the educational radio programming that is offered, as well as how station managers view the Department of Education and SABC cooperation known as Learn 'and Live.

On its ten African language channels, SABC Education Radio has started to build up a sizable body of instructional programmes, although questions remain over their audience appeal and educational efficacy. Only one type of programming—ECD programming—is broadcast directly to formal educational settings, despite the fact that some specialty programming is transmitted (including teacher assistance and early childhood development programmes). Only six of the eight categories of SABC educational radio programmes are relevant to the teaching and learning processes in schools. These are:

1. Early childhood development: These programmes target children in reception year.

2. Curriculum support: These programmes cover a range of different topics in the eight learning areas, namely:

- Science and technology
- Human and social science
- Art and culture
- Life orientation
- Literacy and language
- Economics and management sciences
- Natural sciences and
- Communication

(The curriculum support programmes which have been developed in 1998 are listed in appendix five.)

3. Youth and career counselling: These programmes address subjects like study techniques, time management and career counselling.

4. Educator training: These programmes address subjects including professional development, parental involvement in school governance and entire school development and are aimed for school administrators and teachers.

5. Technology and science: These programmes are intended for adult listeners but a knowledgeable teacher could find some use for higher, primary and secondary schools.

6. Learning and teaching cultures: Although, they are aimed at a broad audience, these programmes are pertinent to what occurs in classrooms and have the potential to spark conversation about significant problems.

CHECK YOUR PROGRESS

Q. 1. List at least five advantages of educational radio.

Ans. The following are limitations of the radio:

(i) A flexible medium cannot be used with radio. The listener and the speaker/producer do not converse or discuss in person. The learning environment is not particularly favourable in the absence of inspiration, direction and monitoring and the teaching/learning process turns into a one-way transfer of knowledge.

(ii) A learner's questions and misgivings can wait till later to be addressed. As a result, neither quick feedback to the learner nor assessment of the value of the content are provided.

(iii) It may not be an effective medium for all types of course material for example, the subjects which need demonstration/visual illustrations cannot be taught effectively through radio.

(iv) There aren't enough people with the necessary qualifications to create educational programmes. Personnel with both production and academic training are required for radio programming. Finding someone with experience in this area is challenging. Coordination within the team is challenging when individuals from either line are selected to work together and the output quality falls as a result.

(v) Educational radio programmes haven't gotten enough and the right amount of airtime. The learners are inconvenienced by this situation because they must be available during the broadcast time, regardless of their current commitments.

(vi) In the majority of emerging nations, educators must build curricula for diverse populations (such as the illiterate, school dropouts, the unemployed, etc.). A radio programme of universal utility or appeal is harder to make the more diverse audience.

(vii) A learner's attention span is limited, thus factual information retained after the programme's initial few minutes is typically poor unless additional efforts are made from time to time to maintain attention. Additionally, the radio setup's primary areas of programming do not include instructional broadcasts.

(viii) The technical team involved in the development and production of radio programmes frequently lacks sufficient knowledge of the pertinent pedagogical requirements of the students and their characteristics. The difficulties of programme production are not well-known to the subject experts. Therefore, no successful manufacturing could ever be accomplished without complete coordination and understanding between the two groups.

Q. 2. Define the objective and scope of radio developmental education briefly.

Ans. The knowledge imparted to the audience during developmental education might not be covered by any set curriculum. The goal of development is to bring about both social and economic transformation in a society. It is a frequently utilised participative approach. In poor nations, radio is frequently used for development education. Radio has long been utilised for social, political, cultural and economic development education all across the world. The radio is seen as a potent, direct tool for growth. It performs the function of a one-way, linear transmitter of developmental messages from the governmental entities to the populace. The radio programmes for development are broadcast alongside regular programming. Discussions focus on issues of general interest and those that require media attention. The majority of radio transmissions now in existence are of a developmental character. Sensitizing individuals to their issues and inspiring them to come up with a solution are the primary objectives of developmental education. These could include initiatives to boost agricultural output, enhance peoples' overall health, combat social ills, end illiteracy, spread social education and more.

According to Jamison and McAnany (1978), the three main goals of radio developmental education are as follows:

***(i)* To inform:** The radio has far better access to the outlying regions. The radio's feature aids in the messages' widespread distribution. Regular radio news programmes include topics like the availability of social services, disaster warning and international and national events. Radio thus, has the ability to increase the accessibility of developmental messages to an infinite audience.

***(ii)* To inspire:** One of the main goals of radio programmes is to inspire listeners to act in a way that is socially accc^table. The radio programmes' objectives include enhancing listeners' quality of life and inspiring them to fight against social ills like drug addiction.

***(iii)* To instruct:** The radio aids in organising the provision of educational services. It aids in the teaching of basic skills, such as those taught in vocational courses on food and nutrition, pickle making, biscuit making and other similar topics. Making people speak up is one of the radio broadcast's key purposes. The radio literacy programme was started by Radio Santa Maria in 1964. The literacy programme has thousands of adult participants who benefited from it. A wide range of children's programming is carried by AIR. The broadcast fare for kids includes, in addition to programmes on their schoolwork, shows about health, hygiene, national integration, etc. On the radio, general interest programmes are discussed for young people. The major goals of these programmes are to instil in young people socially desirable behaviours, to integrate them into society, to make them productive, etc. For the adult audience, programmes on agriculture and related topics, health and hygiene, social education, mass literacy, etc., are transmitted.

AIR's farm and home departments create programming for listeners in rural areas. The majority of radio stations offer specific programmes for teachers. The goals of these broadcasts are to improve teaching abilities, to inform teachers on innovations in teaching techniques, curricular changes, new fields of knowledge and other related topics. Programs on a range of subjects are broadcast on the conventional radio networks to keep their expertise current. These facts make it simple for us to draw the conclusion that the radio is utilised for both formal and developmental education. As you just saw, the majority of radio programmes fall under the umbrella of developmental education, which primarily tries to affect socio-cultural and economic changes in society.

Q. 3. Give three advantages which audiocassettes have over radio broadcasts.

Ans. As opposed to transient radio broadcast, pre-recorded sound distribution on audiocassettes is the main focus. As a result, the word "cassette" acquires significance. A cassette is a storage medium for information that will be used repeatedly in the future. In India, audiocassettes were first used in the early 1980s. The Government of India's open electronic policies from the middle of the 1980s fostered cooperation with the developed nations, particularly Japan, for the production of audiocassettes. As a result, the Indian market saw the sale of thousands of audiocassettes. By producing countless audiocassette recorders, indigenous industrialization boosted the audiocassette market. The audiocassette recorder is mostly used to listen to music and is more of an urban phenomenon. The majority of audiocassettes in use in India are filled with music, including film, popular and classical music. This indicates that in India, audiocassettes are not employed or are not widely used as a teaching tool. Perhaps the first institution to make extensive use of audiocassettes for educational reasons is IGNOU.

The students have a lot more freedom with audiocassettes than they would with a regimented radio broadcast, since they can choose to listen whenever it is convenient for them. They can use the audiocassettes that are available to them. As a result, the audiocassette more effectively meets their unique demands because it is more convenient. With audio cassette players, the technical tools (stop, pause, replay) are available. These tools make it easier for students to study in accordance with their needs. One can learn at their own pace and according to their preferred learning method. Learning from audiocassettes is not limited by time or location. The pupils can listen to a cassette again until they are comfortable with the programme's material. It means that even complex material, which calls for more work from the students, can be covered on audiocassettes. Certain learning tasks and exercises can be browsed, skipped and renewed by the students. The audiocassettes allow the pupils the freedom to read only what they want to. These audiocassette features provide all the benefits of printed text. The control that the students enjoy when using the audiocassettes is the key takeaway if you consider all three of the aforementioned criteria. The students have more control over their education and move on at their own pace and according to their own needs. The educational needs of the pupils, such as individualization, self-pacing, selective reading and others, may not be met by the broadcast programmes.

Q. 4. Write two functions of the pre-listening activities.

Ans. Two functions of the pre-listening activities are as follow:

(i) The pre-listening activities get the students psychologically ready to learn from the programme. If the programme is about 'Solar energy' for senior secondary students, they (listeners) can read the prescribed lesson in their course and when they listen to the radio programme, they will easily understand it.

(ii) These activities may also include necessary guidance/instructions to help the students learn smoothly. The students will know how their learning can be effective.

Q. 5. Write three functions of the post-listening activities.

Ans. The functions of the post-listening activities can be:

(i) The post-listening tasks at the end of the programme assist the students in evaluating their performance development. By answering a few questions in writing or taking a quiz on the subject being covered, students can assess their understanding.

(ii) These exercises aid students in reviewing and recapitulating what they have learned throughout the programme.

(iii) Effective use of the audio programmes can be ensured by thoughtful post-listening exercises.

OTHER IMPORTANT QUESTIONS

Q. 1. Write a note on the growth and development of All India Radio.

Ans. A little over 13 years have passed since broadcasting first started in India. The nation's first broadcast was made by the Radio Club of Bombay in June 1923. The Calcutta Radio Club was then established five months after that. The Indian Broadcasting Company (IBC) was founded on July 23, 1927 but it was forced to file for bankruptcy in less than three years.

The Department of Industries and Labour's Indian Broadcasting Service launched its trial run of operations in April 1930. August 1935 saw the appointment of Lionel Fielden as the first Controller of Broadcasting. Akashvani Mysore, a private radio station, was established the next month. All India Radio replaced the Indian State Broadcasting Service on June 8, 1936.

In August 1937, the Central News Organization (CNO) was founded. The Department of Communications took over AIR the same year and the Department of Information and Broadcasting four years later. There were six radio stations in India at the time of its independence, located in Delhi, Bombay, Calcutta, Madras, Tiruchirapalli and Lucknow. In Pakistan, three were present (Peshawar, Lahore and Dacca). At that time, only 2.5% of the territory and 11% of the population were covered by AIR. The News Services Division (NSD) and the External Services Division (ESD) were formed from CNO the next year. In 1956, the National Broadcaster was given the name AKASHVANI. When the Vividh Bharati Service was first introduced in 1957, its primary feature was popular cinema soundtrack.

All India Radio is now among the biggest media organisations in the world because of its amazing expansion. Today, almost all of the people and about 92% of the country can receive AIR, thanks to its network of 262 radio stations. A massive broadcasting organisation, AIR currently broadcasts in 146 dialects and 23 languages, serving a huge range of socio-economically and culturally diverse audiences.

The External Services Division broadcasts its programmes in 11 Indian and 16 other languages, reaching more than 100 nations. These international broadcasts attempt to enlighten listeners on events in the nation, while also offering a wide variety of entertainment.

The News Services Division of All India Radio broadcasts 647 bulletins every day in roughly 90 languages and dialects in Home, Regional, External and DTH Services for a total of almost 56 hours per day. Additionally, 314 news headlines from 41 AIR Stations are displayed on FM mode on an hourly basis. 469 daily news bulletins in 75 different languages are produced by 44 regional news units. The News Services Division also produces a number of news-based programmes on current events from Delhi and its Regional News Units, in addition to the daily news bulletins.

AIR currently broadcasts 18 FM stereo channels called AIR FM Rainbow that target the urban consumer in a novel manner. AIR FM Gold, a group of four additional FM channels, offers a mix of news and entertainment programming from Delhi, Kolkata, Chennai and Mumbai. AIR is enhancing its Medium Wave transmission with more FM transmitters at Regional stations as the FM wave sweeps the nation.

In accordance with the government's intention to move to digital broadcasting, AIR is making the shift from analogue to digital gradually. The DRM, or Digital Radio Mondiale, is the technology used. The goal is to fully digitise everything by 2017, so listeners may anticipate significantly improved broadcast quality soon.

Q. 2. Discuss some major educational radio projects in India.

Ans. A brief summary of a few major radio projects undertaken in the field of education are given below:

(i) **School Broadcasts:** Even before the AIR was created, there were intermittent transmissions from Bombay and Calcutta for schools. In 1937, Calcutta started broadcasting in classrooms. Radios were bought with money allocated for schools. AIR launched a school programme from Delhi, Calcutta, Madras and Bombay. AIR produced educational programming for schools with the assistance of government

organisations like the NCERT's Central Institute of Educational Technology (CIET) and other like entities.

***(ii)* Adult Education and Community Development Project:** In 1956, a broadcasting campaign was started to connect with rural communities. The "Radio Forum" programme was trialled in 144 communities near Poona. This kind of software was initially created and tested in Canada. With the help of UNESCO, India decided to give it a try and in each of the 144 villages "Radio forums" with a capacity of about 20 people each, were established. Before considering whether to implement an agricultural or community development programme in their local village, the participants were instructed to listen to a radio broadcast about it for thirty minutes.

***(iii)* Farm and Home Broadcasts:** AIR launched the farm and home transmissions in 1966. These broadcasts were made to provide advice and details on farming and related topics. The goal was to educate farmers and assist them in implementing cutting-edge practices on their properties. Also, infrequently offered by the officials are agricultural radio schools, which have had great success.

***(iv)* University Broadcasts:** Radio programmes on scholarly subjects have been broadcast by AIR stations ever since the advent of organised broadcasting. According to studies conducted in 1965 to assess the impact of these broadcasts on students, there was little interest among the students. As a result, "general" and "enrichment" programme categories were established. Issues of public concern are covered in regular programming. The enrichment programmes help colleges that offer correspondence education in their respective jurisdictions. The University of Delhi's correspondence school in Delhi works out the specifics in collaboration with the AIR to offer choices for using radio for its courses. Additionally, the Central Institute of English and Foreign Languages in Hyderabad produces and airs its programmes via AIR.

***(v)* Language Learning Project:** In 1979-1980, the AIR created and ran an experiment to use radio broadcasts for language training. The project was run in conjunction with the Department of Education for the Government of Rajasthan. It was attempted to teach Hindi to school-aged children. The goal of the effort, known as the Radio Pilot Project, was to communicate with 500 elementary schools in the Jaipur and Ajmer regions. Studies have showed how the initiatives grew children's vocabulary and kids thought they were useful. Later, it was replicated in the Hoshangabad area of Madhya Pradesh.

Q. 3. Write the advantages and disadvantages of radio educational programmes.

Ans. Advantages of radio educational programmes:

- It can communicate with a large audience over any distance that reception will support.
- It is cost-effective since the material can be prepared, recorded and used as often as necessary. Repeats are now affordable and feasible.
- Receiving sets are widely accessible and affordably priced.
- The greatest instructors can be applied throughout a broad spectrum.
- The programmes are more practical because they can, if necessary, be heard inside the house.
- Sets are now portable, thanks to the invention of transistorised radios.
- Programmes can be utilised in conjunction with distance education courses, as standalone teaching courses, as part of in-person teaching courses, or as standalone teaching courses.

Disadvantages of radio educational programmes:

- Radio can be impersonal and kids who spend a lot of time listening to a voice from a box, may rapidly lose interest.
- Although, the usage of listening groups and remote education courses can help to address this disadvantage, there may not often be any spontaneous student input.
- Because radio programmes cannot use visual aids, the range of subjects that can be taught is constrained.
- Interruptions in radio programme reception can result in continuity loss.
- Long regular radio programmes that aren't supplemented in other ways, make it harder for kids to maintain self control.
- Because radio programmes are broadcast to a huge audience and "anybody" could be listening in, tutors who are unfamiliar with the medium are frequently, initially hesitant to commit to the radio.

Q. 4. Differentiate between radio educational programmes and radio general programmes.

Ans. There are two categories of radio programmes: The first category includes programmes of general interest that are broadcast to the general public. These might include news articles, opinions and programmes that prioritise amusement over true instruction, such as forums, conversations and quizzes. The second type is an instructional broadcast that is targetted at a particular audience and has a high level of educational content. These include broadcasts for farmers, teachers, engineers and other specialised organisations, as well as broadcasts for youngsters attending schools. While primarily serving educational purposes, these programmes may also entertain and for the best results, they should.

Programmes of general interest have planning, content and assessment issues. There are two approaches to find a guide to the most popular general interest programme types: experience and listener surveys. Risk-taking must be done, while experimenting with novel concepts if new forms are to become widely accepted. Evaluation is challenging because there is frequently no feedback and the only benchmarks are recurrent listener polls that gauge programme popularity.

All forms of education can benefit from using strictly educational broadcasts. It has been argued that using them in underdeveloped nations is one of the only approaches to have a significant impact on their widespread issue with educational supply. Educational programming cannot stand alone. However, they can be effectively incorporated into both traditional class meetings and distance-learning courses. Distance learning courses are extremely impersonal and need a great level of self-discipline to successfully complete. When included into a distance education instructional system, regular radio broadcasts can add a more personal touch and stimulate regular student study. Regular and frequent face-to-face lessons are challenging to schedule, especially in remote locations where there are few teachers and few students in higher-level classes.

Programmes might only realistically be able to accommodate regular monthly weekend sessions. The best radio teachers can be used and educational radio broadcasts can once more be used to provide continuity during the extended times when teacher and student cannot meet in person. According to Usha Rao, using radio in a creative way to spice up an instructional broadcast has proven to be an effective teaching strategy. The use of radio cannot be avoided in emerging nations when a low level of education needs to be quickly and widely rectified. With creativity and careful planning, this mass communication medium can serve as the foundation for mounting and successfully completing any kind of extensive instructional programme.

MULTIPLE CHOICE QUESTIONS

Q. 1. A radio broadcasting effort for adult education was initiated in __________ to reach out to rural residents.

(a) 1946 *(b)* 1947
(c) 1956 *(d)* None of these

Ans. *(c)* 1956.

Q. 2. The programme, dubbed "Radio Forum", was tested in 144 villages close to:

(a) Pune *(b)* Nagpur
(c) Indore *(d)* Bhopal

Ans. *(a)* Pune.

Q. 3. The farm and home transmissions were started by AIR in:

(a) 1956 *(b)* 1962
(c) 1966 *(d)* None of these

Ans. *(a)* 1966.

Q. 4. Which is related to the development of educational radio in India?

(a) The establishment of the broadcast network
(b) The preparation and production of specific educational programmes
(c) Both *(a)* and *(b)*
(d) None of these

Ans. *(c)* Both *(a)* and *(b)*.

Q. 5. The technique of radio-vision was pioneered by:

(a) BBC *(b)* AIR
(c) SABC *(d)* None of these

Ans. *(a)* BBC.

Q. 6. Which is an advantage of Radiovision?

(a) It is economical
(b) It can cater to different categories of learners
(c) It is easy to produce such programmes at the institutional level or at the learning centres
(d) All of these

Ans. *(d)* All of these.

Q. 7. The potentials of radio broadcasting stem from which source?

(a) Its low capital requirements, low-operating costs and wide coverage
(b) Its pedagogical values
(c) Both *(a)* and *(b)*
(d) None of these

Ans. *(c)* Both *(a)* and *(b)*.

Q. 8. Which country designed Radio Primaria (1969) to extend access to elementary schooling in the rural areas?

(a) Mexico *(b)* USA
(c) Switzerland *(d)* India

Ans. *(a)* Mexico.

Q. 9. Radio Santa Maria is a successful example of:

(a) Adult education *(b)* Distance teaching
(c) Formal teaching *(d)* None of these

Ans. *(b)* Distance teaching.

Q. 10. A project entitled the Radio Pilot Project was started jointly by the Department of Education (Government of Rajasthan), AIR, Jaipur and:

(a) NCERT *(b)* Delhi University
(c) IGNOU *(d)* None of these

Ans. *(a)* NCERT.

Q. 11. Which AIR is engaged in producing and broadcasting programmes for the students of the Madurai Kamaraj University?

(a) AIR, Delhi *(b)* AIR, Madras
(c) AIR, Tiruchi *(d)* None of these

Ans. *(c)* AIR, Tiruchi.

Q. 12. When did the Government of India's liberal electronic policies encouraged collaboration with the developed countries, specifically Japan for manufacturing audiocassettes?

(a) Mid-1980s *(b)* 1970s
(c) Mid-1960s *(d)* None of these

Ans. *(a)* Mid-1980s.

Q. 13. Which will play a vital role in the future of educational radio?

(a) The emergence of DAB technology
(b) The development of fibre technology
(c) Both *(a)* and *(b)*
(d) None of these

Ans. *(a)* The emergence of DAB technology.

■■

Television and Video Components

7

INTRODUCTION

This chapter will examine the audio-visual media, which transmits learning messages through visual signals backed by auditory elements. This media has grown in popularity as a means of instruction all around the world because of its auditory and visual potential. A range of visual media, including computer, videotext, videocassettes, video discs, television broadcast and video are now included in multimedia packages used in online teaching and learning, thanks to advancements in communication technology. In this chapter, we'll talk about the video elements and their numerous delivery methods.

CHAPTER AT A GLANCE

POTENTIAL OF EDUCATIONAL TELEVISION

If used creatively, television may be a powerful tool in the hands of educators. It has demonstrated its superiority and efficacy in teaching a variety of subjects, including agriculture, science, geography and oceanography.

Strengths of Television

***(i)* Social Equality in Education:** The majority of people from rural backgrounds and those who reside in urban slums are served by television programmes that advocate for the ideal of social equality in education. Television improves education's effectiveness and lowers the dropout rate.

***(ii)* Higher Quality of Instruction:** Compared to the typical classroom lesson, television shows are more prepared, organised and presented.

***(iii)* Reduce Dependency on Teacher:** Students actively participate in their own learning through television. If television is used, they only need the teacher's bare minimal assistance.

***(iv)* Flexibility:** Educational television enables quick and ongoing adjustment in curricula and teaching techniques. The ongoing development of knowledge and the changing requirements of society can both be included into courses as they are updated.

***(v)* Use of the Best Available Teacher:** The country's educational chances are equalised by educational television. The education received by students in rural and underdeveloped areas of the nation, where educational resources are scarce, is of an equivalent standard to that received by students in urban centres. For any pupil, the best teacher is readily available.

***(vi)* Cost Effectiveness:** When used extensively, television shows its cost-effectiveness. Without sacrificing instruction quality, it can affordably provide education for the entire nation. Of course, the initial cost will be substantial.

***(vii)* In-service Training:** In-service training for teachers can be conducted outside of school hours using educational television. Every week, a programme is broadcast by NCERT, India, to help teachers develop their instructional strategies and abilities.

***(viii)* Logistically Simple:** Educational television makes running an efficient remote learning system logistically very easy. Teaching through television can help to a certain extent overcome the challenges of arranging and managing distance learning.

***(ix)* Combination of Audio and Video Components:** The audio and video capabilities of television are advantageous. Because of this, it is more appealing than radio and print media.

***(x)* Stimulation:** We can manage the stimuli (auditory and visual) through educational television to elicit a reaction (learning).

***(xi)* Mass Education:** Educational television can cater to the explosive increase in student numbers.

Limitations of Television

Some of the disadvantages of television are as follows:

***(i)* Limitations of One-way Communication:** Since television is primarily a one-way communication medium, it does not allow for interaction or conversation and hence cannot provide quick feedback on students' emotions, concerns and uncertainties.

***(ii)* Problem of Pacing Learning:** Every student learns at a different pace and in a different way. Each student is expected to pay attention, while watching television and the teacher moves through his lessons at a pace that he believes is generally appropriate for an average learner.

***(iii)* Poor Accessibility:** The average person still cannot afford television. As a result, it cannot be a popular medium.

***(iv)* Insufficient Viewing Conditions:** The programmes cannot be viewed in universities or schools due to a lack of suitable arrangements.

***(v)* High Cost:** Televised instruction is costly. Due to the high cost of complex electrical devices, production and broadcasting costs must be quite high.

***(vi)* Tough to Integrate:** It is difficult to make television a regular part of a 'classroom' or school' activity. The challenges arise from the lack of a standardised curriculum and of instructors with comparable qualifications.

***(vii)* Images become Distracting:** On occasion, the visuals themselves can be distracting and impair learning.

THE INDIAN EXPERIENCE: A HISTORICAL PERSPECTIVE

It is our intention to give you an overview of experiments in technology within the context of a developing country. We present some specific Indian cases below.

***(i)* Secondary School Television Project (1961):** In Delhi, school television programmes were first introduced in October 1961 on an experimental basis with three physics and chemistry classes each week and one lesson each in English and Hindi for Class XI.

***(ii)* Delhi Agriculture Television (DATV Project: Krishi Darshan (1966):** Encouraged by the success of the school telecast, Krishi Darshan, an experimental TV programme, was launched on January 26, 1966, with the goal of providing farmers with agricultural knowledge.

***(iii)* Satellite Instructional Television Experiment (SITE) (1975):** On August 1, 1975, SITE, one of the largest techno-social experiments ever done in human communication, was launched for a year. It is a turning point in the employment of cutting-edge technology for education. The major goals of this project, which was carried out in 2330 villages throughout six states, were to investigate how rural communication currently operates, how television functions as a new educational medium and how community television is changing rural society. A lot of people in the most remote locations might be reached with the new technology, as demonstrated by SITE. Two types of programmes were telecast:

(i) Developmental educational programmes in the fields of agriculture and related subjects, health, family planning and social education were broadcast in the evening for community viewing.

(ii) The school programmes, each lasting 22 1/2 minutes, were broadcast each school day for rural primary school students in the age range of 5 to 12 years in Hindi, Kannada, Oriya and Telugu.

***(iv)* Post-Site Project (1977):** A new SITE continuity project was initiated in March, 1977 when a terrestrial transmitter was commissioned at Jaipur. Developmental programmes were telecast by this project.

***(v)* Indian National Satellite (INSAT) (1982):** The introduction of satellite technology has significantly boosted educational television. Launched on April 10, 1982, the domestic multipurpose satellite INSAT-1A was ruled useless on September 6, 1982. Later, on October 15, 1983, INSAT-1 B, which had been launched on August 30th, 1983, was completely operational. ETV broadcasts, however, were launched and continued by terrestrial broadcasting from August 15, 1982 in Orissa and Andhra Pradesh as part of the INSAT for Education programme.

***(vi)* UGC—Higher Education Television Project (1984):** On August 15, 1984, the UGC-INSAT educational television initiative, commonly known as "nationwide classroom", was launched. The University Grants Commission actively manages the development and production of the programmes. Under this programme, an hour-long English programme covering a range of topics is offered with the aim of providing general enrichment for undergraduates, the educated public and teachers as well. These initiatives are designed to raise the standard of higher education and foster engaging learning environments.

SOME RECENT DEVELOPMENTS IN COMMUNICATION TECHNOLOGY

Satellite based Comunication

Some cutting-edge technological technologies are used by developed nations in their educational institutions. In 1975, the first educational project in India was conducted to take advantage of satellites' potential for information dissemination. The experiment, known as SITE, proved that satellite-based television programmes may also reach the most isolated rural populations. After that, INSAT-1A and INSAT-1B gave India's distance education programmes the tools they needed to grow. The following are some of the primary benefits of satellite-based communication systems:

***(i)* Geographical Coverage:** Satellite communication has shown to be especially beneficial and efficient. It can transmit TV signals over long distances, including via mountains, where a terrestrial system is unable to operate.

***(ii)* Modernization:** It is particularly effective in encouraging quicker social change growth in underdeveloped nations. It has widened the door for innovation and change, hastening the modernization process.

***(iii)* Immediacy in Implementation:** The preparation and execution of educational innovations take a minimum amount of time. Any educational programme's implementation time can be shortened by it.

***(iv)* Cost Effectiveness:** A more affordable alternative to the current terrestrial educational system is offered by satellite technology because of the satellite's ability to cover big areas over great distances.

Videotapes

The use of videotape technology offers all the benefits of television, while doing away with its main drawback—imposing a strict time schedule on viewers. Additionally, for learners who rely on spoken words and visual images for communication, the videotape may be a useful medium. When needed, educational videotapes can be used in a variety of teaching-learning contexts and preserved for later use. Due to the user-controlled presentation of the media, videotape offers variable learning opportunities. Students can keep track of the repetition of the course material according to their own learning speed.

Compressed Video Technology

A standard for digital transmission of video signals is video compression technology. With the use of compression, eight programmes might now broadcast simultaneously in the same area as one. As a result, satellite stations may now broadcast more content, while utilising less space. It is referred to as a "codec" (short for compression and decompression) instrument. A video camera's analogue signals are transformed into digital signals via a codec.

TELEVISION BROADCASTS

In comparison to other media, television transmission has unequivocally demonstrated better effectiveness as an agent for social reform. The television broadcast is increasingly playing a significant role in distance teaching and learning systems in both developed and developing nations. It is utilised by the vast majority of open colleges for their online students. In this way, India is not an exception. Since its inception, television has been seen as a powerful tool for education and national development. Additionally, the television broadcast is unquestionably a stronger instrument in the hands of educators and media planners to bring about the necessary changes in society due to its enormous viewership, which includes the general public.

Variety of Television Broadcasts

There can be a variety of educational television broadcast delivery systems. The three main varieties are as follows:

***(i)* Live Broadcast:** Advanced broadcasting technology is needed for live broadcast. More live broadcasts may now be possible in our nation, thanks to the DJSAT. In India, live transmission is not frequently used for educational purposes. However, it is very helpful for educational programmes that do not have clear learning objectives but still have educational value, such as those that use renowned people to speak to pupils or provide information on current events. Live broadcasting allows for the presentation of far clearer visual imagery than is otherwise feasible.

Limitations: Live broadcast has the following limitations:

In our situation, it is quite challenging for all of the pupils to watch the same programme at the same time. It is challenging to offer print supplemental resources that the students could use in conjunction with the live broadcast. It is challenging to plan a suitable conversation on the topic because the teacher is unable to preview the live broadcast.

***(ii)* Recorded Broadcast:** Pre-recorded shows are broadcast in accordance with the transmission schedule. The currently available educational television services rely primarily on already generated content. Although, it is typically the convenience of the broadcasting agency that prevails, recording offers the ability to plan and produce programmes according to the convenience of the producers and to transmit during times that are convenient for students or educational institutions. Such programmes can be carefully prepared and assessed at each level of growth. Thus, since all resources, including time, people and equipment, are used to produce recorded programmes, they may be of higher quality than live broadcasts.

***(iii)* Closed Circuit Television Broadcast (CCTV):** The pre-recorded and/or live programmes are broadcast over a closed-circuit television system under this technology. Closed circuit television uses cables installed in a building to transmit educational programmes as the medium between the studio and a number of classes. A transmission from any of the classroom studios is possible because to the system's ability to connect several classrooms or institutions. In India nowadays, the method is employed in commercial institutions like hotels and train stations but not for educational purposes.

Difficulties in Using Television Broadcasts

Here are some of the challenges associated with using TV broadcasts to provide information.

***(i)* Inadequate Coverage:** In India, only 81.5% of the population has access to television. However, a sizable portion of students are unable to hear the transmission. Many households are unable to purchase televisions.

***(ii)* Complexity of Viewers:** Both scholars and programme producers find it difficult to understand the viewers of TV shows. It is challenging to create a programme that is equally satisfying for the audience and the students.

***(iii)* High Transmission Costs:** Another significant barrier is the high expense of using broadcast technology.

***(iv)* Insufficient Time:** Given the abundance of courses offered by open universities, more transmission time is needed.

***(v)* Inappropriate Telecast Timings:** It is very difficult to find the appropriate telecasting time for all the students in the regular transmission slots.

Status of Television

Many South American countries only have one agency, either the government or the public service, that provides a broadcasting service to the entire country. While some countries have hundreds of private commercial broadcasting organisations, many others only have one. India currently has one of the largest television networks in the world. According to estimates, 90% of the nation's population will be served by Doordarshan. In contrast to barely 25% in 1981, it now covers 81.5% of the population, including a sizeable population in rural areas. In India today, there are 529 transmitters in operation. The number of TV sets increased from 41 in 1962 to around 2,78,200 in 1990.

The rapid spread of TV networks in India is due in part to the availability of the necessary equipment as well as the variety of programmes and longer transmission times. The Doordarshan broadcasts programmes in seventeen Indian languages, including English, to fulfil its primary objectives of informing, educating and entertaining the nation's multilingual and multiethnic population, as well as its diverse social, political and economic systems, particularly the rural-urban divide. Two different services have been used to make this possible:

***(i)* Regional Service:** The regional language programmes are shown in the nights to accommodate the people living within each television centre's effective coverage area, which includes both rural and urban areas. These include instructive and educational programmes targetted at both general and niche groups, such as children, young people, women, farmers and industrial workers. Additionally, local programmes that educate viewers about and make them aware of different regional developmental challenges are broadcast regionally. Educational programmes are also broadcast in the appropriate regional languages to support pupils.

***(ii)* National service:** Daily telecasts from Delhi are provided via a common national service and are concurrently carried by all transmitters spread across the nation. Higher education programmes are included in this service along with local, national and international news updates. Doordarshan currently has six channels. A network of more than 700 terrestrial transmitters presently provides access to doordarshan programming to more than 85% of the nation's 900 million residents. The Indian television landscape is currently covered by satellite networks. People have access to about 30 satellite channels.

VIDEO CASSETTES

The television broadcast is thought to be less effective than the video cassette. Because students have complete control over their speed of learning in terms of the time and location at which they use the video cassettes, they are more flexible and convenient in their use. Furthermore, the replay feature has improved its suitability for personalised learning. The usage of video programmes in the classroom is beneficial both for in-person instruction and for remote learning.

Videotape: Types and Standards

There are typically two types of videotapes: VHS and U-matic. While the latter is the preferred option for master copies because of its greater quality, the former is typically employed for mass distribution. The videotapes are available in PAL, SECAM and NTSC, three different colour standards: one videotape recorder cannot play the tape of another standard because both standards are incompatible with one another.

PAL (Phase Alternate Line): This is the system employed in Britain.

NTSC: This is the US standard, which stands for National Television.

Standards Committee: In both PAL and NTSC, the three primary colours (red, green, blue) from which all the other colours are made, are transmitted simultaneously.

SECAM: This is the French standard. It stands for Sequential Couleur a Memoire. As the name suggests, SECAM does not transmit the primary colours simultaneously, it transmits them in sequence.

Strengths and Weaknesses of Video Cassettes

In comparison to television transmissions, video cassette technology has its own advantages for distance learners. The practical benefits and some of the disadvantages of video cassettes.

The video cassette offers structured learning and considerably reduces the amount of study time needed.

***(i)* Minimum Time:** The ability to request knowledge or information repeatedly gives us the ability to get what we need. Saving time, money and resources is made possible by using video cassettes for learning.

***(ii)* Multiple Mode Communication:** The content can be delivered in engaging ways to keep students' attention and hence motivate them. This can assist the students retain and recall knowledge they are exposed to through the programmes. Additionally, there are other ways to watch video cassettes that are not constrained by defined viewing times.

***(iii)* Standard:** All students are exposed to the same high-quality material in the same manner.

***(iv)* Flexibility:** Individualized instruction is made possible by cassette technology. The medium and hence the rate of learning, is under the students' control. You can pause and repeat a tape as often and for as long as you need to.

***(v)* Case Study:** case study may be reordered, depending on the location. Through the movie, each stage of the case's development may be seen. For distance learners, learning through case studies has proven to be highly beneficial and this is possible with the use of cassettes. Additionally, the video cassette offers all the same educational benefits as a television broadcast.

Additionally, the video cassette has some flaws, particularly in the context of India. We are unable to guarantee that every distance learner will have access to replay equipment in the near future, which is necessary for using the video cassette. In order to solve this issue, study center-based learning has taken precedence over learning at home.

Video Programmes in Indira Gandhi National Open University (IGNOU)

In addition to written texts, IGNOU uses video cassette and broadcast technologies and these programmes have grown to be crucial parts of the IGNOU course materials. In order to better support its students, IGNOU anticipates seeing an increase in the use of video cassettes. Through a nationwide network of more than 350 study and job centres, cassettes are made available to pupils. For students who desire to use the programmes, audio and video cassette recorders are provided at the study centres. Efforts are being made to design programmes allowing enhanced control to students such as:

- Clear stopping points
- Use of learning activities
- Close integration with the text.

The video cassette is a recent development in instructional technology, which aims to overcome some of the limitations of television broadcast.

FUTURE TRENDS IN EDUCATIONAL TELEVISION

Various specialists, either as individuals or as representatives of institutions, have conducted a few trials on educational television. Effective tactics can be developed to make the best use of this medium based on the empirical data that is already available.

***(i)* Research:** This could point us in the direction of more effective teaching-learning techniques for television. Long-term research activities should be acknowledged by educational institutions. To accommodate our unique circumstances, we must create research models.

***(ii)* Training:** In our nation, little thought has been devoted to teaching the staff about the function of television and how to use it for educational purposes. When creating and using television for educational purposes, human resource development and training are crucial elements.

***(iii)* Software:** This development is a significant challenge for educators all over the world. Here, the television programmes are referred to as the software. India needs affordable, high-quality software that requires commitment and a sense of teamwork from the agencies and workers involved in the project.

***(iv)* Two-way Systems:** These systems are gaining popularity. Therefore, a system must be created to turn the television into a two-way communication device.

***(v)* The Current Scenario:** The proliferation of information technology and the accessibility and widespread use of electronic media are now recognised as global phenomena. However, in the context of emerging nations, the focus should be on utilising these resources for economic development and socio-political stability.

TELETEXT AND VIDEOTEXT

Making education more accessible to a significant portion of the population is one of the key goals of an open learning institution. The availability of teletext and videotext resources at residential, community and study centres can increase the accessibility and vibrancy of distance learning. The information that will be provided by the college is immediately available to the pupils.

Teletext

The term "teletext" refers to the digitised signals used to transmit pages of text across a broadcast media. It transforms the typical television receiver into a computer interface that can retrieve text and graphics from a distant database. Teletext employs television hardware but limits what it shows to text and visuals for its audience. Teletext operates on straightforward tenets. Similar to textbook pages, a distance database stores a number of pages of text or visuals. The digitised text messages or informational pages are circulated continually in a cycle. The teletext service and the regular programming on a particular channel can be switched between using a control pad, which is commonly found on a remote control device. A viewer can view all the messages in a cycle.

Advantages of Teletext

Its advantages for distance teaching are:

- It makes use of the televisions that are already in homes or community centres.
- Information is considerably more readily available because to it.
- It's simple to edit and update the teletext script. Data can be modified instantly.
- The teletext's concise and useful content makes learning more engaging and less taxing.
- With the aid of this technology, information regarding courses, careers and employment prospects may be simply transmitted.
- It is helpful for disseminating knowledge about industries, libraries and agricultural farm management. These organisations may become more effective and economical as a result.

Teletext Application in India

Delhi Doordarshan launched the teletext service in India on November 14, 1985. Its name is "INTEXT" (meaning Indian teletext). Teletext services provide information about news stories, sporting events, financial trends, the arrival and departure times of significant trains, the weather forecast, city events and AIR and TV programmes that will be broadcast. Four hotlines connecting the teletext information room to the meteorological department, the northern railway central enquiry, the Indian Airlines enquiry (for domestic departure) and the Air Traffic Control are used to collect the information (for international arrivals).

Teletext service can thus, be used to deliver additional information, utilising the current television broadcast.

Videotext

In two-way interactive videotext, users can send requests to a central database from students and other users. A huge master computer meets all of the users' demands at once. Teletext, in contrast, is a one-way system where signals are sent from a source to a user who may then read the desired information on a television stream. Videotext is far more expensive and comprehensive than teletext. While videotext provides more specialised information, teletext typically emphasises the information with broadcast appeals (such as weather, sports and news headlines) (e.g., educational features, financial data, classified advertisements).

In contrast to teletext, which sends a single set of electronic text to all users at once, videotext enables students to ask questions of or request information from databases or other sources to obtain specific information. A student can choose the text they need from the continuously cycling pages of data that appear on the screen by using a special fixture attached to the receiver. The phrases "videotext" and "teletext" are interchangeable when referring to videotext. As a result, one shouldn't be perplexed by their application.

Technology of Videotext

A system for interactive information retrieval is called videotext. Videotext enables the home television to perform the same functions as a computer terminal, retrieving text and graphics from a distant database. As a result, these technologies provide affordable residential power. A keypad or keyboard, a TV display unit, a decoder, a telecommunication link (modem) and a central computer housing a database make up the fundamental components of a videotext system. Access to the computerised information is made possible by videotext using the telephone and television. The keypad, a compact frame with numeric buttons, is used to ask a remote computer for pages of necessary data.

The television is attached to the computer via a telephone line and when the recordings are played, a decoder adapts the television so that they are displayed on a videotext. The home television set is converted into a terminal in this way. The decoder enables a TV to show text and graphics from digital signals sent over the phone line and to communicate information keyed into a keypad back to the user. The computer and the decoder can communicate digitally over phone lines intended for speech, thanks to a modem.

Applications of Video Text

There are several uses for videotext, including word games, teaching a second language and deaf training. Videotext can be utilised in remote learning for the transmission and two-way exchange of general or specialised information. The level of knowledge of potential students about a topic or subject can be determined by using a videotext system, which is especially helpful for general information on programmes and courses. As they could access the type and volume of knowledge currently found in areas with huge libraries, the system with a considerable can be very beneficial to students in remote locations. Due to its lack of a time schedule, videotext has an advantage over other time-bound communication mediums like radio, television and telephone.

Limitations of Videotext

While the videotext system includes graphic capabilities, it does not include audio. Its cost-effectiveness cannot be determined because it is still in the experimental stage. The success of this technology in developing countries remains in doubt. Until both the institution and the students create the necessary infrastructure, the use of videotext and teletext will be limited.

OPTICAL DISCS

High storage capacity optical discs are utilised as interactive media. Additionally, it has the ability to function as a complete multimedia technology with text, voice, pictures and full motion video. There are two types of optical discs: digital video discs and compact disc read-only memory. The amount of data that can be stored on a CD-ROM, 60 MB, is roughly 475 high density floppies. In other words, it can hold around 70 minutes of audio, about 23 minutes of video, or about 275,000 A4-size pages of text. DVDs, on the other hand, can hold around 300 minutes of video, or about 8GB of data. Typically, a DVD can store between 3.95 GB of information each side and as it supports two ROMDVD is 12cm in diameter and a total of 7.9GB can be stored in a single DVD.

Characteristics of Video Disc

The following are some qualities of video discs and their educational implications:

(i) **Automatic Frame Stop:** The first frame on the disc is the start of a formal instructional sequence, to which the student may be requested to reply. The microprocessor unit inside the video disc player allows for this capacity.

(ii) **Frame Number:** Students can conduct research because each (image) has a unique frame number.

(iii) **Dual Audio Tracks** are a possibility for the video disc.

(iv) **Adjustable Forward and Reverse Timing:** The pupils can watch any sequence in slow motion in order to better understand it and pick up some of the information.

(v) **Still Frame:** By concentrating on still images, the video disc allows pupils to pay closer attention to specific details.

(vi) **Chapter Stop:** Chapters are predetermined locations that can be reached by using the fast forward and backward functions.

(vii) **Interaction:** Students can engage with the subject at their own pace and according to their own preferences, thanks to the video disc and the computer.

Limitations of Video Disc:

(i) The absence of the courseware, without which the video disc is of limited utility in education, is one restriction on using the video disc in distant learning.

(ii) It needs really advanced machinery. The price of the tools and textbooks is very high.

(iii) It is unable to re-record television shows.

Advantages of Video Disc

Video can be used at a low cost if the discs are mass made. Additionally, the discs take up less space in storage. These two elements enable the collection of a large course library on compact discs. The discs also make it simple to access and retrieve the content of our choice. Rapid frame search is made possible by the random access function. The video disc can be utilised to boost student productivity by providing more material in appealing presentation modes, quick access (forward and backward) to various disc sections and the ability to repeat lessons to master them.

Courseware Development

The laser beam technique is used for both writing to and reading from video discs. Premastering is the term used to describe the advised procedure for the video disc formats. There are four steps in this. Putting the information together for the disc is the first step. The second stage of the material evaluation process involves employing specialised electrical equipment to imitate the functioning of a video disc player before disc mastering and duplication. The effectiveness of the content is assessed in relation to the instructional design goals by a representative target audience. The final modification is the coding instructions for the video disc, which are made in the third stage. After then, copies of the master video disc are made for wide dissemination. Because of the high cost of making the master disc, the cost effectiveness of the video disc depends on the market size.

ACTIVITIES

Q. 1. Undertake the following small survey on television broadcasts. Take an appropriate sample of ten respondents and ask them the following three questions:

(i) **What is the most suitable time for you to view the educational programmes?**

(ii) In which language would you prefer to view the educational television programme?

(iii) What are the weaknesses of the television as an educational medium?

Analyse the responses, *i.e.*, data and compare and discuss your findings with those of other students during a contact programme or measure them with the details and discussions presented in the unit.

Ans. *(i)* Most of the respondents (six) say the most suitable time to view the educational programmes is the evening time. Four say, they can watch it in the afternoon.

(ii) Seven respondents say they want the educational television programmes in their mother tongue – Hindi, while three respondents say – the language should be English.

(iii) On the weakness of the television as an educational medium, the respondents provided different points. The weaknesses are:

(a) **Inappropriate telecast timings:** The educational programmes are telecast at odd time during the day when the students are in their schools and colleges or when they are busy with their study.

(b) **Inadequate coverage:** Many respondents say the TV coverage is not sufficient and they do not rely on it for the study.

(c) **Language is an issue:** Many want that the programme should be telecast in Hindi or their mother tongue.

(d) **Insufficient time:** More transmission time is required because TV telecasts minimal topics.

CHECK YOUR PROGRESS

Q. 1. Briefly comment on the common objective behind the projects listed above.

Ans. The common objective is to assist students in learning their courses effectively in order for the country to develop and thrive.

(i) On an experimental basis, the secondary school television project started in Delhi in October 1961 with three physics and chemistry lessons each week, as well as one session in each of English and Hindi for Class XI. These shows were broadcast during school hours and adhered to the curriculum as an essential component of learning. The use of television in the educational system was meant to improve instruction due to a lack of suitable science laboratories, equipment, and space as well as a paucity of qualified science professors. The initiative served as an experiment to determine what may be done to alleviate the special difficulties higher secondary schools in Delhi, particularly those related to the teaching of science, encounter.

(ii) On January 26, 1966, an experimental TV show called Krishi Darshan was introduced with the intention of educating farmers about agriculture. This was motivated by the success of the school telecast. In the union territory of Delhi, there are public viewing sites in 80 villages. The experiment was successful, and there was a considerable increase in understanding about agricultural practises, according to the research on "Krishi Darshan".

(iii) One of the most extensive techno-social experiments in human communication, SITE, was established for a year on August 1, 1975. The use of cutting-edge technology in education has reached a tipping point. The main objectives of this project, which was conducted in 2330 villages throughout six states, were to look at the existing state of rural communication, the use of television as a new educational tool, and the impact of community television on rural society. A lot of individuals in the most remote locations might be reached with the new technology, as demonstrated by SITE. There were two kinds of programmes broadcast:

For rural primary school pupils in the age range of 5 to 12, 224-minute instructional programmes in Hindi, Kannada, Oriya, and Telugu were broadcast each school day. These programmes emphasised social education, health, family planning, and development in the fields of agriculture and associated fields. The goal of school television programmes was to "help the youngsters realise that science is omnipresent and that they may question, understand, explain, and influence their environment using scientific method." In rural primary classrooms, television was welcomed since it was valued as a teaching tool.

(iv) As a terrestrial transmitter was put into service in Jaipur in March 1977, a brand-new SITE continuity project was launched. This initiative broadcast developmental programmes. The primary goals of the SITE continuity project were to *(i)* familiarise the rural populace with the improved and scientific knowledge of farming, the use of fertilisers, and the maintenance of health and hygiene; *(ii)* promote national and emotional integration; and *(iii)* make rural children aware of the value of education and a healthy environment.

(v) Educational television has grown tremendously since satellite technology was introduced. The domestic multifunctional satellite INSAT-1A, which was sent into orbit on April 10, 1982, was declared unusable on September 6, 1982. Subsequently, on October 15th, 1983, the August 30th, 1983 launch of INSAT-1 B was fully operational. Nevertheless, as part of the INSAT for Education initiative, ETV transmissions began and were carried on by terrestrial broadcasting starting on August 15, 1982, in Orissa and Andhra Pradesh. Six other states—Andhra Pradesh, Bihar, Gujarat, Maharashtra, Orissa, and U.P.—were added to the INSAT service later, in June 1983. Based on their level of deprivation, the existence of suitable development infrastructure, and their ability to utilise existing industrial facilities, a group of three to four districts in each state were picked.

The INSAT service's main objective is to integrate rural and underdeveloped areas into the nation's mainstream by accelerating development efforts there with media assistance. The service's objective is to keep rural residents informed of the most recent developments in agricultural production, cleanliness, and health. Every day, educational television programmes (ETV) are broadcast for two different age groups of schoolchildren (5-8 years and 9-11 years), as well as community viewing developmental programmes. A 45-minute capsule that alternates between two unique shows, one for a younger audience and the other for an older audience, is regularly shown. Each programme has a time slot of twenty minutes, with a five-minute break between each age group.

These ETV programmes are now being shown in Oriya, Telugu, Marathi, Gujarati, and Hindi for a huge audience of elementary school pupils. The northern belt's Hindi-speaking states all get programming in that language.

(vi) In 1984, the UGC-Higher Education Television Programme (HE Tv) began. The UGC-INSAT educational television programme, also referred to as "nation wide classroom," was introduced on August 15, 1984. The creation and production of the programmes are actively managed by the University Grants Commission. This programme offers an hour-long English programme on a variety of topics with the intention of educating undergraduates, the educated public, and teachers alike.

These programmes aim to improve higher education standards and provide stimulating learning environments.

A network of over 20 audio-visual media Mass Communication Research Centers have been formed at various colleges across the country, and the UGC has established an inter-university Consortium for Educational Communication (CEC) to assist this effort. Along with the programmes developed at these centres, some are imported from other countries and modified to suit the needs of Indian students.

The "country-wide classroom" programmes are designed to increase their impact while enriching, modernising, and improving education. The shows are designed to peak viewers' curiosity, whet their appetite, and broaden their outlooks. Instead of satisfying, they are intended to provoke.

Q. 2. Attempt to list down the considerations that make satellites relevant to the Indian situation.

Ans. The following are some reasons why satellites are important to the Indian situation:

***(i)* Geographical Coverage:** Satellite communication has proven particularly helpful and effective in poor countries where geographical and other considerations make it difficult to construct a statewide network. It can transmit TV signals over long distances, including via mountains, where a terrestrial system is unable to operate.

***(ii)* Motivation for Modernization:** Satellite communication technology is highly useful in fostering quicker social change growth in poorer nations. The communication infrastructure has opened the door for innovation and change, hastening the process of modernization, by bringing the world to the villages through television.

***(iii)* Immediate Implementation:** Because the satellite communication system is centralised, it only needs a short period of time to develop and put new educational initiatives into place. Any educational programme's implementation time can be shortened by it.

***(iv)* Cost-effectiveness:** Satellite technology offers an alternate educational system that is less expensive than the terrestrial system due to the satellite's ability to cover big areas across great distances. Since the price of sending signals is independent of geography, rural villages can be reached for the same price as those in more centralised areas without having to pay additional fees for cables, station construction, etc.

Q. 3. List at least four advantages, which recorded programmes have over live television broadcasts.

Ans. Pre-recorded shows are broadcast in accordance with the transmission schedule. The country's current educational television services rely primarily on already generated content. These programmes are built around a set of precise goals that the students must attain. Although, it is typically the convenience of the broadcasting agency that prevails, recording offers the ability to plan and produce programmes according to the convenience of the producers and to transmit during times that are convenient for students or educational institutions. Such programmes can be carefully prepared and assessed at each level of growth. For instance, formative evaluation might be done when the programmes are still in the planning stages. Thus recorded programmes could be of a better quality than live broadcasts because all facilities in terms of time, manpower equipment, etc., are exploited for producing these programmes.

Q. 4. What are the strengths of the video cassette? List any four.

Ans. Compared to television transmissions, the video cassette technology has its own benefits for distance learners.

***(i)* Minimum Time:** he video cassette offers structured learning and considerably reduces the amount of study time needed. Because of this feature of the video cassette, the programmes are more suited for educational reasons. It takes little time to provide the necessary knowledge. The ability to request knowledge or information repeatedly gives us the ability to get what we need. Saving time, money and resources is made possible by using video cassettes for learning.

***(ii)* Communication in Multiple Modes:** The video programmes can be shown in a variety of ways. The content can be presented in engaging ways to keep students' interest and as a result, motivate them. This can assist students remember the information offered in the programmes. Video cassettes can also be viewed in a variety of ways that are not limited by specified watching times, unlike television.

***(iii)* Common Content:** Subject-matter specialists created the video cassettes. The curriculum is delivered to all pupils in the same manner and is of the same calibre. Otherwise, face-to-face instruction would only allow a select few kids to receive a high quality education because not all teachers are equally qualified.

***(iv)* Flexibility:** Individualized instruction is made possible by cassette technology. The medium and hence the rate of learning, is under the students' control. A tape can be paused and played back as often and for as long as is necessary.

A case study may be reordered depending on the location. The movie can be used to show how the case was handled at each stage. For remote learners, learning through case studies has been quite successful and using of cassettes can assist make this happen. The video cassette offers all the same educational benefits as a television broadcast.

Additionally, the video cassette has some flaws, particularly in the context of India. We are unable to guarantee that every distance learner will have access to replay equipment in the near future, which is necessary for using the video cassette. Therefore, relying solely on video cassette technology is not recommended. A tape replay machine's price and lack of availability in the homes of the majority of students are significant obstacles to its widespread adoption. In order to solve this issue, study center-based learning has taken precedence over learning at home. In other words, we must rely on the collective viewing of video content.

The study centres make the video cassette recorders available for viewing. It is possible to counter that giving students in a large country like India, easy access to study centres is difficult. Therefore, there are some restrictions associated with using the video cassettes through the network of study centres. Experience has shown that only approximately a third of the enrolled students actually use the resources at the study centres.

Q. 5. Keeping in view the current scenario and future trends in educational television, list three important areas which need urgent and sustained attention from academics and electronic media specialists.

Ans. Since television was first used in the educational setting, there has been much debate over whether or not it helps pupils think. The topic is still up for discussion. However, there is sufficient research to support the claim that watching TV helps pupils learn, improving their focus, understanding, assimilation and application of new information. Given that the public uses television primarily as an entertainment medium, connecting television to education is a challenge. It should assume the position of a teacher, as desired. However, children who have always learned through print media might not feel at ease using television as a teaching tool. In order to get the most of TV use, it is required to persuade students and professors (including those who teach remotely). The students need to be prepared to learn from television. For this, the television and video programming must be engaging, visually stunning, interactive and focused on user needs. Various specialists, either as individuals or as representatives of institutions, have conducted a few trials on educational television. We can plan and develop effective ways to make the best use of this medium based on the empirical evidence now available in India and in those nations that have successfully used television in the service of education but nothing noteworthy has emerged so far. We must also consider some of its drawbacks, in order to ensure proper use of television in the future for educational purposes. Let's talk about a couple of them.

***(i)* Research:** The most neglected section is this one. We haven't yet been able to effectively focus our thinking and mobilise our resources to create a scientific connection between research and the efficient use of this media in our circumstance. We all have a big duty to do comprehensive formative and summative research studies as we design, produce and use television as a learning tool.

This might enable us to come up with better TV-based teaching and learning methods. Long-term research activities should be acknowledged by educational institutions. Instead of relying on research studies carried out in western nations where the surroundings, both educational and technical, are different from ours, we need to construct research models to suit our own conditions. Besides, research will help us to produce programmes, which are suited to the requirement of the target students. The programmes will be able to reflect our social reality and meet actual educational needs.

***(ii)* Training:** In our nation, little thought has been devoted to teaching the staff about the function of television and how to use it for educational purposes. When creating and using television for educational purposes, human resource development and training are crucial elements. The bulk of those working in educational television are insufficiently skilled. All persons participating in distance education require thorough training, both in theory and in practice, prior to entering the workforce and regarding television-mediated education. More experts are needed to oversee the televised instruction at various educational levels if we wish to use television on a wide scale. This can be achieved only if adequate infrastructure for training is created to meet the increasing demands for skilled human power.

***(iii)* Software:** For educators worldwide, creating software is a significant challenge. Here, the television programmes are referred to as the software. India needs affordable, high-quality software, which calls for creative planning, commitment and a sense of teamwork from the agencies and workers involved in the project. Because of how quickly technology is advancing, we have not been able to give software development the attention it deserves. It is past time for us to focus our efforts on creating suitable software banks.

***(iv)* Two-way Systems:** We are gradually transitioning from a single print medium to fresh, engaging non-print media, which should guarantee the students' active engagement. Interactive two-way systems are gaining popularity. In the not-too-distant future, interactive technologies are anticipated to rule the distance-learning mode. Therefore, a system must be created to turn television into an efficient two-way communication tool in situations like ours. We are completely aware that the interactive systems cost more and the distribution systems become intricate and challenging to operate as we make this suggestion. We are also aware that we cannot employ the systems on a wide scale because the nation lacks a suitable technological infrastructure. But we must not lose sight of the fact that pupils will learn more effectively when there is two-way pedagogic contact. Therefore, we must start moving in this direction, no matter how modestly.

(v) **The Current Scenario:** The proliferation of information technology and the accessibility and widespread use of electronic media are now recognised as global phenomena. The emphasis should instead be on using these resources to foster economic development and socio-political stability in developing nations. It is important to keep in mind the enormous reach and educational potential of the electronic media.

Q. 6. On the basis of what you have studied in this section, list three disadvantages/limitations of teletext.

Ans. Its disadvantages are:

(a) This is not easily accessible to learners. Only a small number of centres have access to the equipment that produces the output.

(b) Due to its page count restriction, it is unable to offer all relevant information on a subject.

(c) The machine cannot store abundant.

However, it has a number of benefits: It's simple to edit and update the teletext script. Data can be modified instantly. The teletext's concise and useful content makes learning more engaging and less taxing. With the aid of this technology, information regarding courses, careers and employment prospects may be simply transmitted. It is helpful for disseminating knowledge about industries, libraries and agricultural farm management. These organisations may become more effective and economical as a result.

Q. 7. Distinguish videotext from teletext by listing at least four characteristics of the former.

Ans. Students and other users can transmit requests to a central database via videotext, which is a two-way interactive communication. A massive master computer satisfies all of the users' needs at once. Teletext, however, is a one-way system in which signals are sent from a source to a user who may then read the desired information on television broadcasts.

(i) Videotext is far more expensive and comprehensive than teletext.

(ii) While videotext provides more specialised information, teletext typically emphasises the information with broadcast appeals such as weather, sports and news headlines e.g., educational features, financial data, classified advertisements.

(iii) In contrast to teletext, which sends a single set of electronic text to all users at once and requires a special fixture attached to the receiver in order for a student to select the necessary pages of the text from the continuously cycling pages of data appearing on the screen, videotext enables students to ask questions of or request information from databases or sources in order to obtain specific information.

(iv) The phrases "videotext" and "teletext" are interchangeable when referring to videotext. As a result, one shouldn't be perplexed by their application.

Q. 8. How does use of video disc enhance learning?

Ans. If the CDs are produced in bulk, video may be utilised at a reasonable cost. The CDs also take up less room in storage. These two components make it possible to compile a sizable course library on CDs. Also, accessing and retrieving the content of our choosing is made simple by the discs. The random access function enables fast frame search. By offering more content in engaging presentation styles, rapid access (forward and backward) to multiple disc parts, and the option to repeat lectures until you understand them, the video disc may be used to increase student productivity. It also has a large storage capacity, is portable, and is easily available in all stores. At the moment, inexpensive, mass-produced DVDs have high data stability. They are suitable for sound and video because of their excellent audio and video quality.

OTHER IMPORTANT QUESTIONS

Q. 1. Discuss different types of TV broadcasts. What are the difficulties in using television broadcasts?

Ans. Television broadcasting has categorically shown greater effectiveness as a social reform tool than other media. In both industrialised and developing countries, the television broadcast is becoming an increasingly important component of distance learning and teaching systems. For their online students, the vast majority of open colleges use it. India is not an exception in this regard. Television has long been seen as a potent medium for education and societal advancement. Due to its massive audience, which includes the general public, television broadcasts are certainly a stronger tool in the hands of educators and media planners to bring about the required changes in society.

There are numerous delivery methods for instructional television broadcasts. The three main varieties are as follows:

(i) **Live Broadcast:** For live broadcast, sophisticated broadcasting technology is required. Thanks to the DJSAT, more live broadcasts might now be feasible in our country. Live broadcasts are not typically used for educational purposes in India. It is very helpful, though, for educational programmes that don't have definite learning goals but nevertheless have educational value, including those that invite well-known figures to talk to students or deliver news about current events. Live streaming makes it possible to show much clearer visual imagery than would otherwise be possible.

Live broadcast has the following limitations: The students in our position find it difficult to watch the same programme at the same time. Offering print extra materials that students could utilise in conjunction with the live broadcast is difficult. The teacher cannot preview the live broadcast, making it difficult to prepare a meaningful dialogue on the subject.

(ii) **Recorded Broadcast:** Shows that have already been recorded are aired in accordance with the transmission schedule. The educational television services that are currently offered, rely mostly on pre-produced content. Even though it is usually the broadcasting agency's convenience that takes precedence, recording allows producers to plan and produce programmes according to their own convenience and transmit at times that are convenient

for students or educational institutions. At each stage of growth, such programmes can be properly planned and evaluated. Recorded programming may therefore be of higher quality than live broadcasts because all resources, including time, personnel and equipment, are utilised to create it.

***(iii)* Closed Circuit Television (CCTV) Broadcast:** Under this technology, prerecorded and/or live programmes are sent via a closed-circuit television system. Cables connected in a building are used by closed circuit television to broadcast instructional programmes between the studio and various courses. The system's capacity to connect many classrooms or institutions enables a transmission from any of the classroom studios. Currently in India, the strategy is used in for-profit establishments like hotels and train stations but not in educational ones.

Here are a few difficulties in using TV broadcasts to disseminate information:

***(i)* Insufficient Coverage:** Only 81.5% of Indians have access to television. A significant number of students, though, are unable to hear the message. Many households lack the funds necessary to buy televisions.

***(ii)* Consumer Complexity:** It might be challenging for academics and programme creators to comprehend TV viewers. Making a programme that is equally gratifying for the audience and the kids is difficult.

***(iii)* High Transmission Costs:** The high cost of using broadcast technology is another key impediment.

***(iv)* Not Enough Time:** More transmission time is required, given the variety of courses offered by open universities.

***(v)* Inappropriate Telecast Timings:** It might be very challenging to locate a time during the usual transmission intervals that works for all of the pupils.

Q. 2. What is teletext? Write its advantages and applications in Indian context.

Ans. The digitised signals used to send pages of text through a broadcast medium are referred to as "teletext". It converts a standard television receiver into an interface for a computer that can get text and images from a distant database. Teletext uses television technology but it only allows its viewers to see text and images. Teletext runs according to simple rules. A distant database stores numerous pages of text or images, much like textbook pages. The informational pages or digitised text messages are cycled continuously. A control pad, which is typically found on a remote control device, can be used to switch between the teletext service and the conventional programming on a certain channel. Viewers get access to all of the messages in a cycle.

Its advantages for distance teaching are:

- Information is much easier to access as a result of it because it uses televisions that are already in households or community centres.
- The teletext script is easy to change and update. Instant changes can be made to data. Learning is made more interesting and less tiring by the teletext's succinct and practical content.
- With the help of this technology, information on courses, careers and employment prospects may be easily transmitted.
- It is useful for spreading information about businesses, libraries and farm management. As a result, these organisations might become more efficient and cost-effective.

Application of Teletext: On November 14, 1985, Delhi Doordarshan introduced the teletext service to India. It is called "INTEXT" (meaning Indian teletext). The arrival and departure timings of significant trains, news items, athletic events, financial trends, the weather forecast, city events and upcoming AIR and TV shows are all provided by teletext services. Information is gathered via four hotlines that connect the teletext information room to the following departments: the meteorological department, the northern railway central enquiry, the Indian Airlines enquiry (for domestic departure) and the Air Traffic Control (for international arrivals).

The present television broadcast can therefore, be used to convey supplementary information via teletext service.

Q. 3. Discuss technology of video text and its applications.

Ans. Users can send requests from students and other users to a central database via two-way interactive videotext. All user demands are simultaneously met by a massive master computer. As opposed to teletext, which is a one-way system, teletext sends signals from a source to the user, who can then view the desired information on a television stream. Teletext is far less expensive and limited in scope than videotext. Teletext often emphasises the information with broadcast appeals such as weather, sports and news headlines, whereas videotext offers more specialised information e.g., educational features, financial data, classified advertisements.

With videotext, students can query databases or other sources for information to get specific answers, as opposed to teletext, which provides a single set of electronic text to all users at once. Using a particular fixture linked to the receiver, a pupil can select the text they require from the continuously cycling data pages that appear on the screen. When referring to videotext, the terms "videotext" and "teletext" are synonymous. One shouldn't be confused by their application as a result.

Videotext is a system for interactive information retrieval. With the help of videotext, a home television can carry out computer terminal-like tasks by accessing text and images from a distance database. Therefore, these technologies offer reasonably priced household power. The basic building blocks of a videotext system are a keypad or keyboard, a TV display unit, a decoder, a telecommunication link (modem) and a central computer with a database. Videotext over the phone and television enables access to the computerised data. The keypad, a small frame with numeric buttons, is used to request pages of necessary data from a distant computer.

When the recordings are played, a decoder modifies the television so that they are displayed on a videotext. The television is connected to the computer via a telephone line. In this approach, the home television set is transformed into a terminal. A TV may display text and graphics from digital signals delivered over the phone line when using a decoder and it can also transmit information entered into a keypad back to the user. A modem enables digital communication between the computer and the decoder across voice-only phone lines.

Videotext has a variety of applications, such as word games, teaching a second language and deaf education. For the transmission and two-way exchange of general or specialised information, videotext can be used in remote learning. Using a videotext system can help identify a potential student's degree of understanding about a subject or topic, which is especially useful for general information on programmes and courses.

The system with a significant can be highly helpful to students in remote locations, since they could access the type and volume of knowledge currently found in areas with enormous libraries. Videotext offers an advantage over other time-bound communication channels like radio, television and telephone due to its lack of a time schedule.

Videotext works better when used as a part of a multimedia system to convey educational content. It provides strategies for getting instructional resources to those who favour online learning. Currently, the majority of educational applications of videotext and teletext systems use a catalogue listing the courses offered or services given by the institution as their information source. Some developed countries, like the UK, France, Japan, Canada and the USA, use videotext for a variety of purposes. Some universities in Canada and the UK employ videotext to help their students who have access to a wider variety of study and research tools.

MULTIPLE CHOICE QUESTIONS

Q. 1. SITE was launched on:
(a) July 1, 1975 *(b)* August 1, 1975
(c) Sept 1, 1978 *(d)* August 1, 1978
Ans. *(b)* August 1, 1975.

Q. 2. When was UGC-INSAT educational television initiative launched?
(a) August 15, 1984 *(b)* September 15, 1984
(c) August 15, 1985 *(d)* September 15, 1984
Ans. *(a)* August 15, 1984.

Q. 3. Which of the following is known as "nation-wide classroom"?
(a) SITE *(b)* UGC-INSAT
(c) CIET *(d)* None of these
Ans. *(a)* SITE.

Q. 4. In India, only 81.5% of the population has access to:
(a) Television *(b)* Radio
(c) Internet *(d)* None of these
Ans. *(a)* Television.

Q. 5. Which of the following is a type of videotapes?
(a) VHS *(b)* U-matic
(c) Both *(a)* and *(b)* *(d)* None of these
Ans. *(c)* Both *(a)* and *(b)*.

Q. 6. PAL stands for:
(a) Primary Alternate Line
(b) Phase Alternate Line
(c) Phase Alternate Link
(d) Primary Alternate Link
Ans. *(b)* Phase Alternate Line.

Q. 7. PAL is the system employed in:
(a) Britain *(b)* America
(c) India *(d)* None of these
Ans. *(a)* Britain.

Q. 8. SECAM is the standard of:
(a) France *(b)* Britain
(c) India *(d)* America
Ans. *(a)* France.

Q. 9. SECAM stands for:
(a) Sequential Couleur Memories
(b) Serial Couleur a Memoire
(c) Sequential Couleur a Memoire
(d) None of these
Ans. *(c)* Sequential Couleur a Memoire.

Q. 10. Teletext transforms the typical television receiver into a:
(a) Computer interface
(b) Phone interface
(c) Both *(a)* and *(b)*
(d) None of these
Ans. *(a)* Computer interface.

Q. 11. Teletext employs hardware of:
(a) Television *(b)* Computer
(c) Phone *(d)* None of these
Ans. *(a)* Television.

Q. 12. ___________ launched the teletext service in India on November 14, 1985.
(a) Doordarshan Bombay
(b) Doordarshan Delhi
(c) Doordarshan Calcutta
(d) Doordarshan Madras
Ans. *(b)* Doordarshan Delhi.

Q. 13. Videotext is a:
(a) Two-way interactive medium
(b) One way platform
(c) Both *(a)* and *(b)*
(d) None of these
Ans. *(a)* Two-way interactive medium.

Q. 14. Videotext is used in:
(a) Games
(b) Teaching a second language
(c) Deaf training
(d) All of these
Ans. *(d)* All of these.

BLOCK-3: AUDIO AND VIDEO PRODUCTION (PART A)

Production of Audio-Video Programmes: An Overview

8

INTRODUCTION

The creation of audio and video programming is a human-made system in which various sub-systems and their components, including people, machines, materials and procedures, work together in harmony and synchronisation. We will cover a number of stages in making audio and video programmes in this chapter. We want to offer a specific knowledge based in the field. The main goal is to add to this body of knowledge so that you may use the various media in educational contexts. It draws attention to some important topics, including the systems approach and the production process as a team-based operation.

CHAPTER AT A GLANCE

MATERIALS PRODUCTION: A SYSTEMS APPROACH

A media package's creation is a complex task. Its complexity is primarily attributable to the variety of inputs it requires. To comprehend its fundamental structure, consider the entire production of media materials as a "system" in which numerous sub-systems and elements work in tight coordination and harmony. The phrases "system" and "in close synchronisation and harmony" need to be clarified in this context.

Systems Approach

A system is made up of a number of subsystems and components that work together as an integrated whole to accomplish some pre-established and particular goals. Systems can be classified as either natural or man-made. Natural systems include the solar system and galaxies. Machines, media, education and postal systems are a few examples of man-made systems. The creation of audio and video programming is a human-made system in which various sub-systems and their components, including people, machines, materials and procedures, work together in harmony and synchronisation.

Audio-Video Programme Production System: A production of an audio-video programme typically consists of the following two key components:

(i) The most fundamental physical assets or infrastructure, such as tools, machinery, supplies, structures, studios, or a production complex.

(ii) People or human resources: This refers to the skilled workers needed to oversee the procedure, run the machinery and offer suggestions, knowledge and services for the creation of programmes.

The amateur and professional are the two different levels of production. For a basic audio programme creation at the amateur level, all you need is a microphone, a recorder and a few blank tapes. A playback feature can be utilised to edit the recorded programme if necessary.

A camera, a recorder, a microphone, a few lights (depending on the area), some blank cassettes and a straightforward editing console are required for a video production of this calibre. Both audio and video productions demand skilled workers and highly specialised equipment at the professional level.

Major Strands of TV Production

Creating television is ultimately a collaborative activity. It functions as a cohesive system in which numerous specialists from various professions and with various backgrounds and levels of expertise interact closely with one another, pooling their talents and services to contribute to the creation of a chain effect and to ensure the overall quality of the final programme. The following actions are taken during production:

A. Programme Planning and Research:

- Ideas, briefs, synopsis, academic note for programme.
- Programme Research: re-examining of the needs of viewers, context of viewing — specific research on content and its enrichment.

B. Message Planning and Script Development:

- Programme design and presentation strategy.
- Visual possibilities of the medium.
- Selection of materials.
- Programme shape and structure-format and style.
- Story board and final script.

C. Production Planning and Scheduling:

- Planning, budgeting and scheduling of production.
- Designing the production script.
- Organising various production resources/facilities.

D. Casting and Directing Performers and Artists:

- Identifying and casting performers.
- Directing artists/talent-dry runs, rehearsals.

E. Final Production, Editing and Capsuling:

- Studio/field recording.

- Editing and capsules designing, previewing and evaluation.

F. Transmission/Differentiation:

- Designing transmission schedule.
- Telecast and circulation of programmes.

G. Utilization and Evaluation:

- Mounting utilization and evaluation studies.
- Monitoring transmission and obtaining feedback from the field.
- Feeding research findings back into the system.

PRODUCTION: A TEAM MODE APPROACH

Effective cooperation is essential to the creation of audio-visual programmes. A wide variety of specially qualified individuals with artistic, technical, managerial, communicative and other creative abilities come together, work cooperatively and contribute their particular specialties at various phases of the development of a programme in any educational media production.

Functions of the Team Members

The people working on different production jobs and those connected to programme development at various stages are crucial to the production process. Their duties and responsibilities are all more or less well defined and they all collaborate with the director or programmer at the centre of the stage.

***(a)* Producer:** The producer, who reports to the head of production or programmes, is ultimately in charge of ensuring that a programme is successfully produced. She or he oversees all activities and is involved in the production process from the conceptualization stage on, when the media curriculum is prepared and thorough programme briefs are created.

***(b)* Researcher:** The researcher conducts fundamental investigation for an audio-visual production. He conducts research on student profiles, needs analysis and script and prototype programme testing. Additionally, he creates programme briefs, which aid in the creation of the programme scripts. Thus, the researcher serves as a conduit between the production crew and the intended audience of students.

***(c)* Script-writer:** The script writer creates the programme's screenplay and makes recommendations for visuals, graphics, music and effects. According to the programme's goals and the information that is currently accessible, he writes all of the conversation. Some programme creators create their own scripts from scratch.

***(d)* Subject Specialist:** The appointment of a topic expert to provide advice on the presentation of the material, the accuracy of the facts and concepts presented in the programme is a regular and required practice in educational and technical programmes.

Professional inputs from Producers and Academics

Academics frequently serve as the foundation and launching point for the creation of instructional media products of all kinds. They create the curriculum, analyse its underlying assumptions and philosophies, set broad educational objectives, choose the right subject matter, and provide instruments and methods for measurement and evaluation. The academic community is also expected to recommend appropriate teaching-learning strategies, including the use of audio-visual materials, and to offer advice for a smooth curriculum exchange in the classroom. Nonetheless, academics and producers collaborate to build successful multi-media course packages, whether they are high-cost, technologically advanced alternatives or low-cost, less advanced ones. Together, they work to create the curriculum, arrange it, and make sure it functions properly. Similar to academics, producers and their associates work to support the teaching-learning process and try to increase its effectiveness and the learners' enjoyment of it.

Characteristics of the Team

Every individual has a unique history and received different types of schooling and professional training. Each person has perceptions and attitudes unique to his or her area. Each of them has a unique vocabulary and register. If the team members do not have a solid understanding of one another's lingo, this might very easily lead to pandemonium. The media (radio, film, and television) have developed their own vocabulary and terminology over time. It is a system of signs, signals, and acronyms that makes it possible for the members of the production team to communicate clearly with one another. This language has gained currency and recognition across the world. If we are to work in efficient coordination as a team, it is imperative that we have a working understanding of the language of film and television. In other words, teachers and academics who plan to use these media in their teaching-learning transaction should have a functional understanding of shot sizes and abbreviations, camera movements and floor manager's cues.

PROGRAMME PRODUCTION PROCESS

The process of producing a television show comprises a variety of specialised tasks and several odd jobs. Each of these jobs is complex in its own right and necessitates thorough planning in advance and careful consideration. It is important to plan, oversee, coordinate and manage a variety of production components, jobs and personnel at each stage, frequently in parallel and always within a strict time schedule. The producer is the key player and makes all the decisions during the process. He or she needs to have a thorough understanding of all of the duties, which include mastery of media terminologies, visualisation, script preparation, directing and editing techniques, budgeting both time and money and most importantly, good public relations and social intelligence to get along with many people of various backgrounds and professions.

Student Profile

The producer, scriptwriter, and other team members should have as much knowledge as they can about their target audience. We must gather important data about our students, including their age, sex, attitudes, beliefs, and aspirations; socioeconomic background; life styles (urban/rural); current knowledge and skills; language; vocabulary; literacy level; and information needs and preferences, in order to improve the effectiveness and relevance of our programmes. Knowing the circumstances in which the programmes will be heard or seen is equally crucial. For writers and producers of scripts, this type of knowledge about the target audience is highly helpful.

It helps them develop more focused student profiles, get more confidence and understanding when dealing with the communication issues of their viewers and listeners, and identify the best material and presentation forms. It also helps them formulate and refine exact learning objectives. In addition to personal field trips to representative locations for audience interviews, audience information may also be found via publications, census reports, gazetteers, research monographs, etc.

Need Assessment

Studies on needs assessment assist in identifying the precise genuine needs of the target groups and are crucial in establishing the proper educational objectives. It is easier to choose appropriate programme subjects, themes, and content sections when you are aware of the audience's specific, accurate wants. The necessary data are gathered through interviews and scheduled periods of observation during need assessment studies, which are carried out by professional research workers. It is beneficial to communicate extensively with teachers, parents, and other community groups in order to get extra information or to verify and validate already gathered data. Such need assessment studies should also engage the team's researchers, media producers, and scriptwriters since they should be aware of the overt and covert demands of their target audience for particular programmes.

Programme Briefs

Media programmes often have a concept or a topic at their core. So, the first stage in the planning and production of a media show is to identify concepts and topics. After being approved, programme concepts and topics are further examined, investigated, and extended into what is sometimes referred to as a "programme brief" or "programme outline." This framework is frequently enough to allow the playwright and producer to create a script around it. However, organisations involved in large-scale production and frequent distribution of programmes adhere to a more standardised process for creating detailed programme briefs on multiple series. A written, typewritten, or printed statement of purpose is known as a programme brief.

It acts as a foundational document that compiles all pertinent details, concepts, references, and recommendations in a logical order. Such prepared resources are readily available for producers, researchers, and scriptwriters to use when creating screenplays and programmes. The creation of programme briefs does not follow a set format. Yet typically, a radio or television program's programme brief should contain the following details:

- Title of the programme or series (working title only).
- Short content outline.
- Target audience.
- Programme length or duration.
- Programme objectives (expressed in behavioural terms), suggested therapy.
- Potential production resources.

Scriptwriting

The most crucial step in the audio and video production process is writing the screenplay. The manufacture will be carried out according to this plan. It serves as a vehicle for relaying the message or instruction. Writing scripts requires a high level of skill. In reality, it is the creative process of translating ideas into images. In this block's unit 3, further details on scriptwriting are provided.

Production Process

The producer receives the final draught of the screenplay and uses it to carry out the production of the programme. The act of producing anything is intricate and multifaceted.

Feedback and Evaluation

The creation and implementation of programmes increasingly include evaluation and feedback as a crucial component. It is currently customary to assess media projects at many levels, including the following ones:

(i) original concept or programme planning stage;

(ii) narrative board or screenplay stage; and

(iii) post-production stage (field-testing). Formative evaluation is another name for pre-production evaluation. Formative evaluation's primary goal is to test scripts and concepts for programmes while they are being created in an effort to raise the quality of the final result. The system and the components and products it is associated to get feedback from the results or feedback data obtained via such formative assessment to ensure higher quality.

Some methods of media assessment include script content analysis, programme field testing, broadcast monitoring, and programme use. Programs are rescheduled, plotlines and scripts are revised, characters are changed or added, themes of programmes are revised, other intriguing and novel ideas are introduced into programming, and holes in materials or content organisation are filled using the results of assessment. Evaluation must be incorporated into the system of media production from the very beginning. Teams responsible for developing the script and arranging the programme should comprise researchers and evaluators. In reality, there is a need for more frequent communication and interaction between assessors and producers, authors, and other production team members.

CHECK YOUR PROGRESS

Q. 1. List some of the major steps in the production process.

Ans. The major steps in the TV production process include:

1. Pre-production: This stage includes the develop-ment of the idea for the show, writing the script, casting the actors, scouting locations, and planning the overall production.

2. Production: This stage involves filming the show, which includes setting up the lighting, sound, and camera equipment, directing the actors, and capturing the footage.

3. Post-production: This stage includes editing the footage, adding special effects, color correction, sound mixing, and music composition.

4. Distribution: This stage involves distributing the final product, which could be in the form of broadcast television, streaming, DVD, or Blu-ray.

5. Marketing and Promotion: This stage involves promoting the show, which could include advertising on television, social media, and other mediums, creating trailers and teasers, and working with media outlets to generate buzz.

Broadcasting: This stage is the final step, where the show is aired on television or released on a streaming platform for viewers to watch.

Q. 2. Why is a basic working knowledge of media terminology essential for all those associated with media planning and production?

Ans. A basic working knowledge of media terminology is essential for all those associated with media planning and production for several reasons:

1. Clear communication: Understanding media terminology helps to ensure that there is clear communication between all parties involved in media planning and production. This is because specific terms are used to describe different aspects of media production and planning, and it's important that everyone understands what these terms mean.

2. Efficiency: When everyone involved in media planning and production understands the terminology being used, it makes the process more efficient. This is because there is less time spent explaining concepts and terms, and more time can be spent on actually producing the media.

3. Accuracy: Having a basic understanding of media terminology ensures that all parties involved in media planning and production are on the same page in terms of what is being produced. This helps to avoid misunderstandings and mistakes, which can lead to inaccurate or incomplete media products.

4. Professionalism: Knowing media terminology is also important for demonstrating professionalism in the industry. It shows that individuals have a solid understanding of the industry and are committed to producing high-quality work.

Overall, having a basic working knowledge of media terminology is essential for effective communication, efficiency, accuracy, and professionalism in media planning and production.

Q. 3. Describe 'above-the line' and 'below-the line' aspects of TV production.

Ans. "Above-the-line" and "below-the-line" are terms used in the television production industry to differentiate between the two main categories of expenses incurred in the production process.

Above-the-line (ATL) expenses refer to the costs associated with creative elements of a production, such as the script, direction, and talent. These expenses are usually the highest in a production budget and often determine the overall quality and success of the program. Above-the-line expenses are considered non-variable and are fixed costs.

Examples of above-the-line expenses include the following:

1. Talent Fees: This includes the costs associated with actors, presenters, and hosts.

2. Scriptwriting and Development: This includes the costs associated with developing the storyline and writing the script.

3. Directing and Production: This includes the costs associated with hiring the director and the production crew.

4. Pre-production and Post-production Costs: This includes the costs associated with location scouting, editing, and post-production.

Below-the-line (BTL) expenses refer to all other expenses that are not directly related to the creative aspects of production. These expenses are considered variable and can be adjusted during the production process to stay within budget.

Examples of below-the-line expenses include the following:

1. Equipment and Props: This includes the costs associated with renting or purchasing cameras, lighting, and other equipment.

2. Set Construction: This includes the costs associated with building the sets and creating the production design.

3. Sound and Music: This includes the costs associated with sound mixing and composition of music.

Travel and accommodation: This includes the costs associated with travel and accommodation for the production crew.

In summary, above-the-line expenses are the creative and non-variable costs, and below-the-line expenses are the variable and non-creative costs in TV production.

OTHER IMPORTANT QUESTIONS

Q. 1. Define system. Differentiate between natural system and man-made system.

Ans. A system is made up of a number of subsystems and components that work together as an integrated whole to accomplish some pre-established and particular goals. The phrase "in close accord and harmony" is significant in this context since it is a requirement for the proper operation of each component of the system, both individually and collectively. This means that no one part, or even a few parts acting independently, can complete the production process. Additionally, it cannot be done simply eliminating one or more components of the system. Systems can be classified as either natural or man-made. Natural systems include the solar system and galaxies. Machines, media, education and postal systems are a few examples of man-made systems. All such systems are purposefully created, run and managed by people in order to address a particular set of issues or fulfil specific predetermined goals. It is possible to predict, manage and modify the behaviour of man-made systems to a certain extent.

Q. 2. Define production of audio and video programmes as a system. Discuss its elements. What are different levels of production of audio and video programmes?

Ans. The creation of audio and video programming is a human-made system in which various sub-systems and their components, including people, machines, materials and procedures, work together in harmony and synchronisation. It can also be explained in terms of the fundamental components of a system, such as input, process, output, environmental context and feedback. The materials production system, which is essentially developed along the systems approach, strives to achieve specific stated objectives and outputs while functioning within the restrictions of the existing environmental constraints. Additionally, it includes assessment and feedback mechanisms built into it so that any flaws in the system can be fixed, in order to assure optimal effectiveness and error-free functioning.

A production of an audio-video programme typically consists of the following two key components:

(i) The most fundamental physical assets or infrastructure, such as tools, machinery, supplies, structures, studios, or a production complex.

(ii) People or human resources: This refers to the skilled workers' needed to oversee the procedure, run the machinery and offer suggestions, knowledge and services for the creation of programmes.

The amateur and professional are the two different levels of production. For a basic audio programme creation at the amateur level, all you need is a microphone, a recorder and a few blank tapes. A playback feature can be utilised to edit the recorded programme if necessary.

The equipment needed for a video production of this calibre includes a camera, a recorder, a microphone, a few lights (depending on the setting), a few blank cassettes and a straightforward editing console. Both audio and video productions at the professional level demand highly skilled workers and advanced machinery. In a fully functional media production setup, the number of people needed to supply ideas, guidance and management inputs, operate and maintain machinery and equipment, provide and manage various services and resources and carry out and oversee multiple production tasks, would expand proportionally. In other words, the production system expands and becomes larger as the programmes become more complicated and numerous and vice versa.

The production of media materials uses a systems approach because it is only through this approach that a large number of diverse production elements and tasks can be identified, managed and completed through collaborative effort and creative interaction among a large number of people who are all experts in different fields. It should be stressed that the creation of audiovisual content, whether for radio, film, or television, is fundamentally a cooperative activity in which all the system's components—people, tools, resources and methodologies—are interconnected at every stage, from conception to execution. Television, however, is more complicated than other forms of communication, since it incorporates radio and film to a large level.

Q. 3. Discuss the major strands of TV production.

Ans. Creating television is ultimately a collaborative activity. It functions as a cohesive system in which numerous specialists from various professions and with various backgrounds and levels of expertise interact closely with one another, pooling their talents and services to contribute to the creation of a chain effect and to ensure the overall quality of the final programme. In Herbert Zettle's opinion, "Television is a creative process in which humans and technology interact to provide the viewer meaningful experiences, not just a pipeline through which hardware developers can push software. Therefore, producing television demands a deep understanding of the creative interaction between machines and humans." Production involves a large number of independent processes, each linked to the other and all interacting with one another in varying degrees:

***(i)* Programme Planning and Research:** For writers of television scripts and producers of television programmes, comprehensive media, curricular and programme briefs are important sources of reference. The initial written statement that serves as the foundation for a television programming script is the programme brief, often known as the academic note. It provides a detailed description of a programme's title, target audience, duration, goals and summary or outline of its content. At this point, it is crucial to take another look at the target audience's unique requirements, including their preferences, unique traits, prior knowledge, entry behaviour, etc. It is equally crucial to have a full understanding of the circumstances, under which the audience will receive the programme. More detailed study data about the programme's theme must be added to these specifics. In fact, this form of programme study must be done as soon as a programme proposal is made and is extremely necessary.

***(ii)* Message Planning and Script Development:** It is a pivotal and innovative stage in the creation and production of a programme. Always bear in mind the audience's interest, the programme's goals and the visual and other options the medium can provide when creating a screenplay or designing a programme. It's crucial to go through a vast collection of information and choose only the most pertinent ones. You should also look for tools and concepts that complement the goals of the programme. Anything that is not immediately pertinent to the programme is eliminated. The programme's shape or structure starts to take shape as a result of these ideas and inventive choices. At this point, issues like the following are addressed: How will the show get started? What should be the conclusion? What sequences will make up the programme's main body? How will the audience's interest be captured and kept throughout the programme? In order to gather important and fascinating information on the issue, one should look for visual resources on the subject, examine books, journals and other references, as well as connect with informed people.

It is advisable, especially for beginners, to develop a storyboard before a whole script is worked up. On a piece of paper separated into two vertical columns for audio and video content and a description of the programme's specifics, the storyboard is a thorough, shot-by-shot explanation of the show.

***(iii)* Production Planning and Scheduling:** The producer must start concurrent activity on planning, budgeting and scheduling of the production as the final screenplay of the programme develops and assumes some definitive shape. The producer must spend a lot of time at the table and attend numerous planning sessions with technical, programme and resource personnel. A production or camera script including floor drawings and camera cards, as well as other technical needs for studio recording and/or location filming, must be prepared by the producer. He or she consults with camera crew, technical staff and the floor staff who help in the studio during separate and collaborative planning meetings with other programme support staff from different units to finalise graphics, pictures, slides, costumes, make-up, sets and lighting arrangements. Final adjustments are made to the script and its numerous production specifics during a joint planning meeting that the producer calls with the participation of the whole production team. Booking resources, facilities, equipment, studios, production teams and programme talent are tasks that producers prioritise and require extensive planning.

The producer, who frequently also serves as the director of a television or radio programme, is responsible for organising rehearsals and dry runs for the participating actors and artists. The producer is supported by all other members of the concerned units, while receiving primary assistance from his or her production assistant(s) in organising and coordinating all these responsibilities. The producer must estimate all potential inputs, resources and services for budgeting purposes and get in advance the financial approval of the relevant authority. Budgeting for a programme also entails planning for the time and materials needed to plan and execute specific production operations in accordance with the set deadlines.

***(iv)* Casting and Directing Performer Artist:** Prior to beginning the actual recording or filming of various production sequences, the producer must find, choose and reserve the most appropriate performers, artists, or experts for the programme. In fact, one of the keys to great productions is smart casting. The producer-director must pick the talent team members carefully, paying attention to their features, expressions, voices and other necessary characteristics. We need presenters or anchor persons, teachers, specialists, actors and students for instructional productions. Most professional, seasoned performers and artists are familiar with the studio staff and signals. It's important to treat kids and inexperienced, beginning artists with compassion and tolerance. The producer-director should direct the cast to ensure that they carry out the production's goals precisely and in the necessary way. During this phase of production, the producer works closely with artists and performers, guiding them during first briefings, practice runs, camera rehearsals and final recordings. In this situation, a producer needs to have confidence, patience and clear communication. Leading actors and other members of the production team, such as the technical staff, is part of directing.

***(v)* Final production, editing and capsuling:** Finally, the major event is about to begin. That is, the actual production, which includes sound mixing and post-production editing after studio recording or field location shooting, or both. In actuality, this is the final phase of production, during which all operations, personnel and procedures must function as "a dedicated team," completing numerous duties in a coordinated manner. Here, the production process activity as "an integrated system" becomes clearly audible and pronounced. The standard schedule for a studio production of average length includes the set and lighting, camera rehearsals and real recording operations, all of which take place over the course of two to three hours. In complex productions involving outdoor shooting and complex post-production editing, the process may well stretch over several hours, on different working days.

***(vi)* Transmission/dissemination:** Following final production, a programme is capsuled for transmission or dissemination with other programmes and series, in accordance with the transmission or implementation plan of the production centre of the relevant institution. Each programming is typically previewed both after it is produced and before it is broadcast or captured. Any media system for proper storage and simple content retrieval must include a cataloguing system and a video tape recorder (VTR) library for amassing a large number of audio and video tapes in a clean, air-conditioned space.

***(vii)* Utilization and Evaluation:** The effectiveness and worth of programmes, which require ongoing revision for improvement, can only be assessed through a well-designed sub-system of reviewing and getting feedback on programme strengths and defects.

You just learned that the creation of audio-visual programmes is a "man-made" system in which a number of sub-systems and their constituent parts, including people, tools, materials and procedures, are interconnected at every stage from design to implementation. A media production system can be explained in terms of its fundamental components, input, process, output, environmental context and feedback. These components were primarily designed to achieve specific aims.

Q. 4. Discuss production of audio-video programmes as a team approach. What are the functions of the team members?

Ans. Effective cooperation is a must for producing audio-visual programmes. Any educational media production involves a wide range of specially qualified individuals with artistic, technical, management, communicative and other creative talents who come together, work cooperatively and contribute their particular specialties at various stages of a programme's creation. Of course, there are some machines and pieces of equipment that must be used effectively and kept in top shape. However, the people and their collaboration with one another as a team are more crucial to the process than the machinery itself.

The design and production of educational audio-video programmes is often handled by a production team or several teams, working on a single task.

Depending on the size of the production setup and the resources available, different numbers of people operate in production teams. According to the demands of the project, their titles and functions also change from circumstance to scenario.

The individuals working on various production activities and those connected to the various stages of programme development are crucial to the production process. They all operate as a team, with the programme producer or director at the centre of the stage and their duties and responsibilities are more or less well-defined:

***(a)* Producer:** The producer is ultimately responsible for the successful production of a programme, while working under the direction of the head of production or programmes. She or he is in charge of overseeing all operations and is involved in the production process from the beginning, when the media curriculum is defined and specific programme briefs are created. She or he consults the researchers and writers of the screenplay, creates the camera script, selects the format for the programme, manages the production budget and expenses and coordinates with everyone else involved in the programme in any way. The producer also works with the cast, managing their rehearsals and real recording under their direction.

She/he engages with the team's other members and plans their actions.

***(b)* Researcher:** For an audio-visual programme, the researcher does fundamental research. He carries out studies on student profiles, needs analysis and script and programme prototype testing. He also creates programme briefs, which aid in the creation of the scripts for the programmes. As a result, the researcher acts as a conduit between the production crew and the intended audience. Producers and show writers occasionally conduct their own research. Researching your programme is essential if you want to find fresh concepts, intriguing scenarios and stunning visual content. The basis for any compelling and timely programming is research. Research might not necessarily be an essential stage in the entire production process for a discipline-based programme, though.

***(c)* Script-writer:** The programme's script is created by the script writer, who also makes recommendations for visuals, graphics, music and effects. He creates all of the discussion, in accordance with the programme's goals and the information that is currently accessible. Some programme producers develop the scripts for their own shows.

***(d)* Subject Specialist:** Appointing a subject expert to provide advice on the presentation of the material, the accuracy of the facts and concepts provided in the programme is a common and required practice in educational and technical programmes. Regardless of the amount of research information the producer and scriptwriters may have gathered, errors could still appear. Therefore, the position of a subject specialist is crucial and really valuable. So much so that using a skilled subject expert may become necessary in order to provide current knowledge after conducting research.

MULTIPLE CHOICE QUESTIONS

Q. 1. Selection of materials is done during which of the following stage?

(a) Programme Planning and Research
(b) Message Planning and Script Development
(c) Production Planning and Scheduling
(d) Casting and Directing Performers and Artists

Ans. *(b)* Message Planning and Script Development.

Q. 2. Ideas, briefs, synopsis and academic notes for programme are developed during which of the following stage?

(a) Programme Planning and Research
(b) Message Planning and Script Development
(c) Production Planning and Scheduling
(d) Casting and Directing Performers and Artists

Ans. *(a)* Programme Planning and Research.

Q. 3. Designing the production script is done during which of the following stage?

(a) Programme Planning and Research
(b) Message Planning and Script Development
(c) Production Planning and Scheduling
(d) Casting and Directing Performers and Artists

Ans. *(c)* Production Planning and Scheduling.

Q. 4. Directing artists/talent-dry runs, rehearsals is done during:

(a) Programme Planning and Research
(b) Message Planning and Script Development
(c) Production Planning and Scheduling
(d) Casting and Directing Performers and Artists

Ans. *(d)* Casting and Directing Performers and Artists.

Q. 5. Who provides advice on the presentation of the material, the accuracy of the facts and concepts presented in the programme?

(a) Producer *(b)* Researcher
(c) Script-Writer *(d)* Subject specialist

Ans. *(d)* Subject specialist.

Q. 6. Who conducts fundamental investigation for an audio-visual production?

(a) Producer *(b)* Researcher
(c) Script-writer *(d)* Subject specialist

Ans. *(b)* Researcher.

Q. 7. Who creates the programme's screenplay and makes recommendations for visuals, graphics, music and effects?

(a) Producer *(b)* Researcher
(c) Script-writer *(d)* Subject specialist

Ans. *(c)* Script-writer.

Q. 8. Who reports to the head of production or programmes and is ultimately in charge of ensuring that a programme is successfully produced?

(a) Producer *(b)* Researcher
(c) Script-writer *(d)* Subject specialist

Ans. *(a)* Producer.

Q. 9. Formative evaluation is another name for:

(a) Pre-production evaluation
(b) Post-production evaluation
(c) Production evaluation
(d) None of these

Ans. *(a)* Pre-production evaluation.

The Language of Television

9

INTRODUCTION

It was clear that one of the crucial steps in the entire production process is the writing of the script. One needs to be familiar with the special language of television, which all production personnel speak, in order to execute the screenplay in terms of a visual show for television. Television shows us images of items captured at various angles, at various locations and of various sections of the objects. When these images are modified and organised to create a structured programme, the desired mood is created and the pertinent information is presented. In this chapter, the fundamentals of television will be thoroughly covered. By doing so, you will be better equipped to communicate with the personnel that produce television shows.

CHAPTER AT A GLANCE

THE LANGUAGE OF TELEVISION

Today media production has advanced to the point that it is recognised as a separate field on a global scale. With its own register and grammar, it now has a distinct language. Internationally, this is used and understood. Media like film and television communicate mostly through images. The following subsections make an effort to acquaint you with some of the fundamental concepts of film and television language.

Basic Television Shots

The smallest practical visual unit in television or movies is a shot. In a programme, we employ shots of various sizes. The many types of shots are categorised based on the "field of view", or the view in front of the camera. When a subject is present in this setting, the position of the subject presented serves to describe the shot. For the cameraperson, the shots can also be classified by the quantity of objects or things presented and the camera angle. In terms of "field of view", the five fundamental shots utilised in television are as follows:

***(i)* A Long Shot (LS):** It is a picture frame that has its complete background in focus. To make sure that the spectator is facing the area, a long shot may occasionally be replayed. There are more options, such as Very Long Shots (VLS) and Extreme Long Shots (ELS). Such shots are also known as wide shots.

***(ii)* Medium Long Shot (MLS):** It is a shot in which the principal subject (e. g. a person) is shown from the knee upwards with the background in the picture.

***(iii)* Medium Close Up (MCU):** Here, the figure is displayed from the waist up. Although, the background can be seen in some detai l, the subject is the main focus of this sort of photograph. A mid shot is another name for this. When used in programmes with a demonstration style, this shot is quite helpful. An example of this would be someone describing or displaying a model.

***(iv)* Medium Close Up (MCU):** It is cut at the subject's lower chest level or the breast pocket beneath or above the armpit. Here, the subject is the main point of interest and the background is less significant. These images are helpful in panel discussions, interviews and other presenter-based programme formats.

***(v)* Close Up (CU):** This image captures the subject up close, as the name suggests. It is cut at collar level if the topic is a human. The main attention is on the subject. In dramatised genres, where facial expressions are important, these pictures are helpful. They can also be used to draw attention to specifics.

***(vi)* Big Close Up (BCU):** This photograph is helpful for emphasising small features. This shot is typically employed to examine extreme facial emotions, in order to heighten the drama in formats that demand such details.

Camera Angles

We can describe a shot in terms of camera angles in three major ways. They are: *(i)* the normal angle shot, *(ii)* a low-angle shot and *(iii)* a high-angle shot. The high-angle shot, if taken from the air or a high vantage point, will be called an aerial shot. A view taken from the subject's eye level is the typical camera angle. In this instance, the person just so happens to be gazing directly into the viewer's eyes. A low-angle shot places the camera lens a few feet below the average eye level. The opposite occurs with a high-angle shot. The camera is physically lifted and positioned at an overhead angle for an aerial shot, though. Such pictures are probably, frequently used in the coverage of sporting events

Subjectivity and Objectivity in Shots: An objective shot is one in which the camera is 90 degrees away from the action. This is done to project the image from an objective viewpoint. A typical illustration would be the referee's perspective of a tennis match. The start of a subjective shot is indicated by the same shot moving in an arc to look over one of the players' shoulders. An arbitrary camera angle depicts one of the players' physical viewpoints. By unable to virtually step into one of the players' shoes, the viewer is forced to sympathise with their situation.

Complementary Shots: These photos are composed in a way that they interact with the previous objective shot in a certain programme in reverse order. One player's set above his or her head and shoulders, for instance, needs to be paired with another player's same shot. These shots are very helpful in formats like drama, interviews, presentations and discussions. In these formats, the action shots are complemented with reactions from the audience, like in the case of shots of spectators at a tennis match. Cut-away shots are reactions that occur at the same time period as the main picture but are not in the same place. This picture is typically employed to break up the monotony of action and temporarily detract from the main event. It is also useful in cases, where the total time of action needs to be condensed, yet continuity of action is to be maintained.

Picture Composition

Picture composition comprises headroom, illusion of depth and framing. The three elements listed above are actually more applicable to still photographs because, as you must keep in mind, television is focused on moving imagery. They do, however, serve as the cornerstone of every effective television picture arrangement.

A Rule of Thirds: The rule of thirds is a concept that is commonly mentioned in writing about picture composition. Simply said, this rule advises the cameraperson to divide the screen into three equal sections, horizontally and vertically and to try to find the main points of interest in the subject at the four spots where the lines meet. Here, the positioning of the object—a horse's head with room to look—creates depth. The dotted lines demonstrate how a poor positioning could ruin the frame.

Psychological Closureμ: This is yet another framing argument that argues the human mind is able to complete the gaps in familiar things that we perceive. The positioning of the object is only one aspect of the psychological closure concept. Inadvertently cutting the subject at one of the subject's natural joints can result in bizarre impressions. The cameraperson would be wise to stay away from these "amputee shots." When the framing is adjusted, the other foot is visible and an image of the ball being dribbled appears even if the player is not visible. So that the subject can experience psychological closure, the subject should either be well-framed or transported far from the frame.

Headroom: The term "headroom" describes the space between the subject's head and the frame's "ceiling." Crowding at the top of the frame might distract from the photo for aesthetic reasons, in addition to the requirement to leave some room around a subject owing to the possibility of cropping. We are accustomed to seeing some room around people. Therefore, a lack of headroom may give the sense that the subject is attempting to lift the ceiling with his or her head. Too much headroom has the same kind of effect. However, there are no set guidelines on how much space should be offered. The cameraperson's aesthetic judgement is left up to them. The phrase "headroom" refers to issues with vertical framing. This entails leaving more space in front of the person's head than behind it and is also known as nose room, take space, or lead space.

Impression of Depth: The cameraperson may occasionally make little adjustments to the camera angle and position to create the illusion of depth and three-dimensionality in order to minimise the two-dimensional features of the TV screen. With the director's permission, the cameraperson may include a foreground object to serve as a point of comparison for the viewer to determine the relative size and proximity of things in the middle and background. There are several techniques to provide the appearance of depth to a scene, including using doorways, windows, table corners and objects in the foreground like a person's shoulder. To prevent an inadvertent, awkward alignment of the subject with the background, the cameraperson should be vigilant.

Camera Movement

When the image on the programme line is altered, the cameraperson should be able to see both his or her personal viewfinder and the studio monitor. Under the direction of the director, the cameraperson should try to merge their pictures with those from the other cameras so that the shots may be taken1 seamlessly. In order to *(i)* represent activity onscreen and *(ii)* offer the maximum information, a variety of camera motions are used.

***(i)* Static or still shot:** Regardless of movement in the visual, this shot is seen from a static camera perspective.

***(ii)* Pan shot (also known as a panning shot):** A shot with a straightforward camera movement in which the camera head is moved (pivoted) upward or to the right on the horizontal plane with the camera base remaining stationary. (also known as a panoramic photo).

Right panning shot: To achieve a right panning shot, press the panning handle to the left. The camera head is rotated horizontally to the right, or clockwise.

Left panning shot: To get a left panning shot, push the panning handle to the right. The camera head is rotated horizontally to the left, or anticlockwise.

***(iii)* Tilt (up and down):** A straightforward camera action that causes the camera head to move vertically up or down. With a tilt-up, the camera is shifted progressively higher. The camera is progressively turned to point downward during a tilt down.

***(iv)* Crab (Crab left and crab right):** the entire camera is moved sideways on a dolly or set of wheels. Crab left refers to shifting the camera mount to the left of the camera. The term "crab right" refers to turning the camera mount to the right.

***(v)* Truck (Truck in and Truck out):** Moving the camera on its mount either towards or away from the subject is referred to as trucking. Truck in and truck out refer to my movement towards and away from the issue, respectively. This is comparable to "dolly in" and "dolly out" (Also called track in or track out).

***(vi)* Dolly (in/out):** Moving the camera forward towards or away from a scene or subject in a mostly straight path while using its wheels or a dolly. Bringing the camera in closer is known as "dollying in." Moving the camera away from the subject is known as "dolly out" (for dolly back).

***(vii)* Crane (up/down):** The entire camera may be moved up and down on a camera crane. Crane-up and Crane-down motions are compared favourably to "pedestal-up" and "pedestal-down" movements.

Transitions

When becoming familiar with images and camera movements, the desire to seamlessly combine photos or visuals to convey a theme or series of events develops. This takes us to the part of the television production scenario including post-production. The grammar of production defines a number of transitional methods that may be used to seamlessly juxtaposition or dovetail the shots.

These are

- the cut
- Audio and Video Production (Purl A)
- dissolve (mix)
- superimposition (super)
- fade
- wipe
- chroma key.

Let us take a quick look at what each of these devices entails.

The switching procedure known as a cut is used in all "reality" programmes, news, interviews, panel discussions, and quiz shows that try to depict something truly occurring without the use of production method embellishment. A cut is defined as an instantaneous transition from one camera's image to another camera's image. Today's viewers are more observant than ever before, though, thus a cut can also be utilised to indicate a shift in setting or mood. These "special effects" switching techniques are employed in "illusion" programmes like theatre, dance, and music, among others. A fade-in is a smooth change from a black 110 image to a picture.

A slow change from an image to no picture is known as a fade-out (black). The dissolve is a very gradual cut. If you don't move the roll of film forward when using a still camera, a double exposure will happen and your photo will be damaged! An international double exposure is a super in TV switching. Two different cameras' images are simultaneously displayed in the air. For instance, if a vocalist is performing in front of a black background, camera 1 might only show the vocalist's face in the lower third of its frame, while camera 2 would show the singer's complete body in the top third.

When both of these photos are displayed simultaneously on the monitor, just the two different perspectives of the performance are visible since black does not "photograph" on TV. Other special effects include the "wipe," which substitutes an image from one camera for one from another electronically, and the "chrome key," which electronically chooses any colour from the TV spectrum and substitutes it with a picture from another camera.

Cues and Commands/Symbols and Signals

There are a lot of cues and directives, acronyms, symbols, and signs used in television. The producer's instructions, the floor manager's signals used in the studio or on location, and the symbols and abbreviations used on scripts, camera cards, floor plans, and cue sheets should all be understood by everyone. Similar to this, the producer or director must speak clearly and rapidly with a huge group of people. Hence, all members of the production team must be able to accurately understand the language he or she employs while making decisions from the gallery.

The symbols, abbreviations, and marks used on TV/video scripts, floor plans, camera cards, etc. as well as several significant signals used by the floor manager and other members of the floor staff during the midst of a programme recording are all reproduced in this subsection.

Throughout a recording, the floor manager also communicates via recognisable signs. Figure 36 below shows important signals.

Producer's Commands

Verbal commands	Commands meant for
Stand by	Studio/Camera/VCR/Sound/ Talent (for rehearsal/recording/ final take)
Silence on the floor	Everybody
Roll/Start	Camera/VCR/Film/Sound tape
Action	Presenter/talent
Ready	Camera (1/2/3)
Cut	Camera (1/2/3) or VT/Film
Dissolve/Mix	Camera (1/2/3) or VT/Film
Cue Music	Start music (live or taped)
UP/Down/Under Music	Camera (1/2/3)....
Pan (Right/Left)	Camera (1/2/3)........
Tilt (Up/Down)	Camera (1/2/3)............
Zoom (In/Out)	Camera (1/2/3) or Sound/ Tape/Music
Fade (In/Out)	Camera (1/2/3)
Focus (In/Out or Defocus)	Camera 1 or 2
Super	(on 1/2/3)
Lose Super	Presenter/talent/tap
Change Caption	

Cue/Q	
Hold It	
Pack Up/Wrap Up	
Fade Sound & Vision	
Thanks Everybody	

Abbreviations for TV/Video Scripts: Some widely used abbreviations on video scropts are as follows:

Abbreviation	**Full form**
PA	Production Assistant
FM	Floor Manager
AFM	Asstt. Floor Mager
CAM	Camera
MIC/MIKE	Microphone
VT / VTR	Videotape / Recorder
TC / TK	Telecine
C / S	Caption Scanner
Cap	Caption
PIX	Photo caption
PIC	Picture / graphic
BP / RP	Back / Rear Projection
A / B	As Before
SI	Slide
VD	Video disc
O / C	On Camera
Q	Cue
S / B	Stand By
To CAM	To Camera
S / I	Superimpose
Lose	Lose super
CK :	Chroma Key
S / S	Split Screen
O / S (OSS)	Over Shoulder Shot
Cut	Cut
Mix / Dis.	Dissolve
Wipe	Wipe
FU / FI	Fade up / Fade in
FO	Fade out
X - Fade	Cross fade
F / B	Fold back
FX	Effect
SFX	Special effect
Anno Pres:	Presenter
SOF	Sound on Film
SOT	Sound on Tape
Mute	Silent / Without sound
MOS	Man on the street
Prop:	Property
Ext	Exterior
Int	Interior
Mon	Monitor
Roller	Roller Caption
TX / TXN	Transmission
FS & V	Fade sound and vision

Floor Manager's Signals

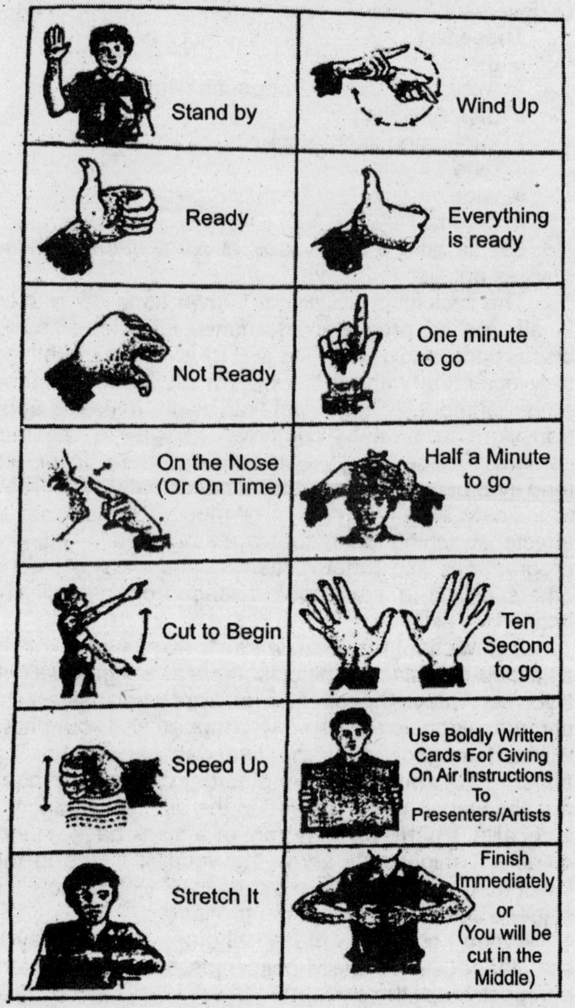

CHECK YOUR PROGRESS

Q. 1. Define 'a shot' in relation to the production process.

Ans. In TV production, "a shot" refers to a continuous sequence of film or video that is captured by the camera from the time it starts recording to the time it stops. A shot is typically defined by its composition, camera movement, and duration, and it is used as a building block for creating scenes and telling stories. Each shot in TV production is carefully planned and executed by the director, cinematographer, and other members of the production team, who work together to achieve the desired visual and emotional impact. Shots can vary in length and complexity, ranging from simple static shots to complex tracking shots and elaborate camera movements. By combining different shots and editing them together, TV producers can create a variety of visual effects, convey emotions, and tell stories in unique and engaging ways. The use of different types of shots, such as close-ups, medium shots, and wide shots, can also help to convey different aspects of a scene and provide important context for the viewer.

Q. 2. List the basic kinds of shots in video production.

Ans. There are several basic kinds of shots in video production that are commonly used to convey different aspects of a story or message. These shots are:

Wide shot or establishing shot: This shot establishes the setting and context of the scene by showing a wide view of the location.

Medium shot: This shot is used to show the subject from the waist up, and is often used for interviews or conversations.

Close-up shot: This shot is used to focus on a specific detail or feature of the subject, such as their face or hands.

Extreme close-up shot: This shot focuses on a very specific detail, such as the eyes or mouth of the subject.

Over-the-shoulder shot: This shot is used to show the perspective of a character in a conversation, with the camera positioned behind one character's shoulder.

Point-of-view shot: This shot shows the perspective of a character, as if the viewer is seeing the scene through their eyes.

Cutaway shot: This shot is used to show something else in the scene, such as an object or a reaction shot, while still maintaining the context of the scene.

These are some of the most common types of shots used in video production, but there are many more techniques and variations that can be used to create different effects and convey different emotions.

Q. 3. What do you mean by the term 'transitional device'?

Ans. In TV production, a transitional device refers to any technique or element used to smoothly transition from one scene or segment to another. These devices help to maintain a seamless flow and continuity in the program, and prevent jarring jumps or interruptions that can disrupt the viewer's experience.

Examples of transitional devices in TV production include:

Dissolves: This is a technique in which the first shot gradually fades out while the next shot fades in, creating a smooth transition.

Crossfades: This is similar to a dissolve, but the two shots are overlapped for a brief moment, creating a blending effect.

Cutaways: These are shots that show something else in the scene, such as an object or a reaction shot, while still maintaining the context of the previous or upcoming scene.

J-cuts and L-cuts: These are audio editing techniques where the audio from the next scene begins before the video, or the audio from the previous scene continues while the video switches to the next scene, creating a seamless audio transition.

Graphics and animation: These can be used to visually transition between scenes, such as using a map to show the location of the next scene, or animating a graphic to transition between two related topics.

Overall, transitional devices in TV production are used to create a sense of continuity and flow in the program, and to help guide the viewer through the various segments and scenes.

Q. 4. Describe 'fade', 'dissolve' and 'super'?

Ans. In TV production, "fade," "dissolve," and "super" are three common techniques used in video editing and post-production. Each of these techniques serves a different purpose in creating a smooth transition between shots or adding visual information to the scene.

Fade: A fade is a transition where the image slowly fades to black or white, or to another color. A fade-out is used to end a scene or segment, while a fade-in is used to start a new scene or segment. Fades can also be used to create a dreamlike or nostalgic effect.

Dissolve: A dissolve is a transition where two images gradually blend into one another, with one image slowly disappearing as the other image becomes more visible. Dissolves are often used to show the passage of time or to indicate a change in location.

Super: A super (short for "superimposition") is a technique where text, graphics, or other images are overlaid onto the video footage, usually in the lower third of the screen. Supers are commonly used to display titles, captions, or other information related to the video content, such as the name of the speaker or the location of the scene.

Overall, fades, dissolves, and supers are effective tools in creating smooth transitions and adding visual information in TV production. By using these techniques appropriately, producers can create a more engaging and dynamic viewing experience for their audience.

OTHER IMPORTANT QUESTIONS

Q. 1. What do you understand by language of television? Discuss briefly on basic television shots.

Ans. Today, media creation has developed to become recognised as a distinct field on a global scale. As a result, it now possesses a unique language with a unique register and syntax. This is accepted and utilised all over the world. Media like film and television, mostly use images to communicate. The primary argument for why we should be familiar with the language of media if we want to work with any of the media components is that this aspect of commonality has created the foundation for its language and grammar. You can become more familiar with certain fundamental facets of cinema and television language by reading the subsections that follow.

Basic Television Shots: In television or movies, a shot is the smallest practical visual unit. In a programme, shots of various sizes are used. There are many different types of shots and they are categorised according to the "field of vision", or the view in front of the camera. When a subject is present in this setting, the shot is defined by the subject's position. The amount of objects or subjects visible in the pictures, as well as the camera angle, can both be used by the cameraperson to describe the views. According to "field of view", the five most common television shots are as follows:

(i) **A Long Shot (LS):** The location where the main action is taking place is described in this image. It is a picture frame that has its complete background in focus, in other words. To make sure that the spectator is facing the area, a long shot may occasionally be replayed. There are more options, such as Very Long Shots (VLS) and Extreme Long Shots (ELS). These images are also known as wide shots.

(ii) **Medium Long Shot (MLS):** It is a shot in which the background is visible and the main subject is seen from the knee up.

(iii) **Medium Close Up (MCU):** Here, the figure is displayed from the waist up. Although the background can be seen in some detail, the subject is the main focus of this sort of photograph. A mid shot is another name for this. When used in programmes with a demonstration style, this shot is quite helpful. An example of this would be someone describing or displaying a model.

(iv) **Medium Close Up (MCU):** It is cut at the subject's lower chest level or the breast pocket beneath or above the armpit. Here, the subject is the main point of interest and the background is less significant. These images are helpful for panel discussions, interviews and other presenter-based show formats.

(v) **Close Up (CU):** This image captures the subject up close, as the name suggests. It is cut at collar level if the topic is a human. The main attention is on the subject. In dramatised genres, where facial expressions are important, these pictures are helpful. They can also be used to draw attention to specifics.

(vi) **Big Close Up (BCU):** This photograph is helpful for emphasising small features. This shot is typically employed to examine extreme facial emotions in order to heighten the drama in formats that demand such details.

However, shots may also be addressed in terms of what the complete house or the visual contents look like from the perspective of the cameraperson. A one-shot, for instance, is a photograph of a single person or thing. Two individuals are framed in a two-shot image. A three-shot will contain three individuals or things and so forth. The term "group-shot" will be used for groups of more than four persons. A crowd shot is a picture of a larger group.

Q. 2. What are different camera angles?

Ans. The camera serves as a supplement to the human sight. Without moving from his or her place, the spectator can watch any object of study or human subject expression. The human eye can observe an angle of 120 degrees, compared to the camera's meagre 54 degree field of view. This is why understanding camera motions is crucial for production. To take pictures from various angles, the camera must be moved frequently. In general, there are three main ways to categorise a photograph in terms of camera angles. They are the standard angle shot, the low-angle shot and the high-angle shot.

An aerial shot is one that has a high-vantage point or was taken from the air. Shots taken from the standard camera stance are taken at the subject's eye level. Here, the subject just so happens to be looking into the viewer's eyes. When taking a low-angle shot, the camera lens descends a few feet below eye level. Here, a typical example would be placing the camera so that the toddler is staring up at an adult from the level of the camera. With a high-angle shot, the opposite occurs. But in an aerial image, the camera is actually raised and set up at an angle above the ground.

Q. 3. What is the difference between subjectivity and objectivity in shots?

Ans. An objective shot is what is referred to in technical terms as a camera that is 90 degrees away from the action. This is done in order to project the image from a distance. A typical illustration would be sitting in the referee's seat and watching a tennis match. The identical shot signals the start of a subjective shot if it moves in an arc to a view over one of the players' shoulders. A player's physical perspective is depicted by a subjective camera angle. Due to the viewer's inability to virtually step into one of the players' shoes, they are forced to sympathise with their situation.

Q. 4. Write a note on complementary shots.

Ans. This is a common "over the shoulder" shot. These photos are composed in a way that interacts in reverse order with the subjective shot that came before it in a particular programme. For instance, it will be necessary to contrast one player's set above his or her head and shoulders with another player's equivalent shot. In drama, interview, presentation and debate forms, these shots are especially helpful. In such formats, the action shots have contrasting reactions, such as the audience shots during a tennis match. Cut-away shots are reactions that take place at the same moment as the main shot but are taken elsewhere. This picture is typically employed to break up the monotony of action and temporarily detract from the main event. It can also be helpful when actions need to be completed in a shorter amount of time, while maintaining continuity.

Q. 5. Write a note on picture composition.

Ans. Television is a form of media that combines audio and visual elements. It is up to the filmmaker to decide what belongs in a picture frame. In order to achieve the desired effect, the cameraperson arranges the elements or details. In other words, the composition of a photograph is influenced by both the camera's framing and the filmmaker's vision. The technique of photograph composition includes things like framing, headroom, and the illusion of depth. While TVs are designed to display moving images, the three factors mentioned above are more applicable to static pictures. All successful television visual compositions are built on top of them.

A rule of thirds: One idea that is frequently brought up in literature about image composition is the rule of thirds. This rule instructs the cameraperson to divide the image into three equal pieces, both horizontally and vertically, and to look for the subject's key areas of interest at the four locations where the lines converge. Here, depth is created by the placement of the item, a horse's head with space to stare. The dotted lines show how the frame might be ruined by bad placement.

Psychological closure: This is another another framing argument supporting the notion that the human mind is capable of filling in the blanks in the familiar objects we encounter. One part of the psychological closure idea is the placement of the object. It can leave strange imprints if you accidentally cut the patient at one of their natural joints. It would be good for the cameraperson to avoid these "amputee pictures." When the frame is changed, the other foot becomes visible and, even if the player is not visible, an image of the ball being dribbled emerges. The topic should either be well within the frame or well outside of it for the spectator to have a feeling of closure.

Headroom: The distance between the subject's head and the "ceiling" of the frame is referred to as "headroom." In addition to the need to leave some space around a subject due to the potential of cropping, crowding at the top of the frame may detract from the image for aesthetic reasons. A shortage of headroom may give the impression that the individual is trying to lift the ceiling with his or her head because we are used to seeing space around people. The result is same when there is much headroom. How much room should be provided, nevertheless, is not governed by any rules. It is up to the cameraperson to make aesthetic decisions. Concerns with vertical framing are referred to as "headroom" problems.

Impression of Depth: Occasionally, the cameraperson can make little adjustments to the angle and location of the camera to provide the appearance of depth and three-dimensionality while minimising the two-dimensional characteristics of the TV screen. A point of reference for the viewer to judge the relative size and proximity of objects in the centre and background may be placed by the cameraperson with the director's approval. A window or doorway, a corner of a table, or a subject's shoulder in the foreground from which the viewer can see the main image can all give the sense that the scene is deeper. The cameraperson must use caution to avoid unintended, incorrect subject alignment with backdrop components.

Q. 6. Discuss different types of camera movements.

Ans. When the picture on the programme line changes, the cameraperson should be able to see both their own viewfinder and the studio monitor. When it comes to picture composition, the cameraperson should make an effort, under the director's supervision, to blend shots with those of the other cameras so that the shots can be taken1 smoothly. A variety of camera movements are employed to *(i)* display action on screen and *(ii)* provide as much information as is practical.

***(i)* Static or still shot:** Despite the movement in the visual, the camera angle for this shot is fixed.

***(ii)* Pan shot (or panning shot):** Shot with a straightforward camera movement in which the camera head is moved (pivoted) upward or to the right on the horizontal axis with the camera's base remaining still, also known as a panorama picture.

Pan right: By pushing the panning handle to the left, you can get a right panning shot by turning the camera head horizontally to the right, or clockwise.

Pan left: A left panning shot is created by pulling the panning handle to the right, which rotates the camera head horizontally to the left, or anticlockwise.

(iii) **Tilt (up and down):** A straightforward camera movement that causes the camera head to move vertically up or down. In a tilt-up, the camera is shifted progressively higher. The camera is gradually turned to point downwards during a tilt down.

(iv) **Crab (crab left and crab right):** The entire camera moving sideways on its wheels or dolly. Crab left refers to shifting the camera mount to the left of the camera. The term "crab right" refers to turning the camera mount to the right.

(v) **Truck (Truck in and truck out):** Moving the camera on its mount either towards or away from the target is referred to as trucking. Truck in and truck out refer to any movement toward and away from the issue, respectively. This is comparable to "dolly in" and "dolly out" Also called track in or track out.

(vi) **Dolly (in/out):** A more-or-less straight line movement of the camera on its wheels or dolly, either towards or away from a scene or subject. Bringing the camera in closer is known as "dollying in." Moving the camera away from the subject is known as "dolly out" (for dolly back).

(vii) **Crane (up/down):** Up and down movement of the whole camera on a camera crane. 'Crane-up' and 'Crane down' movements are seen as very similar to 'pedestal-up' and 'pedestal-down'.

Q. 7. Explain 'Transitions' in video production.

Ans. The desire to seamlessly combine photos or visuals to convey a theme or series of events arises after becoming accustomed to images and camera movements. This gets us to the stage of the television production process where post-production is concerned. A variety of transitional tools are specified by the production language and can be used to dovetail or juxtapose shots in an elegant way.

The cut: All "reality" programmes, news, interviews, panel discussions, and quiz shows that attempt to represent something actually occurring without production style embellishment employ the switching technique known as a cut. An instantaneous switch from the view of one camera to the view of another is known as a cut. Yet because viewers are more perceptive than ever, a cut may also be used to suggest a change in scene or mood.

Drama, dance, and music are just a few of the "illusion" programmes that use these "special effects" switching tactics. A seamless transition from a black 110 image to a picture is called a fade-in. A fade-out is a gradual transition from an image to no picture (black). The cut is very gradually dissolved.

While using a still camera, if you don't advance the roll of film, a double exposure will occur and your picture will be ruined! A twofold exposure from abroad is excellent for TV flipping. Images from two distinct cameras are simultaneously shown in the air. If a vocalist is singing in front of a black background, for example, camera 1 might only show the singer's face in the lower third of its frame while camera 2 would show the singer's entire body in the top third. Black does not "photograph" on television, thus when both of these images are shown at once on the monitor, just the two distinct perspectives of the performance are discernible. The "wipe," which electronically switches an image from one camera for a picture from another, and the "chrome key," which electronically selects any colour from the TV spectrum and switches it with a picture from another camera, are further special effects.

MULTIPLE CHOICE QUESTIONS

Q. 1. The high-angle shot, if taken from the air or a high vantage point, is called an:

(a) Aerial shot *(b)* Very long shot
(c) Large shot *(d)* None of these

Ans. *(a)* Aerial shot.

Q. 2. Which shot places the camera lens a few feet below the average eye level?

(a) Normal angle shot *(b)* Low-angle shot
(c) High-angle shot *(d)* None of these

Ans. *(b)* Low-angle shot.

Q. 3. In which shot, the camera is physically lifted and positioned at an overhead angle?

(a) Normal angle shot *(b)* Low-angle shot
(c) High-angle shot *(d)* None of these

Ans. *(c)* High-angle shot.

Q. 4. When the camera is 90 degrees away from the action, the shot is called:

(a) Objective shot *(b)* Subjective shot
(c) Both *(a)* and *(b)* *(d)* None of these

Ans. *(a)* Objective shot.

Q. 5. Picture composition comprises:

(a) Headroom and illusion of depth
(b) Headroom and framing
(c) Illusion of depth and framing
(d) Headroom, illusion of depth and framing

Ans. *(d)* Headroom, illusion of depth and framing.

Q. 6. Which rule advises the cameraperson to divide the screen into three equal sections, horizontally and vertically?

(a) A rule of thirds
(b) Psychological closure
(c) Headroom
(d) Impression of depth

Ans. *(a)* A rule of thirds.

Q. 7. Which of the following describes the space between the subject's head and the frame's "ceiling"?

(a) A rule of thirds
(b) Psychological closure
(c) Headroom

(*d*) Impression of depth

Ans. (*c*) Headroom.

Q. 8. Which of the following implies the human mind is able to complete the gaps in familiar things that we perceive?

(*a*) A rule of thirds
(*b*) Psychological closure
(*c*) Headroom
(*d*) Impression of depth

Ans. (*b*) Psychological closure.

Q. 9. Which shot is seen from a static camera angle, irrespective of the movement within the visual?

(*a*) Static or still shot
(*b*) Pan shot
(*c*) Tilt (up and down)
(*d*) Crab (crab left and crab right)

Ans. (*a*) Static or still shot.

Q. 10. __________ is a simple camera movement in which the camera head is made to move up or down vertically?

(*a*) Static or still shot
(*b*) Pan shot
(*c*) Tilt (up and down)
(*d*) Crab (crab left and crab right)

Ans. (*c*) Tilt (up and down).

Q. 11. Which is a sideway movement of the whole camera on its wheels or dolly?

(*a*) Static or still shot
(*b*) Pan shot
(*c*) Tilt (up and down)
(*d*) Crab (crab left and crab right)

Ans. (*d*) Crab (crab left and crab right).

Q. 12. Which means moving the camera on its mount towards or away from the subject?

(*a*) Trucking (*b*) Tilt up
(*c*) Crab left (*d*) None of these

Ans. (*a*) Trucking.

Q. 13. Up and down movement of the whole camera on a camera crane is called:

(*a*) Camera crane up/down
(*b*) Tilt up/down
(*c*) Crab left/right
(*d*) None of these

Ans. (*a*) Camera crane up/down.

Q. 14. Movement of the camera on its wheels or dolly is called:

(*a*) Camera crane up/down
(*b*) Tilt up/down
(*c*) Crab left/right
(*d*) Dolly in/out

Ans. (*d*) Dolly in/out.

■■

Writing Scripts for Audio and Video Programmes

10

INTRODUCTION

Writing scripts is a necessary task on a distance educator's agenda, albeit it may appear difficult at first. The specifics of how to approach it are covered in this chapter. In regard to audio and video programmes, we discuss style, formats and the goals of the mediums. The main topic of discussion is the writing process, which includes the steps of generating a script. The course's second block of lessons focused on the use of audio and video programmes in the development of instructional materials for distance-learning systems.

CHAPTER AT A GLANCE

EDUCATIONAL PROGRAMMES

A group of educational activities that are planned to achieve a specific goal or complete a set of educational tasks is referred to as an educational programme. The basic goal of education is to give people the chance to acquire the knowledge and skills they need to reach their full potential and contribute successfully to society.

The Nature of Educational Programmes

A programme or movie must satisfy two requirements in order to be considered educational: *(i)* it must investigate a topic or develop a treatment in a methodical, planned manner; and *(ii)* it must seek to permanently increase the knowledge of the audience.

Newscasts do not provide information in an ordered way, but rather skip around from story to story based on the current events. Information is presented in quizzes, but aimlessly and randomly. In a way, the information presented by newscasts is only useful in the short term, lasting only until the next news programme airs. The knowledge offered by quiz shows is either completely useless or of very little use.

As a result, the broadcast and quiz programmes fall short of the two requirements we outlined. Newscasts would be considered educational, and quiz shows would be considered entertainment. Quiz shows are more accurately referred to as "info-tainment" programmes since they combine fun and education..

Types of Educational Programmes

One that directly teaches a lesson from the normal curriculum is the most regimented kind of educational programme. Direct teaching is exemplified by television programming that explains fractions in an elementary school math lesson or covers topics not included in the traditional curriculum, such as a foreign language. The term "instructional television" is another name for this kind of broadcasting. A different kind of educational programme serves as an addition to the instruction given by the usual teacher. For instance, a class of elementary school students studying American history might see a movie or television show on a particular event in George Washington's life. A film named Geronimo Jones, which illustrates the emotional harm brought on by the stereotyping of native American Indians, might be shown to a university class interested in how movies and television portray stereotypes of certain populations. The programme that combines entertainment and education falls under a third category. Sesame Street, in particular, occasionally engages in what might be called direct instruction in an effort to teach pre-school children to recognise numbers and letters but both programmes also contain segments that are obviously intended to be entertaining. Programmes like Captain Kangaroo and Sesame Street have clear educational objectives. The television programme Victory at Sea educated viewers about World War II's naval history, while also providing them with top-notch entertainment.

Advantages and Limitations of the Media

The use of multiple media for teaching has benefits and drawbacks, which writers should be aware of. The following are a few benefits:

In certain cases, broadcasting is more current than written books and movies. It is beyond the capacity of the classroom instructor to represent famous individuals, foreign locales, and an accurate picture of events in television and movies.

By dismantling the rigid divisions into which much education is divided, broadcasting and cinema can integrate learning by simulating the situation that exists in real life, when individuals perform tasks like reading and spelling together rather than individually as students do in school.

The writer has access to a variety of unique tools and methods for achieving educational goals through broadcasting and cinema, which, when utilised creatively, may frequently make an idea or function plain in a manner that no other teaching approach can equal. By offering a change from the conventional method of instruction and by promising the enjoyable experiences most people associate with television and the movies, broadcasting and movies may make learning more engaging.

While television shows and movies are typically solitary experiences, educational content only works to the degree that viewers integrate it into the larger context of their life. This is vital to understand if these benefits are to be achieved.

Preparation, appreciation, and follow-up are all aspects of integration that are necessary for instructional programmes in particular. Instructors lose efficacy when they don't include educational programmes into the full learning process. Authors contribute to the creation of use materials.

Some of the following media negatives balance out these benefits:

The presenter and the audience don't communicate well with one another. Presenters are actually both blind and deaf since they cannot tell when they have entirely lost the audience because they cannot hear the sound of television knobs moving or the click of switches shutting off sets.

A two-way communication system that enables viewers to ask questions and, in some situations, even participate in debates has been used in certain attempts to address this issue. This is only conceivable in broadcasting, though, if the Instructional Television Fixed Service (ITFS), which is offered by the FCC for engineering instruction to employees of enterprises 40 miles distant in Detroit, is used. Those who receive education through cable television services occasionally have the same chance. While a programme or movie's audience is diverse in terms of background and interests, it is set in terms of substance and approach.

One audience member may feel that it hits the audience where it is most needed, another may think it is above their heads, and a third may feel let down by its obviousness. This lack of individualised attention to needs is a major issue. It might imply that some audience members receive instructional value from a presentation while others do not. Hence, although a music appreciation course may teach people whose preferences are still developing, it may just serve to amuse those who already have a strong appreciation for good music.

Scheduling programmes for schools at the best time for all courses is challenging or impossible. Classes for different courses meet at different times, even within the same school system, due to schedule variations. Even when courses meet at the same time, there are large differences in how quickly they progress through a given course of study. Because of this, broadcasters prioritise content that just enhances or supplements the curriculum rather than attempting to deliver exact, direct instruction.

Films can be screened whenever it is most conducive to the study course, unlike broadcasts, which are limited in their scheduling options. The rigidity of broadcast schedules is especially problematic for shows aimed at wide audiences. While planning and composing them, authors always keep in mind that viewers are unlikely to watch every episode of a given series.

The fact that radio is only compatible with one physical sense is a drawback. It is not unexpected that a significant number of educational radio programmes are about music since music, of course, suffers the least from this constraint and may even gain from it by focusing attention on the sound. However because most subjects need to be taught by visualisation or example, radio lessons have mostly been replaced by video teachings in the classroom.

Defining Goals

Writers need to be very aware of the objectives they are aiming for in order to plan and produce a good instructional series. Goal definition in the educational profession is more difficult than in other fields. Dramatic writers are aware of their goal, which is to entertain an audience while maintaining their interest. The aim of a comedy writer is quite obvious: to make people laugh.

Of course, achieving these objectives is difficult, but identifying them is simple. On the other hand, educators have a wide range of objectives to select from. They must decide if their goal is only to increase audience information or if they also aim to advance comprehension of a subject.

They can want to establish a particular attitude or set of ideals. Its objective may be purely utilitarian, such as instructing viewers on how to perform a certain task or teach them a new skill. They could want to develop their preferences and enthusiasm for music, theatre, or literature. Because achieving these numerous goals necessitates using a variety of strategies, authors must be aware of their goals before beginning programme development.

One of the most popular educational children's television programmes ever created, Sesame Street, is a great illustration of the need of carefully outlining goals.

The Children's Television Workshop, which created the series, conducted a meticulously organised study effort prior to the first episode airing.

A list of objectives that detailed in detail what the programmes should attempt to accomplish resulted from this work. The recognition of letters and numbers by preschoolers was foremost among these objectives. The Workshop continued by outlining in great detail the circumstances under which this recognition should occur. There were further objectives. Children were taught how to identify and name the parts of their bodies, differentiate between distinct visual shapes, tell one sound from another, comprehend size connections, classify and organise items, solve problems, and understand causality using these programmes. Also, the programmes provided information on the social and physical environments and promoted fruitful and fulfilling social engagement.

Youngsters watching Sesame Street on television may have been looking for fun. They received unrestricted entertainment, but they also profited greatly from well crafted programmes that served certain educational goals.

Fred Rogers, the creator and producer of Mister Rogers Neighborhood, also meticulously defined his objectives before to writing the screenplay. One of his goals was to instill in kids the kind of attitudes that would enable them to deal with some of the issues that worry them while still feeling good about themselves and the world around them. Studies conducted at many universities revealed that young programme watchers enhanced or acquired traits including rule adherence, delay tolerance, and task perseverance.

The aims of an educational programme geared for adults should be defined just as carefully as those of programmes for youngsters. On the adult level, when it is thought that fundamental attitudes and values have already been developed, this work could be a little bit simpler. So, the focus is typically on disseminating knowledge that will broaden and deepen knowledge in a particular topic or on offering instruction targeted at refining or improving a skill.

Writing Educational Programmes: An Overview

In the broadcasting industry, "educational" programmes have a terrible reputation since education is typically associated with tedium.

Broadcasters started refraining from using the phrase a long time ago. NBC renamed its "education" branch to its "public service" division early on in its history. Non-commercial radio and television stations have started referring to their broadcasts as "public" rather than "educational" in recent years.

It is unavoidable that many educational programmes and lectures are uninteresting. But, dullness is not unavoidable. Educational programming may be just as thrilling and intellectually interesting as anything on television or in movies. The approach that writers use is essential.

They will inevitably bore their viewers if they use conventional strategies. On the other hand, they can hold the interest and attention of their audiences while educating them if they creatively and resourcefully employ the audio and visual medium. For television and film instructors, arousing and maintaining attention is significantly more important than it is for classroom educators. One explanation is that it's simple for spectators whose attention wanes to exit the room by flipping a switch. Even though they might be inclined to do so, students seldom leave during a boring lecture.

The fact that most people turn on their televisions expecting to be amused is a second reason why capturing their interest is crucial. Commercial television programmes successfully capitalise on this expectation in shows like The Electric Company and Sesame Street.

Choosing the Presentational Framework: The most apparent method for delivering instructional content on film and television is to mimic the standard lecture format used in the classroom. Individuals who do this are sometimes criticised for using a "talking head" to communicate their content. The issue with this strategy is that it fails to take use of what visual media has to offer. A speaker who spends the entirety of a show lecturing while only standing in front of a camera is virtually certain to be uninteresting. Nonetheless, it has proven to be challenging for educational script-writers to completely eradicate talking heads. Information-presenting programmes often require a presenter or narrator to deliver the material and give connectivity as the programme transitions between segments.

This method is perfectly appropriate as long as these parts make engaging and exciting use of the media's varied resources. At times, talking heads by themselves can be effective. Every episode of Mister Rogers' Neighborhood has Mr. Rogers speaking directly to his young viewers in a shot that frequently remains static for a significant amount of time. Here is a perfect example of how well they are used. The reason this strategy works is because Mr. Rogers has built a reputation as a trustworthy, compassionate person who speaks about issues that are immediately relevant to children's life, such the anxieties related to what he refers to as "the universal developmental demands of human development." Youngsters consequently observe with awe and fascination.

It resembles a personal visit via technological means. There are additional options for designing educational programmes than the host-narrator model. The show may centre on interviews with subject-matter specialists or it may include panel discussions with knowledgeable people, like PBS's The Week's News in Review. By airing the arguments that were published in the Congressional Record, several stations have addressed public problems. Even to introduce a serious topic for debate, a quiz style has been employed. Good programmes typically employ still images as their main visual component. In this manner, biographies of Mark Twain and Abraham Lincoln have been presented.

Pierre Berton's City of Gold, which combined still images and poetic narrative, was a spectacular movie that brought the Yukon gold rush to life with such vivid realism that its players appeared to be breathing.

Writing the Script: Clarity should be your top priority while developing an instructional programme. Your secondary objectives should be to sustain interest and make something memorable.

Each is necessary for the creation of a successful programme. You must make creative and innovative use of the audiovisual media's resources in order to accomplish these aims. The first step is to familiarise yourself with the materials completely.

You can only gain the knowledge required to use items like cameras, slides, switching methods, and film inserts in a practical and inventive way by actually witnessing them being used.

The Budget Situation: The financial constraints you face are one aspect you cannot ignore. It will decide which resources you might think about employing. Making an animated video is a great approach, for instance, to illustrate a process. Yet because this is a costly endeavour, only the most well-funded production companies can afford it. You must choose less expensive means of achieving your objectives if animation is out of your price range. Some production companies have created graphics with movable pieces that may be dragged to depict the phases in a process as a considerably less expensive alternative to animation.

You must have a comparable capacity for creativity in coming up with a range of effective ways to communicate information. Don't forget to keep in mind the programme participants when you do this. They are most likely your most valuable resource, therefore you need to employ them as effectively as you can.

Opening the Script: It's important to start the show off right since many listeners will choose to flip to something else or continue listening at that moment. You have to instill interest and an air of expectancy. Educational broadcasters frequently use the "teaser," a theatrical programme beginning approach used by numerous programmes. A teaser may be a question that piques your interest and for which the programme promises to provide a solution. A show on medicine, for instance, may begin by asking, "Are we winning the battle against cancer?" and then answer "Yes" by outlining recent developments in leukaemia therapy.

Opening the show with an intriguing section selected from the script's body is another technique to entice viewers to watch. But, this method has two drawbacks: some people could find its artifice too blatant, and because it offers information out of context, the audience might become confused. Due of this, some people prefer a straightforward opening that tries to pique attention using classic techniques like a provocative phrase, a quotation, a nod to something well-known, a promise of something uncommon, or a description of a recent occurrence. The opening should not only grab viewers' attention but also specify the topic of the show.

It is important to keep in mind that not everyone who has tuned in will be interested in viewing your presentation. You must explain the program's premise to potential viewers, keeping in mind that while some may object and say, "This is not for me," others could be drawn in by the information you offer.

The Body of the Script: We want to stress once more that being clear is your main duty while producing an instructive script. Your audience can only comprehend what you are providing if you are clear. And they are only inclined to keep listening if they comprehend. So, it is crucial to be clear if you want to capture and retain the audience's interest. Moreover, there are other characteristics that make instructional programmes more interesting. There are several of them that we connect with theatrical literature. In reality, while presenting information in instructional programming, writers frequently utilise a dramatic approach, especially when the content is biographical or historical.

To use a dramatic format, however, and to achieve many of the qualities we associate with drama, just as suspense writers do, you should try to gradually build up expectations and even suspense throughout the programme so that complete satisfaction does not arrive all at once but is instead given gradually. You might even be able to mention a contentious scenario sometimes. In a way, the program's climax can be provided by the last reveal. Thus, you should structure an instructional programme similarly to how you would a play, on a level that increases in fascination till the end.

Special Problems: Writing instructional programmes for kids presents authors with a variety of peculiar challenges. Writers need to be very conscious of the financial constraints they face. Insufficient resources lead to a variety of issues for which there are no obvious solutions. Writers must reply to them creatively. Also, they need to be aware of the circumstances around programme creation. For instance, in the making of Mister Rogers' Neighborhood, Mr. Rogers not only spoke to children personally but also provided the voices for many of the puppets that appeared in a fantastical section known as the Neighborhood of Make Believe.

Naturally, both Mr. Rogers, who is responsible for much of the shows' content, and the other members of the tiny team that compose the scripts are fully aware of this situation. Several parameters were created to help potential new authors get more familiar with the conditions under which Mr. Rogers' Neighborhood is produced.

Script Formats: An educational program's script may be completely written out or it may only be semi-scripted, or only partially written for presentation by a host or narrator who speaks impromptu. The structure of a fully scripted programme frequently resembles that of a documentary. Later in this chapter, when we offer a section of a 1920s screenplay to show the narration used in an information programme, another sort of format is introduced.

In contrast to other types of programmes, educational broadcasting uses the ad-libbed or extemporaneous approach more frequently. A typical structure for semiscripted programmes is shown in the script format below.

You'll see that the sentences serve as signals or reminders of the subject matter, which the narrator subsequently develops into a thorough exposition. To help the director put the films into the programme at precisely the appropriate time, the writer has written down the roll cues for the films in their entirety.

WRITING STYLES

Style typically involves some type of expression, including how we dress, how we live (or "lifestyle"), how we comb (or "style") our hair and how we write. Fashion, which comprises style changes, is frequently distinguished from style itself, which refers to the distinctiveness, individuality and personality of how we express ourselves.

Good Writing vs. Poor Writing

How can you tell the difference between a good writing style and a bad one? That is hard to predict. Below, we make an effort to doodle some broad guidelines that could be acceptable.

Good writing	Poor writing
1. Grammatically correct	Grammatically incorrect
2. Fluid, coherent	Incoherent, Fiagrnented
3. Imaginative	Dull, Prosaic
4. Having personality	Undistinctive

5. With interesting ideas	Expressing highly conventional idea
6. Using figurative language	Having a Simplistic structure
7. Easy to read	Hard to read

Thorough instruction and ongoing practise are necessary for good writing. Moreover, there are several elements that may be used to add colour and personality to one's writing. See what they are together.

Technical Devices

The following are some common methods in this category:

1. Alliteration: Alliteration is a dramatic effect technique. This entails using the same sound to begin many words.

2. Repetition: The deliberate use of specific phrases repeatedly to heighten dramatic effect; this method should be used sparingly.

3. Balance: This technique gives the text a certain amount of order and symmetry when comparing items or discussing concepts.

To provide the writing visual richness, descriptive and figurative language is employed, such as metaphors and similes.

Revision at Post Production Stage

Woody Allen famously referred to himself as a "compulsive rewriter," revising his work an average of five or six times. In this context, coming up with an original idea and writing the initial draught on paper are the most challenging tasks. Hence, revision may be done as many times as necessary to achieve your desired results. Yet in order to achieve so, you must have a comprehensive understanding of the approaches that are accessible as well as the genre- and format-related cues. The former was covered in the earlier subsections. You can learn a little more about the formats in the sections that follow.

GENRES AND FORMATS

A medium is just a vehicle for delivering different popular art forms or genres. These subgenres are frequently referred to as shows or programmes in the electronic media. On the other hand, a format refers to the structure of a screenplay, the particular norms (of writing) that one chooses to fulfil certain aims. Let's take a time to halt and review before moving forward. You must consider elements like the style, the media, and the genre when producing a script. Keep writing no matter what assignment you are working on.

- simple;
- fluent;
- lively;
- natural.

Types of Formats

Educational programme producers and writers frequently choose one format or a combination of two or more forms that best meets their needs for a certain topic or subject. A writer must spend some time considering the selection of an appropriate format for the efficient presentation of his programme content during the first stage of programme production. The exact subject matter, its requirements and aims, audience interests, and—most importantly—the availability of suitable production resources—all play a role in determining the format.

Kind of Programme Formats: Some of the standard formats used for presenting radio and television programmes are:

***(i)* Story/Straight Talk:** The straight talk or tale style often uses one person as the narrator and is better suited to radio programmes but is frequently used on television. This category includes illustrated speeches, special reports, newscasts and presenter-graphic-presenter-type programmes. Sometimes two people or voices are employed to provide information that are backed by suitable graphics, in order to add a little diversity. Stories and speeches, which are meticulously planned in preparation, are frequently employed to offer a range of instructional content via radio and television.

***(ii)* Interview:** In this approach, an interviewer and interviewee converse directly with one another. In order to obtain intriguing information from the interviewee that is pertinent to the subject being discussed, the interviewer converses with them on behalf of the viewers or listeners. The interview style is helpful, when presenting current affairs programmes, as well as informational and instructional programmes where a living scholar, scientist, or expert speaks to the audience to increase the programme's interest and credibility. In general, interviews do not follow a script.

***(iii)* Panel Discussion:** The interview format has been expanded in this way. Here, a chosen panel of three or more experts examines a topic of interest to the public or controversies. People with contrasting perspectives and viewpoints are brought together on a single stage for a panel discussion. Discussions are steered and moderated by the panel chairperson. There is no need for a script but the moderator or host should be well-prepared.

***(iv)* Feature:** In this structure, a single topic or subject is picked and its numerous elements are presented, as well as the same issue's facts, opinions, beliefs, arguments, disputes and counterarguments are discussed. For instance, a piece on Khajuraho's cave paintings may be created that goes into great detail about many elements of the subject.

***(v)* Magazine:** The word "magazine" derives from the print media. A radio or television magazine programme might feature a variety of subjects, often unconnected to one another, just as a weekly or fortnightly magazine section of a newspaper or periodical offers pieces on various topics. The distinction between a "magazine" and a "feature" is that the former covers a variety of topics, frequently with diverse target audiences in mind, while the latter focuses on different facets of the same subject.

***(vi)* Drama:** TV and radio have immediately appropriated this style from the theatre; it is essentially a literary method of story telling. Drama is a very fascinating and enjoyable format and it works especially well when it aims to touch the audience's emotions. Drama allows us to portray and observe individuals, their actions, dispositions and traits under realistic or lifelike circumstances.

***(vii)* Documentary:** The documentary format approaches a subject factually in contrast to drama. Here, a subject is examined in-depth and each of its facets is factually examined. Documenting actual life—real people, genuine events, real noises and real experiences of people—is the core focus of a documentary.

***(viii)* Quiz:** For conveying educational and current topics, it is a helpful structure. The quiz structure is quite engaging and interactive. The audience is engaged, kept actively participating in the programme and their attention is held.

Radio Script Format

When writing a radio script, there are a few essential guidelines to remember. Instructions on the left and discourse on the right should be separated into two columns on the page. Character names, music cues, sound effect cues and other instructions are listed in the left-hand column, double-spaced and in ALL CAPS. Except for dialogue, all text is capitalised and single spaced.

The only place to write dialogue is in the right-hand column. Always double space dialogue and use both capital and lowercase letters (like typical prose). This serves to set it apart from directions. As a result, the cast and crew can identify dialogue from non-dialogue at a look.

Instructions on how to read a line are provided in parenthesis, ALL CAPS and at the relevant locations on the right side of the script. Not only are the instructions for the music and sound effects shown in ALL CAPS but they are also underlined.

Television Script (Documentary) Format

The proposals that follow are grounded in common sense and logic. So, there are no strict guidelines for how television scripts should be formatted.

The page should be divided in half. The audio (and dialogue) is given the right side and the video is given the left side. The terms "video" and "audio" are often written at the top of each page.

The Video Side's Material Is All Typed In Capitals

Both directions and pictures are used in this. On the right side of the page, the audio side, dialogue is usually double spaced and written in both upper and lowercase letters. The rest is written in all caps.

Character names are typed in ALL CAPS and shown on the audio side.

Sound effects and music are each given in separate lines and are shown on the audio side. Physical movements are shown in the caps on the video side.

Documentary Writing Techniques

A documentary, in general, has six major components. A good script achieves a skill ful mix of these six elements. The six major components may be briefly described as follows:

***(i)* Narration:** The narrator sets the stage and helps provide continuity, leading viewers from one scene or interview to the next.

***(ii)* Voice-overs:** Here the narrator speaks but is not shown on screen.

***(iii)* Interviews** are used to give a taste of on-scene events to a documentary.

***(iv)* Graphics:** These may be captions, diagrams, or charts, maps and photographs.

***(v)* Music is used to establish a mood:** Natural sound and sound effects are used to enhance a mood.

In a nutshell, a good script is distinguished by visual complexity (diversity of shots) and cerebral complexity (different perspectives) structural depth (a 'conversation' created by weaving interviews in and out) a harmonious ratio of narration and images.

SCRIPTWRITING

The script is the fundamental cornerstone of every well-executed production, whether it be for the stage, radio, camera, or sellotape. It is a well planned blueprint that outlines the directions for technicians, directors, and performers. Television scriptwriting is primarily a collaborative endeavour. It might be interpreted as a form of conversation between the producer, the scriptwriter, and other members of the production crew. This conversation is mostly a team effort that starts with the finalised programme idea. To put it another way, the screenplays for movies or television shows develop gradually. The crucial terms in the screenwriting process are imagination, creativity, and teamwork.

Television scriptwriting may be seen of as a process with a number of steps or stages that don't always happen in order or independently of one another. In actuality, these actions or procedures work together and frequently cross over. Yet, the fundamental structure of the scripting process mostly stays the same, and TV scriptwriters go through specific stages whether they are aware of it or not. The following stages are described:

- Programme idea
- Programme outlinehrief
- Programme research
- Message planninglprogramme design
- Programme structure and visual treatment
- Story board making
- Draft-script
- Final-script
- camera script

Major stages in the scriptwriting process

1. Programme Idea: Discuss the idea and evaluate it against media selection criteria for video production.

2. Programme Brief Outline: Describe in detail the title, target audience, duration, programme objectives (in terms of behaviour), and content summary or synopsis in the programme brief that results from expanding the chosen and tested programme idea. The first written statement that serves as the foundation for a television or video script is called a "programme brief."

3. Research: The issue and your target audience should be thoroughly researched and planned. Look for graphic resources and other pertinent, fascinating information on the subject.

4. Selection of Materials: Select the most relevant materials, resources and ideas, which match your programme objectives.

5. Programme Design Strategy/Message Planning: Message planning is the most decisive and creative stage of programme development. Here, think about and decide on programme design and presentation strategy.

Programme Structure and Visual Treatment: The point at which the programme starts to take shape or take on its structure. It deals with the creative process of providing the show a distinct form and shape. Plan out a thorough visual treatment for your program's middle sections or sequences.

Storyboard Making: Storyboard means a detailed, shot-by-shot description of the programme on a sheet of paper divided into two vertical columns.

The story board is important because:

- It pushes the writer to think in terms of visuals.
- It is at this stage that the TV video screenplay begins to appear as morphing into a sequence of pictures in sequential continuity, with sound and action described alongside.
- Using a storyboard makes it simple to examine the general structure, growth, and progression of the script.
- If necessary, it is possible and advisable to change the script by adding, removing, moving, or rearranging shots and sequences.
- Everyone on the production crew should review the storyboard.

There are three main stages of script development. These are:

***(i)* Draft Script:** First full-length script with an exhaustive list and description of all visuals, captions, music, sound effects, and any accompanying commentary or dialogue. To collect their feedback and opinions, discuss your draught script with your coworkers, subject matter experts, and members of the production crew. Prepare yourself to take criticism of your rough draught and be receptive to suggestions for improvement.

***(ii)* Final Script:** All comments made during the draught script stage have now been taken into account. The producer then receives the completed script and must analyse it from a production standpoint in order to develop a camera script. By this point, the playwright often leaves the scene and the producer takes control, however communication between the two parties continues until the programme is fully finished.

***(iii)* Camera Script:** The final draught of the screenplay written by the playwright is transformed into a camera script for the producer and his crew to use at this crucial stage of script development. It is true that the screenplay is technical, with shot division, production team instructions, and logical sequences for music, effects, and speech. A camera script, in essence, represents the interrelationships between all resources and programme elements. For the producer, it serves as a crucial working document.

Testing of the Script: The evaluation of the script's efficacy is the final phase of script development. While producing a series of many programmes, it is important to test the script at least once with the intended audience.

The main idea of script-testing is to assess the presentation and \scomprehensibility of the content, the difficulty level of the language and the relevance and variety of materials usedto be used in the programme. When a whole script is used, the target audience is really read the contents to gauge their strengths and shortcomings. Some scholars make an effort to dramatise the narrative sections as they are written in the script. The screenwriter may make changes to the script's organisation and substance, as well as its design, order, and amount of graphics, based on the input it receives from the testing.

Script-testing is a kind of formative assessment that offers fast feedback on a variety of product features that may subsequently be appropriately updated prior to its actual manufacturing.

STAGES OF SCRIPT DEVELOPMENT: THE IGNOU CASE

The process of writing a screenplay for an audio or video show, for instance, may be broken down into three separate steps at IGNOU. These include preliminary research and the creation of a programme brief. the development of the programme brief into a note for academia. the development of the academic note into a script.

Programme Brief

In essence, the programme brief is the beginning of the actual work for an audiolvideo programme. The programme summary provides information on

- the target group
- working title
- objectives
- format and style
- content outline
- any additional information

The Academic Note

In essence, the programme brief is the beginning of the actual work for an audiolvideo programme. The programme summary provides information on

1. Media Content

(i) Self Contained TV.

(ii) TV as part of a multi-media package.

2. Learner's Characteristics.

(i) Age, knowledge, commitment, culture, conditions.

3. Teaching Objectives:

(i) Affective.

(ii) Motivational.

(iii) Experiential.

(iv) Cognitive.

4. Format and Style:

(i) Studio/locatiodmixed.

(ii) Presenter in visiodout of vision.

(iii) Documentry/Docu-drama.
(iv) Demonstratiodillustrated lecture1 case-study.
5. Outline of the content.

CHECK YOUR PROGRESS

Q. 1. List some of the considerations which must be kept in mind while writing for educational programmes.

Ans. When writing for educational programs, it is essential to keep in mind the following considerations:

1. Target Audience: The writer should have a clear understanding of the target audience, including their age, educational level, and background. The content should be tailored to the audience's needs, interests, and learning styles.

2. Visual Aids: As television is a visual medium, the writer should incorporate visual aids such as diagrams, animations, and graphics to supplement the written content. These aids should be simple, clear, and relevant to the topic.

3. Time Constraints: Educational programs usually have a limited amount of time, and the writer must ensure that the content can be covered in the allotted time. The content should be concise, well-structured, and engaging to maintain viewers' attention.

4. Interactive Elements: Interactive elements such as quizzes, polls, and games can be included to engage the audience and reinforce learning.

5. Language: The language used in the program should be clear, concise, and easily understandable by the target audience. Technical terms should be explained, and complex ideas should be presented in a simple and straightforward manner.

6. Cultural Sensitivity: The writer should be aware of cultural differences and ensure that the content is sensitive to the audience's cultural background and beliefs. The program should avoid offensive or controversial material and promote inclusivity and diversity.

Q. 2. Briefly describe the process of writing for an educational programme.

Ans. Writing for an educational program involves several steps. Here is a brief overview of the process:

1. Identify the Topic: The first step is to identify the topic of the educational program. This should be based on the program's learning objectives and the target audience's interests and needs.

2. Research: Once the topic is identified, the writer should conduct extensive research to gather relevant information. This could involve reading books, articles, and online resources, as well as conducting interviews with subject matter experts.

3. Outline: After gathering information, the writer should create an outline of the program's structure and content. This should include the program's objectives, key concepts, and a logical sequence of information.

4. Scriptwriting: The next step is to start writing the script. The script should be written in a simple and straightforward language, with a focus on engaging the audience and reinforcing learning. Visual aids, such as graphics and animations, should be included where necessary.

5. Review and Editing: Once the script is complete, it should be reviewed and edited for accuracy, clarity, and flow. The script should be reviewed by subject matter experts, as well as editors, to ensure that it is error-free and engaging.

6. Production: After the script is finalized, the program can be produced. This involves coordinating with producers, directors, and other members of the production team to ensure that the program is produced to a high standard.

7. Testing and Feedback: Once the program is complete, it should be tested with a sample audience to gather feedback. This feedback should be used to refine the program and make improvements where necessary.

Q. 3. Distinguish between good writing and poor writing by listing any of the three characteristics of each.

Ans. Good writing and poor writing can be distinguished by several characteristics. Here are three characteristics of each:

Good Writing:

1. Clarity: Good writing is clear and concise, making it easy for the reader to understand the message being conveyed. It uses simple language and avoids unnecessary jargon or technical terms.

2. Organization: Good writing is well-organized, with a logical flow of ideas that is easy to follow. It uses headings, subheadings, and bullet points to break up the text and make it more readable.

3. Creativity: Good writing is creative and engaging, using literary devices such as metaphor, simile, and personification to bring the message to life. It is original and fresh, capturing the reader's attention from the first sentence.

Poor Writing:

1. Lack of Clarity: Poor writing is often unclear, making it difficult for the reader to understand the message. It may use complex language or jargon that is difficult to understand or be disorganized and rambling.

2. Poor Organization: Poor writing may lack a clear structure or be poorly organized, with ideas presented in a random or illogical manner. It may jump from topic to topic without a clear sense of direction.

3. Lack of Creativity: Poor writing may be dull and uninteresting, lacking the creative flair that makes good writing engaging. It may be filled with clichés or lack originality, making it predictable and uninspired.

Q. 4. List the major programme formats.

Ans. Some of the standard formats are:

(i) **Story/Straight Talk:** The straight talk or tale style often utilises one person as the narrator and is better suited to radio programmes but is frequently used on television. This category includes illustrated talks, special reports, newscasts, and presenter graphic-presenter-type programmes. Sometimes two people or voices are employed to provide information that are backed by suitable graphics in order to add

a little diversity. Stories and speeches, which are meticulously planned in preparation, are frequently employed to offer a range of instructional content via radio and television.

***(ii)* Interview:** In this approach, an interviewer and interviewee converse directly with one another. In order to get intriguing information from the interviewee that is pertinent to the subject being discussed, the interviewer converses with them on behalf of the viewers or listeners. The interview style is helpful for presenting current events programmes, as well as informational and instructional programmes where a live scholar, scientist, or expert speaks to the audience to increase the program's interest and credibility. In general, interviews do not follow a script. Just the opening and closing comments and questions are prepared in advance and occasionally practised.

The interviewer's confidence, talent, and preparation are heavily reliant on the remainder of the programme, which is extempore and unscripted.

At the core of a successful interview are pertinent questions that are clearly phrased, ordered logically, and addressed with assurance, sensitivity, and spontaneity.

***(iii)* Panel Discussion:** The interview format has been expanded in this way. Here, a chosen panel of three or more experts examines a topic of interest to the public or controversies. People with contrasting perspectives and viewpoints are brought together on a same stage for a panel discussion. Discussions are steered and moderated by the panel chairperson. It requires no script but the moderater or the host should prepare thoroughly. To guarantee a friendly, orderly, and fruitful debate, he should be extremely vigilant, knowledgeable, and tactful while also being fully in control of the situation.

***(iv)* Feature:** In this structure, a single topic or subject is chosen for presentation of its numerous sides and the debate of facts, opinions, \sbeliefs, arguments, disputes and counter-arguments - all about the same issue. For example, a piece on cave paintings, Khajuraho may be prepared dealing exhaustively with many elements of the subject.

***(v)* Magazine:** The word "magazine" derives from the print media. A radio or television magazine show might feature a variety of subjects, frequently unconnected to one another, just as a weekly or fortnightly magazine section of a newspaper or periodical offers pieces on various themes. The distinction between a "magazine" and a "feature" is that the former covers a range of topics, frequently with diverse target audiences in mind, while the latter focuses on different facets of the same subject. A magazine programme is comparable to a trip to a fair or big-box retailer, where we can find materials for a wide range of customers or target audiences.

***(vi)* Drama:** TV and radio have immediately appropriated this style from the theatre; it is essentially a literary method of narrative telling. Drama is a very fascinating and enjoyable format, and it works especially well when it aims to touch the audience's emotions. Drama allows us to portray and observe individuals, their actions, dispositions, and traits under realistic or lifelike circumstances. Developing and producing \sa decent television drama is a demanding endeavour. Yet many academic subjects, including those in history, literature, the social sciences, and other fields, are perfectly suited to dramatic adaptation and presentation. A cast of actors performs drama, which calls for realistic settings to depict circumstances and happenings.

***(vii)* Documentary:** The documentary genre approaches a subject factually in contrast to drama. Here, a subject is examined in-depth, and each of its facets is factually examined. Documenting actual life—real people, genuine events, real noises, and real experiences of people—is the core focus of a documentary. The primary responsibility of a documentary filmmaker is to thoroughly and accurately study and explore all facets of the subject. He employs a variety of presentation techniques, such as narration, montage, interviews, discussions, eyewitness accounts, candid photos and videos of actual events, comments from the "man on the street," and expert opinion—all of which are logically combined.

***(viii)* Quiz:** For conveying educational and current topics, it is a helpful structure. The quiz structure is quite engaging and interactive. The audience is engaged, kept actively participating in the programme, and their attention is held.

It should be noted that depending on the writer and producer of the programme, the majority of the aforementioned forms may be employed separately as well as in combination. Yet once more, the choice of format—or mix of formats—depends on the goals of the particular subject matter as well as the time, money, and resource constraints. You just read about a few of the presenting forms for programmes that writers for radio and television frequently utilise.

Q. 5. State the important factors which determine the choice of a particular programme format by a writer or a producer.

Ans. The choice of a particular programme format by a writer or a producer can depend on a variety of factors, including:

1. Target Audience: The format of a programme may be determined by the target audience that the writer or producer is trying to reach. For example, a children's show will have a different format than a news program aimed at adults.

2. Content: The content of the programme may also dictate the format. A documentary or news program may require a more traditional format with a presenter and interviews, while a comedy show may be more flexible in its structure.

3. Production budget: The budget for producing the programme can also influence the format. Some formats may be more expensive to produce than others, so the budget may dictate what format is chosen.

4. Length: The length of the programme can also determine the format. A short-form programme may require a more concise format, while a longer programme may require a more extensive structure.

5. Platform: The platform where the programme will be aired or distributed can also influence the format. For example, a programme made for streaming may have a different format than one made for traditional broadcast television.

6. Competition: The level of competition in the market can also be a factor in the choice of format. If there are already many programmes with a similar format, a writer or producer may choose a different format to stand out.

7. Creative Vision: Ultimately, the choice of format may also be determined by the creative vision of the writer or producer. They may have a specific idea of how they want the programme to look and feel, and the format will be chosen accordingly.

Q. 6. What are the techniques commonly used in a documentary?

Ans. There are several techniques that are commonly used in documentary filmmaking to tell a story and engage the audience. Some of these techniques include:

1. Interviews: Interviews are a common technique in documentaries. Filmmakers interview people who are experts on the subject matter or who have personal experience related to the topic of the film.

2. Archival footage: Archival footage is often used in documentaries to provide historical context or to show footage from the past. This can include newsreels, home movies, and other historical footage.

3. Voiceover narration: Voiceover narration is often used in documentaries to provide context and to guide the audience through the story.

4. Re-enactments: Reenactments are sometimes used in documentaries to recreate a scene or event that cannot be captured on film.

5. Montage: Montage is a technique in which footage or images are edited together in a sequence to create a specific effect or convey a message.

6. Animation: Animation is sometimes used in documentaries to illustrate complex ideas or to create a visual representation of a concept.

7. Verité: Verité is a technique in which the filmmaker captures events as they happen in real-time without interfering with the subjects or events being filmed. This technique aims to provide a sense of authenticity and realism.

8. Music: Music is often used in documentaries to set the tone and mood of a film, to underscore key moments, or to provide emotional impact.

Overall, the techniques used in a documentary will depend on the subject matter and the creative vision of the filmmaker.

Q. 7. Briefly describe the formats of audio and video scripts.

Ans. Audio and video scripts have different formats depending on their intended use and production needs. Here are some common formats for both:

Audio Script Formats: Two-Column Format: This format has two columns; one for the audio script and another for production notes such as sound effects, music, and narration instructions.

1. Single-Column Format: This format has only one column and is a simpler version of the two-column format. It is ideal for scripts that require minimal production notes.

2. Screenplay Format: This format is commonly used for audio dramas and radio plays. It follows the same format as a screenplay, with scene headings, action lines, and dialogue.

Video Script Formats:

1. Two-Column Format: Like the audio script format, the two-column format includes one column for the video script and another for production notes such as camera angles, transitions, and special effects.

2. AV Script Format: This format is used for video productions that require detailed shot lists and technical instructions for camera operators and editors.

3. Storyboard Format: Storyboards are visual representations of each scene or shot in a video. They are often used as a pre-visualization tool for planning and organizing the video production process.

Overall, the format of an audio or video script will depend on the intended use, the production needs, and the preference of the writer or producer.

Q. 8. Beginning with the programme brief stage, list the major steps involved in the development of a video programme script.

Ans. The development of a video programme script involves several key steps from the programme brief stage to the final script. Here are some of the major steps:

1. Programme Brief: The first step is to establish the programme brief, which outlines the purpose, target audience, and format of the video programme.

2. Research: The next step is to conduct research on the topic and gather information that will be used in the script. This can include interviews, articles, and other relevant materials.

3. Outline: Once research is completed, the writer creates an outline for the script, which includes the main points, themes, and structure of the video programme.

4. First Draft: Using the outline as a guide, the writer creates the first draft of the script, incorporating research and outlining material into the script.

5. Review and Revision: After the first draft, the script is reviewed and revised, with input from producers, directors, and other members of the production team. The script may go through several rounds of revision until it meets the desired standard.

6. Final Draft: After all revisions are completed, the final draft of the script is created, including all necessary production instructions such as camera angles, sound effects, and lighting instructions.

7. Table Read: The script is read aloud by the production team to ensure that it flows well and that all technical instructions are clear and concise.

8. Shooting Script: Finally, the shooting script is created, which includes detailed production notes and instructions for filming and editing the video programme.

These steps are iterative and may involve multiple rounds of feedback, revision, and refinement until the final script is approved for production.

OTHER IMPORTANAT QUESTIONS

Q. 1. What are educational programmes? Discuss types of educational programmes.

Ans. A group of educational activities that are planned to achieve a specific goal or complete a set of educational tasks is referred to as an educational programme. The basic goal of education is to give people the chance to acquire the knowledge and skills they need to reach their full potential and contribute successfully to society.

Types of Educational Programmes: One that directly teaches a lesson from the normal curriculum is the most regimented kind of educational programme. Direct teaching is exemplified by television programming that explains fractions in an elementary school math lesson or covers topics not included in the traditional curriculum, such as foreign language. ITV, another name for this kind of transmission, is instructional television. Similar to how many businesses do, the armed forces employ training films to teach its staff how to perform specific tasks.

A different kind of educational programme serves as an addition to the instruction given by the usual teacher. For instance, a class of elementary school students studying American history might see a movie or television show on a particular event in George Washington's life. A film named Geronimo Jones, which illustrates the emotional harm brought on by the stereotyping of native American Indians, might be shown to a university class interested in how movies and television portray stereotypes of certain populations. The programme that combines entertainment and education, falls under a third category.

Sesame Street, in particular, occasionally engages in what might be called direct instruction in an effort to teach pre-school children to recognise numbers and letters but both programmes also contain segments that are obviously intended to be entertaining. Programmes like Captain Kangaroo and Sesame Street have clear educational objectives. The television programme Victory at Sea educated viewers about World War II's naval history, while also providing them with top-notch entertainment.

Q. 2. What is the procedure to write educational programmes?

Ans. The most obvious method for presenting instructional content on film and television is to mimic the standard lecture format used in the classroom. Those who do this are frequently criticised for using a "talking head" to communicate their content. The issue with this strategy is that it fails to take use of what visual media has to offer. A speaker who spends the entirety of a show lecturing, while only standing in front of a camera is almost certain to be uninteresting. But it's been challenging for educational scriptwriters to completely do away with talking heads. Information-presenting programmes typically require a presenter or narrator to deliver the material and give connectivity as the programme transitions between segments.

This method is perfectly appropriate as long as these parts make engaging and stimulating use of the media's varied resources. At times, talking heads by themselves can be effective. Every episode of Mister Rogers' Neighbourhood has Mr. Rogers speaking directly to his young viewers, frequently in a camera shot that does not move for a significant amount of time. This is a nice example of how they are used well. The reason this strategy works is because Mr. Rogers has built a reputation as a trustworthy, compassionate person who speaks about issues that are immediately relevant to children's life, like the anxieties related to what he refers to as "the universal growth demands of human development."

Children consequently observe with awe and fascination. It resembles a personal visit via electronic means. There are additional options for designing educational programmes than the host-narrator model. The programme may centre on interviews with subject-matter specialists or it may include panel discussions with knowledgeable people, like PBS's The Week's News in Review. By airing the arguments that were published in the Congressional Record, several stations have addressed public issues. Even to introduce a serious topic for debate, a quiz style has been employed. Excellent programmes typically employ still images as their main visual component. In this manner, biographies of Mark Twain and Abraham Lincoln have been presented. Pierre Berton's City of Gold, which combined still images and poetic narration, was a spectacular movie that brought the Yukon gold rush to life with such vivid realism that its players appeared to be breathing.

Writing the Script: Clarity should be your top priority, while writing an educational programme. Your secondary objectives should be to maintain interest and make something memorable. Each is necessary for the creation of a successful programme. You must make creative and imaginative use of the audiovisual media's resources, in order to accomplish these goals. The first step is to familiarise yourself with the resources completely. You can only gain the knowledge required to use items like cameras, slides, switching techniques and film inserts in a practical and inventive way by actually witnessing them being used.

The Budget Situation: This project will cost a lot of money. However, only production companies with the greatest financial resources may afford. You must choose less expensive means of achieving your objectives if animation is out of your price range. Several production companies have created graphics with movable pieces that may be pulled to depict the steps in a process as a considerably, less expensive alternative to animation. You must exhibit a similar capacity for creativity in coming up with a range of effective ways to communicate information. Don't forget to keep in mind the programme participants when you do this. They are most likely your most valuable resource, so you need to employ them as effectively as you can.

Opening the Script: It's important to start the programme off right because many listeners will choose to turn to something else or continue listening at that point. You have to instil curiosity and an air of expectation. Educational broadcasters frequently use the "teaser", a theatrical programme opening approach used by numerous programmes. A teaser could be a question that piques your interest and for which the programme promises to provide a solution. For instance, a medical programme might begin by asking, "Are we gaining on cancer?" and then answer "yes" by outlining recent developments in the treatment of leukaemia. Opening the show with an intriguing section selected from the script's body is another technique to entice viewers to watch. However, this method has two drawbacks: some people might find its artifice too blatant and because it offers information out of context, the audience might become confused. Due to this, some people prefer a straightforward opening, that tries to pique attention using classic techniques like a provocative phrase, a quotation, a nod to something well-known, a promise of something uncommon, or a description of a recent occurrence. The opening should not only grab viewers' attention but also specify the topic of the presentation. It is important to keep in mind that not everyone who has tuned in, will be interested in viewing your presentation. You must explain the programme's premise to potential viewers, keeping in mind that while some may object and say, "This is not for me", others might be drawn in by the information you offer.

Script Formats: An educational programme's script may be completely written out or it may merely be semi-scripted, or only partially written for presentation by a host or narrator who speaks impromptuously. The structure of a fully-scripted programme, frequently resembles that of a documentary. Later in this chapter, when we offer a section of a 1920s script to show the narration used in an information programme, another type of format is introduced. In contrast to other types of programmes, educational broadcasting uses the ad-libbed or extemporaneous method more frequently.

Q. 3. Write a note on radio script format.

Ans. When composing a radio script, the following guidelines should be kept in mind:

Instructions on the left and discourse on the right should be separated into two columns on the page. Character names, music cues, sound effect cues and other instructions are listed in the left-hand column, double-spaced and in ALL CAPS. Except for dialogue, all text is capitalised and single-spaced.

The only place to write dialogue is in the right-hand column. Always double space dialogue and use both capital and lowercase letters (like typical prose). This serves to set it apart from directions. As a result, the cast and crew can identify dialogue from non-dialogue at a look.

Instructions on how to read a line are provided in parenthesis, ALL CAPS and at the relevant locations on the right side of the script. Not only are the instructions for the music and sound effects shown in ALL CAPS but they are also underlined.

Q. 4. Write briefly on television script (documentary) format.

Ans. There are no strict guidelines for how television scripts should be formatted. However, the following style can be followed:

- The page should be divided in to half. The audio and dialogue is given the right side and the video is given the left side. The terms "video" and "audio" are often written at the top of each page.
- The video side's materials are all typed in capitals.
- Both directions and pictures are used in this. On the right side of the page, the audio side, dialogue is usually double spaced and written in both upper and lowercase letters. The rest is written in ALL CAPS.
- Character names are typed in all caps and shown on the audio side.
- Sound effects and music are each given in separate lines and are shown on the audio side. Physical movements are shown in the caps on the Video side.

Q. 5. Discuss different documentary writing techniques.

Ans. A documentary typically consists of six main parts. These six components are skill fully combined in a strong script. The following is a succinct description of the six main components: Setting the scene and assisting with continuity, the narrator guides the audience from one scene or interview to the next. There shouldn't be too much narrative. Characters in a documentary should tie the story together, rather than take centre stage and overshadow the main subject.

Voice-overs: In this instance, the narrator is audible but not shown on-screen. He or she instead offers commentary or clarifies something we see on the television. Voice-overs should mostly be utilised to advance the action.

Interviews are used to give a taste of on-scene events to a documentary.

Graphics: These may be captions, diagrams, or charts, maps and photographs.

Music is used to establish a mood.

Natural sound and sound effects are used to enhance a mood.

To briefly recapitulate what we discussed: a good script is characterised by visual complexity (variety of shots), intellectual complexity (different perspectives), structural depth (interviews weaving in and out to make a 'dialogue') and a good balance between narration and visuals.

Q. 6. Discuss different stages of script development.

Ans. There are three main stages of script development. These are:

(i) **Draft Script:** First full-length script with an exhaustive list and description of all graphics, captions, music, sound effects and any accompanying comments or dialogue. To collect their feedback and opinions, discuss your draught script with your coworkers, subject matter experts and members of the production crew. Prepare yourself to take criticism of your rough draught and be receptive to suggestions for improvement.

***(ii)* Final Script:** All comments given during the draft script stage have now been taken into account. The producer then receives the completed script and must analyse it from a production standpoint, in order to develop a camera script. After this point, the scriptwriter typically leaves the scene and the producer takes control, however communication between the two parties continues until the programme is fully finished.

***(iii)* Camera Script:** The final draught of the script written by the playwright is transformed into a camera script for the producer and his team to use at this crucial stage of script development. It is true that the script is technical, with shot division, production team instructions and logical sequences for music, effects and dialogue. A camera script, in essence, represents the interrelationships between all resources and programme elements. For the producer, it serves as a crucial working document.

***(iv)* Testing of the Script:** The evaluation of the script's effectiveness is the final phase of script development. When producing a series of many programmes, it is advisable to test the script at least once with the intended audience. The major goal of script testing is to evaluate the content's presentation and understandability, the language's level of difficulty and the relevancy and variety of the resources to be utilised in the show. When a whole script is used, the target audience actually reads the contents to gauge their strengths and shortcomings. Some scholars make an effort to dramatise the narrative sections as they are written in the script. The scriptwriter may make changes to the script's organisation and substance, as well as its design, order and amount of visuals, based on the input it receives from the testing. Script-testing is a kind of formative evaluation that offers fast feedback on a variety of product features that may subsequently be appropriately updated, prior to its actual production.

MULTIPLE CHOICE QUESTIONS

Q. 1. The term "instructional television" is another name for:

(a) Educational broadcasting
(b) Religious broadcasting
(c) Training programme
(d) None of these

Ans. *(a)* Educational broadcasting.

Q. 2. Which should be your top priority, while writing an educational programme?

(a) Clarity
(b) To maintain interest
(c) Make something memorable
(d) None of these

Ans. *(a)* Clarity.

Q. 3. Which should be your secondary priority, while writing an educational programme?

(a) To maintain interest
(b) Make something memorable
(c) Both *(a)* and *(b)*
(d) None of these

Ans. *(c)* Both *(a)* and *(b)*.

Q. 4. Which uses one person as the narrator and is better suited to radio programmes but is frequently used on television?

(a) The straight talk or tale style
(b) Interview
(c) Panel discussion
(d) Feature

Ans. *(a)* The straight talk or tale style

Q. 5. People with contrasting perspectives and viewpoints are brought together on a single stage for:

(a) The straight talk or tale style
(b) Interview
(c) Panel discussion
(d) Feature

Ans. *(c)* Panel discussion.

Q. 6. Which of the following approaches a subject factually, in contrast to drama?

(a) Documentary *(b)* Interview
(c) Panel discussion *(d)* Feature

Ans. *(a)* Documentary.

Q. 7. Radio script format should have how many columns?

(a) Two *(b)* Three
(c) Four *(d)* One

Ans. *(a)* Two.

Q. 8. In radio script, instructions should be written on the:

(a) Left column *(b)* Right column
(c) Below or top *(d)* None of these

Ans. *(a)* Left column.

Q. 9. In radio script, discourse should be written on the:

(a) Left column *(b)* Right column
(c) Below or top *(d)* None of these

Ans. *(b)* Right column.

Q. 10. In radio script, character names should be written on the:

(a) Left column *(b)* Right column
(c) Below or top *(d)* None of these

Ans. *(a)* Left column.

Q. 11. In radio script, sound effect cues should be written on the:

(a) Left column *(b)* Right column
(c) Below or top *(d)* None of these

Ans. *(a)* Left column.

Q. 12. In radio script, except for dialogue, all text should be:

(a) Capitalised and double-spaced
(b) Capitalised and single-spaced
(c) Lowercase and single-spaced
(d) Lowercase and double-spaced

Ans. *(b)* Capitalised and single-spaced.

Q. 13. In a TV script, the audio (and dialogue) is given:

(a) On right side *(b)* On left side
(c) At bottom *(c)* None of these

Ans. *(a)* On right side.

Q. 14. In a TV script, the vidoe is given:

(a) On right side *(b)* On left side
(c) At bottom *(c)* None of these

Ans. *(b)* On left side.

■■

Skills and Resources for Video Production

11

INTRODUCTION

A more difficult procedure than audio production is video production. As a result, the production process necessary for the audio components is incorporated into the production of television programmes. Thus, the video production is the focus of this discussion. Our discussion in this chapter will mostly centre on some of the fundamental production techniques required in a studio, as well as field location shooting of educational and developmental programmes. We concentrate on the production's planning, scheduling and execution, as well as the technological resources required for this project. Aspects including screenplay analysis, production and graphics preparation, camera operations and recording will also be covered in detail.

CHAPTER AT A GLANCE

PRODUCTION PLANNING, SCHEDULING AND EXECUTION

After the final script stage, the producer must complete the necessary production activities and responsibilities and coordinate them with other professionals and officials.

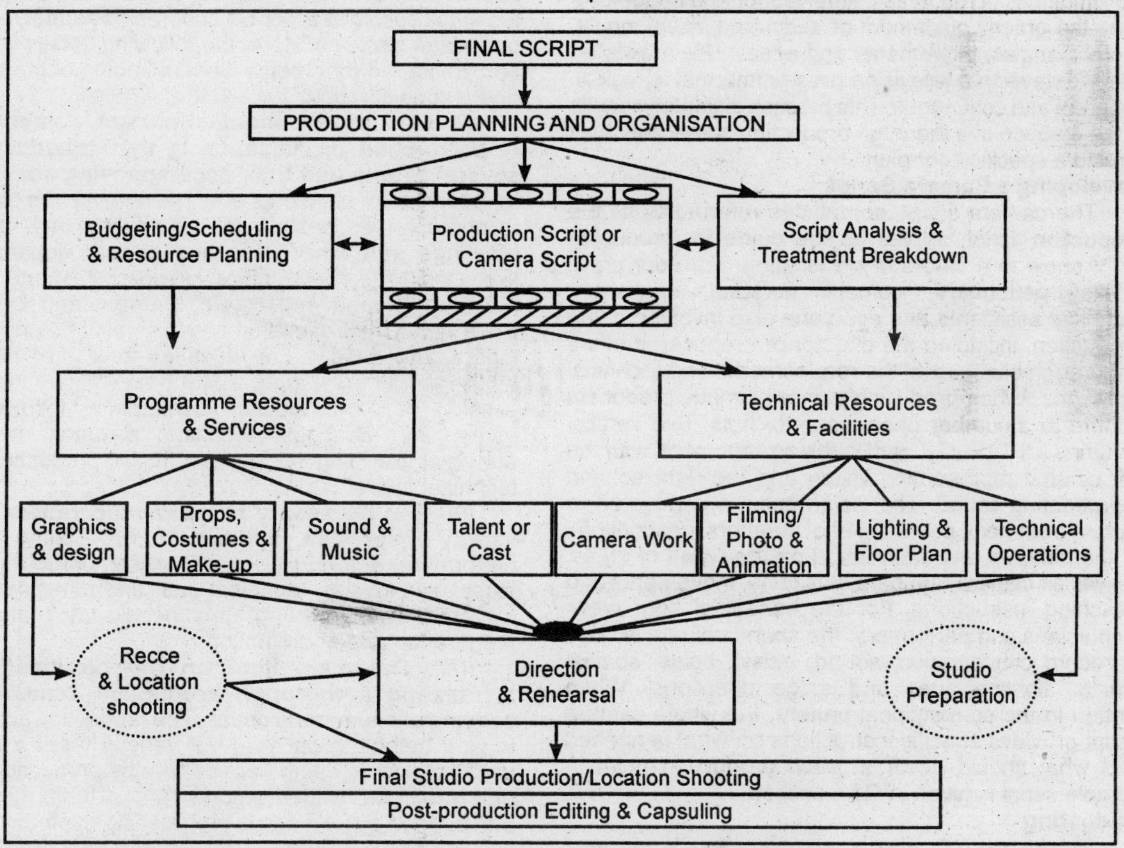

Fig. 1: TV Production: Planning & Organisation

The scriptwriter typically steps down once he or she has completed the final version of the script, with the exception of those media organisations who prioritise team-mode production. However, it is desirable for the scriptwriter and the academic or content experts to be involved with the production process, all the way through in complex educational works. Once the final script has been authorised or approved, the scriptwriter's function may become optional in straightforward production. Frequently, at this point, the producer assumes full control over the production and the nature of their work becomes clear. Teamwork is at the heart of television production, thus a competent producer must learn to interact with a variety of individuals and have the necessary skill and competency in handling people and situations.

Script Analysis

The study and analysis of the programme script is always the first step in any form of professional production planning. The producer examines the screenplay from numerous production vantage points and develops thorough specifications for the programme's various resources, including visual, auditory, technical, human, financial and other ancillary requirements. The producer commits to what is known as a "treatment-breakdown" of various aspects of the programme, while keeping in mind the limitations of resources, time, labour and budget. He sees the orderly placement of audio and visual inputs, camera angles, movements and effects. He makes an effort to develop a television programme that is logical, coherent and continuous. This process ultimately results in the creation of a thorough production screenplay built around a specific floor plan.

Developing a Camera Script

The camera script, sometimes referred to as the production script, serves as the guide for producing a TV show in a studio or on location. For floor crew, artists, performers, camera persons, engineers, technical assistants and everyone else involved in the production, including the director or producer, it offers a thorough blueprint of the requirements and technical directions. When producing camera scripts, producers adhere to a number of common formats. Two vertical columns are typically used in the arrangement, with the left column representing vision and the right column representing sound. The vision column is devoted to picture treatment, providing shot numbers, descriptions of the pictures and information on the types of shots, as well as camera numbers, positions, movements and switching instructions. For the benefit of floor crew, technicians and performers, the sound column is used to record conversation, sound, music, noise, special effects, lighting cues and stage directions. When written in the conventional pattern, the whole camera script provides specific instructions on what is needed and what should occur at each production point. A sample script is given in Q&A section.

Budgeting

Production of media programmes is a very expensive endeavour, so good cost estimation and proper bookkeeping are essential. One of the producer's primary responsibilities is creating and adhering to a budget. Show budget caps are typically set and producers are required to keep their estimations within the overall ceiling outlined for each programme. However, it must be emphasised that in television, the cost of renting out equipment or machinery is calculated by the hour and the cost of operating a studio is assessed in hours, minutes and seconds. Therefore, utilising studios, facilities and equipment for longer than is necessary to produce a show, constitutes criminal waste in the same way that under- or non-utilizing the infrastructure and resources that are already accessible does.

Resources Planning and Scheduling

The creation of media requires a variety of resources and inputs. It demands multitasking and extensive planning in advance, due to the nature of the situation. Therefore, in practice, the planning of programme resources and the scheduling of various production events starts at the very beginning and goes on in parallel with the creation of scripts, setting budgets and other tasks. Two categories of resources, namely: *(i)* programme resources and services, *(ii)* technical resources and facilities, can be used to group the main resources that the producer must plan and schedule for execution. Several of these significant programme and technical resources will be covered separately in this unit's later sections. Here, the following details need to be considered for a better understanding of the theme under consideration.

***(i)* One of the most important components of production organisation is the (scheduling of several events and their accompanying activities).** In addition to choosing and overseeing the cast, it is primarily responsible for scheduling and running meetings with other units and service departments like Design and Graphics, Props, Costumes and Make-up, Sound and Music, Camera and Lighting, Photo, Film and Animation and Technical Planning and Operations. A series of meetings must also be held by the producer, starting with the preliminary planning session or pre-production conference, followed by screenplay meetings, technical planning sessions and joint planning sessions with the production and technical team.

***(ii)* It is necessary to make reservations for a variety of services, facilities,** studios, editing rooms, performers, actors, musicians, artists, camera crews, studio employees, technical staff and other services, well in advance. All of this necessitates intensive preparation and coordination.

***(iii)* The main item on the producer's list is creating a thorough production schedule** for carrying out numerous duties. The production schedule is very helpful in carrying out various tasks and is a useful tool for keeping track of how the production work that has been divided among various team members and support employees is progressing each day.

***(iv)* The overall execution of the total production campaign depends heavily on setting and assigning**

clear-cut tasks to all officials and realistic deadlines. This is when the producer's abilities as a skilled public relations specialist and "manager of men and matters" really shine. One of the best ways to plan and schedule the production of a show is to start with the final deadline (which could be kept a week ahead of the precise preview date) and work backwards, setting a specific time limit for each activity and coordinating different events to reduce the overall production time.

***(v)* The creation and use of proformas, schedules, call sheets, etc.,** greatly eases the life of producers and their production helpers. As efficient communication tools, wall charts, production planners, scheduling charts, artists address lists, facilities request forms, performer's contract proformas, call sheets and many other schedules should be accurately filled out and distributed to the relevant personnel, while stating strict deadlines and time limits.

PROGRAMME AND TECHNICAL RESOURCES

You must have a solid understanding of the programme and the available technical resources before attempting any phase of production. Four primary sources are the topics of our discussion. These are light, sound, camera, and graphics.

Graphics

The design or development of graphics is a technical step in the production of a video. Concepts or information that cannot be clearly expressed or communicated through spoken words or live actions are provided through images. They possess the ability to make knowledge engaging, convincing, attractive, and efficient. You should think about the following three things when you prepare, design, and select the visuals for your video screen.

Aspect Ratio: It speaks about the ratio of the graphic card's width to height. A computer or television display has the proportions 3:4, or three units high by four units wide. Hence, all visual representations should adhere to this aspect ratio.

Essential area: Moreover, it is known as the critical region and safe title area. All necessary information must be contained inside this region in order to prevent visual loss during transmission and playback. The part of the picture that was lost during transmission and scanning is referred to as domestic cut-off. To ensure that no portion of the graphic card is missed on the screen, the scanning and important portions of the graphic must be included in the shot.

Readability: It indicates that the viewer should be able to read the text or other written information as it appears on the screen. Too much information is printed in too-small-to-read fonts for the viewer to completely comprehend. So, we should always use big, bold characters for good reading.

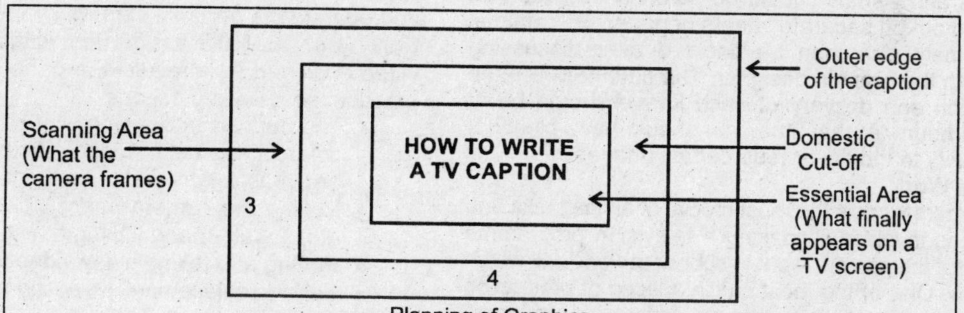

Planning of Graphics

Types of Graphics: Graphics are of five types:

***(i)* Title card:** It is a simple card having information on it, usually written or partially illustrated, such as the title of the show and/or the names of the writer, producer, and programme director.

***(ii)* Key Card:** The "super caption," or "super card," often includes black text on a white background. The black backdrop vanishes and the white letters cover the initial source or scene when superimposing or keying.. A visitor's name is frequently displayed over his or her image on the screen using a key card to identify the person. Information on a key card is always compacted and written in a size that is easy to read.

***(iii)* Slides:** Slides in colour or "black and white" may only be seen on a television if they were taken horizontally. Vertical slides are out of aspect ratio and appear awful on the screen.

***(iv)* Maps, Charts and Photo-captions:** Maps, charts, diagrams, tables, graphs, and photographs are essential visual tools for video programmes because they attempt to communicate the most information possible simply, quickly, and clearly. The degree of attention in a programme may be and often is increased by animated graphics.

***(v)* The Chroma Key Card:** As contrast to a super card's black backdrop, the chroma key card has a blue background. The chroma key card may be keyed into the background scene or image using the chroma key technique, which allows the blue colour to vanish during keying. The chroma key, also known as a "colour separation overlay" or CSO, is really an electrical instrument that "cuts out" any undesired elements of a picture (by colouring them blue) and superimposes the remaining portions over another image or backdrop.

Shooting Graphics

When working with easel graphics in the studio, we should be cautious of two things: Keystoning and glare. Keystoning is an ugly effect that happens when the camera is not exactly perpendicular in both its vertical and horizontal axes to the flat graphic it is photographing! In this case, the floor person should tilt or rotate the graphic up or down to minimise the off-axis angle rather than requesting the camera person to perform the fix. Glare can be avoided by creating the photo's surface with a matte finish as opposed to a glossy one. To reduce glare more quickly, try rotating the graphic at different angles in relation to the problematic light source.

General Rules for Graphics: Graphic designers normally need adequate time to prepare the photos, drawings, maps, and diagrams. It could be required from time to time to recreate certain images or make a few minor modifications here and there. To be on the safe side, a manufacturer must bear in mind the guiding general principles.

As soon as possible, include the graphic designer into your programme. Provide the graphic designer with all the specifics of your special requirements. Throughout the treatment period, always discuss your script with him and pay attention to his advice. Try to make your captions succinct, clear, and legible on screens.

Remove any extraneous information from maps, graphs, diagrams, and tables. Everything should be as straightforward and succinct as feasible. All of your captions and visuals should be carefully outlined and sketched out on separate sheets of paper. The optimal arrangement can then be decided after discussing them with the graphic designer. The time between the production and delivery of each image should be at least 24 hours. At that time, you should have plenty of opportunity to modify or redo certain images.

Camera Work

Camera work is the most crucial of all the tasks and operations involved in making a television programme because if the camera work is subpar, no one will watch the show. One of the most crucial pieces of production equipment is the television camera. Today's TV producers are fortunate to have access to a wide range of electronic cameras, including monochrome, colour, simple, lightweight home camcorders, portable electronics news gathering (ENG) cameras, hefty EFP and other high-tech studio cameras. All electronic cameras share a lot of the same fundamental characteristics.

A standard television camera consists of the following thee main pans:

***(i)* Camera Head:** It consists of *(a)* zoom lens and its attachments, *(b)* camera pick-up tube or the internal optical system, *(c)* the view finder and *(d)* the camera cable.

***(ii)* Panning Head:** It consists of the 'pan handle, and its associated rotating mechanism, which enables the camera head to hit and pan smoothly.

***(iii)* Camera Mounting:** It may consist of a tripod, a leather clamp, a pedestal or a crane to support the camera securely and firmly on the ground or on the shoulder.

The television camera has several other features, connections and controls.

Some of these are — Lens hood, Lens cap, Tally light, Indicator cue lamp, Zoom control (zoom in/zoom out), Focus control, Fade in/fade out (or Aperture control), Headset (intercom), Tilt and Pan Locks, Camera/extension cables, Microphone (built-in), Mic extension cable and Microphone, Camera batteries and Camera carrying case.

How does a Video Camera Work?: The underlying mechanics of all video cameras are the same. They are: *(i)* Converting an optical image or a scene into electrical or video signals and *(ii)* sending these video signals through a network or capturing them on a videotape. These transmitted or recorded video signals can be processed and turned once more by a television or a video monitor into visible screen images via a reverse procedure.

Basic Camera Operations: It has been said that the camera is the producer's language. Numerous camera accessories, movements, transitions, standard shot sizes and picture creation methods have already been covered. Here, we take the risk of outlining a few key stages that can act as a basic blueprint for competent, methodical camera work.

Working with a Portable Video Camera: The producer or cameraperson is typically forced to set up and operate the portable camera by themselves, while working on an ENG assignment without the aid of a video engineer. As a result, she or he must study and practice the following actions:

- Thoroughly familiarising oneself with the various controls, connectors and pieces of the camera and practising how to use them.
- Putting the camera parts, VTR, tripod, cables, etc., together and filming a test clip.
- Putting and taking away video tapes.
- Battery replacement, inspection, connection and charging.
- Verifying the white balance setting.
- Making recordings and playing them back on the baby monitor or viewfinder.

Precautions

- The video camera is an incredibly expensive, delicate and sophisticated gadget. So, handle it with extreme caution and patience.
- If something goes wrong, don't freak out.
- Don't exert pressure on the apparatus.
- Avoid adjusting controls simultaneously or sequentially.
- Report any problems to the technician or engineer so they can inspect and fix the apparatus.
- Don't let the equipment, including the camera, run unattended.
- Keep an eye on all tools and accessories to prevent theft, loss, or forgetfulness.
- Before leaving for a location shoot, make a checklist.

- Before packing up and returning to the studio, make sure that all of the equipment and accessories match those on the checklist.
- Always prepare a shooting script or a shot list before actual shooting to save time in planning camera shots.

Camera Care

There are video camera do's and don'ts. A video camera may or may not be operated by you. But if you're going to work on a production team, it's a good idea to be familiar with certain fundamental operational guidelines for camera care. Here is a short list of items.

- Never point your camera's lens toward the sun or any other bright light to prevent "burn-ins."
- When not using the camera, cover the lens with the lid or lens cap.
- Avoid moving or standing with your camera tube or lens pointed downward.
- Ensure that the camera is mounted firmly on the tripod.
- When you aren't shooting any pictures, firmly tighten the pan and tilt controls.
- Use batteries, leads, lights, microphones (mics) and other equipment cautiously.

Operating a Studio Camera

Before each studio recording, all studio cameras are often routinely maintained and kept in "fault-free" condition. The quick assistance of a maintenance engineer or expert is accessible in the event that any camera experiences a failure, while recording. Though, the studio cameras must be operated with the same care and safety measures as a portable camera. The following guidelines could be helpful to keep in mind and adhere to each time a cameraman uses a studio camera after the video engineer has warmed it up:

- Put on your headset and communicate with the personnel in the control room to ensure that the intercom system is operational. If not, make sure the technician in question turns it on.
- Unlock the camera's pan and controls, then make sure it is appropriately balanced.
- Unlock the pedestal as well and inspect it both up and down, in the same manner.
- Take off the camera cover and make sure the viewfinder image is adjusted properly.
- Verify the lens's sturdiness, zooming capabilities and zoom control setting.
- Verify the studio's objects, graphics and occupants are in focus.
- Each cameraman typically receives a camera card that lists the photos that will be taken sequentially by each camera. Consider practising and framing these pictures beforehand.
- During practice sessions and final recordings, keep a close eye on everything that goes on in the studio.
- Pay close attention to the producer's directions and follow them exactly.
- During practice sessions or recording sessions, never remove your headphones, even for a moment.
- Immediately after finishing the previous shot, move to and line up the following shot.
- To prevent any on-shot jerks or movements, always keep an eye on the tally light on your camera.
- If you are forced to move your camera to a new position during the presentation, properly practice the motion beforehand.
- Verify that your shots have adequate headroom and looking room.
- Remain focused at all times and suggest appealing shots to the producer.
- While rehearsing, notify the producer of any issues or suggestions.
- Only lock and cap your camera once the producer has given the all clear to pack up.

Sound Recording

Sound performs the following functions in a television programme:

- Information is provided by sound. If you pay close attention, you'll see that sound effects, commentary and speech make up the majority of the information elements.
- It increases impact and offers amusement. A programme's enjoyment and interest value are increased by songs, music and other rhythmic sound effects, which increases its appeal.
- It establishes context, period and tone. Different sounds and effects assist establish the scene's setting and period, while setting the correct mood.
- By using the right sound effects and music, it can heighten the activity (as in a race).
- Making meaningful connections between images or graphical sequences also helps.

When editing, it offers logical and intriguing edit points.In fact, sound is an integral element of the video programme and it needs to be given due attention right from the earliest stage of programme planning to recording and editing. To improve a programme's quality, interest factor and overall impact on the audience, a producer should be well-versed in the design, recording and integration of music effects. A producer must be familiar with the fundamentals of audio equipment and its application for sound recording in audio and video programmes. Professional sound recordings and audio operators, sophisticated equipment and facilities are available to ensure sound quality.

Recording Sound for Video Programmes: Broadly, the sound component has the following four elements:

***(i)* Voice:** By far, the most significant component of sound is the human voice. It can be expressed in a variety of ways, including through conversations, monologues, narration or straight talk, out-of-vision comments, recitals, or renditions.

***(ii)* Music:** It consists of background music, theme music and other suggestive music that can be joyful, funny, sinister, etc.

***(iii)* Effects:** These include sound effects, both original and specifically produced ones, like atmospheric noises, footsteps, traffic noises, winds, fire, explosions, sirens and other types of strange and abrupt noises.

***(iv)* Silence:** This category includes jarring pauses that communicate gloom, calm, death and other negative emotions. To enhance and highlight the meaning and impact of a picture, various sound elements—such as music, effects, etc.—may be combined or blended.

The majority of educational programmes typically include background, theme and suggestive music as well as speech, commentary, simple dialogue, questions and answers, songs and poems in addition to other sound effects and sounds. Using the appropriate microphones, recording tools and recording procedures, all these audio components can be recorded in the studio, on location, or from the surrounding area. However, throughout the entire process, the producer is advised by the audio engineer and sound recordist based on their professional judgement. This is obviously dependent upon the type of recording equipment available, the production needs of a specific programme sequence, the situation or setting in which it is to be recorded, including the static or moving position of the sound source.

One of the simplest ways to record the audio for a programme is to simply use microphones to capture all sound and music effects in the studio itself, or to play, insert and mix pre-recorded music, sound and effects on discs and tapes. These pre-recorded music and sound effects are frequently, sequentially put onto a single audiotape to simplify things for everyone. This audiotape is then cued up, played back and combined with the final video recording in the studio. However, it is also possible to combine music and sound effects during post-production editing.

Some operational tips for sound recording: Following are a few general operating standards for sound recording:

***(i)* Take a Level:** Always take a voice level before actually recording, whether you're recording in the studio, on location, or during an ENG shot. To do this, ask the talent to speak a few phrases, adjust the volume within the acceptable range and then control it.

***(ii)* Use AGC:** Use the automatic gain control (AGC) facility when conducting an on-location ENG recording. It aids in enhancing low sound and taming loud sounds.

***(iii)* Rehearse and Record:** Every time you record a sound or commentary sequence, you should first practice it before recording it. This is a good tip to follow.

***(iv)* Match Sound and Picture:** Sound and pictures should fade in together and fade out together. Also use music and sound effects to suggest and enrich the desired meaning and communication.

Kinds of Microphones: Today, a huge selection of microphones are available for television sound recordists. What kind of microphone one should select, mostly relies on the production needs in a specific situation. There are basically three different types of microphones:

***(i)* Dynamic Microphones:** These microphones may be placed close to the sound source and are adequately durable for the majority of recording scenarios. They are safe with really loud noises.

***(ii)* Condenser Microphones:** On the other hand, are quite sensitive to physical trauma but produce sounds of outstanding quality from a distance. A renewable battery is necessary as the power source for a condenser microphone.

***(iii)* Ribbon Microphones:** Despite having a high level of sound quality, these mics are also extremely sensitive to physical trauma. A ribbon mic is quite durable and small and it is perfect for recording regulated and static sounds of speech and music.

Additionally, microphones are categorised, based on how sensitive they are to incoming sound in a particular direction. They are of three types:

***(i)* Cardioid Microphones:** These are sensitive to noises emanating from half of the environments to which they are pointed. These unidirectional microphones are good for capturing interviews since they cut down on background noise. They are referred to as cardioid microphones because of their heart-shaped design.

***(ii)* Omnidirectional Microphones:** These microphones can pick up sound coming from any angle. Additionally, there are bidirectional microphones with a figure-of-eight construction.

***(iii)* Gun Mics:** These microphones, which are also known as rifle mics, only pick up sound from a small angle and ignore background noise in the recording space or location. Gun mics, which have a long, pointed handle or boom and can record sound from a fair distance, are typically used in conjunction with headphones to check the output and confirm that the microphones are in the proper location.

Lighting

In the creation of television, lighting is crucial. It enables the camera to clearly "see" and "capture" a scene or subject. It also aids in creating the illusion of depth, giving two-dimensional images a three-dimensional appearance. Lighting has a bigger part in colour TV programmes when it comes to the surroundings and the clothes. For interior filming of straightforward TV shows, the following three basic lights or light sources are typically employed:

***(i)* Key Light:** It usually comes from a hard source and casts the most light on the object or scene. To brighten the scene, there should only be one primary light present. It is a gentle source of light.

***(ii)* Fill Light:** Its primary job is to fill in and lessen the shadows cast by the key light.

***(iii)* Back Light:** This type of lighting is typically a harsh source that is aimed at a subject from behind. It increases the three-dimensional effect and distinguishes the subject's body from the background.

There may be a need for many lights with varying intensities for elaborate productions. Large television studios, where a range of programmes, including dramatic presentations, can be recorded, typically include intricate "light grids" with multiple lamps and light sources of varying intensities. However, the fundamental lighting pattern is still the same as what was previously described.

Aesthetic Considerations: The television image is two-dimensional and flat. The director determines the viewpoint for us. It can be challenging for the spectator to determine an object's shape, size and distance. The shape, dimension, distance and texture can all be determined by the illumination. Viewers can be aided to perceive depth and subsequently determine the shape, size, texture and relative distance of the object the camera picks up by manipulating light and its absence, or shadows. When necessary, appropriate lighting can create the appearance of fantasy. The length and depth of the shadows being cast can be used to convey the time of day and whether the scenario is occurring inside or outside. Off-camera lighting effects, such as sweeping light if the scene is taking place in a lighthouse, can imply the scene's actual environment. Cutouts in the rear wall's shadows may represent the interior of a cathedral, prison or woodland. The suitable psychological atmosphere can be created and heightened with the use of proper lighting. High key, bright lighting may imply happiness and lightheartedness while low key, gloomy lighting may create a sombre, unsettling atmosphere. For instance, illuminating someone from below, which is a strange, unnatural angle for light, creates an air of mystery and unease. When paired with other production components like a set colour, music and sound effects, lighting can significantly contribute to psychological mood. Lighting alone cannot be expected to produce and maintain the illusion of realism or of imagination, as well as psychological mood.

CHECK YOUR PROGRESS

Q. 1. What is a camera script?

Ans. The director's expected camera movements and exact shot sizes are specified for each camera operator in the camera script. A single camera script outlining each operator's actions will function effectively in live, as-live, or multi-camera studio productions if the director has essentially planned out when s/he will switch from one camera to another. Each operator should have a customised camera script when all cameras are anticipated to record the full scenario during a shot. The instructions are straightforward — keep Rico in a medium close-up throughout the scene. Alternatively, they could involve, intricate shot combinations and camera movements, with each one being triggered by a different sound, movement, or change in lighting and being noted on the camera script by the director. Scripts typically include camera instructions running down the left-hand margin. The number of the camera, its initial (and subsequent) position(s), the starting, interim and final picture sizes and the camera's motion are all included in the directions (s).

Q. 2. Name two major categories of resources for which a producer has to plan and budget.

Ans. A variety of inputs and resources are combined in the production of media. It necessitates not just extensive planning in advance but also the coordination of multiple tasks at once by its very nature. Therefore, in practice, the process of arranging various production events and allocating programme resources starts in the early stages and continues in tandem with budgeting, screenplay development and other tasks. The primary resources that a producer must plan and allocate for execution, can be divided into two groups: *(i)* programme resources and services and *(ii)* technical resources and facilities. In later sections of this unit, we'll deal with some of these significant programme and technical resources separately.

Q. 3. List the major categories of graphics generally used in video programmes.

Ans. Graphics are generally classified under five categories:

***(i)* Title card:** It is a straightforward card with information such the title of the programme and/or the names of the writer, producer, and programme director, and is typically written or partially drawn.

***(ii)* Key card:** The super card, also known as the "super caption," typically has white words on a black backdrop. When superimposing or keying, the black background disappears and the white letters cover the first source or scene. A key card is frequently used to identify a visitor by overlaying his name over his image on the screen. A key card's information is always condensed and written in large, easy-to-read fonts.

***(iii)* Slides:** Slides in colour or "black and white" can only be seen on a television if they were taken horizontally. Vertical slides have an improper aspect ratio and don't display well on screens.

***(iv)* Maps, Charts and Photo-captions:** Since video programmes aim to convey the most information possible clearly, quickly, and simply, maps, charts, diagrams, tables, graphs, and images are crucial visual resources. Animation in visuals may and does raise a program's level of interest.

***(v)* The Chroma key card:** The chroma key card features a blue background, as opposed to a super card's black background. The chroma key technique, which permits the blue colour to disappear during keying, can be used to key the chroma key card into the backdrop scene or image. In reality, the chroma key, commonly referred to as a "colour separation overlay" or CSO, is a type of electronic tool that "cuts out" any undesirable portions of a picture (by tinting them blue) and superimposes the remaining portions over a different image or background.

Q. 4. Name the three basic lights used for indoor shooting of simple TV programmes.

Ans. The three basic lights or light sources are used for indoor shooting of simple TV programmes:

***(i)* Key light:** It is normally a hard source of light and provides main illumination on the subject or scene.

There should be only one key light to illuminate the scene.

(ii) **Fill light:** It is a soft source of light. Its main function is to fill and reduce shadows created by the key light.

(iii) **Back light:** It usually consists of a harsh source of light that is aimed at a target from behind. It improves the appearance of three dimensions by isolating the subject's body from the backdrop.

For complex projects, several lights of varied intensity could be required. Large television studios often have intricate light grids with numerous lamps and light sources of different intensities, making it possible to record a variety of shows, including dramatic presentations. Nonetheless, the underlying lighting pattern is still the same as what was previously stated.

Q. 5. List the major elements of sound as used in television programmes.

Ans. The sound component has the following elements:

(i) **Voice:** The voice of a person is by far the most significant component of sound. It can be expressed in a variety of ways, including through conversations, monologues, narration or straight talk, out-of-vision comments, recitals, or renditions.

(ii) **Music:** It has background music, theme music and other suggestive music that is joyful, funny, ominous, etc.

(iii) **Effects:** These comprise original and professionally produced sound effects like ambient noises, footfalls, traffic noises, winds, flames, explosions, sirens and other forms of strange and abrupt noises.

(iv) **Silence:** It contains brief, sharp silences that suggest calmness, tranquility, death, dread, etc. To enhance and highlight the meaning and impact of a picture, various sound elements—such as music, effects, etc. may be combined or blended.

OTHER IMPORTANT QUESTIONS

Q. 1. Discuss how to prepare a script for a TV programme with an example.

Ans. Producers typically write out camera scripts using one of the many standard templates. The most typical design consists of two vertical columns: the left column for vision and the right column for sound. The vision column is dedicated to picture treatment and provides shot numbers, descriptions and types of shots, as well as camera numbers, positions, movements, switching instructions, etc. The sound column is used to record stage directions for floor workers, technicians and performers as well as dialogue, sound, music, noise, special effects and lighting. The whole camera script, when written in the conventional layout, provides specific instructions on what is needed and what should occur at each production point. Below is a sample script.

Q. 2. Discuss resources planning and scheduling for TV programme production.

Ans. A variety of inputs and resources are combined in the production of media. It necessitates not just extensive planning in advance but also the coordination of multiple tasks at once by its very nature. Therefore, in practice, the process of arranging various production events and allocating programme resources starts in the early stages and continues in tandem with budgeting, screenplay development and other tasks. The primary resources that a producer must plan and allocate for execution can be divided into two groups–*(i)* programme resources and services and *(ii)* technical resources and facilities. In later sections of this unit, we'll deal with some of these significant programme and technical resources separately. Here, the following details need to be considered for a better understanding of the theme under consideration.

(i) One of the crucial elements of production organisation is the scheduling of various events and the countless related activities. Its primary responsibilities include scheduling and running meetings with other units and service departments, including Design and Graphics, Props, Costumes and Make-up, Sound and Music, Camera and Lighting, Photo, Film and Animation and Technical Planning and Operations, in addition to choosing and overseeing the cast. Moreover, the producer is required to hold a number of meetings, including the initial planning session, also known as a pre-production conference, screenplay meetings, technical planning sessions and joint planning sessions with the production and technical team.

(ii) Bookings must be made well in advance for a variety of services, venues, studios, editing rooms, performers, actors, musicians, artists, camera crews, studio employees, technical staff and other services. All of this necessitates, intensive preparation and coordination.

(iii) The producer's first priority also includes creating a thorough production schedule for carrying out numerous activities. The production schedule is very helpful in carrying out various tasks and is a useful tool for keeping track of how the production work that has been divided among various team members and support employees is progressing each day.

(iv) The overall execution of the total production campaign depends heavily on setting and assigning clear-cut tasks to all officials and realistic deadlines. This is when the producer's abilities as a skilled public relations specialist and "manager of men and matters" really shine. One of the best ways to plan and schedule the production of a show is to start with the final deadline (which could be kept a week ahead of the precise preview date) and work backwards, setting a specific time limit for each activity and coordinating different events to reduce the overall production time.

(v) The producers and their production helpers are greatly relieved and have an easier time of it when proformas, schedules, call sheets, etc., are created and used. Many different schedules, including wall charts, production planners, scheduling charts, artists address lists, facilities request forms, performer's contract proformas, call sheets and many others, can be used as efficient communication tools. These schedules should

be accurately filled out and distributed to the relevant personnel, along with strict deadlines and time limits.

Q. 3. While planning, preparing and selecting graphics for video screen, which three points should be kept in view?

Ans. One technical aspect of video production is the designing or creation of graphics. When ideas or information cannot be expressed or communicated effectively through spoken words or live activities, graphics are utilised to present them. They can enhance the effectiveness, persuasion, appeal and power of information. The following three points should be kept in mind when organising, developing and choosing graphics for video screens.

Aspect ratio: It refers to the proportion between the graphic card's height and breadth. The dimensions of a television or computer display are 3:4, or three units high by four units wide. Therefore, this aspect ratio should be followed for all visual graphics.

Essential area: Other names for it include vital area and safe title area. To avoid visual loss during transmission and playback, all pertinent information must be included within this space. The image that was so lost during transmission and scanning is referred to as the domestic cut-off. The scanning and crucial portions of the graphic card must be visible in the shot to guarantee that no part of it is lost on the screen.

Readability: The words or written material should be readable by the viewer as it appears on the screen. When there is too much information presented in small, illegible print, the viewer is unable to fully understand it. For proper reading, we should thus, always utilise large, bold letters.

Q. 4. What steps and precautions should be taken, while working with a portable video camera.

Ans. While working on an ENG assignment without the assistance of a video engineer, the producer or cameraperson is often required to set up and operate the portable camera by themselves. She or he must therefore learn and practise the following skills:

- Get very familiar with all of the camera's controls, connections, and components and practise using them.
- Assembling the camera's components, including the VTR, tripod, wires, etc.; and recording a test clip.
- Placing and removing videotapes.
- The changing, checking, connecting, and charging of batteries.
- Checking the white balance configuration.
- Creating recordings and seeing them on the viewfinder or baby monitor.

The video camera is a highly complex, expensive, and delicate device. Hence, handle it patiently and with considerable caution.

- Be calm if something goes wrong.
- Don't apply pressure to the equipment.
- Steer clear of consecutive or simultaneous control adjustments.
- Inform the technician or engineer of any issues so they can examine and repair the equipment.
- Don't let the equipment, including the camera, run unattended.
- Keep a watch on all tools and accessories to prevent theft, loss, or forgetfulness.
- Always compile a checklist before going out for location photography.
- Prior to packing up and returning to the studio, always compare all equipment and accessories with the checklist.
- Always prepare a shooting script or a shot list before actual shooting. It saves much time in planning camera shots.

Q. 5. Discuss do's and don'ts of camera.

Ans. The video camera is a highly complex, expensive, and delicate device. Hence, handle it patiently and with considerable caution.

- Be calm if something goes wrong.
- Don't apply pressure to the equipment.
- Steer clear of consecutive or simultaneous control adjustments.
- Inform the technician or engineer of any issues so they can examine and repair the equipment.
- Don't let the equipment, including the camera, run unattended.
- Keep a watch on all tools and accessories to prevent theft, loss, or forgetfulness.
- Always compile a checklist before going out for location photography.
- Prior to packing up and returning to the studio, always compare all equipment and accessories with the checklist.
- Always prepare a shooting script or a shot list before actual shooting. It saves much time in planning camera shots.
- All studio cameras are frequently routinely maintained and kept in "fault-free" condition prior to each studio recording. The quick assistance of a maintenance engineer or expert is accessible in the event that any camera experiences a failure while recording. The studio cameras must be operated with the same care and safety considerations as a portable camera, though. After the video engineer has warmed up the studio camera, it may be helpful to remember and follow the following rules each time a cameraman uses it:
- Put on your headset and talk to the staff in the control room to make that the intercom system is working. If not, make sure the technician in question turns it on.
- Unlock the pan and control locks on the camera, then check that it is properly balanced.

- Unlock the pedestal as well, and in the same way, check it from the top and bottom.
- Take off the camera cover and make sure the viewfinder image is adjusted properly.
- Check the durability, zooming abilities, and zoom control setting of the lens.
- Check that the people, graphics, and objects in the studio are in sharp focus.
- Typically, each cameraman is given a camera card with a list of the pictures that will be taken in order by each camera. Try practising and framing these photographs ahead.
- Pay close attention to everything that happens in the studio during rehearsals and final recordings.
- Pay close attention to what the producer says and follow all of his directions.
- Never, not even momentarily, take off your headset while practising or filming.
- Go to and set up the next shot as soon as the previous one is finished.
- Pay close attention to your camera's tally light at all times to avoid any on-shot jerks or motions.
- If you need to move your camera to a new location during the show, practise the motion a lot beforehand.
- Verify again that your images have sufficient headroom and viewing room.
- Maintain your attention at all times, and send the producer appealing images.
- Throughout rehearsals, be sure to let the producer know if there are any problems or suggestions.
- Only lock and cap your camera when the producer gives the all-clear to go.

Q. 6. What are the functions of sound in a television programme?

Ans. Information is communicated through sound. If you listen closely, you'll see that the majority of the informational components consist of voice, sound effects, and commentary.

- It provides entertainment and boosts impact. Songs, music, and other rhythmic sound effects boost a program's enjoyment and interest value, which raises its appeal.
- It establishes context, period, and tone. Various sounds and effects aid define the scene's locale and time while establishing the suitable mood.
- It may heighten the action by employing the appropriate sound effects and music (as in a race).
- Creating connections between pictures or graphical sequences is also beneficial.
- It provides logical and persuading edit points when editing.

In truth, sound is a crucial component of the video show, and it demands careful consideration from the very beginning of programme design through recording and editing. A producer should be knowledgeable in the creation, recording, and integration of music effects in order to raise the calibre, interest level, and overall audience impact of a show. A producer has to be knowledgeable about the principles of audio equipment and how it is used to capture sound for audio and video programmes. To guarantee sound quality, there are expert sound recordists and audio operators, high-tech tools, and facilities at your disposal.

Q. 7. Discuss some operational tips for sound recording.

Ans. Following are a few general operating standards for sound recording:

1. Take a Level: No matter whether you're recording in the studio, on location, or during an ENG shoot, always take a voice level before you start the real recording. To do this, ask the talent to utter a few words, then manage the volume by adjusting it to a suitable level.

2. Using AGC: While filming ENG on site, make use of the automatic gain control (AGC) capability. It helps to amplify low sounds and subdue harsh noises.

3. Practice before recording: You should always record a sound or commentary sequence before practising it. This advice should be heeded.

4. Match sound and picture: Sound and visuals should fade in simultaneously and fade out together. Use sound effects and music to further the intended meaning and communication.

Various microphone types

There are various different types of microphones available currently for the television sound recordist. The ideal kind of microphone to utilise in a particular situation will mostly rely on the demands of the production. Basically, there are three categories of microphones:

***(i)* Dynamic Microphones:** The bulk of recording situations may be handled by placing these microphones close to the sound source. They are resistant to extremely loud sounds.

(ii) Conversely, despite their high sensitivity to physical damage, condenser microphones generate sounds from remote sources with good quality. A condenser microphone needs to be powered by a renewable battery.

***(iii)* Ribbon Microphones:** These microphones have excellent sound quality but are also very sensitive to physical harm. The controlled and static sounds of speech and music are ideal for recording with a ribbon mic since it is both strong and portable. Moreover, the sensitivity of a particular direction of incoming sound is used to classify different types of microphones. They fall into three groups:

(a) Cardioid microphones can pick up sounds coming from 50% of the environments they are pointing at. Interviews may be recorded with these unidirectional microphones since they reduce background noise. Due to their heart-shaped construction, these microphones are known as cardioid microphones.

(b) Omnidirectional microphones are capable of picking up sound originating from all directions. Bidirectional microphones with a figure-of-eight architecture are another option.

(c) Rifle microphones, often referred to as gun microphones, are only sensitive to a narrow sound field and disregard ambient noise in the room or place being recorded.

To verify the output and make sure the microphones are in the right places, people frequently use headphones in conjunction with gun mics, which have a long, pointed handle or boom and can capture sound from a reasonable distance.

Q. 8. Write a short note on Shooting graphics.

Ans. We should watch out for two issues, while handling easel graphics in the studio: keystoning and glare. When the camera is not directly perpendicular in both its vertical and horizontal axes to the flat graphic it is taking, keystoning is an unattractive effect that results! Instead of asking the camera person to make the correction, the floor person should rotate the graphic in this situation either clockwise or anticlockwise or tilt it up or down to lessen the off-axis angle. By having the photo's surface created in a matte, rather than a glossy finish, glare can be prevented. Experiment with rotating the graphic at various angles from the offending light source to reduce glare more quickly.

MULTIPLE CHOICE QUESTIONS

Q. 1. What serves as the guide for producing a TV show in a studio or on a location?

(a) Camera script *(b)* Script analysis
(c) Budgeting *(d)* None of these

Ans. *(a)* Camera script.

Q. 2. Which of the following sometimes referred to as the production script?

(a) Producer's words *(b)* Camera script
(c) Log book *(d)* None of these

Ans. *(b)* Camera script.

Q. 3. Which card has information such as the title of the programme and/or the names of the writer, producer?

(a) Title card *(b)* Key card
(c) Slides *(d)* All of these

Ans. *(a)* Title card.

Q. 4. Which is called the super card?

(a) Title card *(b)* Key card
(c) Slides *(d)* All of these

Ans. *(b)* Key card.

Q. 5. Which is frequently used to identify a visitor by overlaying his name over his image on the screen?

(a) Title card *(b)* Key card
(c) Slides *(d)* All of these

Ans. *(b)* Key card.

Q. 6. Which card features a blue background?

(a) Title card *(b)* Key card
(c) Chroma card *(d)* Super card

Ans. *(c)* Chroma card.

Q. 7. Which card features a black background?

(a) Title card *(b)* Key card
(c) Chroma card *(d)* Super card

Ans. *(d)* Super card.

Q. 8. Which has zoom lens and its attachments?

(a) Camera head *(b)* Panning head
(c) Camera mounting *(d)* None of these

Ans. *(d)* None of these.

Q. 9. Which has the pan handle and its associated rotating mechanism?

(a) Camera head *(b)* Panning head
(c) Camera mounting *(d)* None of these

Ans. *(b)* Panning head.

Q. 10. Which of the following has a tripod, a leather clamp, a pedestal or a crane?

(a) Camera head *(b)* Panning head
(c) Camera mounting *(d)* None of these

Ans. *(c)* Camera mounting.

Q. 11. Which microphones are sensitive to noises emanating from half of the environments to which they are pointed?

(a) Dynamic microphones
(b) Condenser microphones
(c) Ribbon microphones
(d) Cardioid microphones

Ans. *(d)* Cardioid microphones.

Q. 12. __________ are quite sensitive to physical trauma but produce sounds of outstanding quality from a distance.

(a) Dynamic microphones
(b) Condenser microphones
(c) Ribbon microphones
(d) Cardioid microphones

Ans. *(b)* Condenser microphones.

Q. 13. Which microphones may be placed close to the sound source and are adequately durable for the majority of recording scenarios?

(a) Dynamic microphones
(b) Condenser microphones
(c) Ribbon microphones
(d) Cardioid microphones

Ans. *(a)* Dynamic microphones.

Q. 14. Which type of lighting is typically a harsh source that is aimed at a subject from behind?

(a) Key light *(b)* Fill light
(c) Backlight *(d)* None of these

Ans. *(c)* Backlight.

Q. 15. Which light usually comes from a hard source and casts the most light on the object or scene?

(a) Key light
(b) Fill light
(c) Backlight
(d) None of these

Ans. *(a)* Key light.

■■

Production of Television Programmes: The Process

12

INTRODUCTION

Production of television programmes involves creating and producing audio and/or visual content for transmission. This could entail writing, editing, on-location filming, sound recording, graphic designing, lighting and many other things. In this chapter, we take things a step further and go through how audio-video programmes are actually produced. Rehearsal, studio and location preparation, recording and TV programme editing will all be covered.

CHAPTER AT A GLANCE

STUDIO RECORDING

Given below are various stages of the production process:

Studio Preparation

(i) **The Set:** When a programme is recorded in a studio, scenery or a set is constructed there. It provides the tone and style for a TV show or programme to be recorded in the studio, while also creating the proper physical setting. The set could be quite straightforward or extremely complex, depending on the demands of the programme and, of course, the budget. Each time, the set designer must be consulted in order for the producer to receive his input and suggestions. The set designer develops a draught floor plan with everyone's consent before presenting it for discussion in the first planning meeting.

(ii) **The Floor Plan:** The studio's floor plan displays the studio's primary characteristics in scaled diagram form, including the walls, the cyclorama, the entrance doors and the location of the lighting grid. The term "floor plan" is used to describe a design that shows, where furniture and objects will be placed on the studio floor, as well as the scenery or set that will be constructed. The floor plan actually offers crucial instructions for using the studio, including how to put up scenery and props, arrange lights, install microphones, plan different camera angles, positions and movements and indicate the actions and movements of performers and actors on the studio floor.

(iii) **The Camera Cards:** For each of the recording cameras, camera cards are prepared. The producer makes this, while creating the camera screenplay, based on shot divisions. A camera card lists the shots, types of shots, motions, positions and activities associated with a certain camera. During dress rehearsals and the real production, the camera card is pinned or fastened to the camera in front of the cinematographer, who is led by it. One or two days before the recording day itself, camera cards are prepared.

(iv) **Initial Production Conference:** An essential part of studio preparation is the initial production conference or the early planning and marketing. The producer calls the first planning meeting when the comprehensive camera screenplay, production treatment and studio floor plan are completed. Attendees include experts from all relevant departments, including scenic design, graphics, camera, audio, lighting and technical. Copies of the set designer's floor layout and the producer's camera screenplay are sent to everyone. The set designer delivers his floor layout and staging strategy during this conference and the producer provides his production treatment. The producer also requests feedback on numerous production-related issues and discloses the tentative production deadlines.

(a) **Graphics:** A comprehensive catalogue of visuals is created by the creator, along with a description of each. In a separate meeting, the graphic designer discuss these graphics and their content. The artist who starts working on the job against a deadline is also given some references, if necessary. Additionally, if there are any existing visuals, they are found, bought and improved for use in the programme.

(b) **Photo, Film and Animation:** The producer should direct the acquisition of new photos and films if the programme requirements call for the usage of certain images, films, or animation sequences. Filming and printing photos and videos takes time. Therefore, enough time should be available for gathering these resources. You might want to employ a group of slides occasionally in your programmes. Additionally, these must be prepared for in advance: planned, photographed, edited and mounted.

(c) **Props:** A thorough inventory of all objects (also known as props), furniture and other items for decoration, demonstration and other effects must be produced, based on the script's requirements. The props assistant, who is tasked with procuring the necessary goods through hiring or purchasing, may talk through this list with them.

(d) **Costumes and make-up:** Your artists or performers might require some unique attire. These could need to be coordinated through the costumes department, so adequate notice is required. Similar to this, the person in charge of makeup should be informed in advance if one or more of your artists need a unique type of makeup. This is crucial when it comes to different types of beards, moustaches and other odd makeup.

(e) **Sound Effects and Music:** The producer should make sure that all of the programme's audio needs, including the theme song, opening music, background music and any special sound effects, sounds, or songs, are determined, purchased, recorded and preferably placed onto a single audio tape. It should be maintained, prepared, precisely timed and cued for use during actual recording and integration with the application. Music and other audio inserts are recorded by the audio technicians.

(f) **Films and Video Inserts:** It should be previewed beforehand, cued and kept available as an insert through telecine or a video tape source if you have opted to use a segment of a movie or a video clip in your presentation. In the same way, specially made film clips or video recordings—with or without commentary and sound—must be maintained, cued and prepared. In case of copyright materials like movies, videos, slides, photos, etc., the producer must always take proactive measures to secure the required authorization and clearance in each case.

(g) **Casting and Direction:** Casting involves choosing actors and performers who are appropriate for the programme. Actors converse with one another in the studio or speak directly to the camera. They don't take on the roles of other people; they portray themselves as announcers, teachers and anchorpersons. An actor or actress, however, always adopts a persona and performs that role. We need both forms of cast, i.e., performers as well as actors and actresses, for educational programmes.

(v) **Technical Planning Meeting:** The producer calls the second planning meeting, also known as a review meeting, after an interval of 8–10 days to assess the status of the various production activities allocated or started during the first planning meeting. All members of the production team and partners present verbally at this meeting, asking questions and receiving additional clarifications. Any issues or concerns that may arise during this time are resolved. The recording date is established and the producer presents the complete schedule for all events. Decisions made in the meeting are followed by written notes and directions.

(a) **Booking of Studios and Other Facilities:** At this point, prior tentative bookings of studios, technical facilities and other resources are fully confirmed and the production crew is notified in writing of the dates, times and duration of all events. Check the reservations and compliance with all regulations right away, notably the following:

- Scheduling cameramen, floor crew, technical crew and talent.
- Reserving the studio and other technical resources.
- Planning the set building (to be completed one day in advance).
- Planning the lighting (to be completed two to three hours in advance).
- Giving everyone involved copies of the final camera script two days beforehand.
- Preparations for tea/coffee, refreshments, etc.
- Information provided to performers and artists regarding rehearsal and recording dates and times.
  Arrangements for all programme inputs, including graphics, pictures, film and VT inserts, music and sound effects, costumes, props and make-up, as well as the payment of artists' fees shortly after the recording.

(b) **Set and Lighting:** Once instructed and properly briefed the personnel concerned will do the set and lighting on time. However, it is the producer's responsibility to check, supervise and ensure that these requirements are fulfilled well in time and the studio is ready for launching pre-production activities at the time agreed and communicated to all in advance.

Rehearsals

A studio recording is a well-organised process in which many technical and other specialists run numerous machines and high-tech apparatus. Because of this, all studio productions are expensive. We cannot, therefore, afford to hold rehearsals in the studio while everyone waits impatiently. It is wise to do some rehearsals outside the studio to save on the expensive studio time. Simple instructional programmes may not need a lot of rehearsals but complicated plays and dramatic presentations do and the producer should organise more rehearsals if the script calls for it or if the cast members lack confidence. The producers can pick and use one of the following recommendations for practising the shows.

(a) **Script Reading:** Regardless of the type of programme involved, discussing and reading the script with the talent is essential during this first phase of any rehearsal. This technique is especially well-suited to drama productions.

(b) **Dry Run:** Complex projects are typically practiced outside of the studio, in a separate rehearsal space. During a dry run, the producer tests the actor's motions and camera angles. The producer can use his viewfinder to block his shots and camera angles as the locations and motions of the artists and cameras are meticulously practiced.

(c) Walk-through: A walk through is a brief run-through the entire programme or specific segments in the studio before to camera practice and filming. A walk-through is mostly used block actor shots and motions and test out camera positions, microphone placements, zooms, lighting effects and shadow effects.

(d) **Camera Rehearsal:** A camera rehearsal, also referred to as the last dress rehearsal, is conducted right before the final recording. A camera rehearsal can be done in two different ways. One technique is the uninterrupted run through, where you restart from the beginning if a mistake is made anytime along the way. The programme can finally be taped after a successful, error-free camera rehearsal. The alternative way is to pause where the error occurs and restart from a suitable linking point in the script, being careful not to repeat the error. It is known as the stop-start approach.

(e) **Timing the Script:** The producer has an excellent opportunity to schedule their programme scripts more or less properly during script readings and rehearsals. The final programme can be managed to be slightly enlarged or compressed to bring it to its exact or intended duration with a little amount of tweaking.

(f) **Final Planning Meeting:** One or two days prior to the programme's actual taping, producers frequently hold a quick final production meeting. The goal is to make sure that everything is prepared and under control, that all duties have been satisfactorily completed, or are likely to be completed at the appropriate time. Taking a more personal approach, some producers make it a point to speak with or meet with each essential member of the production team separately and to quickly check their level of preparedness for the recording day. The following are some of the most crucial things the producer and his production assistant need to confirm and double check:

- All graphics, photocaptions, film and VT inserts and slides are prepared.
- Sufficient copies of the final camera scripts are made available.
- Camera cards for all studio cameras are prepared.
- All music and sound effects are recorded and cued.
- The set and lighting are either been prepared or will be so well before the recording time.
- Copies of the recording schedule, which includes the date, location and time for various activities, are communicated to all parties involved.
- All technical crew members, including the technical director, vision mixer operator, audio engineer, telecine and VTR operators, lighting supervisor, electricians, technicians and grips, are informed accordingly and placed on studio duty.
- All video and audio tapes, both recorded and blank, have a stopwatch and timer attached
- Plans are made for tea, coffee and light refreshments.

Always keep in mind that nothing would be brought into the studio unless the producer specifically requested it.

Final Production

The final production stage is where all pre-production work and planning processes come together, bringing the efficiency of the entire production crew into clear focus within the confines of the studio. On the production day, the producer and his or her production team must arrive at the studio between 30 minutes and an hour before the scheduled recording time. They must also approach the activities in a laid-back and upbeat manner, making small talk and cracking jokes with everyone. On a typical recording session day, everything ought to go according to the producer's actual schedule. The producer should particularly look to the following aspects before actual production begins making sure that:

- The set has been carefully assembled, painted and cleaned.
- Every prop, piece of furniture and demonstration item is in its proper location.
- Lighting equipment has been set up and the set and other locations are suitably lit.
- All cameras, microphones, monitors and other apparatus have been positioned correctly.
- To ensure proper camera numbers and order, all visuals and captions have been set up on stands in front of the cameras.
- The cameras' cards have all been fixed.
- All blank and recorded audio and video cassettes have been delivered to the studio and given to the technical staff for usage.
- Every camera has been warmed up and set up.
- All artists and performers have arrived at the appropriate time to change into their costumes and put on "make-up."
- All members of the production and technical staff have reported for duty and assumed their respective roles and positions.

Some general guidelines for directing studio productions:

(i) **Studio Rehearsals:** The rehearsal process is a crucial component of every studio production. The technical director should be consulted when the producer is prepared to start rehearsals to determine whether he and his team are prepared. Additionally, he needs to confirm with the floor manager that the

talent and cameramen are all prepared. The producer can start his show in the following way if everyone and everything is prepared on the studio floor and in the technical sections.

- **Blocking:** This refers to the act of successively blocking shots by cameras. Each cameraman receives detailed directions from the producer regarding each shot's size, angle, duration, movements, etc.
- **Staggering:** It means a 'bit-by-bit' rehearsal by actors performing their role in front of cameras and with actions aid movements on the set or floor as directed by the producer often repeating and correcting themselves.

***(ii)* Walk through or run through:** It refers to a fast, frequently unbroken rehearsal of a portion or the entirety of the programme in the studio using all the available tools, actions, movements, effects and music. The producer explains to his artists and technical team what he wants in each frame and action during a walk-through. Everyone now has a thorough understanding of the programme's requirements. The producer can go on to the text stage of full camera rehearsal once a walk-through has been completed in one session. Before the last practice and recording, a 10-minute coffee or tea break is necessary.

***(iii)* Full Camera Rehearsal or Dress Rehearsal:** Everyone returns to the studio and assumes their positions after a ten-minute break. The producer can now practice using the entire camera. All technical operators, cameramen, floor workers and artists must execute continuously and flawlessly throughout. The final recording of the show can begin after one or two full camera rehearsals.

***(iv)* Final Recording:** At this point, one has every reason to believe that everyone will perform at their greatest best. When everything is going well, the producer frequently makes the final recording of his or her programme in only one attempt, starting the countdown. To complete the final creation, he or she may occasionally need to try again.

FIELD/LOCATION RECORDING

All audio-visual programmes had to be created and transmitted from the studios in the early days of broadcasting. However, with the invention of the portable camera, lightweight VTRs and other mobile equipment, it is now possible to simultaneously broadcast programmes from the field, while simultaneously recording them. The majority of audio and video programmes that are produced today are shot on location, returned to the studio for editing and sound mixing and then packaged for transmission or distribution on cassettes.

Types of Field Recording

Field location recording or a remote are terms used to describe when a TV programme (or a segment of it) is filmed outside the studio. These on-site or remote recordings can be divided into the following three categories:

***(i)* Electronic News Gathering (ENG):** One small portable camera, along with a VTR, is frequently used for ENG location recording. Back in the studio, the uncut raw video material is edited and broadcast. It requires quick, adaptable operations, a tiny personnel and excellent mobility. It is best suited for short news gathering or even a live telecast from the location due to its decent but lower quality photographs. However, ENG approaches are now being used more frequently to create educational programming.

***(ii)* Electronic Field Production (EFP):** While keeping some of ENG's flexibility and mobility, electronic field production requires more meticulous planning and advance preparations. Of course, this calls for more personnel, more gear, video switches, an OB van and more cameras but it results in higher-quality images. EFP approach is suitable for filming various field programmes, which may frequently require post-production editing. It may or may not involve direct transmission from the spot.

***(iii)* Big Remotes:** A big remote is a type of field production used to film large events that aren't specifically planned for radio or television. Important events including national or international sporting events, conferences/ seminars, competitions and pageants are covered live and aired directly by large remotes. Such remotes typically involve elaborate arrangements, including multiple high-quality cameras and related audio-video equipment, a multiple VTR setup for recording, instant replay, slow-motion playback and freeze-frame capability, a giant OB van housing a complete, first-rate control room, a mobile microwave transmitter and a sizable contingent of production and technical crew. These remotes are typically planned several weeks prior to the actual event. For large remotes and various kinds of field site recordings, commentators and anchormen are also necessary.

Studio vs. Field Recordings

The studio provides extremely regulated environments for the creation of video programmes. The entire process is well-organised and most outside disturbance has been removed. On the other hand, shooting in the field is seldom done in ideal circumstances. The weather and the amount of daylight are always uncertain. Additionally, there are a number of additional uncontrollable elements that could go awry and ruin your programme. Therefore, producers working on location shoots need to prepare properly in advance, come up with fail-proof backup plans and be willing to accept tiny concessions to resolve issues. Here, we highlight a few key points that producers and everyone else involved with remotes should pay close attention to.

Production Planning: Plan, budget and schedule the production in the same manner as you would for a typical studio production. Dealing with people, scheduling locations, obtaining police or other authorities' approval for shooting, coordinating transportation, lunches and refreshments for your crew, among many other things, may need more of your time. You should have in-depth discussions with your production and technical crew about each and every area of the production and assign the production manager specific tasks for your production assistants, technical crew members and other team members.

Recce or Location Viewing

Recce, short for reconnaissance, refers to a preliminary inspection of the shooting scene. During on-location filming, scouting, or a trip to Double check that *(i)* all relevant parties have been informed and *(ii)* that power will be provided continuously by the closest electric substation as well as *(iii)* that all necessary shooting permissions have been obtained from the appropriate authorities about the actual recording's day, time and date.

The producer's agenda includes the site as a top priority item that must never be overlooked. Along with his cameraman, production assistants, engineers and technical operators, the producer must do a thorough reconnaissance. The following factors are taken into account during a recce:

- Make an appointment with the individuals in question or go to the area beforehand to gather their opinions and comments.
- Observe the location from all aspects and speak with the staff.
- Look for power supply points and create your own or obtain a copy of the site plan.
- Seek for and prepare an acceptable camera position, potential camera angles and fascinating images.
- Monitor the location of the sun during and after production time, including shadow formation and sun brightness.

Shooting Plan

Create a shooting schedule that includes camera positions and potential shot choices from each position. Choose a location for the OH Van, transmitter, generator sets and other vehicles as well. Determine the length of the cable for the cameras, microphones and lights (if needed). Additionally, listen out for any strange noises in the area and take precautions to avoid them during the filming. Pay close attention to the following factors when choosing your shooting strategy:

- Create a list of all the shooting sequences you'll be using and arrange them in the order you want to shoot them.
- Mark the shots that are the most crucial and that you simply can't miss because you can't take another shot at them or it's just not possible.
- Use a still cameraman to record the most significant and captivating scenes on still images.
- Thoroughly go over your shooting strategies with your crew, including the cameramen and engineers.
- Involve the audio engineer and the soundman as early as possible to capture high-quality sound.

Other Arrangements

There are various additional crucial preparations that, if not handled correctly, might lead to significant issues during recording or filming. Here, a few of these are listed:

***(i)* Transportation Facilities:** It's crucial that everyone on the production team has the means to arrive for remote duty on time.

***(ii)* Refreshments and Meals:** If your production will likely go for several hours, make sure to plan for tea, coffee, light refreshments and even meals if the need arises.

***(iii)* Parking of Vehicle:** Make sure all of your vehicles are parked in a convenient location so they are out of the way, while being recorded. It is advisable to set aside one car solely, for use in emergencies.

***(iv)* Equipment checklist:** Guarantee that the technical and production staff have created a thorough checklist for all pieces of equipment and props.

***(v)* Actual Recording/Shooting Operations:** In a field location recording situation, the fundamental shooting procedures employed are much the same as those used in a studio production. However, there are a few variations and unique practices that deserve special attention:

- Keep in mind that weather conditions can change quickly, so you should be ready for a variety of contingencies. Take notes on the opening establishing shots, key covering shots, exteriors, setting and landmarks.
- Make sure one of your cameras captures "master shots" of each portion of the show. The main action of the event may be captured by various cameras in CUs, MCUs, cutaways and reaction shots.
- You don't have to worry much about the shooting sequence during a field production, which entails post-production editing to put the finished programme together. Before switching to a new setup, take a number of potential pictures from each camera location. Always be on the lookout for odd and intriguing images that the environment might spontaneously present to you.
- Give your technical colleagues the responsibility for video recording, lighting and sound quality but keep an eye on every little detail.
- Make sure you have control over the graphics that will be captured.

EDITING

Editing entails putting together and rearrangement previously recorded video content into an ongoing meaningful programme. It encompasses both the technical task of picking and putting together and the skill of arranging the rushes made in the studio or on location to achieve aesthetic effects. The producer can physically put together these audio and video snippets into a cohesive narrative on the videotape through the editing process. Editing is frequently referred to as post-production editing because it happens after (post) production, as opposed to live or most studio productions, when it happens during production. You can look for precise edit points by searching frame by frame using editing software. The producer has the chance to carefully and patiently examine and edit the pre-recorded information during post-production editing. The editing process listed below might be helpful:

(i) Carefully and attentively go over your previously recorded contents once, twice, or even more frequently if you have the time.

(ii) Create a proper "log sheet" and record all significant ideas and specifics that cross your head.

(iii) Spend some time reflecting on the recorded material and defining your thoughts regarding the overall structure of the programme, including its main theme, aims, style, pace, organisation, beginning and end, etc.

(iv) Decide what is significant and pertinent to the goal of your programme and what is not.

(v) Remove any pictures or sequences—no matter how stunning—that do not advance the concept of your show. Choose only the best, most pertinent and highest-quality images.

(vi) Check for any gaps in the material and re-shoot any necessary segments if doing so will improve the programme's quality, relevancy and overall purpose.

(vii) You should have a good sense of the overall plot or shape of your programme and be able to create the final "edit-script".

(viii) You are now prepared to edit your programme in its entirety. Calculate the amount of time you'll need for editing. Try to complete it all at once. Keep close to your final "edit script" as you can, while editing. Avoid jump cuts and keep in mind the fundamental shot progression of LS, MS, then CU. Make good use of reaction shots and cutaways.

(ix) There are other additional things that one learns, while actually editing using the tools and resources.

SOME PRODUCTION TECHNIQUES

Television at first was merely "radio with visuals." Until recently, educational programmes were merely studio-produced "direct classroom telecasts." The term "televised theatre" was used to refer to TV plays and "grade-Z movies" was used to refer to TV shows. However, television has developed into a distinct field in barely 50 years. Naturally, it has taken and incorporated the majority of its elements, methods and techniques from a variety of other media, including radio, theatre and film. In recent years, television has outperformed all other forms of media and has come to have its own distinct identity. As hardware technology has made significant strides, television has also evolved, honed and improved many of its production methods.

Developing Shots and Introducing Movement

Video programmes mainly rely on moving pictures for their impact because static images or non-moving subjects are uninteresting. It is the producer's responsibility to treat static images with visual variation. The following techniques can be used to make the static image appear to be moving or to provide the appearance of movement:

- **By making the Artist Move:** Let's say the setting is a kitchenette's interior. Something is cooking in a pressure cooker, while the gas stove is on. We hear a sudden, loud whistle coming from the stove. A young girl enters through the small side entrance. The whistling ends when she depresses the cooker. Since we planned and created a scenario for the artist to walk, enter the shot and perform an action, even if the camera is fixed in place, there is movement in the shot. Everything seems to make sense, have purpose and be intriguing. It gives the producer the chance to capture the female transitioning from LS to MS to MCU on camera, full of curiosity and impact.
- **By Making the Camera Move:** We may organise our pictures using the same set-up by relocating the camera rather than the artist, who may already be in the kitchen. Of course, we can snap multiple pictures now by shifting the camera to other positions and angles but the outcome won't be as compelling and fascinating as in the first instance.
- **By Making both Camera and the Artist Move:** In this instance, we can begin with a shot of the girl walking through the door and pan along with her as she approaches the stove. The setup is fine but it is also clearly uninspiring and uninteresting. There are many instances of similar circumstances that present opportunities for creating a range of fascinating photos by adding movements to the subject, the camera, or both. However, both the camera and the subject movements must be driven, in order to appear logical and natural.

Maintaining Continuity: One of a producer's main responsibilities is to break down each action into a series of images or shots, capture these shots in the order he chooses and then reassemble the shots in the proper sequence to create a continuous presentation. In other words, from shot to shot and scene to scene, the producer must ensure that the action, dialogue, costumes, props and background, all remain consistent. When shooting intermittently, it's crucial to match elements of continuity like:

- **Technical continuity:** For matching colour, brightness, contrast, light intensity, etc.
- **Video and audio continuity:** For action, shot location, background, atmospheric effects, sound quality and volume and other effects.
- **Continuity of time, direction and movement:**

As an illustration, the spectator will become perplexed if the background in two or more subsequent photos of the same place changes. Similar to this, if we combine an image of a man sprinting from "right to left" with a shot of his legs going from "left to right", the viewer will lose their sense of direction and be unable to connect the two shots. As a result, it's important to check for consistency in each shot's content and preserve it, even when switching between shots. We can continue to cut from one shot to the next as long as the story's action is ongoing. This will guarantee action continuation.

Techniques of Cutting and Mixing

The cut is a very straightforward and energetic mechanism of transition, suggesting an instantaneous and undetectable change from one shot to the next. It is applied to the following circumstances and objectives:

- To maintain action, switch between pictures that depict continuous, step-by-step action.
- To expose details, cut to a closer view that clearly demonstrates the event's or subject's details.
- To increase or decrease impact — cutting to a close shot increases the action, while cutting to a distant shot decreases the impact.
- To establish the rhythm of the event, fast cutting or intercutting between parallel shots gives the impression of vigour and intensity, while slow cutting suggests calm.
- To shift the location and time by cutting to a remote or outer location. When to cut and when not to cut are actually two issues that the cutting technique addresses.

The following two factors should be taken into account by the producer before trimming:

***(i)* Motivating the cut:** Cuts should always be made for a reason or on a motivation expressed, either through the picture or the sound or both.

For example: "In a room we see a man working at his desk. Suddenly there is a gentle knock at the door on his right. As the man turns his face to look up towards the door, it opens and a young girl appears saying. "May I come in.. .?" Man stands up but drops his pen, which breaks, looks at the broken pen and then the girl and mutters - 'Oh dear.. .' The girl

Let's now investigate the predicament outlined earlier. When the door opens and the girl asks permission to enter, the man turns to gaze up after hearing the knock (cut), stands up, drops his pen to the ground (cut), stares at the pen (cut) and then advances to greet the girl (cut), who is now standing and giggles. Here, we discover that we always cut, when there is a justification for the cut, often known as "cutting on reaction"

***(ii)* Disguising the Cut:** Cutting on action is another cutting technique. Always cut during the action or movement of the subject in relation to the object when cutting on action. For instance, if the subject is in a CU and ready to stand up from his seat or sit down in a chair, the optimal time to cut would be just as he is going to perch on the seat. This style of cut is relatively undetectable and smooth. This method is also known as "cutting on action" or "disguising the cut." Here are a few other ideas that producers should keep in mind, while cutting or blending different shots.

Never switch from one of a person's CUs to another of the same person's CUs. In every shot you intend to cut, always look for anything fresh. Always adjust the shot's angle when cutting from LS to MS or MCU to CU (to ensure a natural effect).

Plan for increasingly more close-ups (CUs), while cutting between shots because they add impact and reveal more vivid face expressions and features. Avoid cutting from a very long shot to a close-up, since the audience will be confused by this abrupt change.

Instead, combine an LS with a CU or vice versa by using "dissolve" or "mix." For instance, a close-up of a single singer can be turned into a long view of the entire ensemble (or the other way round). Use a "mix" to imply a change in location or in time, or to imply a close relationship between two things. Avoid using excessive amounts of "mixes" or "dissolves", as a frequent reliance on "mixes" can slow down the pace of the programme and may be impair its continuity.

Crossing the Line

The cameras must be set up to capture the event when filming a public event, such as a football or hockey game. In this case, preserving screen direction and movement continuity becomes very important and the idea of "crossing the line" enters the picture. Let's attempt to comprehend this idea. Consider a situation, where two persons are facing each other and two cameras are set up to photograph them as in the Figure. In this case, the vector line is the fictitious line connecting their eyes. The two people will appear to be staring at each other if we shoot them from the same side of the hypothetical (vector) line and then switch between cameras. This is a recognised television tradition that is often used in setups for interviews, games and other events. The two people will, however, appear to be looking in the same direction if we shift one of the cameras to position X on the opposite side of the hypothetical line and cut images between cameras A and C. As a result of our violation of the vector line's basic premise, the viewers will be completely perplexed.

The viewers won't be able to tell, which team is playing in which way if this rule of shooting from the same side of "the imaginary line" is broken when filming a football game. Therefore, every camera is always set up to film from one side of "the imaginary line" that is drawn up the field and connects the two goal posts. If there are photos of moving things, a more serious issue may develop. Let's say a car is driving down the road or a runner is crossing the ground from left to right. The car or the athlete will appear to have changed direction from "left-to-right" to "right-to-left" if we intercut between photos taken by the two cameras, one of which is positioned on the opposing sides of the motion, crossing the vector line. This screen motion direction reverse is unacceptable because it is quite confusing. However, this accepted practice of "not crossing the line" has two exceptions:

The vector line principle is not broken during a shot if the camera is moved to a new location (across the vector line) and the locations of the persons or objects in the frame are re-established, indicating a changed direction.

The vector line may also be regarded as not having been crossed if the two subjects of the shot change positions. This is a concise description of a few significant television production methods. Other areas of production are seeing the development of more modern methods. Computers have given nearly every aspect of media production a completely new dimension and opened up new vistas. We currently have access to a wide range of computer-generated graphics, instant character generators for creating credits and titles, computer animation, computerised video editing techniques and several types of fantastic electronic effects and innovations, all provided by modern technology to help us master and refine the art of television production.

ACTIVITIES

Q. 1. Here is an outline of a small situation for you to visualize and practice shot development for a one-minute sequence:

"An old man is sitting on a bench in a park. He is immersed in the morning newspaper. Few people (both old and young) are jogging in the park. A dog is moving near the old man reading the newspaper. Suddenly an explosion takes place. The dog runs towards the explosion, bark continuously. The old man is shocked, drops the newspaper, gets up from the bench and starts moving towards the explosion site. Reaching the explosion site, he finds a crowd surrounding a burning car."

Now, on the basis of the above outline, work out a list of possible shots, camera moves and artists' moves covering the entire action from *(i)* a one-camera set-up *(ii)* a two camera set up, both in the field location shooting situation as well as a studio situation, where a set is provided.

Ans. The situation offers the producer an opportunity to take a shot of the spot changing from Long Shot to Medium Shot to MCU.

With the same set-up, we can plan our shots by moving the camera and not the artist who may be already is positioned at the place. We can take several shots by moving the camera to different positions and angles.

In this case, we can start with a shot of the old man sitting. After that a long shot to cover the people jogging in the park. The camera should also capture the dog moving near the old man. A long shot can be taken towards the explosion site, then a close up of the exact explosion spot. After that, the camera can capture the dog running towards the explosion, bark continuously. Then camera should also go to the old man who is shocked, drops the newspaper, gets up from the bench and starts moving towards the explosion site. The camera should also focus on the crowd surrounding a burning car. Here, two camera set ups can work better.

CHECK YOUR PROGRESS

Q. 1. Why is the camera script an essential first step leading to studio preparation?

Ans. The fundamental idea of TV video production should be put into written form as part of the scriptwriting process. It gives a pre-conceived idea of what will be stated and what scenes will be shot to complement the main point you're attempting to make. You can plan ahead as you get ready for the several components that will combine to create the finished product with the aid of the script. You'll have a clearer notion of the course you want to take with your plan after writing a script. It might help you decide more clearly who you want to play and what their function will be in the film.

You can select who will appear in the video, whether it's an actor or the proprietor of the company and whether they'll speak on-screen or in a voiceover. The set must be planned in accordance with the script. The set is a studio's built-in scenery or set that is used to record a programme. It provides the tone and style for a TV show or programme to be recorded in the studio, while also creating the proper physical setting. The set could be quite straightforward or extremely complex, depending on the demands of the programme and of course, the budget.

Each time, the set designer must be consulted in order for the producer to receive his input and suggestions. The set designer develops a draught floor plan with everyone's consent before presenting it for discussion in the first planning meeting. Following approval, various floor requirements are planned and chosen, including camera placements, objects and furniture placements, microphone placements, lighting patterns and actor movements.

The script also affects the floor plan. The floor plan is a representation of the studio's layout. It displays the studio's primary characteristics in scaled diagram form, including the walls, the cyclorama, the entrance doors and the location of the lighting grid. The term "floor plan" is used to describe a drawing of the scenery or set that will be constructed, along with the location of furniture and objects on the studio floor. In actuality, the floor plan offers crucial instructions for studio use, including how to put up scenery and props, arrange lights, install microphones, plan different perspectives, angles, positions and motions of cameras and indicate the actions and movements of actors and performers on the studio floor. It paints a complete picture of what the studio or the setting might seem like during the final recording. Therefore, a floor plan is crucial for the set designer, set erectors, floor manager, lighting technician, audio engineer, producer, director and talent.

Typically, the floor layout is created by the set designer after conversations with the producer. The screenplay specifies how to prepare the camera cards. For each of the recording cameras, camera cards are ready. The producer performs this while creating the camera screenplay, based on shot divisions. A camera card lists the shots, types of shots, motions, positions and activities associated with a certain camera. During dress rehearsals and the real production, the camera card is pinned or fastened to the camera in front of the cinematographer, who is led by it. One or two days before the recording day itself, camera cards are prepared.

Q. 2. List four inputs a producer has to organise before he/she can actually enter the studio for production.

Ans. Prior to entering the studio to begin production, a producer must arrange the following:

Graphics: The producer compiles a thorough list of the graphics along with an explanation of each. I have a separate meeting with the graphic designer to discuss the content of these designs. A deadline and references are provided before the artist begins work on the job. If there are any existing graphics, they are also located, purchased, and modified for use in the programme.

Photo, film and animation: The producer should direct the acquisition of new photos and films if the programme requirements call for the usage of certain images, films, or animation sequences. Filming and printing photos and videos takes time. Therefore, there should be enough time to collect these resources. You might want to employ a group of slides occasionally in your programmes. Additionally, these must be prepared for in advance: planned, photographed, edited, and mounted.

Props: According to the specifications of the script, a complete inventory of all objects (also known as props), furniture, and other items for decoration, demonstration, and other effects must be produced. The props assistant, who is tasked with procuring the necessary goods through hiring or purchasing, may talk through this list with them. Occasionally you might require something that has to be obtained promptly since it has to be fresh. On the other hand, if your presentation incorporates puppets, they might need to be carefully prepared, and the puppet fabricator should be given adequate time for this.

Costumes and make up: Your artists or performers might require some unique attire. This might need to be organised through the costumes department, so enough notice is essential. Similar to this, the person in charge of cosmetics should be told in advance if one or more of your artists need a specific style of makeup. This is important for various beard styles, moustaches, and other unusual cosmetics.

Sound effects and music: The producer should make sure that all of the program's audio needs, including the theme song, opening music, background music, and any special sound effects, sounds, or songs, are determined, purchased, recorded, and preferably placed onto a single audio tape. It should be maintained prepared, precisely timed, and cued for use during actual recording and integration with the application. The audio engineers record any music or other audio inserts.

Set and lighting: The concerned staff will finish the set and lighting on time after being fully instructed and guided. However, it is the producer's duty to examine, monitor, and guarantee that these conditions are met well in advance and that the studio is prepared to begin pre-production operations at the time set and disclosed to all in advance. If the set and lights are running late, you.

Q. 3. State, in brief, the types of rehearsal, which a video producer should ideally go through before recording a programme in the studio.

Ans. An organised studio recording process involves several technical and non-technical professionals operating multiple machines and cutting-edge equipment. All studio productions are therefore costly. Rehearsals cannot be held in the studio while others wait impatiently as a result. To avoid paying for the pricey studio time, it is a good idea to have some rehearsals outside the building. Basic educational programmes might not require many rehearsals, but elaborate plays and dramatic performances do. The producer should schedule more rehearsals if the script requires them or if the cast members lack confidence. The producers can opt to apply one or more of the following procedures depending on the scenario. The following suggestions may be helpful for practising the programmes.

Script Reading: No matter what kind of programme is being worked on, this is the first stage of any kind of rehearsal, and it is crucial to talk and read the script with the talent. Actors who have read the script are better able to depict their characters with assurance, ease, and motivation, which makes it easier for them to say their lines during the final takes. Dramatic productions are especially well-suited to this method.

Dry Run: Complicated productions are often practised in a separate rehearsal room away from the studio. The producer examines the actor's movements and camera positions during a dry run. Given that the positions and movements of the artists and cameras have been properly practised, the producer may utilise his viewfinder to block his shots and camera angles.

Walk-through: In the studio, a walk through is a fast run-through of the entire show or certain portions, just before camera practise and recording. The individual shot blocking and staggered procedures can be followed immediately by a walk-through, during which artists, cameramen, and floor crew get familiar with the nature and flow of the programme. A walk-through is generally used to test the placement of cameras, microphones, zooms, lighting effects, and shadows as well as to block performer shots and moves. Take a little break after the walk-through and before practising with the camera.

Camera Rehearsal: Just before the last recording, a camera rehearsal—also known as the final dress rehearsal—is held. Two methods may be used to practise using a camera. If a mistake is made at any point along the journey, one strategy is the continuous run through, where you start over from the beginning. Finally, following a successful, flawless camera practise, the show may be filmed. Instead, you can pause when the mistake happens and continue from an appropriate linking point in the script, being cautious not to repeat the error. It is referred to as the stop-start method. Both strategies need a lot of work and are exhaustive.

But, the continuous run-through method of camera rehearsal is incredibly stimulating since it involves everyone as a team and gives an electrifying feeling of the program's effect before it is really shot. Also, it is normal and recommended to record continuous camera tests, which occasionally turn out to be better than the final output.

Timing the Script: At script readings and rehearsals, the producer gets a great chance to roughly schedule the scripts for their shows. With a little bit of editing, the completed software may be managed to be slightly expanded or compressed to get it to its precise or intended duration.

Final Planning Meeting: Producers usually have a brief final production meeting one or two days prior to the actual filming of the programme. The aim is to ensure that everything is organised and under control, that all tasks have been successfully done or are likely to be performed at the proper time. Some producers make it a point to talk with or meet with each significant production member separately and do a quick informal appraisal of their level of readiness for the recording day in an effort to be more accessible. The producer and his production assistant must be certain of and confirm the following, to name just a few of the most important things:

- All graphics, photocaptions, film and VT inserts, and slides have been created; there are enough copies of the final camera scripts; camera cards have been created for all studio cameras;
- All music and sound effects have finally been recorded and cued; the set and lighting have either been created or will do so well in advance of the recording time;
- Copies of the recording schedule, which details the date, location, and time for various activities, are available. The recording is in perfect condition.
- All members of the technical crew, such as the technical director, the vision mixer operator, the audio engineer, the telecine and VTR operators, the lighting supervisor, the electricians, technicians, and grips, have been notified and assigned to studio duty;
- A stopwatch and timer are connected to every video and audio recording, both completed and unfinished; tea, coffee, and light snacks are on the schedule.

Never forget that nothing would be brought into the studio unless the producer requested it directly. He must be absolutely assured that he has filed his request or the appropriate requisition form on the day of the recording for any service or facility he needs in the studio. The producer can decompress after finishing these tasks and get ready to organise and direct the grand finale, which is the program's final in-studio recording.

Q. 4. List the three types of location recording situations. How is a big remote different from the other two?

Ans. When a TV programme (or part of it) is shot outside the studio, it is called a field location recording or a remote. These location recordings or remote can be classified into the following three types:

(i) Electronic news gathering (ENG)

(ii) Electronic field production (EFP)

(iii) Big remotes

One small portable camera, along with a VTR, is frequently used for ENG location recording. Back in the studio, the uncut raw video material is edited and broadcast. It requires quick, adaptable operations, a tiny personnel and excellent mobility. It is best suited for short news gathering or even a live telecast from the location due to its decent but lower quality photographs. However, ENG approaches are now being used more frequently to create educational programming.

Although EFP still has some of the flexibility and mobility of ENG, it requires more thorough planning and advance preparation. Of course, this calls for more personnel, more gear, video switches, an OB van and more cameras but it results in higher-quality images. EFP approach is suitable for filming various field programmes, which may frequently require post-production editing. It may or may not involve direct transmission from the spot. A huge event that is not specifically planned for radio or television can be recorded using a field production operation called a "big remote."

For live coverage and direct broadcast of significant events, such as national or international sporting competitions, conferences and seminars, contests and pageants, large remotes are organised. Such remotes typically involve elaborate preparations, including numerous high-quality cameras and related audio-video equipment, a multiple VTR setup for recording, instant replay, slow-motion playback and freeze-frame capability, a gigantic OB van housing a full, first-rate control room, a mobile microwave transmitter and a sizable contingent of production and technical crew.

Additionally, it requires a 3-phase power supply and backup generators for automatic takeover in the event of an unexpected power outage. For major remotes and other kinds of field location recordings, commentators and anchormen are also necessary (and in some situations, participating talent as well).

Q. 5. What is meant by the term 'recce'? Why is it important?

Ans. Recce, an abbreviation for reconnaissance, describes an initial examination of the shooting scene. Double check that I all pertinent parties have been notified, *(ii)* that power will be continuously provided by the closest electric substation, *(iii)* that all necessary shooting permissions have been obtained from the relevant authorities, and *(iv)* that during on-location filming, scouting, or a trip to, all relevant parties have been informed. the day, time, and date that the recording was actually made.

The location is a top priority issue on the producer's agenda that should never be disregarded. The producer must do a comprehensive reconnaissance along with his cameraman, production assistants, engineers, and technical operators. During a recce, the following considerations are made:

- schedule a meeting with the folks in issue or visit the place beforehand to get their feedback;
- look around the area from all angles and talk to the employees;
- find power supply points, make your own, or get a copy of the site plan;
- Monitor the location of the sun during and after production time, including shadow creation and sun brightness, in order to find and prepare a suitable camera position, prospective camera angles, and intriguing photographs.

Q. 6. Explain briefly what is meant by the term 'post-production editing'. What is its main objective?

Ans. Editing transforms the raw material into the finished software. It requires combining and rearranging already-existing recorded video resources into a continuous, impactful show. It includes both the meticulous expertise of rearranging the rushes made in the studio or on location to achieve visual effects, as well as the mechanical action of choosing and combining them. Most television programmes nowadays are usually made with just one video camera, in a filmic style, and with minimal consideration given to the order in which images and scenes would appear as they are being shot. During the editing phase, the producer may physically place these audio and video snippets together to build a coherent story on the videotape.

The editing process is referred to as post-production editing since it takes place after (post) production as opposed to live or during most studio productions. With editing software, you may search frame by frame for specific edit spots. During post-production editing, the producer has the opportunity to scrutinise and work with the pre-recorded materials in a more thorough and patient manner. Effective editing takes considerable planning. Of course, there may be times when it takes longer than shooting. The primary objective of editing is to put together a video programme with elements that promote clarity, consistency, and impact. To do this, the editing procedure listed below could be useful:

(i) Once, twice, or even more frequently if you have the time, carefully and attentively review the contents of your prior recordings.

(ii) Establish a suitable "log sheet" and include all relevant thoughts and facts that come to mind.

(iii) Take some time to consider the recorded material and formulate your opinions on the program's general structure, including its principal subject, objectives, style, pacing, organisation, beginning and conclusion, etc.

(iv) Determine what information is important and relevant to your program's purpose and what information is not.

(v) Delete any images or video clips, regardless of how magnificent they are, that do not enhance the theme of your programme. Only the finest, most relevant, and best-quality photographs should be used.

(vi) Examine the content for any gaps and re-shoot any needed sections if doing so will enhance the program's calibre, relevance, and overall goal.

(vii) At this time, you need to be able to write the final "edit-script" and have a solid understanding of the main storyline or structure of your programme. The careful sequencing and continuity of shots, the merging of sound and music, and the use of transition, cut-aways, and reaction shots that may create a fluid flow and the desired impression are all examples of this.

(viii) At this point, you're ready to alter your programme completely. Determine how much time you will need for editing.

Attempt to finish it in its entirety. During editing, try to stay as near to your final "edit script" as you can. Stay away from jump cuts and remember the LS, MS, CU shot process. Use reaction shots and cutaways to your advantage. By really using the tools and resources for editing, one learns a great deal more.

The basic phases in the video editing process are shown in this flowchart. Naturally, the actual editing procedures will vary greatly between machines. Depending on the editing technique chosen, some of the steps described below can be avoided.

Q. 7. List some of the important production techniques a producer should learn and master.

Ans. Television has created, improved and perfected many of its production procedures as a result of the significant developments in hardware technology. The following are some typical production methods that a producer ought to understand and master:

Advancing shots and adding motion: A producer is frequently obliged to arrange and choose from among the different shots that are accessible to his single or multiple camera setup in a given setting that may lend itself to still images or moving pictures. Video programmes mainly rely on moving pictures for their impact because static images or non-moving subjects are uninteresting. It is the producer's responsibility to treat static images with visual variation.

The following techniques can be used to make the static image appear to be moving or to provide the appearance of movement:

Making the performer move: Let's say the setting is a kitchenette's interior. Something is cooking in a pressure cooker, while the gas stove is on. We hear a sudden, loud whistle coming from the stove. A young girl enters through the small side entrance. The whistling ends when she depresses the cooker. Since we planned and created a scenario for the artist to walk, enter the shot and perform an action, even if the camera is fixed in place, there is movement in the shot. Everything seems to make sense, have purpose and be intriguing. It gives the producer the chance to capture the female transitioning from LS to MS to MCU on camera, full of curiosity and impact.

By shifting the camera: We may organise our pictures using the same set-up by relocating the camera rather than the artist, who may already be in the kitchen. Of course, we can snap multiple pictures now by shifting the camera to other positions and angles but the outcome won't be as compelling and fascinating as in the first instance.

Making the artist and the camera move together: In this instance, we can begin with a shot of the girl entering the door and pan alongside her to the stove. The setup is fine but it is also clearly uninspiring and uninteresting. There are many instances of similar circumstances that present opportunities for creating a range of fascinating photos by adding movements to the subject, the camera, or both. However, both the camera and the subject movements must be driven in order to appear logical and natural. A producer or director should actually practice mentally transforming a situation into television images and the associated sounds. He should be positioned in relation to the cameras or know how the cameras should be placed in relation to the main event, which is to be shot. In this way, peoples' actions and movements can be worked out and camera positions and angles can be estimated.

One of a producer's main responsibilities is to break down each action into a sequence of images or shots, capture these shots in whichever order he chooses and then reassemble the shots in the proper order to present a continuous presentation. In other words, from shot to shot and scene to scene, the producer must ensure that the action, dialogue, costumes, props and background all remain consistent. It is crucial to maintain technical continuity for matching colour, brightness, contrast, light intensity, etc., when filming in a discontinuous manner.

Action, shot location, background, ambient effects, sound quality and loudness and other effects are all kept consistent in the video and audio.

Continuity of time, direction and movement: As an illustration, the spectator will become perplexed if the background in two or more subsequent photos of the same place changes. Similar to this, if we combine an image of a man sprinting from "right to left" with a shot of his legs going from "left to right", the viewer will lose their sense of direction and be unable to connect the two shots. As a result, it's important to check for consistency in each shot's content and preserve it even when switching between shots. We can continue to cut from one shot to the next as long as the story's action is ongoing. This will guarantee action continuation.

Techniques of cutting and mixing: The cut is a very straightforward and energetic mechanism of transition, suggesting an instantaneous and undetectable change from one shot to the next. The cut is applied to the following circumstances and objectives:

- By switching between frames that depict continuous action being taken step-by-step.
- By cutting to a closer view that clearly reveals the event's or subject's details.
- To increase action or decrease effect, switch to a close-up shot. Conversely, go to a longer view to lessen impact.
- By quickly switching to a close-up shot that makes the specifics of the event or topic evident.
- By switching to a close-up shot, you can heighten action or lessen impact. To decrease impact, though, switch to a longer view.

Motivating the cut: Cuts should always be made for a reason or on a motivation expressed either through the picture or sound, or both.

Disguising the cut: Cutting on action is another cutting technique. Always cut during the action or movement of the subject in relation to the object when cutting on action. For instance, if the subject is in a CU and ready to stand up from his seat or sit down in a chair, the optimal time to cut would be just as he is going to perch on the seat. This style of cut is relatively undetectable and smooth. This method is also known as "cutting on action" or "disguising the cut."

Crossing the line: The cameras must be set up to capture the event when filming a public event, such as a football or hockey game. In this case, preserving screen direction and movement continuity becomes very important and the idea of "crossing the line" enters the picture.

OTHER IMPORTANT QUESTIONS

Q. 1. Write a note on filed location recording.

Ans. All audio-visual programmes had to be created and supplied from the studios in the early days of broadcasting. But, with the advent of portable cameras, lightweight VTRs, and other mobile equipment, it is now feasible to broadcast and record programmes concurrently from the field. The bulk of audio and video programmes produced today are created on location, edited, and mixed in a studio, then packaged for broadcast or distribution on cassettes.

Field location recording or a remote are terms used to describe when a TV programme (or a segment of it) is filmed on site. These local or distant recordings can be categorised into the following three categories.

***(i)* Electronic news gathering (ENG):** One tiny portable camera and a VTR are often used for ENG location recording. At the studio, the uncut raw video footage is edited and transmitted. It calls for quick, adaptable operations, a small staff, and extraordinary mobility. It is best ideal for short news gathering or even a live transmission from the scene because to its acceptable but lower quality photographs. ENG approaches are being used more frequently to create instructional programmes.

***(ii)* Electronic field production (EFP):** Although keeping some of ENG's flexibility and mobility, electronic field production requires more exact planning and advance preparations.

It goes without saying that this calls for more personnel, tools, video switches, an OB truck, and cameras, but the finished product is better-looking footage. Filming a variety of field programmes, which typically require post-production editing, is suited for the EFP approach. Direct transmission from the area may or may not occur.

***(iii)* Huge remotes:** A type of field production utilised to record noteworthy events that aren't meant for radio or television is an example of a large remote. Big remotes broadcast key events live, including contests, pageants, conferences and seminars, as well as regional, national, and worldwide sporting events.

Such remotes frequently call for elaborate setups, such as numerous top-notch cameras and associated audio-video gear, a multi-VTR setup for recording, instant replay, slow-motion playback, and freeze-frame capability, a sizable OB van housing a full, excellent control room, a mobile microwave transmitter, and a sizable contingent of production and technical crew. These remotes are often scheduled a few weeks before the event. Large remotes and different kinds of field site recordings also call for commentators and anchormen.

MULTIPLE CHOICE QUESTIONS

Q. 1. Which of the following provides the tone and style for a TV show or programme to be recorded in the studio?

(a) The set *(b)* The floor plan
(c) The camera cards *(d)* None of these

Ans. *(a)* The set.

Q. 2. Which of the following displays the studio's primary characteristics in scaled diagram form?

(a) The set *(b)* The floor plan
(c) The camera cards *(d)* None of these

Ans. *(b)* The floor plan.

Q. 3. Which of the following shows the shots, types of shots, motions, positions and activities associated with a certain camera?

(a) The set *(b)* The floor plan
(c) The camera cards *(d)* None of these

Ans. *(c)* The camera cards.

Q. 4. Who calls the first planning meeting when the comprehensive camera screenplay, production treatment and studio floor plan are completed?

(a) The director *(b)* The producer
(c) The main actor *(d)* None of these

Ans. *(b)* The producer.

Q. 5. Who delivers the floor layout and staging strategy during the first planning meeting?

(a) The director *(b)* The producer
(c) The main actor *(d)* The set designer

Ans. *(d)* The set designer.

Q. 6. __________ involves choosing actors and performers who are appropriate for the programme.

(a) Set plan *(b)* Floor plan
(c) Casting *(d)* None of these

Ans. *(c)* Casting.

Q. 7. The second planning meeting is also called as a:

(a) Review meeting *(b)* Producer's meeting
(c) Crew meeting *(d)* None of these

Ans. *(a)* Review meeting.

Q. 8. In the second planning meeting:

(a) The status of the various production activities allocated or started during the first planning meeting are assessed
(b) All members of the production team and partners present verbally at this meeting, asking questions and receiving additional clarifications
(c) Both *(a)* and *(b)*
(d) None of these

Ans. *(c)* Both *(a)* and *(b)*.

Q. 9. When does the producer test the actor's motions and camera angles?

(a) Dry run *(b)* Script reading
(c) Walk-through *(d)* Camera rehearsal

Ans. *(a)* Dry run.

Q. 10. Which is a quick run-through of the entire programme?

(a) Dry run *(b)* Script reading
(c) Walk-through *(d)* Camera rehearsal

Ans. *(c)* Walk-through.

Q. 11. Which is also referred to as the last dress rehearsal?

(a) Dry run *(b)* Script reading
(c) Walk-through *(d)* Camera rehearsal

Ans. *(d)* Camera rehearsal.

Q. 12. Which of the following is conducted right before the final recording?

(a) Dry run *(b)* Script reading
(c) Walk-through *(d)* Camera rehearsal

Ans. *(d)* Camera rehearsal.

Q. 13. Recce refers to:

(a) A preliminary inspection of the site, where the shooting will take place
(b) A preliminary inspection of the shooting scene
(c) Checking the readiness of people involved
(d) None of these

Ans. *(b)* A preliminary inspection of the shooting scene.

Q. 14. When shall you remove any pictures or sequences—no matter how stunning—that do not advance the concept of your show?

(a) During editing
(b) During shooting
(c) Just after shooting
(d) None of these

Ans. *(a)* During editing

■■

Pedagogy

Computer usage for pedagogical purposes focuses on enhancing learning through technology. The computer should be viewed as a supplement rather than a replacement for other technology. It is a technological instrument that should be used appropriately at the appropriate time, to the appropriate degree and in the appropriate manner to enhance what has been learned from other media and sources. In an ideal world, it should be up to the teacher to decide when, how much and how to utilise the computer to promote learning. Teachers who want to use computers in the classroom should pay close attention to the following three questions:

- How can students express themselves via computers?
- How can computer systems be adapted to the demands of specific users?
- How can the effectiveness of educational software be assessed?

Given the widespread perception that the rise in the availability and use of computers in education is matched only by a fall in the calibre of educational software on the market, the last question assumes significant significance. However, if the programme is chosen with sufficient quality awareness, this need not be the case.

Nearly all topics, from music (one of the least structured) to mathematics (the most structured), can be learned using computers, according to the spectrum of their pedagogic usefulness. This was extensively proved by the National Institute of Pedagogic Research (NIPR) in France between 1971 and 1976. About 600 instructors from all subject areas, including math, biology, history, geography, literature, physics, foreign languages and music, were trained by the NIPR over the course of these five years.

Computers are used in pedagogy, which calls for the development of computer-related abilities among teachers and students. Computers are currently being used for pedagogical purposes at all educational levels, from elementary school to college, as well as with children who are disabled and have special needs. Because it makes use of widely accessible technology like regular television and telephone, CYCLOPS, for instance, disabled students in many open colleges. A single instructor can monitor multiple students at once using the computer tutorial MERLIN, which also has a telephone function and can conduct a telephone tutorial based on the students' wishes or progress.

The pedagogical applications of computers are particularly important for distant learning for financial reasons. The computer makes it feasible for many distance learners to acquire new abilities at a far cheaper cost than would otherwise be the case with the traditional learning system.

As a result, we discover that the pedagogic applications of computers may be related to enhancing learners' motivation.

Helping recall previous learning:

- Providing new instructional stimuli.
- Activating the learner's response.
- Providing systematic and steady feedback.
- Facilitating appropriate practice.
- Sequencing learning appropriately.
- Providing a viable source of information for enhanced learning.

Training

Computers can be useful in providing training that is effective. The examples that follow show this:

(a) In the computer science department of the University of Karlsruhe in Germany, CAIL (computer-aided laboratory instruction) was developed to provide real-time applications of physics. This was done in an effort to bridge the significant knowledge gap that exists between the knowledge acquired during university education and the knowledge most useful in the workplace. Some students eventually used computerised equipment and experiments in various universities as a result of their participation in CAIL.

(b) Shortliffe, a different German University, created MYCIN, an artificial intelligence programme, in 1976 to teach medical students how to identify bacterial illnesses in blood and recommend the best course of action.

(c) Morris and Stewart-Dore created ERICA (Effective Reading in Content Areas) in 1976 at Brisbane College of Advanced Education in Australia to instruct students in reading. Its emphasis is on the process strategies in four stages, namely getting ready to read, thinking through the information in the text, extracting and organising information and translating the it into one's own words. ERICA presents reading as a continuous linguistic, cognitive and affective interaction with the response to the text.

(d) Although SPACEX has an adventure game-like appearance, it actually offers a whole training programme in language skills, covering reading, listening comprehension, oral expression, writing, art activities (such as drawing, colouring and painting, etc.), dramatisation and more. The kids that utilise SPACEX have to find various spaceship components that have been stashed away on the planet Persephone by its citizens. The game style efficiently stimulates the kids and allows them to practice a variety of linguistic abilities.

These are merely illustrative rather than exhaustive examples but they demonstrate how the computer can be an extremely helpful tool for skill development.

Various areas of professional courses like engineering and teacher training, as well as disciplines like physics and languages can all be learned on computers.

Lifelong Education

Lifelong learning is related to the idea of a learning society. The completion of formal education nowadays does not signal the end of learning. The rate at which new knowledge is created and older knowledge is replaced, necessitates that a person pursues learning throughout their lifetime. Institutions offering distant education, as well as open learning programmes must have resources for lifetime learning. The computer can be a fantastic tool and tutor in this situation. The idea of lifelong learning is founded on post-secondary education and presupposes that students are adults or nearly adults who are capable of managing their learning on their own.

COMPUTERS IN EDUCATION

For efficient learning, "teaching machines" were created in the 1930s. The use of computers in education came next. There are now other terms, including "computer-managed learning (CML)", "computer-assisted instruction (CAI)" and "computer-assisted learning (CAL)". In his framework for understanding computers in education, Romiszowski (1986) divided the topic into two primary categories: informatics as educational content and informatics as educational device. The latter, which uses computers as administrative, educational and learning tools, is what we are worried about.

Computer-Assisted Learning (CAL)

Four paradigms for CAL were promoted by Stephen Kemmis *et. al.*, (1977) are: *(i)* Instructional paradigm, *(ii)* Revelatory paradigm, *(iii)* Conjectural paradigm, *(iv)* Emancipatory paradigm.

(i) The drill-and-practice method and tutorials are part of the **instructional paradigm**. According to Kemmis, the instructional paradigm is predicated on the idea that language can be used to specify the information and the students' need to acquire it and that verbal messages can be transmitted and received to facilitate learning. As a result, the instructional paradigm generally bases how a subject is taught on its content.

(ii) The **revelatory paradigm** addresses learning through experience gained through computer simulation and data processing, as well as learning through discovery. The revelatory paradigm works by gradually revealing to the learner the fundamental ideas associated with the subject in a way that parallels the knowledge structure of the field being learned.

(iii) The **conjectural paradigm** places an emphasis on manipulation, active knowledge and hypothesis testing. According to the conjectural paradigm, knowledge develops via experience and is influenced by psychological and social factors.

(iv) The **emancipatory paradigm**, the fourth paradigm, makes a distinction between information that is valuable in and of itself and knowledge that is valuable for its instrumental purpose. The emancipator paradigm devalues learning that has more practical application and prioritises learning of authentic information.

CAL is divided into two modes by Johnes (1984)– tutorial CAL and simulation CAL. The conversation between the student and the teacher is simulated by the instructional CAL. Cicero, Merlin and Calchem are the three Tutorial CAL systems used by the Open University. Through simulation CAL, students can conduct risky, challenging and/or expensive investigations in a computer-simulated lab or field setting. Students that use simulation CAL have more freedom to design their own experiments and to deepen their comprehension. CAI includes computer use for the entire class, a group of students and the individual learner. Some of the educational activities that are widely employed under CAL include drills, demonstrations, games and programmed learning.

The utilisation of the educational materials produced by computers is encouraged by a generative approach to CAL. The primary consideration in the design criteria ought to be the needs of the learner.

Meeting the Learner's Needs: Hubbard (1988) developed a set of criteria for assessing courseware. This resulted from combining the developer's ideas about how to teach languages with the inherent benefits and drawbacks of using computers as interactive delivery systems. The most important items on this list are:

(i) To provide practice that is meaningful rather than mechanical, contextualised in a coherent discourse longer than a single line.

(ii) To give pupils tips of various kinds to guide them to the right solutions.

(iii) To accept alternate correct responses within the parameters of the question.

(iv) To offer the option of explaining why certain answers are considered correct.

(v) To anticipate incorrect answers and offer explanations concerning them.

The Notion of Intelligence in CAL

In CAL, intelligence is equated with the execution of extremely sophisticated programmes that mimic human intellect or carry out activities that, if performed by humans, would necessitate intelligence. These programmes are built using artificial intelligence approaches. The development of an increasingly complex interaction between "artificial" and "actual" intelligence is the major topic of this article.

Language teachers envision the ideal CALL programme as one that can comprehend spoken natural language. It also has the ability to answer appropriately using a voice synthesiser with a flawless accent in a range of registers, while containing the condensed essence of all the world's top-language instructors.

Expert system-based computer-aided learning (EXCAL) is one of these systems' key advancements. The Australian EXCALIBUR project serves as a particular illustration here. It is designed to be a

general-purpose, intelligent computing environment that will support the creation and delivery of computer-aided learning:

(i) A domain expert system made up of a knowledge base and a suitable reasoning framework makes up the EXCALIBUR project.

(ii) A model of each student's cognitive talents and subject-matter knowledge, such as a representational map or network diagram.

(iii) A teacher with pedagogical expertise in both general and subject-specific areas.

(iv) A natural language interface to synthesise system output into natural language and analyse user input.

(v) A reasoning system capable of working not just from knowledge, in one of the above knowledge bases but also from the student's knowledge, in order to establish a conversation with him/her.

To reiterate an earlier remark, these instances continually show us that the primary goal of using computers as instructional tools is to meet the diverse needs of students.

Computer Managed Learning (CML)

In contrast to CAL, the student is expected to take significantly less initiative and get more support in CML. CML deals with material that is less specific and less dynamic and it has recently come to be more closely linked to individualised learning, where the computer makes information stored on it, accessible to the learners, in order to offer them a variety of learning experiences. These include giving examinations to determine achievement, as well as identifying weak areas and providing subsequent remedial teaching in those areas. An examination of the CML literature finds that CAL has been the subject of much more writing than CML. CAL is more adaptable than CML and offers more room for experimentation. The computer-based interactive video in education is another noteworthy 1980s breakthrough. The end-user, who could be a learner or trainee, the computer system, which includes a knowledge elicitation system and the video disc system are the three key components of the interactive video system. Although, the technology is still in its infancy, an intelligent interactive video system may hypothetically replace the interactive role of the human teacher.

While evaluating CAL, two key aspects must be kept in mind: First off, CAL has been the topic of much more studies in more structured fields than in less structured ones, such as languages and music. These fields include mathematics and physics. Second, practically all of these investigations were carried out in industrialised nations.

Various CAL studies reveal that:

(i) The effectiveness of CAL is far from absolute; it depends on a variety of factors, the most important of which are the subject matter covered in class, the students' academic level and the environment in which instruction is taking place.

(ii) CAL is more effective when used to teach subjects that are comparatively more organised and structured.

(iii) CAL is more effective when it is integrated into the curriculum, rather than being used as a simple add-on to classroom instruction.

(iv) CAL can be introduced profitably in the lower grades, or in primary education. Elementary level students benefit from CAL more than college students do.

Computer-Based Training (CBT)

Computer-based training (CBT) is a method that is essentially personalised for resolving performance issues through training. A typical CBT helps the learners to gain the knowledge and skills necessary for task performance competency.

With CBT, you can get:

(a) Quicker, activity-based tutorials that help you comprehend the material and retain it better.

(b) Drill and practice is one method that enables mastery learning.

(c) Earning by closing: CBT can offer fully experiential learning and learners can hone their abilities by utilising simulated and modelled tasks.

Ravet and Layte (1997) propose six levels of computer activity that can be utilised for creating computer-based training programmes, using the UK-based National Vocational Qualification framework. The table below includes them:

MULTIMEDIA TEACHING-LEARNING MATERIALS

The use of multimedia is an alternative strategy for effective teaching and learning. However, the advent of greater computing power has underpinned the emergence of multimedia as a potential teaching and learning tool in higher education.

What is Multimedia?

Contrary to traditional mass media, such as printed material or audio recordings, which contain little to no user participation, multimedia is a type of communication that combines several content formats, such as text, audio, images, animations, or video into a single interactive presentation. Audio slideshows, animated films and video podcasts are a few common types of multimedia. The fundamentals of software, hardware and other technologies, as well as their applications in interactive communication, are all included in multimedia. On demand or in real-time, multimedia can be recorded for playback on desktops, laptops, cellphones and other electronic devices.

What is hypertext?: A word, phrase, or section of text that can be linked to another text or document is referred to as hypertext. Both text-based and visual linkages are included in hypertext. One of the fundamental ideas that underpins the operation of the Internet, the phrase was first used by Ted Nelson in the

1960s. Without hypertext, one of the main methods of exploring the Web would be impossible: clicking link on a topic to read a related article on that topic. However, Vannevar Bush's 1945 article "As We May Think" in the Atlantic Monthly, where he stated: "Consider a future technology for individual use, which is a sort of mechanised private file and library, may be attributed with the idea of hypertext. To come up with a name at random, "Memex" will work. A memex is a gadget where a person keeps all of their correspondence, books and records. It is automated to allow for incredibly quick and flexible access. It is a more comprehensive supplement to his or her memories'.

What is hypermedia?: Hypertext, or the capacity to launch new Web pages by clicking text links on a Web browser, is an outgrowth of what is referred to as hypermedia. Hypermedia takes this a step further by enabling users to click on images, videos, graphics and other types of media in addition to text to build a non-linear network of information. Although, this term is frequently used interchangeably with "multimedia", other multimedia systems—such as the video disk-based multimedia programme known as the Doomsday Project (UK) do not operate on the concepts of hypertext.

Multimedia Design Issues

Authoring software, sometimes known as authoring tools, is used to create multimedia programmes. The following authoring tools are frequently used in the creation of educational materials: Authorware Professional, Director, Studiomax, Hyper Card, Toolbook, Apple Media Toolkit, etc. When considering the creation of any multimedia teaching or learning materials, the following factors should be taken into account:

- Use a user-centered strategy to enhance student learning.
- Gather user input to determine whether students are happy with the courseware.
- Take learner input into account, while developing new materials.
- Be consistent as you create your style and design.
- Make it participatory.
- Create interactional tools for errors, pace-setting, module selection, etc.
- Disclose information in manageable doses.
- To keep students' interest, the information in multimedia programmes should also be thought provoking.

Applications of Multimedia

Multiple uses can be made of multimedia programmes. They are employed in information kiosks, the delivery of reference materials like encyclopaedias, the distribution of games and the provision of educational and recreational content.

Since it contains a variety of media, it clearly has an edge over resources that just contain one type of media. Because multimedia courseware is made to accommodate various learning styles, the user can somewhat influence how they learn. Phillips has suggested the following instances, where using multimedia as a technology might be appropriate:

- Subject matter that is challenging to visualise, such microscopic processes.
- Three-dimensional content might be challenging to visualise using standard two-dimensional mediums like books and whiteboards. Dynamic processes, which require understanding of the relationships between moving objects.
- Content that focuses on broad settings in which a lot of concepts must be connected in order to build a knowledge of the whole, rather than merely the pieces.
- Why simulations of pricey or difficult processes, where using actual equipment is not an option and understanding may be hampered by the process's mechanical intricacies.

EFFECTIVENESS OF COMPUTER USE

Here we shall deal with two practical aspects of the use of computers in education —administration and cost consideration.

Administration

Computer installation, student management, staff training and software evaluation are administrative facets of computer use in education. Computer use for instructional purposes shouldn't be a hit-or-miss endeavour. Therefore, it is necessary to develop a policy and a strategy for it. The policy regarding when, how and how much computer use should be allowed, should ideally be developed with the help of a group of teachers.

***(i)* Installation of the Computer:** The computer is an expensive piece of equipment, so due care should be taken to maintain its safety. However, accessibility shouldn't be sacrificed for the computer's security. After all, users should have access to the computer. Computers should ideally be connected to an uninterruptible power source.

***(ii)* Pupil Management:** The computer is an expensive piece of equipment, so due care should be taken to maintain its safety. However, accessibility shouldn't be sacrificed for the computer's security. After all, users should have access to the computer. Computers should ideally be connected to an uninterruptible power source.

Second, group organisation encourages conversation. Small group organisation should come after entire group organisation, if at all possible. For a small group, four to six students are ideal. Computer-enhanced collaborative learning (CECL) employing small groups is more effective than solo computer-assisted learning (CAL), since CECL is built on cooperation and discussion.

***(iii)* Staff Training:** When they first start working for the school, not all teachers may be computer savvy

and even those who are, may not be adept at using computers as teaching tools. However, the institution can initially guarantee the systematic computer literacy and skills of one teacher, who can thereafter instruct others. However, institutional policy should be more concerned with the provision for teaching computer literacy and computer-based teaching techniques. The probability of the best increases with the number of teachers who are computer literate and skilled in computer-based education! One of the computer resources the university has accessible.

(iv) **Software Evalutation:** If an institution has computer-based learning capabilities, then some considerations must be taken for the acquisition of suitable and acceptable software. The need for the teacher to assess the software package in terms of its suitability for the pupils persists, even if an institution receives its software supply from a centralised agency. When used, a good software product should engage students' interest and motivation, provide more pertinent information, promote practice, sequence learning and serve as a valuable supplemental learning resource in and of itself. Software packages frequently don't live up to their stated benefits. Software should therefore, be evaluated using these three criteria, as well as its technical aspects and visual appeal. A good programme should be simple for the student to use, since it should place the fewest demands on them and allow them to use it without experiencing any problems. But there are no shortcuts for developing software evaluation skills; they must be practiced over time and cannot be learned quickly or even over a short period of time.

Cost

Cost factors are regularly taken into account, while making decisions about educational innovations and the usage of different educational media. In underdeveloped nations, where education is merely one of many priorities—many of which frequently rate higher than education—this is particularly true. The technical aspects of the various computer manufacturers and models will not be covered in this article. A computer system's price includes peripherals and occasionally, the price of an additional visual displays device or monitor. As a result, the price depends on the computer's capabilities, such as whether it is standalone, networked, or both.

COMPUTERS IN INDIAN EDUCATION

In 1984–1985, the computer made an appearance in a few Indian schools as a result of a national initiative to promote computer literacy and studies in classrooms (CLASS). Therefore, the computer is a relatively new technology in Indian classrooms and project CLASS itself represents its history. The computer continues to be a fantastical, enigmatic high-tech object that needs respect and careful handling for millions of Indian pupils. The kids involved in the CLASS experiment are essentially an affluent minority. Even though they are small in number, the CLASS-trained teachers are projected to play a significant part in creating the multiplier effect. A 12-inch colour monitor, a 5-1/4" floppy drive, an 80-column dot-matrix printer and an 8-bit microprocessor with 32k RAM made up the computer hardware that was delivered to the 750 schools participating in CLASS. Undoubtedly, a system with relatively little configuration by today's standards.

To demystify the computer and foster a level of comfort and familiarity with it that should be conducive to developing individual creativity, Project CLASS had four goals—(1) to give students a broad understanding of the computer and its use, (2) to provide hands-on experience, (3) to familiarise the students with the range of computer applications in all facets of human activity and the computer's potential as a controlling and information processing tool and (4) to provide hands-on experience.

The majority of software applications included in CLASS are related to science and mathematics. The majority of the computer custodian teachers have backgrounds in mathematics and physics. Computer literacy classes have been offered for about eight years and the experience has shown that *(i)* the computer as a tool won't be readily available in all Indian schools in the near future, *(ii)* the computer is now treated as a prestige symbol and owning one has become more important than using it effectively, *(iii)* unless adequate precautions are taken right away, practical use of the computer in schools will decrease and computer literacy will become by and large an obsolete skill, *(iv)* despite being a neglected subject, teaching students how to programme is crucial from a pedagogical perspective because it gives students a different approach to problem-solving and *(v)* because computer networks and CAL are largely nonexistent in schools, computer use in Indian classrooms is still in its infancy.

Any efficient educational system depends on the instructor and in this case, the teacher must ensure that computers are used effectively in classrooms. The effectiveness with which a computer is used for educational purposes is, however, determined by the teacher's attitude, regardless of whether computers are used or not.

COMPUTER MEDIA IN DISTANCE EDUCATION

Chacon (1992) provides a fascinating taxonomy of computer media in distance learning. He supports more fundamental computer usage as an extension of appropriate student and teacher conduct. He also lists the three modes of computer use: information processing, interaction and communication.

Information Processing: 'I learn by doing' is a principle that is used in the information processing technique of computer use in distant learning. Memory, sorting, calculation, relationships, matching, reading

and writing are a few intelligence-related skills that are involved. A computer is used in these activities as a tool.

Interaction: The concept of "I teach things to myself" is used when using computers in an interactive manner for remote learning. Interaction between a person and a machine. Chacon claims that when a student is given the chance to have a conversation with a computer over which they have significant control and when they are exposed to stimuli across a range of media types, interactive computing in education takes place. The most common place for interactive computer use is in educational settings. The computer becomes an experienced teacher in this mode.

Communication: The notion of "I learn from others" is used in the computer communication technique used in distant learning. It anticipates the use of computers to facilitate communication between people. The communication method application in distance education may be predominating due to its worth in supporting far-off students. Email and computer conferencing software are the employed technologies.

CHECK YOUR PROGRESS

Q. 1. List the three basic issues related to the pedagogic uses of the computer.

Ans. There are various challenges and issues related to the pedagogic uses of the computer. Some of them are discussed below:

***(i)* School with Limited Technical Support:** Teachers cannot be expected to get through the barriers stopping them from using computers in the classroom without adequate technical support in the classroom and whole-school resources. Lack of technical support was one of the main obstacles to computer use in education. These technical obstacles included things like waiting for websites to load, having trouble connecting to the Internet, printers that wouldn't print, broken computers and having to use outdated computers for teachers. The lesson's flawless delivery and the activity's natural flow in the classroom were both hampered by technical difficulties. Contracts for ICT support or upkeep in schools allow instructors to utilise computers in the classroom without spending time resolving software and hardware issues. If a school lacks technical support, it is likely that technical maintenance will not be performed on a regular basis, increasing the risk of technical failures. Because they worry that the technology might malfunction in the middle of a lesson, technical issues might deter them from using computers in their classrooms. According to various surveys, the primary obstacle to employing computers in education is a lack of technical support. If a technician is not present, it can be difficult to integrate ICT into the classroom because there won't be any technical support.

***(ii)* Lack of Effective Training:** Lack of efficient training is the problem that is most usually mentioned. There weren't enough possibilities for teachers to receive computer-use training in a classroom setting. The topic of training is undoubtedly complicated because it's crucial to take into account a number of factors in order to guarantee training efficacy. It's crucial to give instructors pedagogical training as opposed to only instructing them how to use ICT technologies. Teachers should receive pedagogical-focused training if they want to be persuaded of the advantages of integrating ICT into their lessons. Studies revealed that teachers only knew how to run a computer and set up a printer, not how to use computers in their classes, even after taking professional development courses in ICT. They said that this is the case because teachers were rarely taught how to improve the educational components of ICT in the courses, which frequently, mainly concentrated on teaching teachers how to acquire fundamental ICT skills. They claim that this is so because training programmes put more emphasis on acquiring ICT skills than on instructors' ICT-related pedagogical practices.

Fundamentally, if teachers are to incorporate new teaching methods and tools into their lessons, they must undergo appropriate training.

***(iii)* Limited Time:** Many instructors, according to recent surveys, are competent and confident in using computers in the classroom but they don't always use them since they don't have the time. The use of ICT by teachers in their instruction has been hampered by time constraints and the challenge of scheduling enough computer time for courses, according to a sizable number of academics. Lack of time to design technological classes, browse the Internet, or examine various facets of educational software is the most frequent issue teachers mention. The shortage of time for teachers to complete activities impacts many parts of their work, according to studies. Some of the participant teachers particularly mentioned which computer-related chores take up the most time. These include the time required to research online guidance, plan classes, experiment with and practice using technology, resolve technical issues and obtain the necessary training.

Q. 2. Justify the use of computer as an 'ass-on' device instead of a 'replacing device'.

Ans. The use of computers as an 'ass-on' device means that they are used to augment and enhance human abilities rather than replacing them entirely. This approach recognizes that computers are tools that can improve human productivity, efficiency, and creativity.

Here are some reasons why using computers as an 'ass-on' device is justified:

1. Complementing Human Skills: Computers are powerful tools that can be used to complement human skills, such as decision-making, problem-solving, and analysis. By combining the strengths of humans and computers, we can achieve better outcomes than we could with either one alone.

2. Supporting Human Creativity: Computers can ssist humans in creative endeavors, such as graphic lesign, music composition, and writing. For example, a vriter may use software to help organize their thoughts nd ideas, but ultimately, the final product is still their wn creation.

3. Increasing Efficiency: Computers can perform nany repetitive and time-consuming tasks faster and nore accurately than humans, freeing up time for umans to focus on more complex and creative work.

4. Reducing Errors: By using computers to assist vith tasks such as data entry, calculations, and analysis, ve can reduce the risk of human error, leading to more ccurate results.

5. Improving Accessibility: Computers can nake it easier for people with disabilities to access nformation and participate in activities that would therwise be difficult or impossible.

Q. 3. How does the use of the computer make istance education more open, as well as more exible?

Ans. Less physical interaction between the acher and the student is encouraged in distance arning programmes, which place a heavy emphasis electronic communication. As a result, computers e now a crucial component in distant learning. udents can access online information sources like D-ROMs, the Internet, the Online Public Access atalogue (OPAC) and other electronic databases anks to computers. As students use word processing ogrammes to type assignments, do classwork and rowse the Internet to get current information for their me-papers and projects, computers help students earn. The availability of electronic resources in university braries, cybercafés, residences and technology entres is extremely important, since it gives students ccess to a wealth of knowledge they need to succeed cademically. The usage of computers by pupils has been the subject of numerous studies. Learning is more flexible and efficient because of computers.

Q. 4. Name two functions of the computer, which justify its use as a training device.

Ans. The trainer can focus on the crucial duties of needs assessment and instructional design, thanks to the computer's capacity to store materials and evaluate data.

You can use a spreadsheet to track all of your training programmes, whether you are an internal trainer or an outside consultant. As we mentioned previously when talking about the computer-managed instruction function of the computer, you can keep an eye on all of the employees as they progress through the various phases of training. You can also keep track of the costs, mileage and other things needed for taxes.

The accounting feature of the computer will be less useful for beginning trainers but if you start with such a programme, you will be prepared as the demand arises. It is preferable to have too much capacity and software than too little and be unable to expand because your computer lacks the necessary capacity, as we have emphasised throughout this chapter.

Your computer's analysis capabilities are a key component of its training capabilities. Consider the scenario where you administered a company-wide attitude survey to all of the staff members. How do you handle the hundreds or perhaps thousands of surveys you gather? You could compile summaries of the responses, based on the averages of all the respondents, or you could detail each respondent's answers to the questions.

You may easily and rapidly analyse survey replies statistically by entering all the data on a computer. Once the data has been entered, the possibilities for analysis are virtually endless. You may learn what the majority of female employees thought about a certain topic or what the more seasoned employees thought in comparison to those who had just started working there. The only restrictions on your analysis will be the data you first provided into the computer. You couldn't compare ages of employees if you didn't enquire about their ages.

After you have examined the data and created a composite image of worker sentiments, to provide the reader of your report with eye-catching visuals, you could use a graphics software programme. There are countless applications for computers in analysis. Communication is one of the newest and most fascinating uses of the computer. While university students have just recently been able to connect with one other via computers, new technology now allows anyone with a computer, a modem, a phone line and money to do so.

Q. 5. Distinguish between CAL and CML.

Ans. Both in the typical classroom and in contexts for language acquisition, computer assisted learning (CAL) and computer managed learning (CML) have drastically updated the way that students learn. Even the most resistant students can become interested in lessons thanks to their increased interactivity and engagement. In contrast to CAL, the student is expected to take significantly less initiative and get more support in CML. CML deals with material that is less specific and less dynamic and it has recently come to be more closely linked to individualised learning, where the computer makes information stored on it, accessible to the learners in order to offer them a variety of learning experiences. These include giving examinations to determine achievement as well as identifying weak areas and providing subsequent remedial teaching in those areas. An examination of the CML literature finds that CAL has been the subject of much more writing than CML. CAL is more adaptable than CML and offers more room for experimentation. The computer-based interactive video in education is another noteworthy 1980s breakthrough.

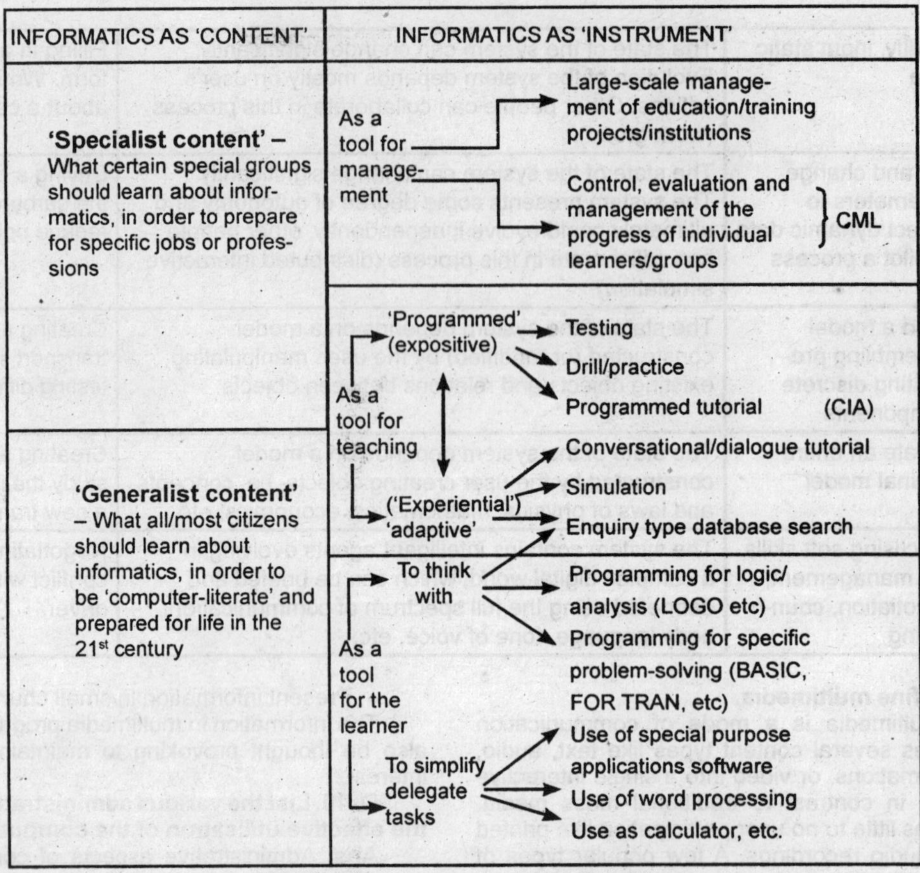

The 'field' of 'computers in education

Q. 6. List any two distinguishing features of Instructional CAL and Revelatory CAL.

Ans. Drill-and-practice and lessons are topics covered by instructional CAL. Based on the premise that knowledge and students' needs to acquire it may be expressed in language and learned through the transmission and reception of verbal messages, instructional CAL was developed. As a result, the instructional paradigm generally bases how a subject is taught on its content. Revelatory CAL focuses on learning via experience gained through computer simulation and data management, as well as learning by discovery. The revelatory paradigm works by gradually revealing to the learner the fundamental ideas associated with the subject in a way that parallels the knowledge structure of the field being learned.

Q. 7. Give three advantages of CBT.

Ans. Computer-based training (CBT) is a method that is essentially personalised for resolving performance issues through training. A typical CBT helps the learners to gain the knowledge and skills necessary for task performance competency. With CBT, you can get:

(a) Quicker, activity-based tutorials that help you comprehend the material and retain it better.

(b) Drill and practice is one method that enables mastery learning.

(c) Earning by closing: CBT can offer fully experiential learning and students can hone their abilities by utilising models.

Six Levels of Computer Activity

Level	User Activity	Computers Reaction to User Activity	Computers Reaction to User Activity
1.	Select, read, listen, watch static data	The state of the system does not change significantly. It is possible to add basic information like a page mark, annotation or users name.	Reading a manual about a car

2.	Modify, input static data	The state of the system can change significantly. Evolution of the system depends mostly on user's actions. Other people can collaborate in this process (work group).	Filling in a registration form. Writing a manual about a car.
3.	Set and change parameters to collect dynamic data or pilot a process	The state of the system can change significantly. The system presents some degree of autonomy and ultimately could evolve independently, other people can collaborate in this process (distributed interactive simulation).	Driving a car. Adjusting the carburetor to reduce pollution.
4.	Build a model assembling pre-existing discrete components	The state of the system depends on a model constructed (or modified) by the user, manipulating existing objects and relations between objects.	Creating a road transport system and testing different options.
5.	Create an entire original model	The state of the system depends on a model constructed by the user creating objects, i.e. concepts and laws of physics, mathematics, economics, etc.	Creating a model to study the importance of a new transport policy.
6.	Practising soft skills like management, negotiation, counselling	The system contains intelligent agents evolving in a complex digital world, which can be briefed and debriefed using the full spectrum of communication: body language, tone of voice, etc.	Negotiating during a conflict with a lorry driver.

Q. 8. Define multimedia.

Ans. Multimedia is a mode of communication that integrates several content types like text, audio, graphics, animations, or video into a single interactive presentation, in contrast to traditional mass media, which involves little to no user participation like printed material or audio recordings. A few popular types of multimedia are animated videos, audio slideshows, and video podcasts. Multimedia encompasses the foundations of hardware, software, and other technologies, as well as the uses and ideas behind effective interactive communication. Multimedia can be recorded on PCs, laptops, cellphones, and other electronic devices so that it can be viewed at a later time or immediately.

Q. 9. Identify at least three issues in multimedia design.

Ans. Authoring software, sometimes known as authoring tools are used to create multimedia programmes. The following authoring tools are frequently used in the creation of educational materials: Authorware Professional, Director, Studiomax, Hyper Card, Toolbook, Apple Media Toolkit, etc. When considering the creation of any multimedia teaching or learning materials, the following factors should be taken into account:

- Use a user-centered strategy to enhance student learning.
- Gather user input to determine whether students are happy with the courseware.
- Take learner input into account, while developing new materials.
- Be consistent as you create your style and design.
- Make it participatory.
- Create interactional tools for errors, pace-setting, module selection, etc.
- Present information in small chunks.

The information in multimedia programmes should also be thought provoking to maintain the learners' interest.

Q. 10. List the various administrative aspects of the effective utilisation of the computer.

Ans. Administrative aspects of computer use in education include software review, staff training, student management, and staff installation of computers.

***(i)* Computer setup:** As computers are obviously expensive pieces of machinery, proper precautions should be taken to preserve their security. Accessibility shouldn't be given up in favour of computer security, though. Users should have access to the computer after all. An uninterruptible power supply should preferably be linked to computers.

***(ii)* Student management:** The instructor or counsellor typically acts as a go-between for the computer-using pupils and the device. A reservation for the computer room should be made if the institution has more than one teacher who is computer-capable.

This makes it possible to use computers more effectively and divide the burden involved in computer-based training fairly.

In terms of controlling the pupils, they can employ the computer in big groups, smaller groups, or individually. Whole group organisation is justified in spite of its shortcomings since it may be used to show the program's aims and, thus, serve as a helpful starting point. Second, dialogue is promoted through group organisation. Small group organisation should come after entire group organisation, if at all possible. Four to six students make the perfect small group size. Small-group computer-enhanced collaborative learning (CECL), which is built on cooperation and discussion,

Computer as an Educational Aid

13

INTRODUCTION

The way we gather, process, store and communicate information has been changed by computers. Every account of the accomplishments of the 20th century emphasises gadgets that can store an enormous amount of data but the computer was the creation that made them all possible. Television, print, telephone and computers—the four main ways that information was disseminated—were all independent in the 1960s. Today, computer technology either fully or partially supports everyone. The advancements in computer, transistor and microelectronic technologies have allowed for this confluence. The rise of multimedia programmes is the most recent development in this field. Multimedia programmes offer the ability to navigate swiftly between points, without taking the time to physically view each page. This is suitable for all learners because it accommodates various learning styles and gives the opportunity to read only the sections that pique one's attention and skip others.

CHAPTER AT A GLANCE

COMPUTERS: AN INTRODUCTION

In 1946, the Electronics Numerical Integrator and Calculator, or ENIAC was created. Since then, the era of the fifth-generation supercomputer has begun (based on artificial intelligence). Generally speaking, there are four types of computers: microcomputers, minicomputers, mainframes and supercomputers. The majority of microcomputer used is in the classroom. These are machines that interact between the hardware and software components of a computer to produce features like fast speed, accuracy and versatility. A computer's hardware consists of its physical parts, while its software is its collection of programmes that make it work. One of the most significant components of hardware is the Central Processing Unit (CPU). The CPU's transistor count determines a computer's speed.

Capabilities of Computers

A high rate of speed is used by modern computers. They have a huge number of text, audio, image, and video storage capacity. A laptop-style computer, which typically only takes up the space of one table, is another option. They are able to go about on foot. Even while travelling from Amsterdam to New York for work, a notebook or laptop computer may be used. These are really intriguing and simple to use. Computers are ideally suited for use in education and training because of all of these capabilities.

SPECIFIC USES OF THE COMPUTER

Modern information technology is adaptabl and the computer can be used to store, analyse an retrieve data in a variety of settings. Its uses are thu almost as varied as the situations in which education transactions take place in daily life. Howeve there have been some differences in how differen instructors have responded to using computers as tool for teaching and learning. In many underdevelope countries, the computer is still viewed as a disease tha should be avoided, since it jeopardises the tried-and true educational system there. This only tells a portio of the narrative, though. On the other hand, a growing number of instructors are driven to try out its applicability in almost every subject area by the potential it gives to them as well as their students. It is not necessary to identify or explain each instance in which the compute can be used as a teaching tool. The computer can be used for a variety of tasks and can instruct students in a variety of curriculum at nearly all grade levels utilising both face-to-face and remote learning methods.

Rural Informatics: The Udang Experiment

Udang is a small rural village in West Bengal. This neighbourhood serves as an illustration of how people in rural areas may use computers to build an information system that is shared by 20 surrounding communities. In three days, almost 2000 old and young people living in rural areas had their first encounter with a computer. As the awareness-raising initiative gathered pace, money was raised from the neighbourhood to purchase a computer. There were few persons who regularly attended local teachers' lessons on how to build an information system. The rural informatics experiment produced a wide range of results, including *(i)* that anyone and everyone can use computers, *(ii)* that all demographic groups are interested in and benefit from using computers, and *(iii)* that elite urban, developed class individuals, do not have exclusive access to computers.

has been proven in computer-based learning studies to be superior than solo computer-assisted learning (CAL).

***(iii)* Staff training:** Not all teachers are likely to be computer literate when they first begin working for the school, and even those who are might not be skilled at using computers as teaching tools. Yet, the institution can first ensure the systematic computer literacy and abilities of one instructor, who can thereafter train others. Institutional policy should focus more on the availability of computer literacy instruction and computer-based teaching strategies. The likelihood of the best rises as more teachers gain computer literacy and expertise in computer-based education, one of the available computer resources at the university.

***(iv)* Software evalutation:** If a school offers computer-based instruction, there are a few things to think about while buying appropriate and respectable software. Even if a school obtains its software supply from a centralised organisation, the teacher still has to evaluate the software package in terms of its usefulness for the students. When employed, a good software product should pique students' attention and motivation, offer more relevant knowledge, encourage practise, sequence learning, and function as a priceless independent additional learning resource. Software programmes typically fall short of their claimed advantages. These three factors should be used to assess software along with its technical features and aesthetic appeal.

A good programme should be easy for students to use because it should impose the fewest requirements and enable them to use it without any issues. However there are no shortcuts for acquiring software assessment abilities; they must be exercised over time and cannot be learnt rapidly or even over a short period of time.

Q. 11. Briefly describe the various types of pupil management. Which of these is most useful and why?

Ans. In most cases, the instructor or counsellor acts as a middleman between the computer-user kids and the device. A reservation for the computer room should be made if the institution has more than one teacher who is computer-capable. This enables better computer utilisation and equitable division of the workload associated with computer-based instruction. In terms of managing the students, they can utilise the computer in large groups, smaller groups, or individually. Despite its drawbacks, whole group organisation is justified, since it can be utilised to illustrate the programme's objectives and thus, serve as a useful starting point. Second, group organisation encourages conversation. Small group organisation should come after entire group organisation, if at all possible. For a small group, four to six students are ideal.

Computer-enhanced collaborative learning (CECL) employing small groups is more effective than solo computer-assisted learning (CAL), since CECL is built on cooperation and discussion.

Q. 12. Describe the five salient features of the use of computers in Indian schools.

Ans. In 1984–1985, the computer made an appearance in a few Indian schools as a result of a national initiative to promote computer literacy and studies in schools (CLASS). Therefore, the computer is a relatively new technology in Indian classrooms and project CLASS itself represents its history. The computer continues to be a fantastical, enigmatic high-tech object that needs respect and careful handling for millions of Indian pupils.

Except for private schools, which are mostly found in India cities, most public schools there do not offer even the most basic computer education, despite the fact that India has emerged as one of the world's leading players in the use of communication technology. The usage of computers by students as a learning tool is not standardised in these institutions either. Each institution has its unique strategies for instructing pupils or facilitating computer-based learning. The infrastructure and computer laboratories that are offered in the schools, vary from one institution to the next.

Let's examine how computer education is handled in different kinds of Indian schools. Our government-run schools are primarily found in rural areas. These schools have the infrastructure necessary to teach students using computers, either fully or properly. Where computers are offered, even in city government schools, they are either not properly maintained or there are insufficiently qualified teachers to use them as an effective teaching tool. Numerous schools just preserve computers to display statistical data, in order to appease the inspection authority. Many privately run institutions, most of which are found in urban regions, provide students a foundational education in computers. The depth and breadth of computer instruction offered in privately managed schools varies from one institution to the next. The majority of the tiny schools in this category primarily employ computers to teach computer basics or for kids to play common games. The majority of them lack internet access. These schools do not share the same computer-related infrastructure for using and implementing computer-based education.

Electronic interactive white boards with computer-based instructional software are offered by several multinational and corporate schools that charge very high-tuition rates to the students. These businesses include Educomp, Teachnext, Digiclass, Smartech, etc. In some other private schools, when these businesses supply the technology and software for so-called "smart classes", they charge each student an additional cost of roughly Rs. 100 per month on top of the regular tuition. Some schools have their own LCD TVs, projectors and laptops and they have created their own PowerPoint courses based on the textbooks that their pupils utilise in class.

OTHER IMPORTANT QUESTIONS

Q. 1. How can computers help expand access to education?

Ans. Computers are a potentially effective tool for extending educational opportunities, both formal and informal, to previously underserved constituencies, including dispersed and rural populations, historically marginalised groups like ethnic minorities, girls and women, people with disabilities and the elderly, as well as everyone else who cannot enrol in campus due to cost or time constraints:

- **Anytime, anywhere:** The ability of ICTs to transcend location and time is one of their defining characteristics. Asynchronous learning, or learning where there is a delay between the delivery of information and its reception by students, is made feasible by computers. For instance, online course materials are accessible every day of the week, 24 hours a day. ICT-based educational delivery eliminates the requirement for all students and the instructor to be present in the same physical location, such as educational content transmitted by radio or television. Additionally, some ICTs, including teleconferencing technology, allow for the simultaneous delivery of education to several, scattered students.
- **Access to remote learning resources:** For their educational purposes, teachers and students no longer have to rely primarily on printed books and other tangible media kept in libraries (and available in scarce amounts). A plethora of educational resources in practically every subject and in a variety of mediums are now accessible from anywhere, at any time of day and by an infinite number of people, thanks to the Internet and the World Wide Web. This is crucial for many schools in underdeveloped nations, as well as some in rich nations, who have obsolete and insufficient library resources. ICTs also make it easier to connect with global resource people including mentors, experts, researchers, professionals, business leaders and peers.

Q. 2. How can the use of computers help improve the quality of education? How can ICTs help transform the learning environment into one that is learner-centered?

Ans. In particular during a period of educational expansion, improving the quality of education and training is a crucial concern. Computers can improve the quality of education in a number of ways, including by raising learner motivation and engagement, making it easier to pick up fundamental skills and improving teacher preparation.

ICTs are transformational resources that, when properly applied, can support the transition to a learner-centered environment. Encouraging learning ICTs can be utilised to deliver challenging and authentic content that will involve the student in the learning process, such as videos, television and multimedia computer software that combines text, sound and vibrant, moving graphics. The pupils are also motivated by interactive radio, which employs sound effects, music, dramatisations, comedic skits and other performance norms.

According to research, the paradigmatic shift in both content and pedagogy that is at the core of education reform in the 21st century can be catalysed by the effective use of ICTs. ICT-supported education can encourage the acquisition of the information and skills that will equip students for a lifelong learning if it is properly designed and implemented.

When used properly, ICTs—particularly computers and Internet technologies—allow teachers and students to accomplish what they have always done in a better way, rather than only enable new modes of teaching and learning. Constructivist theories of learning serve as the foundation for these innovative approaches to teaching and learning, which represent a shift away from the worst aspects of teacher-centered pedagogy, which are characterised by memorization and rote learning.

ICT-enhanced learning makes use of tools for information examination, calculation and analysis, so giving students a platform for research, analysis and the creation of new knowledge. In order to make learning less abstract and more applicable to the learner's condition in reality, students learn as they go along and where appropriate, work in-depth on real-world situations. In this way, ICT-enhanced learning encourages higher learner engagement in contrast to memorization-based or rote learning. The use of ICT to enhance learning also enables "just-in-time" learning, where students can decide what to learn and when to learn it.

No matter where they are, ICT-supported learning promotes communication and collaboration between students, teachers and subject matter experts. In addition to simulating real-world interactions, ICT-supported learning gives students the chance to interact with people from various cultural backgrounds, fostering the development of their interpersonal and communication skills, as well as their sense of global awareness. By enlarging the learning environment to include mentors and subject-matter experts from many fields in addition to peers, it simulates learning that occurs over the course of a learner's lifetime.

Q. 3. Discuss the application of computer in distance education.

Ans. An intriguing taxonomy of computer media in remote education is offered by Chacon (1992). He advocates a more basic kind of computer use as an extension of how students and educators should behave. Additionally, he lists information processing, interaction and communication as the three modalities of computer use.

Information processing: The information processing mode of computer use in distance education uses the principle - 'I learn by doing'. It has to do with several intelligence-related skills, including memory, ordering, calculating, relationship, matching, reading and writing. These activities involve the use of a computer as a tool. The student uses a computer to complete certain outside tasks, such as writing a project report, creating a balance sheet, or creating a design utilising a set of graphic tools. This means that the following pedagogical tasks can be carried out by computers in distant learning:

- Dissemination of information,
- Development of language skills,
- Learning foreign languages,
- Development of procedural skills,
- Learning problem solving,
- Learning analytical skills,
- Learning presentation skills,
- Learning design skills.

Interaction: The interactive mode of computer use in distance education uses the principle — 'I teach something to myself.' A person and a machine engage in interaction. According to Chacon, interactive computing in education occurs when the student is given the opportunity to build a dialogue with the computer over which they have a lot of influence and when they are exposed to stimuli in a variety of media types. Computer use that is interactive is most frequently used in educational settings. In this mode, the computer transforms into a knowledgeable teacher. CAI, interactive multimedia and CBT programmes are examples of this modality. Drill and practice, problem solving, procedural learning, tutorials, guided discovery learning and decision making are among the instructional activities covered by this style.

Communication: The communication mode of computer use in distance education uses the principle — 'I learn from others'. It envisions using computers to facilitate interpersonal connection. Due to its value in assisting distant students, the communication mode application in distance education may be dominating. Computer conferencing software and email are the technology used. The following pedagogical tasks are carried out via the communication mode:

- Learning verbal communication,
- Developing skills for analysis and synthesis of textual information,
- Development of expression and articulation,
- Developing skills for analysis and synthesis of textual information,
- Motivational support to remote learners,
- Development of critical judgement,
- Participative problem solving,
- Opportunity for incidental learning,
- Substitute for direct experience,
- Presentation of abstract knowledge.

This section calls attention to two effective uses of this mode. Excellent examples of how computers are used as a communication tool in remote education are the Cosy programme created by the University of Guelph (Canada) for computer conferencing and the First Class software used by the UKOU. Apart from this, e-mail and mailing lists, which enable one-to-one and many-to-one contact, are widely used. Collaborative learning has a lot to gain from the communication style.

MULTIPLE CHOICE QUESTIONS

Q. 1. ENIAC stands for:

(*a*) Electronics Numerical Integral Calculator
(*b*) Electronics Numerical Integration and Calculation
(*c*) Electronics Numerical Integrator and Calculator
(*d*) None of these

Ans. (*c*) Electronics Numerical Integrator and Calculator.

Q. 2. In which year, the Electronics Numerical Integrator and Calculator was created?

(*a*) 1945 (*b*) 1946
(*c*) 1947 (*d*) 1948

Ans. (*b*) 1946.

Q. 3. Which types of computers are used in classroom?

(*a*) Microcomputers (*b*) Minicomputers
(*c*) Mainframes (*d*) Supercomputers

Ans. (*b*) Minicomputers

Q. 4. Udang is a village in:

(*a*) Rajasthan (*b*) West Bengal
(*c*) Madhya Pradesh (*d*) Uttar Pradesh

Ans. (*b*) West Bengal.

Q. 5. Teachers who want to use computers in the classroom should pay close attention to which question?

(*a*) How can students express themselves via computers?
(*b*) How can computer systems be adapted to the demands of specific users?
(*c*) How can the effectiveness of educational software be assessed?
(*d*) All of these

Ans. (*d*) All of these.

Q. 6. MYCIN is a/an:

(*a*) Educational software
(*b*) Artificial intelligence programme
(*c*) Training programme
(*a*) None of these

Ans. (*b*) Artificial intelligence programme.

Q. 7. MYCIN was developed to teach:

(*a*) Medical students
(*b*) Primary students
(*c*) Engineers in industries
(*d*) None of these

Ans. (*a*) Medical students.

Q. 8. ERICA was developed at:

(*a*) Brisbane College of Advanced Education in Australia
(*b*) Oxford University in UK
(*c*) Standford University in USA
(*d*) None of these

Ans. *(a)* Brisbane College of Advanced Education in Australia.

Q. 9. For efficient learning, "teaching machines" were created in the:

(a) 1930s *(b)* 1940s
(c) 1950s *(d)* None of these

Ans. *(a)* 1930s.

Q. 10. CML is:

(a) Computer-managed learning
(b) Computer management learning
(c) Computer-managed learners
(d) None of these

Ans. *(a)* Computer-managed learning.

Q. 11. CAL is:

(a) Computer-assistant learning
(b) Computer-assisted learners
(c) Computer-assisted learning
(d) None of these

Ans. *(c)* Computer-assisted learning.

Q. 12. CAI is:

(a) Computer-assistant instruction
(b) Computer-assisted instructors
(c) Computer-assisted instruction
(d) None of these

Ans. *(c)* Computer-assisted instruction.

Q. 13. Which of the following makes a distinction between information that is valuable in and of itself and knowledge that is valuable for its instrumental purpose?

(a) The revelatory paradigm
(b) The conjectural paradigm
(c) The emancipatory paradigm
(d) None of these

Ans. *(c)* The emancipatory paradigm.

Q. 14. Which of the following addresses learning through experience gained through computer simulation and data processing, as well as learning through discovery?

(a) The revelatory paradigm
(b) The conjectural paradigm
(c) The emancipatory paradigm
(d) None of these

Ans. *(a)* The revelatory paradigm.

Q. 15. Which places an emphasis on manipulation, active knowledge and hypothesis testing?

(a) The revelatory paradigm
(b) The conjectural paradigm
(c) The emancipatory paradigm
(d) None of these

Ans. *(b)* The conjectural paradigm.

Satellite Technology and Distance Education

14

INTRODUCTION

An artificial satellite called a communication satellite establishes a channel between a transmitter and a receiver at various points on Earth in order to transmit a signal using a transponder. Satellite communications are used in telephone, radio, television, internet and military applications. In this chapter, we'll concentrate on the factors that contribute to satellite-based communication systems' significance in remote learning. We'll talk about the importance, current state and promise of these systems, as well as potential applications for underdeveloped nations. Due to their unique value in remote learning, the talk-back devices—teleconferencing and the phone—will receive more attention.

CHAPTER AT A GLANCE

COMMUNICATION SATELLITES

A communication satellite is a spacecraft that collects signals from an earthly transmitter, amplifies them, modifies the carrier frequencies and then retransmits the boosted signals to the earth's receivers. The majority of the time, communication satellites are put in a particular earth orbit that gives the impression that they are stationary to transmitters and receivers on earth. These communication satellites already number over a hundred and others are constantly being sent into orbit. The launch of Sputnik by the former USSR in 1957 marked the beginning of the space age. Many satellites have been launched since then for a variety of uses, including telecommunications, meteorology and remote sensing, disaster warning, defence and other services. The satellite itself is not the key to satellite-based communication; other components are also important, including an uplink station on the ground and a downlink disc. The direct receiving disc, also known as the satellite, amplifies and retransmits signals to the downlink, which in turn feeds a local station, via the uplink.

Launching of Satellites: Either a reusable piloted space shuttle or an unmanned spacecraft can be used to launch a satellite into a geostationary orbit. The device, also referred to as the Satellite Launch Vehicle (SLV), is equipped with one or more rocket stages that offer the acceleration required to launch a satellite into the desired earth orbit. The SLV typically places the satellite in a spherical earth orbit before moving, shifting, or fixing it into a geostationary orbit. The impulse required to move the satellite from a circular orbit into a geostationary orbit is provided by a specific rocket within the spacecraft. An alternate means of launching communication satellites is the space shuttle. Because a space shuttle can launch multiple satellites on a single flight and can be reused, it is less expensive to launch satellites using one of them than with an unmanned launch vehicle. After being locked into the geostationary orbit, the satellite rotates in the same direction as the earth and at a speed equal to that of the planet. Communication satellites have quickly taken over as the main long-distance communication carriers. The majority of domestic and international communications are now handled by the satellite sector, which has flourished since the first commercial satellite, INTELSAT, was launched on April 6, 1965.

In several nations, direct broadcasting is done via satellite. In order to perform space science experiments, India's first National Committee on Space Research was established in 1982. The main goals of the Indian space programme are to produce scientific workforce for space science and technology, as well as to develop indigenous competence in advanced space technology and engineering to develop capability for diverse uses of space technology for national development. The late Vikram Sarabhai, the founding director of the Indian Space Research Organization, believed that India should take advantage of satellite technology to establish a national television service for instructional, educational and related developmental purposes given its size, population and low economic development. Sarabhai's ambition was finally realised in the form of the INSAT-A multipurpose system after 15 years of work. There are now over 40 television satellites operating worldwide. A summary of some significant satellite operators is provided in the table below, broken down according to their geographic service region.

SATELLITE ORBITS

The orbit that the communication satellite has been fixed into is one of the crucial elements that makes it helpful for particular objectives. Four different orbital types may be used to place satellites in orbit.

(i) **Low Orbit:** Early satellite technologies involved orbits, that were relatively close to the planet's surface. Low-orbit satellites can only be utilised for brief periods of communication since they move from horizon to horizon very quickly. The earth's rotational speed and that of the low-orbiting satellite do not coincide. As a result, low-orbit satellites are not very useful for communication.

(ii) **Medium Orbit:** Higher orbits for the satellite were made possible as space research advanced, thanks to the design and development of more potent satellite launchers. The term "medium altitude orbits" refers to satellite orbits that are between a few hundred and a few thousand kilometres above the surface of the earth. Satellites in these orbits also rotate quickly, therefore we must adjust the antennas on earth stations to follow the satellite in space. In these circumstances, at least two antennas are placed, one of which tracks a setting satellite and the other, a rising satellite.

(iii) **Geo-synchronous Orbit:** An orbiting satellite can move so quickly that it seems immobile to humans on the ground at a distance of around 36,000 kilometres from the surface of the earth. This orbit is also called a geostationary orbit or a geosynchronous orbit. These days, the majority of brand-new satellites for domestic and international communications operate in this orbit, which is advantageous for communications.

The benefit of a geo-stationary orbit is that the earth station antennas can be installed in a fixed location rather than, having to track the satellite. A satellite must meet the following requirements, the in order to maintain geostationary orbit:

(i) The angle of inclination must be zero (*i.e.*, a special orbit directly above the equator).

(ii) The satellite must move in the same direction as the earth's rotation.

(iii) The satellite completes a revolution in 23.94 hours to match the rate of earth's rotation on its axis. The majority of communication satellites are geo-stationary, which means that they orbit the globe every 24 hours. Geosynchronous satellites of the Indian National Satellite series are also present in orbit due to the fact that geosynchronous satellites are used for communications.

(iv) **Special Orbit:** For various services like meteorology, remote sensing and natural resources, there are a variety of useful specialised orbits in space. The medium altitude sun-synchronous polar orbit, which covers the same regions of the earth's surface twice daily, is one of these.

CHARACTERISTICS OF SATELLITES

Communication satellites share the following traits:

(i) **Power:** A live satellite does not need conventional power to maintain its place in orbit, with the exception of very small quantities of energy required to periodically correct its position and check for errors brought on by the gravitational pull of the moon, sun and earth. The satellite's solar batteries provide electricity for both signal reception and transmission.

(ii) **Large Coverage:** Communication using satellites is not affected by distance. A satellite-based communication system can simultaneously service rural and urban, central and far-flung places, in contrast to a terrestrial system that often originates from the more central urban centres. At one moment it can serve large dispersed people. This feature of the satellite is beneficial for distance learning.

(iii) **Multi-purpose Uses:** Satellites can be utilised for a variety of purposes at once, including radio, telephone, television and data communication. The satellites are utilised for remote sensing, which is necessary for soil assessments, flood control, forestry and oceanography, in addition to supporting communication needs.

(iv) **Cost:** Developing and launching a satellite requires a significant initial financial outlay, particularly for developing nations. A significant amount of money was needed to build and deploy a multipurpose spacecraft like INSAT. But after INSAT-IB was launched and put into operation, all communication needs were satisfied without the need for additional investment. To accommodate a nation's growing information needs, the terrestrial system, including the microwave, required more infrastructure.

(v) **Planning:** It is essential for the implementation of satellite-based communication. Compared to terrestrial communication, it requires greater preparation time. As a result, the usage of satellites ought to be related to the nation's overall socio-economic and educational development.

(vi) **National and Region-specific Communication:** Satellite-based communication can meet a nation's demands on both a national and regional level. Even though it's thought of as a centralised communication system, it can also be regionalized. Regional production and distribution hubs could offer service tailored to a particular region.

(vii) **Life of a Satellite:** The life of a satellite is determined by the use of solar panels or cells. Age affects a solar cell's ability to produce electrical energy; after 8 to 10 years, the electrical output will have decreased by roughly 20%. Typically, the communication satellites are replaced after 10 to 12 years of non-stop use.

SATELLITE VERSUS TERRESTRIAL COMMUNICATION

The use of satellite-based communication is particularly beneficial for online learners or the online learning system. The unique advantages of satellite communication, including its great distance, high performance, networking and one point to multi-point to one point transmission capabilities, have been acknowledged since the invention of communication satellites. However, non-satellite methods are crucial in helping a nation achieve its communication needs. In actuality, satellite and terrestrial systems complement one another to improve communication.

Satellite and Terrestrial Communication: A Comparison

Forms of communication, satellite and terrestrial systems do not compete with one another. The ability of both systems to increase communication accessibility and cost-effectiveness is complemented by one another.

Satellite	Terrestrial
(i) It is not dependent on ground-based, high-power, high-tower systems.	*(i)* Requires high-powered, tall systems (The height of the transmitter at Pitampura, Delhi is 235 metres).
(ii) Does not require a lot of ground-based equipment; satellite-direct television sets can receive signals directly.	*(ii)* Requires multiple transmitters for widespread coverage (at present Doordarshan has a network of 529 transmitters spread all over the country).
(iii) The price of equipment is high but it is now becoming less expensive and it is also becoming less expensive quickly.	*(iii)* The equipment is inexpensive.
(iv) Because it is a highly-centralised system, the developing process may be paced and controlled more effectively.	*(iv)* Occasionally challenging due to management and technical barriers to system cooperation. Additionally, it might be challenging at times due to the stance local authorities have adopted in limiting the information flow at the regional level.
(v) Because satellite technology brings the entire globe into a small community, it may inspire instructors, students and parents to embrace modernity.	*(v)* It has several disadvantages due to its restricted scope.
(vi) Planning and execution demand more foresight.	*(vi)* Relatively takes less time.
(vii) Useful for a sizable nation or a collection of nations.	*(vii)* Appropriate for a tiny nation or a region of a nation.
(viii) Independent of distance.	*(viii)* Limited geographic coverage.
(ix) Unaffected by the terrain's characteristics.	*(ix)* Difficult in coastal and mountainous regions.
(x) Has the ability to fulfil rising communication demands without incurring additional costs.	*(x)* The implementation of the regional system limits the communication capacity and adds to the cost.
(xi) More successful in addressing the general requirements of the populace on a national scale.	*(xi)* Better meets local information needs.
(xii) A satellite failure may render the entire system inoperable, which would put a great deal of demand on communication during the readjustment process.	*(xii)* System failure would not be as severe as it was in the case of the satellite system, since it would be possible to manage the damage after adjustments and repair.
(xiii) Parking places for the geosynchronous satellite, which are getting harder to find, are needed.	*(xiii)* Does not require a parking place.
(xiv) Global network connections are made possible by satellite can solve the issue of unequal educational chances and enable the exchange of educational resources for international education on a truly global scale.	*(xiv)* Networking is only feasible at the regional level.

Type of Television Sets

Different television sets use different technology to receive signals from a satellite or terrestrial transmitter. Depending on the type of broadcasting — satellite or terrestrial, there are two types of receivers used:

(a) Direct Reception System (DRS)

(b) Very High Frequency (VHF)

DRS: Although the satellite sends out pretty strong signals, typical television sets used to watch regular broadcast programming cannot pick up these signals. We must install a low-noise pre-amplifier converter and a parabolic antenna. A compact antenna with a parabolic reflector is called as parabolic antenna. The parabola's focus point is where the antenna is situated. Due to its physical characteristics and shape, a parabolic antenna is frequently referred to as a dish antenna. DRS refers to such TVs that receive signals directly from the satellite.

VHF: The alternative technique makes use of a regular VHF television set, which gets signals from terrestrial transmitters after those transmitters have received them from satellite through TVRO (Television Receive Only device). We all have such TVs in our homes, where we watch shows that are broadcast on the standard networks.

SATELLITE-BASED COMMUNICATION AND DISTANCE EDUCATION

The capacity of the telecommunications network and the information flow are improved by satellite technology, which, among other things, helps a nation's educational advancement. In large geographic areas with dispersed people, satellite technology is more useful. Because of this, it will be helpful to students who are studying remotely from remote locations. The satellite can be utilised more widely to give students who reside on small islands access to possibilities for a university degree. For instance, the University of the West Indies connects its three main campuses—located on the islands of Jamaica, Barbados and Trinidad—with smaller extramural campuses in St. Lucia, Dominica and Antigua.

In large nations, satellite-based communication is a practical substitute for reaching the thousands of dispersed, remote areas that would otherwise be prohibitively expensive and technically impractical to access. Its accessibility is its key benefit. Second, the high expense paid can be easily justified, given the huge and dispersed nature of the target audience for distance education programmes offered by open universities. Studies conducted elsewhere have demonstrated that satellite transmission is considerably more affordable and that all areas of the nation can more easily access the system.

The satellite can be used for education in at least three different ways: broadcasting educational and developmental content for the general public (as part of a national discipline-based learning initiative); broadcasting pre-recorded content for students at all educational levels as part of the routine/regular learning system and broadcasting live educational content with two-way interaction. Radio and television are employed as general media in the first two cases. In the third instance, the satellite is used to support some of the two-way communication systems that are already in use, including computers, videotext, teleconferencing, telephones, etc. Teleconferencing and phone-based instruction are two common uses of telecommunication. Teleconferencing and training conducted over the phone may have a wider audience and be more successful thanks to the communication satellite.

TELECONFERENCING

Three main types of teleconferencing are: *(i)* audio teleconferencing, *(ii)* video teleconferencing and *(iii)* computer teleconferencing.

Technical Description of Teleconferencing

In order to debate or share the usage of two-way and one-way video, both full motion and slow scan, electronic blackboards, facsimiles, computer graphics, radio satellite and videotext, three or four individuals can be brought together via teleconferencing. The most important component of all teleconferencing methods is a good audio system, which facilitates quick communication and information sharing between participants. A multi-telephone line electronic switch or connector device known as a "bridge" is needed for audio teleconferencing, to which the user can connect a variety of telephones and data transfer equipment. The typical handsets, speakerphones, radio telephones and microphone speaker units (commonly referred to as "conveners") are utilised for audio with the bridge. Regular telephone lines provided by regional public telephone providers are used for audio teleconferencing. If the local telephone system includes these features, setting up a private audio teleconferencing system at a university or college won't be expensive:

(i) A relatively quiet line

(ii) Ready accessibility and

(iii) Acceptable local and long distance rates

Interactive Television in Support of Distance Education:

Morocco's Ministry of Education has joined forces with UNESCO and the International Telecommunication Union (ITU) to create a pilot programme for distant education there. The goal is to connect the audio-visual and telecommunication industries and investigate how they may be used to improve the nation's educational system. The initiative will work to address the most urgent educational demands as well as the issue of budgetary restrictions. At the Jomtein World Conference on Education for All, several issues were raised. The potential of interactive television in relation to education and teacher preparation was subsequently estimated by UNESCO and ITU in 1995, leading to the creation of a plan of action. The duration of this project is three years. Studies on the viability of expanding the programme to other developing nations, including Bangladesh and Cape Verde, are currently being conducted.

Advantages of Teleconferencing

The advantages are:

***(i)* Effective Support for Distance Learners:** Teleconferencing can be highly helpful when the majority of potential students are dispersed over numerous remote communities.

***(ii)* Cost-effectiveness:** When compared to other available options for supporting remote learners, the start-up and operating costs of an audio teleconferencing system are rather cheap.

***(iii)* Flexible System:** The system can be readily modified to accommodate both large and small groups.

***(iv)* Familiar Instructional Mode:** The form of education is comparable to that of a seminar, with the instructor in charge of the discussion and able to encourage multi-location engagement.

***(v)* Simple Scheduling Adjustments:** Changes to the schedule can be made almost as easily as they are for the on-campus classrooms.

***(vi)* Multiple-location Access Control:** A select few off-campus centres can be used to restrict access to the programme's instruction.

***(vii)* High-quality Instruction:** The necessity for meticulous and early planning allows for the maintenance of high-quality teaching materials.

***(viii)* Immediate Feedback:** The teleconferencing system enables the learners to receive immediate feedback and communicate their thoughts to the tutors.

Types of Teleconferencing

Depending on the use of hardware, there can be three types of teleconferencing:

***(i)* Audio Teleconferencing:** Audio-teleconferencing is teleconferencing in which the audio medium is employed for two-way communication. The majority of audio teleconference communication is spoken. A more cost-effective approach of academic contact is two-way audio. Other institutions in affluent nations use audio teleconferencing for academic purposes but there aren't many of these instances around right now.

Audiographics: The simultaneous use of datagraphics and sound in audioconferencing is a powerful variation. The technology is known as audiographics. A teacher site and many remote sites make up a standard audiographics setup. A speaker phone, a powerful PC-based microcomputer, a modem, flatbed image scanners and a high-resolution display are all included on the instructor site.

***(ii)* Video Teleconferencing:** Two-way video media is used to set up this kind of teleconference. Due to its expensive cost and a number of additional issues, such as the difficulty of using video to connect several places and the lack of hardware, this technology is only occasionally used in schools. However, due to its visual component, video teleconferencing has advantages over audio teleconferencing. Because both the teacher and the student can see each other and communicate their feelings and experiences, video teleconferencing improves the quality of interaction.

***(iii)* Computer Teleconferencing:** Although, it is the most efficient method of teleconferencing, it is also quite expensive, requires a lot of infrastructure, etc. Information can be communicated and received using computers at the convenience of the teacher and the student with the right infrastructure and technology. Both text-based and fully video-based computer conferencing are possible.

Organising Teleconference Sessions

The process of teleconferencing consists of four stages:

***(i)* Planning:** For teleconferences to be successful, careful planning in advance is essential. The session's content must be chosen by you. Along with the needs and attitudes of the kids participating, you also need to be fully aware of any potential discussion topics. You must be aware of the total number of pupils and the length of each class period. It is vital to verify that all conditions are met.

***(ii)* Preparing Materials for the Students:** The students should receive printed resources, such as charts and diagrams, well in advance so they may use them during the teleconference and actively engage in the conversation.

***(iii)* Preparing Students:** An important duty of the remote educator in charge of the conference is to get the students ready for active engagement in the teleconference. The discussion topics, goals and teleconferencing system should all be explained to the students in advance. The preparation exercises should not take too much time and they should be psychologically prepared to learn through talk-back facilities.

***(iv)* Conduct in the Actual Session:** All of the students should be able to actively participate in the sessions and gain as much knowledge as they can from the conference. Some do's and don'ts must be kept in mind. The dialogue should be informal, just like the self-instructional resources. Human touch and humour should be incorporated when needed, so long as they don't compromise the discussion's instructional value. To make the meetings as engaging as possible, it is crucial to allot enough time for questions, responses and debates. Encourage each student to actively participate in the conversation.

***(v)* Feedback:** Following the conference, you should work with the students to meet their unique needs and demands. They should therefore, be given enough time to comment on the conference's quality. The feedback session must also assist the students in understanding their performance. It should take almost exactly the same amount of time to get the students ready for the teleconference and to get their comments. The relevance of the topic being discussed and the creativity of the expert asked to lead the debate are key factors in teleconferencing efficacy.

Limitations of Teleconferencing

Some limitations are:

(i) One restriction is that teleconferencing necessitates a vast and very effective nationwide telephone, radio and television network.

(ii) There is a good risk of a technical malfunction.

(iii) All educational institutions are unable to pay the exorbitant phone costs.

(iv) Teleconferencing is an expensive instructional method. Both advanced technology and skilled human labour are needed. The willingness of each participant is a crucial condition for teleconferencing because it is a kind of group communication, yet this is typically absent, especially among distance learners.

Training and Development Communication Channel

The Electronic Media Production Centre at IGNOU, which was founded by ISRO, is cooperating in the operation of the Training and Development Communication Channel (TDCC). In addition to IGNOU, it is utilised by state government departments public sector banks and professional organisations.

TDCC is being used at IGNOU for:

- Telecounselling to student groups.
- Training of study centre counsellor and coordinators.
- Administrative interaction with Regional Centre functionaries.
- Extended Contact Programmes (ECP) with students.

Special Features of TDCC:

- Provides economies of scale since a single teaching resource person may communicate with any number of participants spread out across the nation.
- Contributes to enhancing the calibre of instruction and training by allowing participation from top specialists.
- Minimizes communication gaps in geographically distributed organisations with many branches.
- Real-time interaction gives online learning a human face.
- By providing a direct contact with the top echelons of the hierarchy, it encourages participative decision-making and the empowering of grossroots functionaries.
- Through a variety of visual aids, including slides, transparencies, pictures, videos and computer data, teaching and learning are improved.
- Asynchronous mode of communication is also possible as the system permits the recording of the entire session, both at the teaching-end and at the receiving end.

Some Low Cost Options: The Video Class

Here, we'll examine a less formal method of using television for education: the video class. This first caught us by surprise in a big way and we have no doubt that it will do the same for you. This is due to the fact that:

(i) The video class system raises questions about some fundamental notions about the use of television in instructional design.

(ii) It indicates very unmistakably that the responsibility for good education lies with the instructor, who must be knowledgeable, dynamic and competent. The frills of commercial production are exactly what they are—side effects of the teaching industry.

TV is considered as expensive, a mass medium, a visual mode of communication and best in the hands of professional producers. The video class system has proven this wrong.

It proves that:

- A plain lecture format can be a very effective teaching tool.
- The 'interactive nature' of educational programmes is highly overrated.
- It is unrealistic and unproductive to expect teachers to conform to the norms of commercial production.

TELEPHONE-MEDIATED INSTRUCTION

Phone-mediated instruction is another instance of satellite-based communication. The most individualised kind of telecom communication used for remote education is the telephone as a teaching tool. Some open colleges in affluent nations use the phone a lot for instructional connection. However, India has yet to fully utilise the telephone's educational potential.

Instead of instructing pupils in person, assistance and direction can be provided over the phone. Talking on the phone is a great tool for distance counselling.

Grammar, vocabulary, oral exams and pronunciation are some areas of language acquisition, where telephone-based instruction is most beneficial.

The advantages of telephone-mediated instruction are as follows:

- Interactive
- Multi-site linkage
- Immediate
- Personal
- Cost effective.

Research on telephone-based pedagogic engagement hasn't been studied all that much up until now. Experience and the results of a few projects carried out in industrialised nations show that telephone teaching has never been found to be worse than in-person instruction and has even been proven to be superior at establishing a successful discussion. Although one-on-one, two-way telephone conversation on a broad scale is impractical, telephone tutorials with the tutor are highly desirable. Telephone-mediated education is a technique to deliver the two-way interactive tutorial if we want to connect with and educate dispersed and isolated pupils but India does not have a telephone system that is widely available and trustworthy enough to be used in this fashion. Rural areas, where telephone use would be most beneficial, have very weak phone infrastructure. Similar to this, the telephone network still does not connect the open university with any of the study centres.

CHECK YOUR PROGRESS

Q. 1. Which orbit in space is most suitable for communication satellites and why? Give three reasons.

Ans. The best orbit for communication satellites is geosynchronous orbit. These days, the majority of brand-new satellites for domestic and international communications operate in this orbit, which is advantageous for communications. The benefit of a geostationary orbit is that the earth station antennas can be installed in a fixed location rather of having to track the satellite. A satellite must meet the following requirements in order to maintain geostationary orbit:

The satellite must move in the same direction as the earth's rotation and the angle of inclination must be zero (*i.e.*, in a specific orbit precisely above the equator).

To match the speed of the earth's rotation on its axis, the satellite completes one revolution in 23.94 hours.

The majority of communication satellites are geostationary, which means that they orbit the globe every 24 hours. Geosynchronous satellites of the Indian National Satellite series are also present in orbit. Due to recent advancements in space technology, it is now possible to broadcast straight to low-cost antennas installed on the rooftops of individual homes using synchronous satellites that are so strong and big. These satellites are independent of receiving and retransmission infrastructure on the ground. This form of satellite offers the possibility of extensive usage in the field of education, particularly that of far isolated communities, because there is no intermediary agent in the receiving of signals. Besides providing regional and local coverage, it can distribute signals at the national level.

Q. 2. A communication satellite is essentially a centralised system of communication. Explain how it can be used at regional levels to meet peoples' information needs.

Ans. The demands of a nation can be met both nationally and regionally, thanks to satellite-based communication. Even though, it's thought of as a centralised communication system, it can also be regionalized. Regional production and distribution hubs could offer service tailored to a particular region. Both national and regional levels can exchange educational materials.

Q. 3. Distinguish between DRS and VHF sets. Give at least two differences between them.

Ans. Different television sets use different technology to receive signals from a satellite or terrestrial transmitter. Depending on the type of broadcasting — satellite or terrestrial, there are two types of receivers used:

(a) Direct Reception System (DRS)

(b) Very High Frequency (VHF)

DRS refers to TVs that directly receive satellite feeds. Although, the satellite sends out pretty strong signals, typical television sets used to watch regular broadcast programming, which cannot pick up these signals. We must install a low-noise pre-amplifier converter and a parabolic antenna. A compact antenna with a parabolic reflector is called a parabolic antenna. The parabola's focus point is where the antenna is situated. Due to its physical characteristics and shape, a parabolic antenna is frequently referred to as a dish antenna.

VHF utilizes the ordinary very high frequency television set, which receives signals from the terrestrial transmitters after the latter have received them from the satellite through TVRO (Television Receive Only device). We all use such TV sets in our houses to view programmes telecast on the regular networks.

Q. 4. You are given a one-hour teleconferencing programme. If the minimum conferencing programme conditions, such as the despatch of supplementary materials, topic outline, physical facilitiese, etc, are provided, how would you plan for a one hour teleconferencing programme? Take three activities - preparing the students, conducting the actual teleconferencing session and collecting feedback - into account. How much time will you allot to each component?

Ans. Here's a possible plan for a one-hour teleconferencing program:

Preparing the Students (15 minutes)

Send out supplementary materials such as readings, videos, or slides to participants in advance so they can review them prior to the teleconferencing session.

Provide a clear outline of the topic to be discussed during the teleconferencing session.

Ensure that all participants have access to the necessary physical facilities and technology needed to participate in the teleconferencing session.

Conducting the Actual Teleconferencing Session (40 minutes)

Begin with a brief introduction and icebreaker activity to set a positive tone for the teleconferencing session.

Lead a discussion on the topic using open-ended questions and encouraging participation from all participants.

Use visual aids and other interactive activities to keep participants engaged throughout the session.

Wrap up the discussion by summarizing key points and providing next steps for further learning or action.

Collecting Feedback (5 minutes)

Conduct a brief survey or provide an opportunity for participants to share feedback on the teleconferencing session.

Use the feedback to improve future teleconferencing sessions.

Overall, this plan provides 15 minutes for preparing the students, 40 minutes for conducting the teleconferencing session, and 5 minutes for collecting feedback. It's important to note that the timing for each component may vary depending on the complexity of the topic, the number of participants, and the level of engagement during the discussion. It's also important to allow for flexibility and adaptability during the teleconferencing session to ensure that all participants have a meaningful and productive experience.

Q. 5. Write down three advantages of teleconferencing for distance education.

Ans. The advantages are:

(i) **Effective support for distance learners:** Teleconferencing can be highly helpful when the majority of potential students are dispersed over numerous remote communities.

(ii) **Cost-effectiveness:** When compared to other available options for supporting remote learners, the start-up and operating costs of an audio teleconferencing system are rather cheap.

(iii) **Flexible system:** The system can be readily modified to accommodate both large and small groups.

The form of education is comparable to that of a seminar, with the instructor in charge of the discussion and able to encourage multi-location engagement.

(iv) **Familiar instructional mode:** The form of education is comparable to that of a seminar, with the instructor in charge of the discussion and able to encourage multi-location engagement.

(v) **Simple scheduling modifications:** Changes to the schedule can be made almost as easily as they are for the on-campus classrooms.

(vi) **Multiple-location access control:** A select few off-campus centres can be used to restrict access to the programme's instruction.

(vii) **High-quality instruction:** The necessity for meticulous and early planning allows for the maintenance of high-quality teaching materials.

(viii) **Immediate feedback:** The teleconferencing system enables the learners to receive immediate feedback and communicate their thoughts to the tutors.

Q. 6. List any three reasons why the video class system is relevant today.

Ans. The following three factors make the video class system relevant today:

(a) The video class system casts doubt on the fundamental arguments in favour of instructional television.

(b) By doing this, it expands the potential uses of the medium that are both affordable and user-friendly for teachers.

(c) This provides a fresh viewpoint on how television is used from the perspectives of instructional design, infrastructure and production costs.

Q. 7. What are the two major weaknesses of the telephone-mediated instruction in the Indian context?

Ans. The following are some drawbacks of telephone-mediated instruction:

(i) Although one-on-one, two-way telephone conversation on a broad scale is just not practical, telephone tutorials with the instructor are highly desirable.

(ii) Telephone-mediated education is a method of giving the two-way interactive tutorial if we want to reach out to and educate dispersed and isolated pupils but India does not have a telephone system that is widely available and dependable enough to be used in this fashion.

(iii) The telephone network is extremely underdeveloped in rural areas, which is the place that might use the phone the most. Similar to this, the telephone network still does not connect the open university with any of the study centres.

(iv) Using the phone for education is an expensive endeavour.

(v) Close coordination is necessary.

OTHER IMPORTANT QUESTIONS

Q. 1. What is satellite communication? How does a satellite work?

Ans. The utilisation of man-made satellites to provide satellite communication links between different sites on Earth is essential to the global communications network. In orbit around the Earth, there are about 5,600 man-made satellites that transmit analogue and digital signals conveying audio, video and data to and from one or more sites around the globe. Communication satellites serve as the connecting points for a variety of specialised commercial and private telecommunications sectors, forging links between countries and enhancing global interconnectivity. The ground segment, which comprises of stationary or mobile transmission, reception and auxiliary equipment and the space segment, which principally consists of the satellite itself, are the two primary parts of satellite communications.

In a conventional satellite link, a signal is transmitted from a ground station to a satellite, which receives and amplifies the signal before relaying it back to Earth, where ground stations and terminals again receive and amplify the signal. Fixed satellite equipment, mobile receiving equipment on aircraft, satellite phones and portable gadgets, all function as satellite receivers on the ground.

How do satellites function?

A standalone system that orbits in space is a communications satellite. It maintains its altitude, withstands the extreme conditions of space and guarantees that the mission devices operate normally for the appropriate amount of time. It also supplies its own electrical power source.

The design of a satellite consists of the conceptual design, the preliminary design and the critical design, based on a plan of satellite communications systems in addition to the design of performance requirements and the construction of various manufacturing models (BBM, board model; EM, engineering model; PFM, proto flight model and FM, flight model). The satellite must pass a simulated thermal vacuum test in a space chamber, as well as vibration and other necessary tests, before being loaded and launched on a rocket.

Main components of a satellite: Communications system includes the antennas and transponders to receive and retransmit signals:

1. Power System: It contains solar panels that provide power; in that sense, during the entire useful life of the satellite, its main source of energy is sunlight. However, it also has batteries on board to provide power when the Sun is blocked by the Earth.

2. Propulsion System: A satellite in geostationary orbit can drift up to one degree per year from north to south or east to west due to the gravitational attraction of the Moon and Sun. It provides the rockets that propel the satellite and is necessary to get to the proper orbital location and make periodic corrections to that position. "Station maintenance" and "attitude control" are terms used to describe maintaining a satellite's orbital position and making necessary corrections. The quantity of fuel a satellite has to run these thrusters affects how long it will last. The satellite eventually wanders into space as its fuel runs out, where it stops functioning and turns into space debris.

Satellite components that would be exposed to radiation are insulated with aluminium and other radiation-resistant materials, since satellites operate in space at temperatures ranging from –150°C (–238°F) to 150°C (300°F). The thermal system of a satellite maintains the satellite at the ideal temperature to ensure continuous operation, while safeguarding its delicate mechanical and electronic components. Similar to how it protects other delicate satellite components from sudden temperature changes, it also turns on cooling systems when it becomes too hot and heating systems when it gets too cold. A satellite's telemetry and control system serves as a two-way communication channel with the Earth.

This makes it possible for a ground station to monitor a satellite's location and manage its systems for propulsion, temperature and other factors. It may also keep an eye on the temperature, electrical voltages and other crucial satellite factors.

Microsatellites, which weigh less than one kilogramme (2.2 pounds) and big spacecraft, which weigh more than 6,500 kilogrammes, are all used as communication satellites (14,000 pounds). Over time, developments in miniaturisation and digitization have greatly enhanced satellite capacity. The Boeing 702 series of satellites can have more than 100 transponders and by using digital compression technology, each transponder can have up to 16 channels, providing more than 1,600 television channels via satellite. Early Bird had only one transponder capable of sending just one television channel.

Satellites operate in three different orbits:

Low Earth Orbit (LEO): They are placed between 160 and 1,600 kilometres (100 and 1,000 miles) above the surface of the planet.

Mid-Earth Orbit (MEO), which function between 10,000 and 20,000 km (6,300 and 12,500 miles) from the planet.

Geostationary or Geosynchronous Orbit (GEO): They orbit the Earth at a height of 35,786 kilometres (22,236 miles) and complete one orbit every 24 hours, staying stationary in one place.

Similar to how 20 or more LEO satellites and 10 or more MEO satellites are required to cover the entire Earth, only three GEO satellites are required to offer worldwide coverage. Additionally, ground tracking antennas are needed for communication with satellites in LEO and MEO to ensure a reliable inter-satellite connection.

At the speed of light, a signal bouncing off at a GEO satellite travels from Earth to the satellite and back in about 0.22 seconds. Applications like voice and mobile telephone services are affected by this delay, which is why the majority of these services often employ LEO or MEO satellites to reduce signal delays. Due to their ability to cover a broader region on the ground, GEO satellites are typically employed for broadcast and data applications.

Q. 2. Write a note on Satellite Orbits.

Ans. One of the essential components that makes the communication satellite useful for specific goals is the orbit that it has been placed in. There are four main orbital types that can be employed to orbit satellites.

Early satellite technologies employed low orbits, which were quite close to the planet's surface. Low-orbit satellites can only be used for short bursts of transmission because of how swiftly they travel from horizon to horizon. The low-orbiting satellite's rotational speed and that of the earth do not match. Low-orbit satellites are therefore, not particularly helpful for communication.

With the advent of more powerful satellite launchers, higher satellite orbits became feasible as space exploration expanded. Satellite orbits that are between a few hundred and a few thousand kilometres above the surface of the planet are referred to as "middle altitude orbits". Because of the rapid rotation of satellites in these orbits, earth station antennas must be changed in order to track the satellite in space. In these conditions, at least two antennas are installed, each of which tracks a satellite that is ascending and setting.

At a distance of approximately 36,000 kilometres from the surface of the planet, an orbiting satellite can move so swiftly that it appears motionless to humans on the ground.

A geostationary orbit or a geosynchronous orbit are other names for this orbit. It is useful for communications that most modern satellites for both domestic and international communication operate in this orbit.

The advantage of a geostationary orbit is that the earth station antennas can be set up without needing to follow the satellite in a fixed spot. The following conditions must be met by a satellite in order to stay in geostationary orbit:

(i) The angle of inclination must be zero (*i.e.*, the spacecraft must be in a specific orbit straight above the equator)

(ii) The satellite must rotate in the same direction as the earth.

To match the speed at which the earth rotates on its axis, the satellite completes one revolution in 23.94 hours. The majority of satellites used for communication are geostationary, which means they orbit the earth every 24 hours. Due to the fact that geosynchronous satellites are used for communications, geosynchronous satellites from the Indian National Satellite series are also present in orbit.

Special Orbit: There are a number of useful specialised orbits in space for diverse services like meteorology, remote sensing and natural resources. One of these orbits is the medium altitude sun-synchronous polar orbit, which travels over the same areas of the earth's surface twice daily.

Q. 3. Discuss the characteristics of satellites.

Ans. The following qualities are present in all communication satellites:

(i) **Power:** A live satellite requires extremely little energy to regularly correct its position and check for mistakes caused by the gravitational attraction of the moon, sun and earth. A live satellite does not require conventional power to maintain its position in orbit. The solar-powered satellite's batteries supply power for both signal reception and transmission.

(ii) **Broad Coverage:** Distance has no bearing on satellite communication. In contrast to a terrestrial system, which frequently originates from the more central metropolitan centres, a satellite-based communication system can concurrently serve rural and urban, central and far-flung locations. It can accommodate many dispersed people at once. Distance learning benefits from this satellite feature.

(iii) **Multipurpose Applications:** Satellites can be used simultaneously for radio, telephone, television and data transmission. In addition to serving communication demands, the satellites are used for remote sensing, which is essential for soil assessments, flood management, forestry and oceanography.

(iv) **Price:** Underdeveloped and deploying a satellite is an expensive initial investment, especially for developing countries. A costly investment was required to create and launch a multifunctional spacecraft like INSAT. However, once INSAT-IB was launched and put into use, all communication needs could be met without the need for more funding. The terrestrial system, including the microwave, needed more infrastructure to meet a country's expanding information needs.

(v) **Planning:** he introduction of satellite-based communication requires **careful planning**. It requires more planning time than terrestrial communication. Therefore, the use of satellites should be in line with the overall socio-economic and educational development of the country.

(vi) **Regional and National Communication:** Regional and national needs can both be satisfied by satellite-based communication. It can be regionalized even though it's often thought of as a centralised communication system. Regional centres for manufacturing and distribution could provide services that are regionally specific.

(vii) **Satellite Life:** The use of solar cells or panels affects a satellite's lifespan. The ability of a solar cell to generate electrical energy is impacted by age; after 8 to 10 years, the electrical output will have dropped by about 20%. The communication satellites are typically changed out after 10 to 12 years of continuous use.

Q. 4. What is teleconferencing?

Ans. The term "teleconferencing" refers to any electronic connection between two or more individuals. The phrase is most frequently used to refer to a conference call involving more than two persons. A more advanced option to a two-way long-distance phone call is teleconferencing (usually allowing more than two participants).

An audio conference call between two different places with multiple people speaking through speakerphones on either end could be an example of a teleconference in its most basic form.

In the past, only voice calls were allowed during these teleconference meetings, which used conventional PBX and PSTN (public switched telephone network) telephone lines.

However, as telecommunications technology has advanced, the phrase is now used more broadly to refer to the various electronic group communication methods that we utilise. Some claim there are six different forms of teleconferences: business television (BTV), voice communication, audio graphic, computer, video and remote education. However, these can generally be boiled down to their bare minimum for the sake of simplicity: voice conferencing and video conferencing. A teleconference is essentially a digital meeting with two or more participants that is typically carried out over an audio or video connection. Teams now have an easy and effective way to connect with one other, as well as with clients and partners, through the internet, thanks to features like VoIP (voice over internet protocol) and video.

Even if landline conferencing is still an option, the majority of contemporary firms will hold teleconference meetings online, using a VoIP handset or softphone as a reliable and effective approach. The more modern, web-based teleconferences that are now often used in our everyday work situations will be the main emphasis of this piece.

Q. 5. How does teleconferencing work?

Ans. Information is exchanged via teleconferencing when two parties are geographically apart. Computer telephone has advanced recently, considerably enhancing the teleconferencing experience for corporate users.

Corporate users can use their business phone system to speak with hundreds of listeners during conference calls. Many companies utilise these conversations to convey updates or news in a more one-sided call format, while others use conference calls to more actively brainstorm and communicate.

Participants dial a predetermined phone number to join a call. Alternative: A conference bridge operator could make separate calls to each member to connect them (or audio bridge). A server that serves as both a phone and a conference bridge, the conference bridge can take many calls at once. Callers on some telephone networks could be required to enter their login information and personal ID number in order to connect to the call, improving security and anonymity.

Businesses have the option of hosting their conference calls on their own bridge or through a telephone service provider. Call recording, in-call operators and attendance polling are just a few of the additional functionality and features that these providers frequently make available to enterprises. Depending on the software, a lot of VoIP phones let organisations hold their own conference calls.

Users of web conferencing can converse using voice only, video and instant messaging. As a result, participants can add textual comments, inquiries, or group discussions to any live video presentation. For an all-encompassing, comprehensive communications session, the majority of modern platforms also include tools like file sharing and screen sharing.

Similar to audio conferencing, companies can decide whether to invest in a hosted telephonic services provider or host their own meetings utilising conferencing software. These services offer the necessary server space and software for hosting video conferences. Businesses in both scenarios need to make sure they have dependable software and enough bandwidth to handle this virtual conference.

Q. 6. What are different types of teleconference?

Ans. Even though there are other ways to hold a teleconferencing, we'll stick to the two most popular audio and visual techniques.

Sound Conferencing: A voice-only virtual conference is an audio teleconference. These conferences can include more participants than a standard phone call but they are still handled much the same manner. This technique, which is frequently referred to as a "conference call", can interactively connect many caller participants who can "dial in" from various locations via their telephone lines.

The majority of landline teleconferences can accommodate up to 100 callers. Given that this figure is considerably greater for VoIP conferencing services, audio conferencing is frequently utilised by organisations as a practical and affordable method of holding large-scale meetings remotely.

Another benefit of audio conferencing is that callers can join by dialling in without requiring an internet connection. This allows organisations to connect those who are travelling or in faraway locations without significantly disrupting the meeting. It would still be possible for people to dial in and even host an audio teleconference utilising a conventional landline telephone system.

Therefore, anyone can participate in an audio conference using any phone that is compatible with current telephony. Callers can now place a call from a computer, a landline, or any mobile device. Teams can connect even when they are frequently on the go by utilising this flexibility.

Video Conferencing: To provide more visual calls, a video teleconference mixes audio and video. With video conferencing, participants can see one another, creating a more immersive conference that feels like it's taking place in person. Video conferencing has just recently become typical due to the greater bandwidth requirements and sophisticated equipment.

These video teleconferences in the past needed IT assistance and a special room with screens on either end for callers to meet via video conferencing equipment. Participants frequently connect to video conferences using their mobile devices. However, connecting using a laptop or computer is typically commonplace.

Video teleconferencing is an efficient approach for both large and small teams to meet in real-time because the majority of services have the capacity to accommodate more than 100 people in each session.

One-way video and two-way audio, two-way video and two-way audio, or any other combination that best meets the meeting's requirements can be used to conduct meetings. Users can deliver a variety of teleconferences because of this versatility, including webinars, web conferences, interactive meetings, brainstorming sessions and even online training and classrooms.

The conference host can use capabilities like screen sharing, whiteboards and live file sharing, thanks to the advanced features and functionalities of more current telecommunications technology, which means nobody will need a written document on the day.

By allowing speakers to share presentation slides, videos and other visual aids, for instance, video teleconferencing is the best approach to offer a live presentation or seminar.

The advantages of online conferencing that can be enabled by various types of video teleconferencing software include:

- Transmit live video using a webcam, or still images for one-way or two-way conferences, meetings and webinars.
- Upload and distribute PowerPoint Presentations.
- Use a virtual whiteboard to jot down ideas, brainstorm, or make notes.
- Real-time annotation of photos and diagrams.
- Screen sharing by the host or moderator.
- Document and file sharing.
- Public and private instant chat among call participants.

Q. 7. Enlist the Satellite Operations in the world.

Ans.

Selected Satellite Operators Around the World

Operators	Organisation	Services	Satellites	Reach
International Operators				
Inmarsat	Founded in 1979 by International Maritime Organisation. Coopera-tion between 179 member states including Japan, Noday, UK and USA.	Telecommunication	Inmarsat 2F I (1990) Inmarsat 2F2 (1991) Inmarsat 2F3 (1992) Inmarsat 3F1 (1996) Inmarsat 3F3	Worldwide
Worldwide	Co-operation of 134 member states: Preparing to change status from 'interna tional public service to commercial. Part of the organisation will remain in the public domain to ensure regional balance.	Telecommunica-tion, Satellite News gathering	24 satellites in orbit. Approximately 1700 terrestrial stations	Worldwide
Regional Operators				
Asiasat	Asia's first regional satellite, totally financed with private fund. Launched in 1990.	Television broadcast.	Asiasat 1 (1990) Asiasat 2 (1995) Asiasat 3	Asia, Arab states, Eastern Europe
Arabsat	International Group of Arab countries	Transmits Arabic public television as well as Interna-tional television, such as CNN and MBC	Arabsat 1A (1985), Arabsat 1B (1985), Arabsat I C (1992), Arabsat ID (1993), Arabsat 1 E (1995), Arabsat 2A (1996), Arabsat 2B (1996)	Mediter-ranean countries and North Africa.
National Operators				
India	Indian Space Research Organisation	Telecommunica-tion, meteorological services, education	Insat 2A (1992), Insat 2B (1993), Insat 2C (1995) IRS 1 A (1988), IRS IB(1991)IRSP2(1994), IRS 1C (1995) IRS P3 (1996)	India and neigh-bouring countries
Brazil	EMBRATEL (National Communications Company)	Data, message, television and voice.	Brazilsat AI (1985), Brazilsat A2 (1986), Brazilsat B1(1994), Brasilsat B2 (1995), Brasilsat B3A (1997).	Whole of Latin America

Source : World Communication Report, 1997. (p. 160-162).

Q. 8. Discuss about Interactive Narrowcasting for Distance Education.

Ans. A brief summary of the paper: "Interactive Narrowcasting for Distance Education" by S.BHATIA

This paper discusses the experience and plans of utilising the network for distance education.

Background: In India, trials were carried out in the years 1975 and 1976 about satellite transmission for rural education. Currently, attempts are being made to develop interactive Narrowcasting Systems for Distance Education using one-way video and two-way audio teleconferencing networks. Today's national and regional telecasts frequently include instructional programming for schoolchildren, college students and students at open universities. In addition, there are ongoing programmes for rural and former education.

Systems Description: The system has gone by a variety of names over the years, including "talkback" network, "interactive TV network" and "interactive narrowcasting", while being essentially a one-way video, two-way audio teleconferencing network. Some user agencies have also used other names, such as SINET (Satellite based Interactive Network). Three key components make up the system — the spacecraft, the classroom serving as the receiving end and the teaching end. A small studio and an uplink earth station make up the teaching end. The training material is created at the teaching end in the form of either "live" lectures or recorded video programmes from a tiny studio. The training end then uplinks these television signals to a geostationary communication satellite using an "uplink" earth station that is situated there. The Direct Reception System (DRS), which consists of an inexpensive dish antenna with a diameter of 8 to 12 feet, front-end electronics and a standard television receiver, can receive these signals from the satellite, amplify them and retransmit them so that they can be picked up in any classroom located within the coverage area.

The IGNOU Experiment: In the period between October 4 and October 13, 1993, this experiment was carried out. The IGNOU campus in Delhi served as the experiment's teaching centre. In one of the IGNOU classrooms, a small TV broadcast facility (studio) with audio-video teaching aids has been set up. The studio was connected via cable to the INSAT-ILIB satellite using the Transportable Remote Area Communication Terminal (TRACT) of the Space Applications Centre (ISRO), which was temporarily parked on the IGNOU campus.

Ongoing System and Future Plans: Given the system's shortcomings, ISRO and IGNOU have recently chosen to operate it continuously and make it available to many organisations engaged in distance education. As a result, the transportable uplink (TRACT) project by ISRO has been established at the IGNOU campus for the following two years and IGNOU has provided a small studio.

Regional Possibilities: Sharing experiences, data and information can help the countries in the Asian area avoid duplication, increase cost-benefit and develop their human resources in the field of distant education.

Q. 9. Give some tips regarding effective utilization for TDCC.

Ans. Tips for Effective Utilization:

- Wherever more than one resource person is anticipated in a single session, an anchorperson must be included.
- The sessions should be scheduled into 1-1.5 hour blocks with 15-20 minute breaks in between. An anchorperson with subject knowledge is preferable.
- Limit the lecture portion of the session to around 15 minutes, during which time important points about the subject matter, the challenges at hand, problem areas that require discussion, or ideas for group decision-making might be highlighted.
- To ensure that each resource person has enough time, a session should only have a maximum of three resource people.
- Avoid wearing outfits that are all black and white. Colours that are more muted make an impact. Do not wear clothing with extremely little stripes. Hair that is dry and non-greasy improves appearance.

To the Anchorperson: The session's start and effective conduct, both in terms of substance and presentation, are the anchorperson's duties. Some of the abilities demanded of an anchorperson include time management, ensuring enough involvement from the nodes, coordinating among the resource people, providing a connecting link if necessary and eliciting feedback on a regular basis. Understanding the subject area will be a distinct advantage. The anchorperson has to:

- Welcome all the participants
- Introduce the theme and resource persons for the session
- Announce the telephone and Fax number for interaction
- Instruct the viewers from time to time

To the Resource Person: It is advised for resource persons to frame their information with appropriate graphics for the medium and to act casually to put the remote participants at ease. They would benefit from being accustomed to the studio setting in advance.

Adopt an interactive and conversational style.

- Establish eye contact with the viewers by looking into the lens of the camera assigned to you.
- Please be brief in your lecture to leave enough time for interaction.

To Coordinators at the Nodes: Each node should have a coordinator to assist in arranging participant seating and controlling interactions. Please make sure that the participants have access to the required readings, prior to the commencement of a session.

- The operation of TV set, telephone, fax is checked for proper working.
- The teaching end is informed at the earliest opportunity of the status regarding the number of participants and their profile.
- This can be best done innocuously through the fax mode.

MULTIPLE CHOICE QUESTIONS

Q. 1. The launch of Sputnik by __________ in 1957 marked the beginning of the space age.

(a) Former USSR (b) America
(c) Japan (d) Britain

Ans. (a) Former USSR.

Q. 2. The first commercial satellite was:

(a) Sputnik (b) INTELSAT
(c) AMSAT (d) Aryabhat

Ans. (b) INTELSAT.

Q. 3. When was first commercial satellite launched?

(a) April 6, 1965 (b) May 6, 1965
(c) April 6, 1966 (d) May 6, 1966

Ans. (a) April 6, 1965.

Q. 4. India's first National Committee on Space Research was established in:

(a) 1947 (b) 1950
(c) 1982 (d) 1985

Ans. (c) 1982.

Q. 5. The main goals of the Indian space programme are:

(a) To produce scientific workforce for space science and technology
(b) To develop indigenous competence in advanced space technology and engineering
(c) Both (a) and (b)
(d) None of these

Ans. (c) Both (a) and (b).

Q. 6. Who was the founding director of the Indian Space Research Organization?

(a) A P J Abdul Kalam (b) Vikram Sarabhai
(c) Homi Bhaba (d) None of these

Ans. (b) Vikram Sarabhai.

Q. 7. Early satellite technologies involved:

(a) Low orbit
(b) Medium orbit
(c) Geo-synchronus orbit
(d) None of these

Ans. (a) Low orbit.

Q. 8. These days, the majority of brand-new satellites for domestic and international communications operate in:

(a) Low orbit
(b) Medium orbit
(c) Geo-synchronus orbit
(d) Special orbit

Ans. (c) Geo-synchronus orbit.

Q. 9. Satellites for meteorology, remote sensing and natural resources operate in:

(a) Low orbit
(b) Medium orbit
(c) Geo-synchronus orbit
(d) Special orbit

Ans. (d) Special orbit.

Q. 10. The life of a satellite is determined by its:

(a) Solar panels or cells
(b) Engine
(c) The outer body resistance
(d) None of these

Ans. (a) Solar panels or cells.

Q. 11. The communication satellites are replaced after:

(a) 5 to 10 years (b) 10 to 12 years
(c) 15 to 20 years (d) None of these

Ans. (b) 10 to 12 years.

Q. 12. The height of the transmitter at Pitampura, Delhi is:

(a) 200 metres (b) 235 metres
(c) 430 metres (d) None of these

Ans. (b) 235 metres.

Q. 13. TVs that receive signals directly from the satellite have

(a) Direct Reception System (DRS)
(b) Very High Frequency (VHF)
(c) Both (a) and (b)
(d) None of these

Ans. (a) Direct Reception System (DRS).

Q. 14. TVs at our homes have which receiver?

(a) Direct Reception System (DRS)
(b) Very High Frequency (VHF)
(c) Both (a) and (b)
(d) None of these

Ans. (b) Very High Frequency (VHF).

■■

Internet for Distance Education

15

INTRODUCTION

This chapter focuses on both of their application related characteristics, which together have given rise to the Internet, a global network of networks. It is quite challenging to stay current in print because of how quickly the Internet is developing. To familiarise you with the Internet's potential for remote teaching and learning, however, is our goal here. We will keep our discussion to the fundamentals that will enable you to use the technology, if it is available to you, as this sector is developing faster, than books can be written about it. Additionally, since more and more courses are offered in an "online" format via the Internet, it is crucial for you, as distance educators to adopt this technology as soon as you can, in order to deliver high-quality instruction in line with the principles of distance education.

CHAPTER AT A GLANCE

COMPUTER NETWORKS

A network of computers is the connection of two or more computers, terminals and peripheral devices. Computers are connected through a network to exchange files, share databases and share resources such as shared printers, hard drive space, modems and CD-ROM drives. Physical devices or data stored in databases may be shared resources in a network. Online data communication enabled by a network enables both a more rapid flow of information and a highly interactive way of conversation. Another crucial aspect of networking is distributed databases and distributed data processing. The expense of maintaining databases and specialist software is decreased by a network.

Advantages of Computer Networking

Some major advantages of computer networking are:

Resource Sharing: On a standalone computer, not every computer user has access to the best computing resources. A main-frame computer cannot ever be a financially viable solution for a single person or a small business. The same prohibitive cost prevents expensive peripherals like high-end printers, sizable hard drives, etc., from being connected to individual PCs. But if we can connect (network) the little computers and terminals to powerful resources connected through a network, such as a secondary storage system, printers, etc., then all of these small computers can make use of the powerful resources.

Global Database: There is no need to store the same or similar information on the storage areas of separate computers when those systems are connected and can share resources. Users can gain access to data that needs to be shared by numerous users by storing it at a global storage area and maintaining it there using their user-ids (user identification codes kept for the computer's unique recognition of the user) and passwords (used to protect a user's data from other users). For instance, if a large number of students need some study or reference materials, they can all access them through a network from one computer storage location.

Powerful Communication Medium: The development and dissemination of information through traditional methods and media, such as print, recorded audio and video, is laborious and extremely sluggish. Due to the ease of editing and ability to get data from all over the world, the storage and dissemination of information through networks has recently become the most common method. Other forms o. communication might be just as quick but they are also very expensive and unable to transport large databases. Students can access university databases through the DE and use them in a variety of ways, including as learning about the most recent research, navigating from one information topic to another and getting online explanations of various subjects.

Information Management: In a networked system, information management in a global database is also simpler. Since there won't be a duplicate copy of any database in this arrangement, all editing, updating, deleting, etc., must be done in one location. This is in contrast to local database management systems, where one information may have duplicate entries in many distinct databases and all the databases that maintain that component of the information, must be updated correspondingly. In a network, data is also protected from any unauthorised usage. Failure to do so will result in ambiguous and therefore, incorrect information.

Online Information Exchange: Any information is kept available for users to use whenever and however they like. One can easily and quickly get the appropriate information using a computer connected to a network, which can be used for further work and quick decision-making.

Saving Money: The cost of information storage and exchange is decreased by a network system's many above mentioned features, including resource sharing, worldwide information maintenance and speedy information exchange. Although a network's initial establishment expenses might seem exorbitant, overall operating and other future costs end up being less expensive.

Data Communication Channels

All computers and other devices are connected to one another through data communication channels in a network. There are two different kinds of these channels: one that uses a physical medium, such as a pair of twisted copper wires (like telephone lines), coaxial cables (like television cables), or optical fibre cables to transmit data and the other that makes use of microwaves and satellite communication systems.

The most frequent medium is two pairs of **twisted wires**. In order to lessen electrical interference from nearby similar pairs, two copper wires are twisted together. Both analogue and digital signals can be transmitted over twisted pairs. It is now the most affordable transmission method.

Coaxial cables have a rigid copper core that is contained in an insulated cover, which is then covered in a woven conductor mesh. A layer of plastic material is used to cover the entire construction. Its transmission speed is faster and its shielding is better.

Optical fibres are extremely efficient transmission mediums. Of all the physical mediums and detectors, they are the priciest. When there is a pulse of light, it is perceived as 1 and when there is none, it is perceived as 0. Any time the density of the medium through which light beams are travelling changes, light is refracted. Light is confined inside the fibre by total internal reflection, where it travels a great distance at the speed of light.

Network Hardware Technology

A network topology is the arrangement of the computers connected by data communication channels. Although, there are many different possible styles, computer networks typically adopt a few conventional structures. The discussion of four network topologies is as under:

Star Topology: In the star network, there is a central computer (referred to as the host) that is linked with every other computer (referred to as a node) in the network and the central computer is the only one through which all of the nodes are connected to one another. Since just the connection between the host and the node may be established or destroyed in this network, adding and removing nodes is significantly easier. A similar network has modest initial setup costs. The major drawback of this topology is that if a host malfunctions, the entire network goes down.

Ring Topology: All of the computers in the network are connected to two other computers in the ring topology. For each individual machine in the ring architecture, data transmission is two-way. Therefore, even if a connection fails for a specific computer, it still has a back end for connecting to others even if the ring structure is broken. The cost of initial setup is cheap and adding and removing nodes is simpler.

Bus Topology: It is also known as the network of linear connections. It is a local area network transmission method that uses broadcasting. Data can only be sent from one machine at a time. Both machines must wait separately for separate random times if they attempt to communicate data at the same moment.

Fully-connected or Mesh Topology: Each computer in this form of technology is linked to every other computer. A node in such a network is expensive to add or remove. The price of the initial setup is likewise rather costly. But because each computer has numerous links, the communication in it is quite reliable.

Network Types

Networks can link computers across the globe or two PCs sharing the same desk. A network can be categorised as a Local Region Network (LAN), Metropolitan Area Network (MAN), or Wide Area Network (WAN) depending on its uses and geographic coverage area.

Local Area Network: A local area network connects computers and electronic devices inside a constrained geographic region, such as building a specific organisational function or a research and development unit. A LAN typically operates within a 10 kilometre radius. Various computer types, mostly microcomputers (PCs) and peripheral devices may be connected to it using various data transmission connections or cables.

Advantages offered by LAN are:

1. It may be set up with a modest expenditure and additional systems can be added as needed.
2. It provides good backup capabilities in the event that one or two network systems fail. This improves the systems' availability and dependability to users.
3. LAN offers a setting for resource sharing. The entire LAN user base may share expensive hosts, peripherals and databases.
4. Multi-vendor systems may be connected to a LAN that complies with a specific standard. As a result, a user is not tied to a certain vendor.
5. In LANs, systems are often chosen so that they can satisfy the majority of user requirements locally and the network is simply utilised to share resources and information. As a result, each user receives a better response than they would in a centrally managed system.
6. LAN allows for device placement freedom. The majority of computers on a LAN are physically located at the user table, which is

most practical for working and greatly boosts productivity.

Metropolitan Area Network: The typical coverage area for a metropolitan area network is 5 to 50 kilometres. The Star, Bus and Ring network topologies used in MAN are comparable to LANs. Such MANs are LAN extensions. Broadband coaxial cable and optical fibres are the transmission mediums that are most appropriate for MANs applications. Wide Area Networks (WANs) are huge area networks that span several cities or nations. Point-to-point transmission is the method used by a WAN. A gateway is a shared processor that serves as a common interface and connects local area networks to wide area networks.

Internetworking

The issues with internetworking are caused by various machine kinds, topologies and networks. Standard protocol designs are employed to address the internetworking issue. These are referred to as protocols or standards. Devices like bridges, routers and gateways can be used to connect LANs. Data Link Bridge is the usual name for a bridge. It links networks utilising appropriate local or remote devices. Two networks with different protocols can be connected using a router. It has the ability to connect two different media types, such as Ethernet and Token ring. Brouter is the name of a multiple router with bridging capabilities. It is quite typical for LAN systems to have equipment from various suppliers in order to provide networking solutions that are affordable. As a result, there are issues with incompatibility when exchanging even the most basic files, as well as issues with different screen and keyboard layouts in a network setting. There are three solutions available to get disparate devices connected in a LAN to communicate logically: Protocol Converter "Gateways", Emulator Sofiare, or OSI standards.

INTERNET

The Internet is an open, non-participatory computer communication system that connects users to information on a variety of topics throughout the world at all times. It is a worldwide network of interconnected networks technically. It enables computer users to exchange tools, software and data found on various websites. The phrase "ultimate information superhighway" is sometimes used to describe it.

The Beginning

At the height of the cold war in the 1960s, the Internet's history began. The USA's Defence Advanced Research Project Agency (DARPA) received funding to develop strategies for sharing costly computer resources across laboratories and scientific institutions. The Advanced Research Project Agency Network (ARPANET), which went live in 1969, was the manifestation of the research. The possibility of a communication breakdown in the event of a nuclear attack caused some concern among employees at the Rand Corporation, the American Army's Research and Development section. At that time, point-to-point connections that were connected in chains, formed the foundation of the communication networks.

The new kind of network resembled a spider web more, since it connected various sites via various pathways. The communication might continue through alternative pathways if one of the parts failed. Four US universities—Stanford Research Institute, UCLA, UC Santa Barbara and the University of Utah—created the, first authentic Internet link.

Growth of the Internet

In 1973, the ARPANET offered, for the first time, an international link to organisations outside of the United States, namely the Royal Radar Establishment in Norway and University College in London, England. As previously stated, the Internet is a global network of networks, where various computer kinds are connected for communication. As opposed to early LANs, which had homogenous network platforms, today's LANs use heterogeneous platforms for communication, including IBM mainframes, VAX machines, numerous LANs with microcomputers, etc. The Transmission Control Protocol – Internet Protocol (TCP/IP) reference model and TCP/IP protocol stack serve as the glue that holds every system on the Internet together. If a device can deliver IP packets to other devices on the network, run the TCP/IP protocol and have an IP address, it can be linked to the Internet. Over the years, the Internet has expanded quite quickly. The DARPANET had grown to 37 computers in 1972 from just 4 hosts in 1969. Later, ARPANET was given the name. It had more than 500 hosts by 1983, resulting in MILNET. Figures 5, 6 and 7 demonstrate the Internet's phenomenal expansion, which currently numbers more than 36 million hosts. The growth has, however, not been evenly spread and has primarily occurred in North America and Europe.

DARPA initially intended to launch a research project to examine methods and tools for tying together different types of packet networks. DARPA's ultimate goal was to create protocols for networked computers to communicate freely across various platforms and networks. So, ARPANET was established. TCP/IP is a series of protocols that were created by ARPANET, now known as the Internet. Until 1986, when the US National Science Foundation (NSF) started the creation of the NSFnet, which is now a key service for the Internet, a small number of government scientists were supported by the Internet. Although NSF's arrival on the scene played a significant role in the growth of the Internet, the biggest watershed year was 1991, when NSF stopped supporting the Internet and relaxed the restriction on commercial traffic. Up until 1991, the US government and educational institutions accounted for all NSF traffic.

The Internet is currently only widely used in large, urban areas of India. By 2000 A.D., it is anticipated to have reached every district headquarters. India is the most Internet-savvy developing nation. Along with the government's liberal policies, the key factors driving its rapid development, include the expansion of the satellite and software development businesses.

India has had access to the Internet for non-commercial purposes, since the late 1980s. VSNL launched a commercial offering in 1995 with its

Gateway Internet Access Service (GIAS). It had 64 consumer lines, 703 members when it first launched and 4 Internet nodes. In November 1998, VSNL had 1,50,000 subscribers and 42 Internet nodes.

How it Works?

Transmission Control Protocol (TCP) and Internet Protocol are used to operate the Internet. These two make up the TCP/IP collective. TCP breaks the data into tiny packets for forwarding to another system and IP labels each packet with the destination address. The Internet addresses come in two different formats, one for human comprehension and the other for computer understanding. An Internet address often looks like this: @host.subdomain.domain as the user. Where host is the local network server divided into domains and username is the user's log-in name. Geographic and non-geographic realms are separated out. The list of domain names is shown in Table.

Table 1: Domain Names in Internet

Geographical		Non-Geographical	
.in	India	.corn	Commercial organisation
.au	Australia	.net	Networks
.de	Germany	gov	Government
.jp	Japan	.mil	Military networks
.uk	United Kingdom	.edu	Educational institute
.ca	Canada	.org	Organisation

The Internet address stride @del2.vsnl.net. in indicates the user group stride in the host de12 server among the server of VSNL, which is a network organisation situated in India. In terms of machine understandable address, the de12 server of vsnl has an IP address 202.54.15.30.

Who Governs it?

The internet has developed into a free, open system that anyone can use to register and get online. There are various organisations that maintain the technical standards for Internet technology. The development of the Internet is supervised by the organisation listed below.

Internet Society: Its members—individuals and organizations—are tasked with ensuring the Internet's long-term viability, since it was established in January 1992 as the body responsible for its development.

Internet Architecture Board: In order to manage the Internet's architecture and protocols, it became a member of the Internet Society in June 1992.

Internet Engineering Task Force: The TETF, which was established in 1986, is in charge of managing the intricate work involved in creating and standardising the Internet Protocol family.

Internet Engineering Steering Group: It provides management of the Internet standard process.

World Wide Web Consortium: Founded in 1994 to develop common standards for the evolution of the web.

Internet Service Providers

There are several companies that offer services and are well-liked. These include AOL, Compuserve, Prodigy and others. Each nation does, however, typically have its own national Internet Service Provider (ISP). Videsh Sanchar Nigam Limited (VSNL) was up until recently the sole commercial ISP in India. Estimates place China's number of ISPs at 30, Japan's at 1,300, South Korea's at 15, Hong Kong's at 90 and Singapore's at 3. In India, the top ISPs are:

***(a)* Education and Research Network (ERNET):** It is based on terrestrial lines and VSATs. It serves more than 50,000 users from 800 organisations with non-commercial access.

***(b)* National Informatics Network (NICNET):** Mainly satellite based, exclusively for government organisations, it allows up to 2.2 mbps and covers 850 centres including 650 organisations.

***(c)* Gateway Internet Access Service (GTAS) of VSNL:** It is based on terrestrial lines and satellite with a user base of 1,50,000.

***(d)* SOFTNET:** Mainly sattelite based and serves the requirements of six 100% export-oriented software technology parks.

INTERNET SERVICES

To send and receive mails (e-mail), support for special interest scholarly lists and newsgroups, remote login to a computer (telnet) and file transfer from remote locations (FTP). In this section, we will discuss some of these services.

Telnet

Telnet, a kind of utility protocol, allows a computer connected to a network to log on to another computer and read the data stored there if it has an account there. In 1974, the public was given access to the ARPANET's first commercial iteration. This also goes by the name "remote log in." In Telnet, the user's computer is referred to as the "local" computer, while the computer they are logged into is referred to as the "remote" or "host" computer. Once the connection is made, the instructions are carried out on the remote computer but the local computer is where the information is shown as a result. It makes no difference how close or far apart the local and remote computers are physically. They could be located hundreds of kilometres apart or only a few feet apart.

File Transfer Protocol

To copy files from one Internet-connected computer to another, the File Transfer Protocol (FTP) programme is used. Articles, databases, and other resources are uploaded to FTP sites so that others can browse and download them by people who enjoy sharing their resources. The fact that the information is available in electronic form is FTP's major benefit. A telnet server connection and an FTP server login are similar. FTP is a dependable, rapid, and effective means of sending data. There are billions of files stored online at FTP sites. As many of them are only available to permitted persons, it is not possible to access them all. The great majority of FTP sites, however, are open to the public and available to everyone.

Electronic Mail

A mailing system called Electronic Mail (E-mail) makes use of a variety of data communication devices as its medium. The ability to create, transmit and receive mail using electronic means is known as email. Unlike telnet and FTP, sending an email does not need logging onto the host computer. Through the Internet Protocol Address, the machine on the network finds routes and is quickly forwarded.

Components of any e-mail:

- The recipient's address.
- The sender's return address.
- The subject of the message.
- The body of the message.
- Enclosure consisting of one or more file (optional).

E-mail Etiquette and Emoticons: Email messages cannot be formatted in bold, italic, or other styles, since the message body is sent as a standard text file. However, throughout time, various acronyms and emoticons have been utilised in email messages for the benefit of clarity and brevity. Additionally, as messages go across borders, netiquette has grown in significance. For instance, typing in capital letters is considered offensive because it is the equivalent of screaming. Here are a few acronyms and emoticons:

	Abbreviations	Emoticons
BTW	By the way	:-) smiling
IMO	In my opinion	:-i Semi-smiley
RE	Regarding	:) Big smile
FAQ	Frequently Asked Questions	: (Angry
FYI	For Your Information	:-o Surprised
OTOH	On the other hand	

Personal E-mail accounts: You will receive one email account from your ISP. However, if everyone in your organisation needs a unique account, this is still achievable with just one llaterfiet address. Numerous web-based email services are readily available and cost nothing to use online. One of these has the following address:

- Yahoomail www. yahoo.com
- Rocketmail www.rocketmail
- Rediffmail www.rediff.com.

Internet Chatting

Internet chatting is a type of online communication that allows for the live streaming of text messages from sender to receiver. Online communication is sometimes referred to as point-to-point, one sender to one receiver, or one sender to many receivers. Additionally, audio, video and web-conferencing capabilities are provided. Both chat and video can be used for communication (using webcams). Nowadays, there are many chatting platforms available for users. Some of them are mentioned below: Facebook, WhatsApp, Skype, Telegram, Snapchat and Hike.

Mailing Lists

These lists of email addresses are referred to as *listserv* and have common interests. LISTSERVJ, newsgroups and email all develop time-delayed communication features. i.e., users can choose when to communicate, rather than having it happen in real time. The group is a "virtual group" even if all of the group's users are members due to the way the group interacts and responds at the users' leisure. Because users can respond to questions and read answers at their convenience, such a group can be of tremendous assistance in remote learning.

The following are a few useful mailing lists for open and remote learning:

- **DEOS-L:** Distance Education Online Symposium (listserv@lists.psu.edu)
- **DE-L:** Forum for instructors of Distance Education (listserv@pdomain-uwindsor.co)
- **Itde:** Instructional Technology and Distance Education List (listserv@pulsar.acast.nova.edu)
- **Networking:** One-way list covering post-secondary Distance Education (listserv@, node. on.ca).

Cu-SeeMe

CU-SeeMe is a platform for online video conferences. Without a server, CU-SeeMe may make point-to-point video calls, or it can make multi-point calls with server software that was once referred to as a "reflector" and is now known as a "conference server" or Multipoint Control Unit (MCU). Tim Dorcey of Cornell University's information technology department created CU-SeeMe in its initial iteration. In 1992, it was initially created for the Macintosh, then in 1994, it was created for the Windows platform. It was initially only available in video, with audio being introduced in 1994 for Macintosh and 1995 for Windows.

World Wide Web

The World Wide Web (WWW) was first developed in 1989 at the European Centre for Nuclear Research

(CERN) as a hypertext-based application, or a system that links different documents dispersed across millions of devices connected via the Internet. However, it wasn't until December 1991 that the application started to function. A powerful Graphically User Interface (GUI) called Mosaic, which was introduced in February 1993, was the following significant advance in WWW. The WWW contributed to the Internet's emergence as a resource for everyday information. Three criteria that distinguish web protocol are as follows:

- The use of URLs as addressing system (a typical URL starts with http://)
- The Hypertext Transfer Protocol (HTTP) by which the delivery of requested information is transacted.
- The Hypertext Markup Language (HTML) through which the links between documents and parts of documents are made.

Web has the following features:

- It benefits students and contributes to its effectiveness as a suitable style of course delivery.
- Facilities for handling forms, as well as input to forms that are useful for course registration, evaluation and other types of questionnaires and examinations.
- Support for showing tables, footnotes and mathematical symbols.

USING WORLD WIDE WEB

Hypertext linkages are what hold the WWW network as a whole together. Together, the World Wide Web Consortium (W3C) and the Internet Engineering Task Force (IETF) ensure that the WWW's technology functions and that users may use its services from anywhere in the world without becoming divided into local organisations. A web browser is necessary to connect to the WWW. Netscape and Internet Explorer are two popular web browsers. These browsers give you access to the world of online documents. You must know the page's Universal Resource Locator (URL) address, which you must type into the browser, in order to access a specific page or document.

Search Engines

Search engines are automated information retrieval devices that make it simple to find information on the Internet. Through the use of word strings and operators, they enable searching (and, or, not, near, etc.). The six most popular search engines are Webcrawler, HotBot, Excite, Infoseek, Lycos and Altavista. A quick summary of various search engines can be found in Table 2.

Table 2: Search Engines

Search Site	URL	Summary	Pros	Cons
Altavista	http://www.alta-vistn.com	Large as well as fast	Returns many hits; option for advanced search	Low relevance.
Excite	http://www.exite.com	Launched in 1995. It is a web directory as well. It is fast, current and large.	Concept search technologies, personalised option.	Delivery of duplicates.
Infoseek	http://www.infoseek.com	Started in 1995 along with a directory easy to use.	High relevance.	Limited database size.
HotBot	http://www.hotbot.com	Launched in May 1996 High speed, Strong product information	Drop-down menu for search options; high speed.	Delivery of duplicates.
Lycos	http://www.lycos.com	One of the oldest search engine dating back to May 1994.	Also searches graphics, sounds and video.	Slow.
Webcrawler	http://www.webcrawler.com	Started in April 1994, it has a large database.	Easy to use, relatively fast.	High number of hits; low relevance.

IMPLICATIONS OF INTERNET FOR DISTANCE EDUCATION

Users of a network are no longer required to buy copies of software or content. The students in DE have access to and usage of online resources. Since most distance learners are employed, their study schedules can be highly flexible. Online education is not limited by strict time constraints. The user is free to learn whenever is most convenient for them. The schedule for visiting the library or talking to professors or classmates is flexible. One can approach them whenever suits them. Collaborative learning opportunities, web-based teaching and interactivity for learning are all made feasible by the Internet and WWW.

Web-Based Education and Training

One of the most widely used platforms for delivering programmes for distant learning is the World Wide Web (WWW). The web can transmit multimedia content, as was already established and this feature makes it ideal for distance-learning courses. A website for education can assist students in reading, viewing, hearing and interacting with online content. It may also enable student interaction. The web makes it possible for educators to create informational modules for their students. Learners can perform the following in an effective online course:

- Navigate between chunks with ease, both within and between websites.
- Scroll through the material or use links to jump to different sections of the website.
- Understand where information is located and how to use it.
- See the relationships between different types of information.
- Upload and/or download information.

While designing web-based courses, the following issues should be looked into critically:

Administrative questions:

1. Who should have access to the complete materials?
2. To whom should samples be made available?
3. How will access be constrained?
4. Who will make the website's content updates?
5. Who will keep an eye on the website?
6. How long is the course going to remain accessible?
7. Where should the entrance and exit be located?

Academic questions:

1. What kinds of content—text, images, audio, video, animation and quizzes—should be present?
2. What connections will be made between the materials and internal and external resources?
3. How will the students interact with the website's materials?
4. What forms of communication may we expect from the students?

Some educational websites are as under:

IGNOU, India: http://www.ignou.org

USQ, Australia: http://www.usq .edu.au

Athabasca University, Canada: http://www.athabascau.ca

IET, UKOU: http://www-iet.open.ac.uk/iet

NIIT Netversity: http://www.niitnetversity.com

Interactivity and Collaborative Learning

The Internet offers the much-needed engagement that education needs. Additionally, because it is interactive, it gives students the chance to interact not just with their teachers but also with peer groups or other students. Real-time communication may take place throughout this contact over an app like CUSeeMe or IRC. Additionally, mailing lists and email are options. Additionally, examinations in web-based courses offer immediate feedback. As a result, the print medium's check-your-progress activities could be made more interactive, since students can now submit assignments online and get feedback right away. Through a variety of instruments for sharing each person's concept, collaborative learning through computer-mediated communication also improves team performance.

STRENGTHS AND LIMITATIONS OF THE INTERNET

Given below are the strengths and limitations of Internet:

Strengths

- The multimedia capabilities of the Internet to store, process and disseminate information in a number of formats make it highly useful for education and training.
- The Internet offers a vast range of information resources in nearly all domains of expertise.
- The system's characteristic is its simplicity and accessibility.
- The Internet has a broad reach and offers a quick and dependable communication infrastructure that delivers current and nearly real-time information.
- As technology advances, costs decrease as well.
- A global group of professionals is continuously developing this technology.

Limitations

- Unwanted and pointless e-mails are a constant problem in institutions with Internet access. The subscriber must spend a lot of time on this.
- The importance of internet security cannot be overstated. Internet e-mail and downloaded files from the WWW have been known to contain viruses; when messages span many backbone infrastructures, there is the potential for hacking and the leakage of sensitive information through the network.
- This mandates that antivirus software be set up on every computer. Everyone can participate in the public forum that is the Internet, since it is open to all. The debates are frequently not taken too seriously.

COMPUTER AND COMMUNICATION SKILL FOR TEACHERS

Teachers should have the following skills:

1. Navigate desktop settings.
2. Make use of WWW services to copy and move files.
3. Read and write files in HTML.
4. Work with both compressed and uncompressed files.
5. Take part in online conferences.
6. Talk on a web phone.
7. Use domestic and international communication networks to send and receive letters.
8. Become familiar with a few programming languages.
9. Employ authoring software.

10. Create a student, teacher and school home page.
11. Use a PC to take part in interactive satellite classes that are both one-way and two-way.
12. Email sending and receiving.
13. Access FTP files through the internet.
14. Create a lesson plan video that will be used in a computer-based presentation.
15. Use a DOS or Windows word processor.
16. Make use of spreadsheet and database programmes.
17. Install and load.

CHECK YOUR PROGRESS

Q. 1. What are the advantages of computer networks?

Ans. A collection of linked autonomous systems that enable dispersed information processing makes up a computer network. It produces greater performance with a rapid processing rate. Computer networks' key benefits are:

***(a)* Files can be kept in a Central Location** (the file server), where they can be shared and made accessible to all users within an organisation.

***(b)* Anyone can Connect to a Computer Network:** Only a small set of skills are needed to access a contemporary computer network. Even young children can start utilising the data because to how simple it is to enrol.

***(c)* Quicker Problem-solving:** Because a lengthy procedure is broken down into several smaller procedures, each of which is handled by all the related devices, a specific problem can be resolved in less time.

***(d)* Reliability:** Reliability necessitates information backup. When equipment malfunctions, crashes, etc. and information on one PC becomes compromised or unavailable, another copy of the same information is available on another workstation for future use, enabling uninterrupted functioning.

***(e)* It is Incredibly Adjustable:** This innovation is renowned for being incredibly flexible, since it gives users the ability to learn everything there is to know about core concepts like programming without affecting how useful they are.

***(f)* Security through Authorization:** The system also handles information security and protection. No one else can breach the information security or protection, since only authorised system users have access to certain records or applications.

***(g)* It increases Storage Capacity:** Since you will be sharing data, records and assets with others, you need to make sure that all information and material are properly stored in the system. You can handle the majority of this with no problems, thanks to this advancement in system administration and you'll have all the room you need for capacity.

Q. 2. Which of the following statements are true and which false?

(i) The twisted pair cable can transmit both digital and analog signal.

(ii) In ring to pology, the breakdown of a system causes failure of the network.

(iii) The geographical coverage of a MAN is usually within 5-50 kms.

(iv) Interconnection of networks and devices is done through standards and protocols.

Ans. *(i)* True, *(ii)* False, *(iii)* True, *(iv)* True.

Q. 3. Identify the different parts of the following Internet address.

rse @pcquest.com

ignou @gaisdlOl.vsnl.net.in

Ans.

- rse@pequest.com

rse = Username
pcquest = Host
Com = Domain

- ignou@goisdlO1.vsnl.net.in

ignou = Username
gaisdlOl = Host
vsnl = Subdomain
net = network
in = India

Q. 4. Identify which of the following are True or False.

(i) Telnet is used to connect to a LAN.

(ii) FTP is a programme to download files from remote computers.

(iii) While sending e-mail messages capital letters should be avoided.

(iv) Internet Relay Chat is a time delayed communication.

(v) Listservs are great ways to communicate with people of similar interests on the net.

(vi) WWW is capable of multimedia facilities.

Ans. *(i)* False, *(ii)* True, *(iii)* True, *(iv)* False, *(v)* True, *(vi)* True.

Q. 5. How would you find material on distance education in WWW?

Ans. By using search engines, we may use the WWW to obtain information on distance learning. In order to do that, we must enter the URL of a search engine. Once the search engine is running, we may enter the string "distance education" to find the needed materials.

Q. 6. List the three most significant effects of the Internet on remote learning.

Ans. The internet is helpful for distance learning. There is no longer a requirement for network users to purchase copies of software or material. Online materials are available to and used by the DE students. Since, most distance learners have day jobs, they often have very flexible study schedules. Online learning is not constrained by stringent time restrictions.

Anytime that is most convenient for the user, they are free to learn. The timetable for going to the library, speaking with lecturers, or interacting with classmates is flexible. They are approachable anytime it is convenient. The Internet and WWW provide interactive learning, web-based teaching and collaborative learning opportunities all possible.

The World Wide Web (WWW) is one of the most popular distribution channels for programmes for distance learning. As was already known, the web can convey multimedia content, which makes it the perfect platform for online classes. A learning website can help students read, watch, listen to and engage with online content. Student interaction may also be made possible through it. The internet enables instructors to produce educational modules for pupils.

Learners can perform the following in an effective online course:

- Navigate between chunks with ease, both within and between websites.
- Scroll through the material or use links to jump to different sections of the website.
- Understand where information is located and how to use it.
- See the relationships between different types of information.
- Upload and/or download information.

The Internet provides the crucial interaction that is required for education. Additionally, because it is interactive, it offers pupils the option to communicate with others besides simply their teachers or peer groups. Throughout this encounter, real-time communication might be possible via an app like CUSeeMe or IRC. Email and mailing lists are further alternatives. In addition, exams in online courses provide quick feedback. As a result, since students can now turn in assignments online and receive immediate feedback, check-your-progress activities in the print medium may become more engaging. Collaborative learning through computer-mediated communication enhances team performance by using a variety of tools for communicating each person's concept.

OTHER IMPORTANT QUESTIONS

Q. 1. What is computer networking? What are the types of computer network architecture?

Ans. Computer networking is the term for a network of connected computers that may communicate and share resources. These networked devices transmit data through wireless or physical technologies using a set of guidelines known as communications protocols.

Computer networking's fundamental building components are nodes and links. A network node could be data terminal equipment (DTE), which includes two or more computers and printers, or data communication equipment (DCE), which includes a modem, hub, or switch. The transmission medium that connects two nodes is referred to as a link. Links can be vacant spaces used by wireless networks or they can be physically present, such cable wires or optical fibres.

The rules or protocols that specify how to transmit and receive electronic data over the links are followed by nodes in a functioning computer network. These physical and logical components' designs are determined by the computer network architecture. It offers the standards for the physical elements, operational structure, protocols and practices of the network.

In the late 1950s, the first computer networks were developed for use in defence and military applications. They initially had limited commercial and scientific applications and were used to transport data via telephone lines. The development of internet technologies has made computer networks essential for businesses. More than just connectivity is provided by contemporary network systems. They are essential to modern company performance and the digital transformation of industries.

Underlying network capabilities have become more programmable, automated and secure.

Computer network design falls under two broad categories:

(a) **Client-server Architecture:** Nodes in this kind of computer network could be clients or servers. Client nodes receive resources from server nodes, such as memory, computing power, or data. Client node activity may also be controlled by server nodes. Although clients can interact with one another, they do not exchange resources. For instance, some computers in business networks save information and setup preferences. The network's servers are represented by these devices. Clients can request access to this data from the server machine.

(b) **Peer-to-peer Architecture:** The connected computers in a peer-to-peer (P2P) architecture share the same rights and privileges. No centralised server is present for coordination. Each computer network device has the option of serving or acting as a client. A portion of each peer's resources, such as memory and processing power, may be shared across the entire computer network. For instance, several businesses host memory-intensive programmes, including 3-D graphic rendering, across multiple digital devices using P2P architecture.

Q. 2. What is network topology? What are different types of network topology?

Ans. Network topology refers to how nodes and links are organised. They can be set up in many ways to get various results. Examples of:

(a) **Point-to-Point:** A point-to-point network consists of exactly two hosts, such as servers, switches, or routers, which are connected back-to-back by a single cable. The sending end of one host is frequently connected to the receiving end of another and vice versa. If the hosts are logically connected point-to-point, then there might be several intermediate devices. However, the end hosts perceive one another as though they are directly connected and are not aware of the underlying network.

***(b)* Bus Topology:** A single communication line or cable is shared by all devices in a bus topology. It might experience issues when several hosts are sending data simultaneously.

Therefore, to address the problem. Bus topology either uses CSMA/CD technology or designates one host as a Bus Master. It is one of the straightforward networking models, where a device's failure has no impact on the other devices. However, if the shared communication channel fails, all other devices could become inoperable.

***(c)* Star Topology:** All hosts in a star topology are linked together by a point-to-point connection to a hub device in the centre. In other words, the hosts and hub are connected point-to-point. Any of the following can serve as the hub device:

Layer-1 device such as hub or repeater,
Layer-2 device such as switch or bridge,
Layer-3 device such as router or gateway.

***(d)* Ring Topology:** In a ring topology, a circular network structure is formed by each host machine connecting to exactly two more machines. Data passes via all intermediate hosts if one host tries to communicate with or send a message to another host that is not nearby. The administrator may simply require one more cable to connect one more host to the current structure.

***(e)* Mesh Topology:** A host is connected to one or more hosts in this form of architecture. Hosts in this topology may be connected point-to-point to every other host or they may only be connected point-to-point to a small number of hosts.

- **Full Mesh:** Each host in the network has a point-to-point link with every other host. Therefore, n(n-1)/2 connections are needed for every new host. Of all network topologies, it offers the most dependable network structure.
- **Partially Mesh:** Not every host is connected to every other host on a point-to-point basis. Hosts connect to one another in a random manner. In this topology, we must give certain hosts out of all the hosts reliability.

***(f)* Tree Topology:** This type of network structure, also referred to as hierarchical topology, is the most popular one currently in use. This topology mimics an extended Star topology and inherits bus topology characteristics.

The network is divided into several tiers or layers by this topology. A network is divided into three different types of network devices, primarily in LANs. The access-layer, to which computers are connected, is the lowest. The distribution layer, which sits between the top and lower layers, is the middle layer. The core layer, which is the top most layer and the layer from which all nodes fork out, serves as the network's central node.

There is a point-to-point connection between each neighbouring host. Similar to the bus topology, the entire network is affected if the root fails. Even though there are other points of failure. Every link acts as a potential point of failure and when one fails, a portion of the network becomes inaccessible.

***(g)* Daisy Chain:** With this topology, all hosts are connected to one another linearly. All hosts, with the exception of the end hosts, are connected to just two hosts, similar to the ring topology. This indicates that a daisy chain has a ring topology if the end hosts are connected.

In a daisy chain topology, every link is a potential single point of failure. The network is divided into two sections for each broken link. For its immediate hosts, each intermediate host serves as a relay.

***(h)* Hybrid Topology:** A hybrid topology is a network structure that incorporates many topologies into its design. The benefits and drawbacks of each incorporating topology are carried over into the hybrid topology.

Q. 3. Explain the term enterprise network. Discuss types of enterprise networks.

Ans. The physical, virtual and logical design of a mid-size to large organisational network is referred to as an enterprise network. It deals with how protocols, hardware and software interact to:

- Communicate,
- Share information,
- Run programmes,
- Analyze system performance.

Types of Enterprise Networks:

1. Local Area Network (LAN): A building, office, or residence is the actual site, where a LAN is physically located. It contains access points, cables, routers, switches and other connected components. Any size LAN is possible (e.g., an office with multiple departments and thousands of users or a small home network with just a few users). The greatest distinguishing feature of a LAN, regardless of size, is that it is contained to a single, predefined area.

LANs are often configured logically or virtually within a business network (as in a VLAN). As an illustration, each department (such as accounting, processing, etc.) runs on its own little LAN that connects all of its computers to a single switch that is isolated from all other departments.

2. Wide Area Network (WAN): A WAN is a network that extends across several floors of a building or buildings in various geographic areas, sometimes even on opposite sides of the world, as is typical with global corporations. A WAN is essentially a network of networks. Across the Open Systems Interconnection (OSI) Reference Model layers, WANs use many protocols and parts. Additionally, WANs set up communication in the following ways, whereas LAN technology is utilised for high-speed data transfer from a single location:

- Long-distance,
- Energy efficient,
- Secure,
- Dependable.

A WAN can be installed as either a private or public network and is most commonly set up by an Internet Service Provider (ISP).

3. Cloud Networks: According to recent figures, 94 percent of businesses were using cloud services as of 2019 and by 2025, an incredible 100 Zettabytes of data are expected to be stored in cloud data centres. An IT infrastructure known as "cloud networking" hosts some or all of an organization's networking resources in a public, private, or hybrid cloud (*i.e.*, a combination of public or private).

Large businesses or their cloud service providers may build, configure and operate sophisticated networks using only an internet connection, thanks to cloud networking. A cloud can host a variety of network resources, including:

- Bandwidth,
- Connectivity,
- Content Delivery Networks (CDNs),
- Domain Name System (DNS),
- Firewalls,
- Load balancers,
- Network management software,
- Virtual Private Network (VPN),
- Virtual routers.

Additionally, a variety of network security options are available with cloud networking, including firewalls, distributed denial of service (DDoS) and AI-based threat detection monitoring.

Cloud-based and cloud-enabled networking are the two basic forms.

Network architecture for these networks is located on-site at the business, while some (or all) of the other network resources are hosted in the cloud.

Cloud-based Networks: Using this technique, the complete network is based in the cloud.

Why Enterprise Networks are Important?

It is impossible to exaggerate the significance of enterprise networks. Enterprise networks make it possible for businesses with branches spread across several cities or nations to connect swiftly and effectively. Without this crucial technology, every division of the business would have to function independently.

Fast, organised and secure information transmission is essential in today's digitally-oriented organisation because it affects revenue. Productivity suffers immediately when a network section (or, God forbid, the entire network) goes down or is compromised. The seamless facilitation of corporate activities including internal supply chains, purchasing, production, sales and distribution via an enterprise network must be underlined. Every piece of information used in a company's business planning and execution, literally travels across the network.

Additionally, a company's enterprise network is essential to its continued existence. For instance, a corporate network is crucial to the proper operation of business continuity, disaster recovery, high availability cluster nodes and cloud-based failover servers.

Q. 4. Write a note on FTP.

Ans. FTP (File Transfer Protocol) is used to communicate and transfer files between computers on a TCP/IP (Transmission Control Protocol/Internet Protocol) network, aka the internet. Users, who have been granted access, can receive and transfer files in the File Transfer Protocol server (also known as FTP host/site).

FTP connection needs two parties to establish and communicate on the network. To do that, users need to have permission by providing credentials to the FTP server. Some public FTP servers may not require credentials to access their files. The practice is common in a so-called anonymous FTP.

There are two distinct communication channels, while establishing an FTP connection. The first one is called the command channel, where it initiates the instruction and response. The other one is called a data channel, where the distribution of data happens.

To get or transfer a file, an authorized user will use the protocol to request on creating changes in the server. In return, the server will grant that access. This session is known as the active connection mode.

The distribution in active mode might face a problem if a firewall is protecting the user's machine. The firewall usually does not allow any unauthorized sessions from an external party.

The passive mode is used if that issue occurs. In this mode, the user establishes both command and the data channel. This mode then asks the server to listen, rather than to attempt to create a connection back to the user.

Q. 5. How is computer networking evolving?

Ans. Today's networks offer more than just connectivity. Organizations are starting their digital transformation. Their networks are essential to both their success and this transition. The following are the several sorts of network designs that are developing to fulfil these needs:

1. Software-defined (SDN): Network architecture is evolving to meet new demands in the "digital" era by becoming more programmable, automated and open. Software-based techniques are used in software-defined networks to centrally manage traffic routing. This enables the network to respond swiftly to evolving circumstances.

2. Intent-based: Intent-based networking (IBN), which is built on SDN concepts, not only adds agility but also configures a network to achieve desired goals by heavily automating operations, reviewing its performance, identifying problem areas, offering all-around security and integrating with business processes.

3. Virtualized: Multiple "overlay" networks can be created by logically dividing the underlying physical network architecture. It is possible to adjust each of these logical networks to satisfy certain security, quality-of-service (QoS) and other needs.

4. Controller-based: Network growth and security depend heavily on network controllers. By translating business purpose into device configurations, controllers simplify networking tasks. They also regularly check on devices to assist maintain performance and security. Controllers streamline processes and assist businesses in adapting to shifting business needs.

5. Multidomain Integrations: For their offices, WANs and data centres, larger businesses may build separate networks, often known as networking domains. Through their controllers, these networks talk to one another. In order to ensure that targetted business outcomes that span network domains are realised, such cross-network, or multidomain, integrations typically entail sharing pertinent operating parameters.

MULTIPLE CHOICE QUESTIONS

Q. 1. In which of the following approach, the information is preserved in an archive for future researchers, historians and the public?

(a) Online chronicle approach
(b) New medium methodology
(c) Distributing intermediation approach
(d) Dynamic and without a moment to spare methodology

Ans. *(a)* Online chronicle approach.

Q. 2. Who developed World Wide Web?

(a) Tim Berners-Lee and his colleagues
(b) Claude Shannon and his colleagues
(c) Konrad Zuse and his colleagues
(d) Tommy Flowers and his colleagues

Ans. *(a)* Tim Berners-Lee and his colleagues.

Q. 3. The WWW became popular with the development of:

(a) Mosaic (b) Safari
(c) Internet Explorer (d) Google Chrome

Ans. *(a)* Mosaic.

Q. 4. Before the introduction of HTTP, which of the following was used to retrieve files from a server?

(a) File Transfer Protocol
(b) The Gopher Protocol
(c) Both (a) and (b)
(d) None of these

Ans. *(c)* Both *(a)* and *(b)*.

Q. 5. Which element allows the visitors to easily locate what they are looking for on a website?

(a) Logical layout
(b) Clean navigation
(c) Details of the website
(d) White space

Ans. *(b)* Clean navigation.

Q. 6. Which of the following is not a web browser?

(a) Internet Explorer (b) Firefox
(c) Google Chrome (d) Facebook

Ans. *(d)* Facebook.

Q. 7. In HTTP, URL begins with:

(a) "http://" (b) "https://".
(c) "www://". (d) None of these

Ans. *(a)* "http://"

Q. 8. Which site is trusted by its users?

(a) Authority website
(b) Lead-generation website
(c) Sales website
(d) Utility website

Ans. *(a)* Authority website.

Q. 9. OTA is an:

(a) e-publishing tool
(b) e-banking software
(c) e-travelling aggregator
(d) e-library tool

Ans. *(c)* e-travelling aggregator.

Q. 10. Which of the following is a feedback channel?

(a) Phone number (b) Emails
(c) Live chat links (d) All of the above

Ans. *(d)* All of the above.

Q. 11. Presenting the right thing at the right time in the right way on a website implies:

(a) Clean navigation (b) Beautiful typography
(c) White space (d) Logical layout

Ans. *(d)* Logical layout.

Q. 12. The Planning step comes after, which step in website development process?

(a) Innovative Requirement
(b) Information Gathering
(c) Web Design
(d) Web Development

Ans. *(b)* Information Gathering.

Q. 13. Which of the following is not an e-governance?

(a) Government-to-Citizen (G2C)
(b) Government-to-Business (G2B)
(c) Government-to-Employee (G2E)
(d) Consumers-to-Business (C2B)

Ans. *(d)* Consumers-to-Business (C2B).

Q. 14. VPS is:

(a) Virtual private service
(b) Virtually private server
(c) Virtual private server
(d) Virtually private service

Ans. *(c)* Virtual private server.

Q. 15. Facebook is a:

(a) Utility website
(b) Authority website
(c) Lead-generation website
(d) Sales website

Ans. *(a)* Utility website.

■■